V&R

Forschungen zur systematischen und ökumenischen Theologie

Herausgegeben von
Reinhard Slenczka und Gunther Wenz

Band 100

Vandenhoeck & Ruprecht

Per Lønning

Is Christ a Christian?

On *Inter*-Religious Dialogue
and *Intra*-Religious Horizon

Vandenhoeck & Ruprecht

Bibliografische Information Der Deutschen Bibliothek
Die Deutsche Bibliothek verzeichnet diese Publikation in der Deutschen
Nationalbibliografie; detaillierte bibliografische Daten sind im Internet
über <http://dnb.ddb.de> abrufbar.

ISBN 3-525-56225-X

Satz: Text & Form, Garbsen.
Druck- und Bindearbeiten: Hubert & Co., Göttingen.

Gedruckt auf alterungsbeständigem Papier.

Contents

Acknowledgements

Particular gratitude is owed to The Institute for Ecumenical Research, Strasbourg, France, where the first preparations for this work started during my term as research professor (1981–87), and where I have had several opportunities to come back in the meantime and take advantage of the library and other working facilities. I am also obliged to the Christian Michelsens Institutt, Bergen, Norway, for valuable support in the years following my retirement as bishop in 1994, when again I had the opportunity to return to full time academical studies. This gave me possibilities for exchange with surroundings geared to studies of international relations other, and in some ways more comprehensive, than my own. It provided me with important technical assistance, and – more important still – supported study tours to Germany, Switzerland and the USA.

I am particularly indebted to the professors Notto Thelle and Oddbjørn Leirvik of the Theological Faculty, University of Oslo, and Tormod Engelsviken and Arild Romarheim of the Independent Theological Faculty, Oslo, for interesting comments and advice – without making any of them responsible for reflections where my stubbornness may have led me on controversial paths of my own. – Mr. John Kaufmann deserves thanks for a scrupulous control of my use of the English language, and Mr. Trygve Smebye for valuable assistance with the electronic completion of the manuscript – a technological test which tends to transcend the working routines of my generation.

And – last but not least – thanks to my dear Ingunn, who had certainly looked forward to retirement years with a relaxed husband having left the worries of demanding studies behind, but who never refused me the understanding and support necessary in order for me to to carry on and to accomplish a challenging task.

Oslo, in January 2002   Per Lønning

0. De-Mystification

0.1. The Question in the Question

'Is Christ a Christian?' The question definitely sounds rhetorical. Just another attempt to catch attention, saving the book from anonymous disappearance on the more and more insurveyable ocean of dialogue studies? In any case, our guiding question should be answered: yes *and* no, depending on the meaning – provided that there is some. But is there?

Certainly. – In order to prevent possible misunderstandings: 'Christ' refers to the focal figure of historical Christian faith, presented by the ancient Ecumenical Symbols and taken to be identical with Jesus of Nazareth, key figure of New Testament proclamation. Critical research about "the historical Jesus" lies outside our actual horizon, to the extent that the topic is beyond the agenda of contemporary interfaith exchange. The only major exception from this may be a not uncommon Muslim reference to Western historical criticism in order to question the reliability of the Bible versus that of the Qur'an.

The purpose of our question, then, is to question a supposition frequently and uncritically taken as the basis of *intra*-religious and even of *inter*-religious discourse by Christians. Namely that claims made by believers on behalf of Christ and claims made on behalf of some sociologically or socio-psychologically objectifiable "Christianity" necessarily coextend. Provided that Christ is confessed as unique, this is frequently and uncritically assumed to imply that Christianity also, in essential regards, claims uniqueness. Conversely, if plain observations must deny the epithet "unique" to empirical Christianity, Christians are expected to disclaim uniqueness not only for themselves, but also for the Christ in whom they believe. A corresponding dialectic may obviously apply to the concept of 'God', as principally represented by an overwhelming segment of the world religions. Too often an intended relationship with God, the expression of ultimate perfection, is, without further examination, taken to warrant the perfection of the relationship – i.e. of a concrete religious practice including the corresponding community of worshipers, as such.

In recent literature, attempts to distinguish claims in favor of Christ from claims in favor of Christianity are increasing in number, preferably with authors wanting to combine openness to dialogue with the historical Christian understanding of Jesus Christ as The Savior of (all) humankind. – The provocative title of the present study is by no means without topical precedence. This time, however, it is raised with a new emphasis, with an extended review of critical premises, and – hopefully – with new and thought-provoking elements of an answer.

Our provocative guiding question, then, presents a real question and not a hidden proposition. This question arises immediately from the contemporary debate, as we shall see, while at the same time trying to sharpen what may be more and more discernible as 'the question within the question'. The major claim enwrapped in the wording is that of an ultimate issue worth serious consideration.

Precisely the exploration of the issue indicated will in the long run prove decisive for a theologically justifiable Christian integration of dialogue. If all attempts at such a distinction fail, a simple choice will open up between all and next-to-nothing: either unrestricted conversation between specialists with restricted grass-root contact to their respective communities, or undialectical emphasis on Christian particularity with accordingly restricted space for dialogical listening. Most likely other faith communities expected to participate will, for their own part, find themselves exposed to some corresponding intrinsic dilemma. Relativism is as damaging to human exchange as is absolutism.

The challenging distinction behind our question "Is Christ a Christian?" has, for that reason, important implications which could be equally pursued under the headlines "Is Buddha a Buddhist?" or "Is Muhammed a Muslim?" This comparison obscures by no means the insight that, at the same time, the three versions of the question must lead to the exposure of assumptions highly different already in premises. In any case, awareness of "the distinction behind" may be of fundamental importance for a meaningful dialogical orientation of any religion. Seen in this perspective, our reflections from a Christian background may be of assistance to other faith communities in their preparation for dialogue, not only as information about a Christian thought pattern, but as an invitation to discover (corresponding dynamics of) their own.

0.2. "Interreligious" and "Intrareligious"

What, then, is intended by an inquiry about "*inter*religious dialogue and *intra*religious horizon"? 'Interreligious' has for decades been agreed as signifying what is common to different religions, bilaterally, multilaterally, universally. 'Intrareligious' is not equally established in scholarly terminology and may for that reason be subject to different understandings. As it is used in the present study, it fixes attention on developments within each religion regarding its relationship with other religions.[1]

---

[1] Definitely different is the programmatic use of "intrareligious" in PANIKKAR's study (1985), endorsed and developed in a wider systematical context by BASSET 1996, 353–355.

"Intrareligious" is here defined as "a fundamental human phenomenon" to be distinguished from "religion in its doctrinal, communitary or confessional diversity." More precisely: "Le dialogue intrareligieux est la rencontre d'expériences et d'intuitions relative au sens de l'existence humaine, à la limite des mots et de l'intelligible" (BASSET, 354). Distinct from the issue of terminology, there will be occasion to discuss Basset's theory of a pan-religious spiritual encounter later.

'Intrareligious' as a distinctive area of concern, then, will develop in dialectical interaction with 'interreligious' involvement and will accommodate its meaning accordingly. 'Intrareligious', as the word will be used in the following, may be an unrivaled philological vehicle to designate activities in the constituency of one religion with the purpose of clarifying its relationship with other religions.

The interaction between "intrareligious" and "interreligious" may seem complex, but the principal coordination of the two concepts should be clear enough. In order to become operative, the interreligious adventure must be preceded, surrounded and followed by a network of intrareligious reflections. This observation reflects the indispensable presupposition of all authentic dialogue: the partners reciprocally ready to recognize each other as people of conviction and integrity. Also the other religions will, for the sake of logical consistency, have to subject their participation in common interreligious conversation to constant intrareligious scrutiny.

This equips the concept "intrareligious horizon" in our headline with a certain, hopefully stimulating, ambiguity. As a matter of fact, the eye-catching orientation of the study is 'intrareligious'. But at the same time its superior purpose is to lay foundations essential for 'interreligious' dialogue, presented through the premises of one particular religion – Christianity: how should Christians, taking their own faith commitments seriously, conceive, and engage in, dialogue with other faiths? In this perspective intrareligious exchange, even if quantitatively dominant, becomes subordinate while essentially instrumental.

Already preliminary 'intrareligious' reflection may integrate a remarkable element of 'interreligious' orientation. As dialogue develops, growing reciprocal confidence may hopefully encourage non-Christian conversation partners to voice challenging observations to the ways in which Christians profess and practice Christianity. Conversely, the Christian part may be welcomed to comment on the partner(s): "This is how your message appears to us! We don't want to compromise your identity, but would like to inquire how you yourself view elements and circumstances which seem astonishing to us."

From a linguistic point of view, "intra-religious" could, of course, designate an "inside" orientation common to all religion (viewed as one universal sphere), just as well as some process of reflection going on within the premises of each religion separately. "Intra-" as understood by Panikkar/Basset introduces a last, conclusive stage to all dialogical procedure, a stage, the meaning and relevance of which will be differently assessed in various religions and – supposedly – between various schools of theology within the same religion. Regardless of our yes-or-no to such an idea of a trans-verbal fulfilment of dialogue, other designations would probably distinguish the phenomenon more clearly than "intrareligious". If some dialectical tie is sought between "intra-" and "inter-religious", it must in any case be of importance to let "-religious" reflect corresponding notions of "religion". As "inter-religious" immediately evokes the idea of "religions" in the plural (inter = between, presupposing two or more identifiable partners), there is no such correspondence unless the "intra" (= within) relates to concrete religions viewed one by one. – Besides, it is hard to fancy a meaningful dialogue between religions unless escorted by a reflective dialogical process within each of them, evaluating external dialogue in relation to its experience of own identity. There could scarcely be invented a set of referential terms more apt to present this dialectic than the conceptual interaction of inter- and intrareligious.

At the same time, even 'intrareligious' may have a universalizing function: it implicitly refers to the internal conversation of any faith community. So doing, it will not unilaterally signalize the preparation of particular strategies for one's own religion in its approach to others. It must also presuppose and will – hopefully – detect orientative patterns of principal importance for any religion/ideology reviewing the interaction between own specificity and universal quest for communion, an issue never more urgent than in our world of today.

In this perspective we cannot come to terms with Christian distinctiveness, unless we presuppose historical distinctiveness as a universal concern, not only of religious traditions, but of ideological movements and of cultures at large.

On this background, the present study, even in its most stubborn insistence on intrareligious authenticity, does not address itself exclusively, nor even predominantly, to a Christian readership. As already stated in the review of our provocative question about Christ, also our stress on the inter/intra dialectic, aside from bringing information about Christian reflections to potential dialogue partners, and to any engaged observer of interfaith relations, it hopes to communicate certain insights about the interaction of 'intra-religious' and 'interreligious' dynamics which may be as relevant to other religions/ideologies as it is to Christianity. The reciprocal recognition of such an interaction may finally be indispensible for any prosperous development of interreligious dialogue.

0.3. Why "Religion" and "Religious"?

The World Council of Churches (WCC) in 1971 termed its first dialogue program *Dialogue with People of Living Faiths and Ideologies*. At that time, that may have been a rather conscious choice. The Roman Catholic Church had already in 1964 organized its *Secretariat for Developing Relations with Non-Christian Religions*, and one could have expected that the WCC in the spring of blooming ecumenism might have adjusted its vocabulary correspondingly and thus emphasized harmony between the two enterprises. So, why 'faith' instead of 'religions'?

In 1988 the Roman secretariat was replaced by a more impressive structure, the *Pontifical Council for Dialogue Between Religions*. One observes how the somewhat confrontative perspective: "relations with non-Christians" is replaced by the WCC term "dialogue" = an exchange between partners on equal footing. At the same time "religions" is preserved, which, apart from all theological implications of this term, sociologically suggests conversation between structural bodies of a recognizable and, in certain easily recognizable regards, comparable format. Such a suggestion is lacking in the sociologically more open-ended "faith".

In the case of the WCC, "faith", at the first stage of events, may have been preferred for several reasons. Not only might the choice of "living faiths", in harmony with good Protestant tradition, indicate a less structure-oriented approach. More important was probably the fact that in Western theology the word 'religion' had a dubious taste since the age of Neo-Orthodoxy (approximately 1930–1965).

> In a subsequent review of this preparative history, we shall return to this observation and try to accommodate it into a more comprehensive assessement of the BARTH / KRAEMER era in Occidental theology as a whole.[2] We shall also look at the idea of a collapse of religion in the modern world – as eloquently stated in the prison diary of the German martyr theologian DIETRICH BONHOEFFER[3], and its continuation. – The influential historian of religion W.C. SMITH in 1962 announced "The End of Religion" (i.e.: as a general concept, neglecting the peculiarity of living faiths).[4] About the same time his colleague A.TH. VAN LEEUWEN presented the liberating impulse of biblical secularization as an uncontradictable challenge to the 'ontocratic' structure of pre- and extra-biblical religion.[5]

In 1992 the WCC, as part of a comprehensive reform of structure, decided to remodel its dialogue engagement, and a new *'Office on Inter-Religious Relations'* was organized within the WCC general secretariat. As to the wording 'Interreligious Relations', it may partly be explained by a remarkable comeback of 'Religion' in Occidental theology from the 1970's onward. But there is also reason to mark that the adjectives "religious" and "inter-religious" are less bent towards structure than the noun 'religions'. At the same time 'relations' is a more open-ended word than 'dialogue', because it may invite issues and programs beyond a process of verbal exchange.

Our study will not make terminology an important issue in itself. We could for that matter have chosen "inter-faith"/"intra-faith" in the title of the work. That might even have underlined an important perspective underscored by the WCC report "Dialogue in Community" (report, Chiang-Mai 1977): dialogue is essentially something more than officially organized negotiation between establishments: the burden of it takes place on a local level in everyday contact between persons of living faith commitments.

In our present context, however, primary attention will be given to a different aspect. Even if contact between believers of different religions in our contemporary world neither could nor should be restricted to official program activities, it is important that dialogue as an item of critical reflection transcends a casual communication of observations and impressions between single believers and within local communities. Also the dialectic "inter"/"intra" loses a good deal of its meaning if limited to a perspective of subjective "faith" or informal everyday conversation. So, concerning the word 'religion' let us wholeheartedly endorse the observation by HANS KÜNG:

> "Gibt es aber kein Wort, das den so missverständlichen Begriff Religion ersetzen könnte? Bisher hat sich keines gefunden, das sich hätte durchsetzen können. Auf einen generellen Oberbegriff wird man aber aus praktischen Gründen kaum verzichten können ..."[6]

---

[2] In the case of BARTH, this particularly applies to his (countless) writings in the 1930s, with his violent attacks on 'natural theology'. Cf. KRAEMER 1938. – We return to the complex influence of the two in 1.1. (cf. our note 4) and 4.3.2. (particularly note 229).

[3] BONHOEFFER 1951.   [4] SMITH 1962 and 1982.

[5] VAN LEEUWEN 1964.   [6] C 1/1986, 2.

1. Toward a Joint Enterprise?

Interreligious Dialogue, as shaped during the last third of the 20th century, must first of all be seen as a response to the urgency for new paths to worldwide understanding and cooperation. This urgency again is generated by the revolutionary technological, political and socio-cultural development of the era, a picture which is observed in highly different manners by nations and civilizations in different parts of the world, depending not at least on their location in the historical face-to-face of industrialized / non-industrialized, colonizers / colonized of various kinds and of varying social repercussions.

A variety of spiritual commitments interact with this pattern, making the relationship between politics and religion more complex than ever in history. Not least, we see traditional religious ideas and values reconquering influence in wide parts of the world, sometimes escorted by frightening irruptions of political unrest and even militancy. In many cases religion less than anything else seems to forward peace and cooperation. The role of interreligious dialogue under such circumstances may be as complex as it is vital.

1.1. Two Hundred Years of Wrestling with "Religion"

In "the Christian world", readiness to dialogue depends not only on the challenges of a complex world scenario, but on more than two hundred years of critical, self-examinatory discussion on the fundamental conditions of divine truth as a topic of human discourse. The ordeal of 18. century "Enlightenment" has, with its remaining effects, become an integral part of Occidental identity.

The meaning of this may be illustrated in the contemporary confrontation of Christianity and Islam. Islam, except for minor occurrences in limited parts of the Muslim world (especially Mediterranean Africa), was never exposed to the scrutinizing questions of critical philosophy[1] or of methodical historical research, and can as to socio-cultural framework rather be compared to European Christianity in ages prior to the French Revolution. The same will generally apply to other religions of a non-European extraction.

According to the 18th century Enlightenment, "Truth" in its plenitude is accessible to the human mind, basically independent of revelation and of religious institu-

---

[1] This may, to a remarkable extent, have been different in the blooming age of Hispanic Muslim culture in the 11. and 12. centuries, with "progressive" critical philosophers like Averrhoes and Avicenna exercising an important influence even on nascent Scholasticism in Christian Europe.

tions, warranted, as it is seen, by "nature", and by nature alone. A given civilization with its particular ideas and practices may contribute to obscuring or to illuminating human concepts of truth, but can never affect truth as timeless given. Truth resides in the human mind as a universally given possibility, equally present, as it were, always and everywhere.

Nevertheless, such a theory was, and is, easily linked with an all-encompassing idea of historical progress. The final criterion for comparing and ranking actual religions may then be their respective degrees of perfectibility (= potentiality of progress toward pure rationality). Truth as essentially and unchangeably the same thus announces its arrival in an unmistakable pattern of developmental progress.

In such a framework, a comparison of "living faiths" tends to end up in one of two opposite constructions, both discriminatory and this in rather lamentable ways. The judgement will either proceed – consciously or unconsciously – from the religious culture of one's own environment, a maneuver which will generally end up with negative judgements on foreign faiths in the name of seeming objectivity, or a judge preponderantly negative to domestic spiritual inheritance may choose an image of some foreign civilization (or of a pure utopia) as the critical standard. Maybe he/she will even universalize the negative observations from his/her own environment as characteristic of "all religion". These "Enlightenment" paths of discriminative "non-discrimination" seem today to be as present as ever.

A turning point was reached with Romanticism around 1800. A new era was proclaimed above all with SCHLEIERMACHER's *'Reden über die Religion'*. Schleiermacher vigorously distinguished religion not only from theoretical knowledge (a distinction already made by Kant), but also from morality ('weder ein Wissen noch ein Tun') and saw it as the fundamental mood of immediate self-consciousness, defined as the sensation of absolute dependence.

This made of religion a personal-emotional experience, transferred in and through spiritual communities (the Synagogue, the Church, Buddhist monasticism), each of them issuing from the impulse of some distinctive historical event. Here we observe a turn towards history and differentiation profoundly different from the rigid "universality" of the Enlightenment. In Christianity that impulse is the redemptive experience offered to posterity in the consciousness of divine presence communicated by Jesus of Nazareth. In principle this vision does not deny the possibility that salvation (= human experience of an unconditional come-to-rest in all-sustaining divine actuality) could be communicated through other divine interventons manifesting themselves through religious communities other than the Church.[2] But in the world anno 1800 this was not an issue of much practical consequence. In any case, the explosion of Christian world mission would be a fact only a few decades later.

---

[2] See: Friedrich Daniel Ernst SCHLEIERMACHER: Reden über die Religion, 1799, 'Fünfte Rede: Über die Religionen' – and same author: Der christliche Glaube, 1830², 'Erstes Kap., II: Von den Verschiedenheiten der frommen Gemeinschaften überhaupt' (§§ 7–10).

SCHLEIERMACHER's vision gave direction to mainline Protestant theology up to the First World War: religion is a matter of strictly personal experience, but available only through mediation by some distinctive historical community. Even in this perspective, a dialogue between extant religious traditions is not particularly urgent, for the prospect is not one of different 'faiths' as neighbours obliged to share common ground, but more of streams, each with a source and a flow of its own, although water may in any case be water, if not always of an equally unpolluted quality.

When the reborn idea of evolution enjoyed its full triumph in all areas of human observation in the latter half of the 19th century, a tendency evolved to integrate each single religion as "higher" and "lower" on a common scale of "development", an orientation which for good reasons came to invite anything but dialogue. Nor was it mere chance that the heyday of evolution coincided with the triumphal season of Western colonialism. The Darwinian "Survival of the fittest" not only explained the dynamics of evolutionary progress; as "Social Darwinism" it could easily be mobilized to justify oppressive exploitation of some peoples/cultures by others!

Around 1900, the relationship between the world religions – if any there were[3] – was structured precisely by the fact of *Western colonialism*, accompanied by a generally accepted image of 'Christian' cultural dominance. The countries setting the theological agenda of the day were generally identical with the big colonial powers. Christian mission was indirectly, but effectively supported by a general longing to share the technological, economic and intellectual progress of the West in peoples which for generations had been paralyzed by an image of themselves as not only economically, but also spiritually underdeveloped.

Correspondingly, the Occidental churches, not-with-standing a genuine missionary fervor, could barely help but evolve a feeling of superiority, which also, with or without reflection, colored even their approach to non-Christian religion. There was not only the gulf between the Gospel and "blunt paganism", so strongly emphasized by conventional preachers, but also the concept of progress with distinctive levels of development, infinitely dear to theological and political liberalism. "Progressives" could be no less condescending than "conservatives".

With all this, *a split* was starting to manifest itself. I am not primarily referring to the growing confrontation between colonizers and colonized, world opinion and power balance having to undergo impressive changes in the decades to come. I refer to a tension challenging (Western) Christian identity from within.

In order to consolidate its alliance with the progressive powers of the day, the liberal wing of Christianity, dominating the academical and political West in the last decades before World War I, needed to clothe itself in a lofty and not too discriminatory idea of 'comparative Religion'. New disciplines of study: history, phenomenolo-

---

[3] The World Parliament of Religions, in Chicago 1893, and the scattered flora of international organizations for interreligious understanding which emerged during the following 60 years, can hardly be said to modify the image of interreligious dialogue as a process first taking off along with the last third of the 20. century, cf. BAYBROOKE 1980 and 1992.

gy, psychology, sociology ... of religion, were generally geared to legitimize Christianity as the highest known expression of religious life – a life understood as the most basic of human concerns. Dominant in the religio-cultural image of the day was Christianity in its remarkable historical adaptability – until then unmatched by any tradition of faith.

One important circumstance escaped observation, however: the fundamental self-contradiction of such superiority. Its lofty idea of humanity should supposedly have undermined any celebration of own superiority and restricted all "comparative" approaches based on near-sighted criteria of evaluation. "Religion" as the paramount expression of humanity should dissuade any quest for a religious ranking list. Precisely the evolutionary perspective, however, produced a paradoxical obstacle to any progress of interreligious understanding: the dogmatic idea of progress itself. At the same time a most intricate threat to fellowship developed: the complacent indulgence in one's own alleged tolerance.

A remarkable wave of general pessimism and critique seized the Occident in the decade following World War I – discernible not least in Continental uneasiness about Western culture (Spengler), literature (Kafka), philosophy (Heidegger) and theology (Barth). This explains to a certain extent why the reflection on religion(s) and the quest for a wider ecumenical space in the period between the two great wars so manifestly had to depart from the previous, "liberal" celebration of human accomplishment. The intrinsic contradiction of modern faith in progress had become apparent, and so had Western self-glorification, sticking as it was to its evaluative approach to "comparative religion".

The new concentration of main-line theology on a Bible-based demarcation of Christian identity, advocated above all by "Dialectical theology" – KARL BARTH and his followers – soon gained control also of the new ecumenical movement in its process of formation. In the age of developing dialogue half a century later, this "neo-orthodox" breakthrough in the 1920–30's was widely frowned upon and even seen as a regrettable setback. Karl Barth the dogmatician and his follower HENDRIK KRAEMER – the great name in missiology and ecumenical theology – were generally regarded as main respondents. In recent years, attempts have been made to acquit both the two from the most robust accusations, and reference has been made to indications of a more "open" orientation in their later, supposedly more mature works (from the post-war period).[4]

What might have been proven by the critics in the 1970's and later, is, however, that the post-World War I reaction was less directed against Non-Christian religions than against what seemed to be the exploitation of "religion" for domestic Christian purposes, namely (1) the downgrading of Christian soteriology on modernistic premises, (2) the overrating of the human species as capable of administering its own

---

[4] The unmitigated anti-dialogue profile of Barth and Kraemer is still taken for granted by ARIARAJAH, former leader of the WCC Dialogue Unit, PD 1998, 258ff. – For a more complex understanding of the contributions of the two: SCHOEN 1984, 88–97; KÜNG, C 1986, 2–4; BRAATEN 1992, 49–63.

salvation, and correspondingly (3) the equally undue elevation of Western cultural superiority.

The eclipse of "religion" in Western thought – including Christian theology – during most of the second and third fourths of the 20th century gradually turned and took on a more complex character. In the 1960's a somewhat surprising interaction emerged between aging 'Neo-orthodoxy', with its classical accent on Christian uniqueness, and new-appearing 'Secular theology', with its praise of a desacralized modern world. But already around 1970 this somewhat unexpected partnership rapidly lost momentum, as well as the partners individually. Detection and denunciation of Occidental arrogance, such as it had now again come to the light in Western "Secular theology", was inescapable both in light of the political development (decolonialization) and of the growing self-confidence of the 'Third World' which, through the ecumenical movement, was also to gain a more and more audible voice within worldwide Christian conversation.

Simultaneously, the 'Green Wave' again brought the long forgotten doctrine of creation to the fore in theology, as a visionary rediscovery of God-given resources, this time as a universal realm of natural resources, which again opened up for a reinterpretation of religion – as the underlying integrative factor in human history.[5] Ecology became as candid a threat to the intellectual establishment of theological modernity as already was anti-colonialism.

1.2. The Break-Through of Dialogue

"Most interreligious dialogue has unto now been initiated by Christians", writes PAUL J. GRIFFITHS 1990 in the introduction to his anthology 'Christianity through Non-Christian Eyes'.[6] This observation has been confirmed by some dozens of other authors, but the fact is too evident to need further testimonies. At the same time, it is obvious that there are two sets of dynamic factors behind the breakthrough of dialogue.

First, there are the circumstances challenging humankind as a whole, leading to a quest for universal fellowship and intercultural cooperation in face of arms' race, socio-technological disintegration, economic underdevelopment, environmental crisis etc.

Second, there may be dynamics proper to the world religions, reciprocally and individually. This is already suggested in a preliminary look at Christian history, as just presented by our superficial sketch of a couple of centuries' prior reflection. These theological dynamics relate to, but are by no means a mere function of, the more general features of society so far brought to attention. Dynamics in other faiths – to a considerable extent geared to the same observations – obviously play a corresponding role in their respective constituencies.

[5] Cf. LØNNING 1989, particularly 5–24.
[6] GRIFFITHS 1990, 3.

Contemporary dialogue has been inspired by a new and more concrete vision than ever of religions as vehicles of human fellowship. Such a vision could materialize only through an obliging face-to-face exchange between people of differing commitments, ready to recognize each other as equally sincere, and equally dedicated to the cause shared by the human community. A joint concern of incalculable importance is becoming more and more accepted.

Eloquent testimonies of this new orientation and its expansion in contemporary Christendom can be observed already in the 1980 series of *"How My Mind has Changed over the Last Ten Years"*, a column presented at the end of each decade in *The Christian Century*. For the decade thus observed – the 1970s – one could freely state as the most remarkable trend a rediscovery of "religion" accompanied by the concern for a new exchange across religious borderlines.[7] The most characteristic headline in this collection may be the opening one, by the renowned sociologist of religion PETER L. BERGER: *"From Secularity to World Religions"*.[8] Several of the contributions profess a conversion from depreciative, pessimistic attitudes regarding religion(s) and worship, to an attitude of appreciation and hopeful expectation.

In recent literature on interreligious dialogue, numerous presentations of the authors' own paths to dialogue make impressive elements, often reflecting real conversion stories: the formation of a new alertness with a more deep-going acceptance of faiths differing from one's own. In several cases, the actual story is one of growing up, or of living a long time (in some cases: as a Christian missionary) in cultures stamped by foreign faiths, thus learning from close observation to appreciate patterns of spirituality other than one's own.[9]

"Crossing the Rubicon" is an expression that has come in use about the reorientation of someone who for the first time ventures to express a 'pluralist' acclamation of truth as – in principle – equally present in all faiths sincere. Evidently, this expression was first launched by one of the most candid pluralist advocates, the Roman Catholic theologian of religions PAUL KNITTER. His idea was to challenge a fellow in faith – another powerful proponent of dialogue: HANS KÜNG – to take a more powerful stand on principle. During a conference at Temple University, October 1984, Knitter attacked a paper of Küng's:

[7] WALL 1981.

[8] Ibid. 21(–28). – Cf. MOLTMANN, ibid. 107(–112).

[9] Particularly impressive are a number of testimonies by Christians with personal roots in India's fertile religious soil. Cf. PANIKKAR (who presents himself as "a Hindu Catholic"), in HICK & KNITTER 1987, 89–116. Further SAMARTHA (director of the WCC dialogue program 1971–80) 1996 – M.M. THOMAS (moderator of WCC Central Committee 1968–75) in D'COSTA 1990, 49–62 – and J. RUSSEL CHANDRAN, PD 98, 197–200. Other striking testimonies of attitudes changed (in addition to the Christian Century series referred to in note 7), are found in the works of Hick, especially 1985, 1–15, who also points to W.C. Smith as an influential model, ibid. 28–45. – Instructive is also the story of ECK, American hinduologist with Scandinavian background, sketching her own "spiritual journey from Bozeman to Benares," 1993. – A similar conversion story, but with explicit Catholic background and interpretative framework is presented by HILLMAN, 1989, cf. especially his preface.

"I am really asking HANS KÜNG to step across the Rubicon ... from an earlier inclusivist
position of viewing Christianity as the necessary fulfillment and norm of all religions, to a
more pluralist model that affirms that other religions may be just as valid as Christianity
..."[10]

The Rubicon image has exercised some orientative influence in the successive debate,
mainly in connection with the global scheme elaborated by JOHN HICK and PAUL
KNITTER:[11] a triple division of alternative approaches: *exclusivism – inclusivism – pluralism*, to which we will have ample occasion to return. "Crossing the river Rubicon"
then signalizes transition from 'inclusivism', a standpoint recognizing the faithful of
other religions as undoubtedly qualified for salvation by Christ – to 'pluralism', a full
admittance of equal truth and same salvatory power in every religion.

HANS KÜNG's critical response to the Rubicon invitation: *'What is True Religion?
Toward an Ecumenical Criteriology'* came at a follow-up seminar in Tübingen the
following year, and is included in the volume of the Temple papers.[12] Küng there
pleads in favor of "a generous, tolerant inclusivism" and states his warning: "What
looks like tolerance" may in practice be "a kind of conquest by embrace." GAVIN
D'COSTA's remark about the Rubicon image in the illustrious "Uniqueness debate" a
few years later goes in a similar direction: "Caesar's crossing of that same river in 49
BCE was a forceful attempt to encompass the 'other' within his own framework ...
some of the proposals put forward (i.e. by the 'pluralists') are as triumphalist and
imperialist as the old solutions being criticized."[13]

1.3. Personal Paths to "Dialogue"

On the whole, it is striking how the dialogue on dialogue, more than theological
discourse in general, tends to reactivate memories of some personal paths to the topic, and to challenge critics, encouraging them to biographical self-examination and
to rethinking of fixed attitudes.

In the setting of the present volume it can also be a challenge for the author to
recall his own involvement with dialogue and dialogue debate. It may be of limited
interest that I served as a member of the Structure Committee which among several
other initiatives proposed a particular Dialogue Unit in the World Council of
Churches (WCC) 1971. My role may have been less anonymous in the heated discussions at the WCC Assemblies in Nairobi 1975 and Vancouver 1983, and in the
meantime as a participant at the Chiang Mai consultation in 1977, where the dialogue program was substantially reviewed and reshaped. As a member of the Central

---

[10] KNITTER: 'Hans Küng's Theological Rubicon', in: SWIDLER 1987, 229 (224–230).
[11] HICK 1985, 31ff. – KNITTER 1985, Preface & 73–167. The latter refers to Race 1983, as the one
having first proposed this terminology.
[12] SWIDLER 1987, 231–250.
[13] D'COSTA 1990, IX.

Committee between Nairobi and Vancouver I was also in that period in a favorable position to observe and to comment on the program development.

As the official Assembly report confirms, I was the one who in Nairobi 1975 proposed to send the dialogue report back to Section III for revision, a proposal which was adopted by the plenary "by a large majority" (PATON). That precisely the same thing came to pass in Vancouver 7 1/2 years later, was as much of a surprise to me as, probably, to anyone else.[14] On that occasion the idea to intervene came to me in the last minute, the plenary having reached a state of deadlock on the report "Witnessing in a Divided World", where some spontaneous initiative was acutely needed to open a lane for continued procedure. Observations of the Vancouver episode have not been so vividly recorded and commented as Nairobi, obviously because my 1983 intervention was geared to assembly procedure more than to principles. At that time the adopted Guidelines (proposed by the Chiang Mai consultation 1977 and adopted by the Central Committe in Kingston, Jamaica 1979) were no actual topic of discussion.

The immediate involvement of the author with the WCC Dialogue program ended when my membership in the Central Committee expired in 1983. In the following four years I had a more indirect, but in itself quite stimulating occasion to follow the dialogue discussion as it was carried on within the ecumenical family worldwide, namely in my daily occupation as research professor at the Institute for Ecumenical Research in Strasbourg, France. My main responsibility here was a comprehensive study on 'Creation – An Ecumenical Challenge?'[15] In analyzing the comeback of creation thought in recent theology – an event very much parallel to, and partly linked with, the resurgence of religion in the same period – the study forced me to reflect a good deal also on the contemporary development of dialogue in the perspective of a global theological concern.

In connection with a series of reports from the Strasbourg study which I offered through the 'Ecumenical Review' (official publication of the WCC), I was asked to contribute to a special issue of this review dedicated to the dialogue discussion. Maybe I was invited also because of my past, which could make me a suitable 'advocatus

---

[14] David M. PATON (ed.): 'Breaking Barriers – Nairobi 1975', Geneva 1976, 70. – David GILL (ed.): 'Gathered for Life' – Vancouver 1983, Geneva 1984, 31.– Cf. BAYBROOKE 1980, 100f; MULDER, SID 2/ 1 1992, 145ff; ZEHNER 1992, 82ff; BASSET 1996, 226–235. – I must, however, protest the Nairobi scenario in ECK 1993, 198: "A bishop of the Church of Norway led the attack, calling dialogue a betrayal of Christian mission. The Church should be engaged in proclaiming the Gospel to the ends of the earth and making disciples of all nations, not in interreligious dialogue, he said." – As the only person present to whom this remark can possibly refer, I do not remember, there or anywhere else, to have described mission and dialogue as mutually exclusive. How could my proposal of returning the actual draft to the committee for revision – if based on such an argument – have obtained "a large majority" in an Assembly which finally came out with a clear pro-dialogue declaration?

[15] Cf. the reports: LØNNING 1989, and idem (ed:) 'Selected Papers', LWFD 28, May 1990; further David G. BURKE (ed.) 'Creation and Culture: The Challenge of Indigenous Spirituality and Culture to Western Creation Thought', an integral element of the recorded Strasbourg study, LWM Studies 1987. More about this: 5.2.5.4., cf. our note 131.

diaboli'. From ecumenical observers in various quarters I received words of surprise that my contribution "Dialogue: A Question about 'Religiology'"[16] was rather balanced and my conclusions fairly sympathetic in their assessment of the contemporary development.

After having finished my years in Strasbourg, I was determined to take up a study on dialogue and theology of religions as soon as time might permit, having already collected a good deal of the material substantial to such a project. For the following 7 years, however, obligations in domestic church life heavily restricted academical activities, and I had to leave anymajor study project aside. Retiring from my episcopal duties in Bergen in 1994, I received an unexpected invitation from the renowned Christian Michelsen's Institute (CMI) in that city – which is strongly involved in studies on international relations and human rights – inviting practical cooperation.

Three years of valuable contact with the CMI provided new possibilities for my work, among others three interesting study tours (Tübingen, Geneva, round-trip USA). From this cooperation there first emerged a study on 'fundamentalism', in the Norwegian language – focused on the origin, developments, transformations and communicative complications of that term and of movements associated with it.[17] Also the collection of material for the dialogue study was largely completed during that period. I am very grateful to the CMI for these opportunities.

Having observed the development of dialogue for a quarter of a century, and appearing as a "bad guy" in several records of that history, the question of how my attitude to dialogue may have changed over these years may be of interest not only to myself. I am not one of those champions of dialogue who have a remarkable conversion story to report. But nor can I say that my reflections have remained unaffected by the observation of shifting tides. To me as, hopefully, to many, the picture of an ever shrinking world with ever expanding needs for communication – in a deeper and more authentic sense than hitherto produced – has become ever more impressive.

Trying to stick to a vision of theology as a global enterprise (in more than one sense!), not to be disintegrated by isolated concerns, it is not difficult to see that a concrete experience of practical commitment may challenge an abstract formulation of however legitimate principles. In straight terms: a pragmatic quest for dialogue should not in itself dictate theology, but in a situation of live encounter it may well open minds for vital theological self-examination. Such examination is not only needed. In the world of today it must be classified as urgent.

If I for my part have one specific sin to confess in this connection, I am one of the many who for several years – following the "syncretism" debate invited by the moderator M.M.Thomas at the WCC Assembly in Nairobi – cherished the term "syncretism" as a negative heuristic principle. Such a methodological move demands a good deal more care and reflection than conservative participants in the debate were for a

---

[16] ER 1985, 506–511.
[17] LØNNING 1997.

long time prepared to admit. This is the only observable issue where my reflection on interreligious dialogue may have bluntly changed over the years, as will hopefully be proven by the present study.

1.4. "Dialogue" and Conceptual Modesty

Some reservation must be taken in light of epistemological temptations commonly attached to the term "Dialogue". The word itself echoes two highly different, both well-observed and important trails of communication. The widespread efforts of our day for revitalizing strategies of exchange in all areas pertaining to human community may be the one most familiar to contemporary observers. But the philosophical tradition dating back to Old Greece (Plato!), of exploring truth by consciously relating it to logical laws seen as constitutive of dialogical exchange, has been tested out over a much longer course of time is a. In classical Greek the noun διάλογος as much as the adjective διαλεκτικός correspond with the verb διαλέγομαι.

It goes without saying that our approach to the term so far – like the majority of recent responses to "dialogue" and human coexistence – has entered the communicative context of contemporary pragmatics first mentioned, without taking much notice of the classical Greek inheritance.

When, at this stage of reflection, we make a short break and ask about the possible advantages of a more philosophical approach to our key term, this is no direct consequence of the deliberations presented so far. We do so because a speculative orientation, supporting a universal theory of dialogue as a hermeneutical clue to contemporary interreligious dialogue, is already on the arena. And it has been launched with so emphatic an argument and with so impressive consequences, that it will need some examination.

I am again referring to JEAN-CLAUDE BASSET: *Le dialogue inter-religieux, Histoire et avenir* (1996). This comprehensive, well-informed and existentially engaging study may, in terms of concern, be seen as belonging to what we shall later examine as "pluralist" theology of religions.[18] Methodologically, however, it moves along a distinctive path of its own, to a certain extent guided by RAIMUNDO PANIKKAR's mystical understanding of "intrareligious dialogue", which we have already made the object of critical comment, although, so far, just from a consideration of terminology.[19]

Basset starts his study by developing, at a considerable length, a general theory of dialogue. This part of his reflection proceeds from an observation of the expanding contemporary use of the notion "in all domains of human existence" and moves on to the author's development of his own "hermeneutic of dialogue".[20] When, in this perspective, "interreligious dialogue" is presented as "in certain regards a prolonga-

---

[18] Here, 4.1.
[19] Cf. our comment, 0.2., note 1.
[20] BASSET 1996, 11–63.

tion of the ecumenical intrareligious dialogue,"[21] he evidently proposes to extend the
experience of spiritual fellowship as a dimension transcending argument and opinions – an experience rather common today in the domestic "ecumenism" of single
religions – and claims its validity also between supporters of different religions.

What this means, he more thoroughly explains in a later chapter on "Typologie du
dialogue".[22] We have already seen how BASSET there attempts to present and promote
RAIMUNDO PANIKKAR's mystical concept of "intrareligious dialogue" as a pan-
religious event.[23] So he goes on:

> "C'est assurément le niveau le plus profond du dialogue interreligieux ... Avec la dimension
> intérieure ou intrareligieuse, le dialogue touche sa propre limite, au-delà de laquelle nous
> parlons, faute de mieux, d'ultra-communication, par analogie avec les rayons ultraviolets ...
> la rencontre interreligieuse devient une expérience commune de méditation silecieuse, de
> contemplation infinie, d'accord intime et d'adhésion à l'être des choses ... À ce dépassement
> des mots et des représentations corresponde la théologie apophatique de la tradition chré-
> tienne qui rejoint l'affirmation advaïta de la non-dualité et la quête zen de la non-discrimi-
> nation" [24]

This quotation takes us some miles away from what we have for our own part presented as "the ecumenical intrareligious dialogue". We have already questioned the
clarifying value of Panikkar's extended terminology and indicated our reasons for
using the word "intra-religious" with a more simple, verifiable meaning, to cover the
more or less structured dialogue within each religion in order to clarify its own dialogical relationship with other faiths, which also seems to be the most widespread use
of the term in contemporary discussion.

Our objection this time is not concerning terminology. Nor is it about the issue in
a strict sense: whether some apophatic communication based on a universal concept
of religion could, and eventually should, be invited as the final integrative aim of
dialogue. The adequacy of such a claim may be proven if (after so substantial a dialogue as possible) it is universally accepted by the dialogue partners as not infringing
upon anyone's conviction. On these conditions there will be ample occasion to reflect
in a broader exposé on "religion" versus "religions" at a later stage of our study.[25]

The decisive observations at this stage of events are on methodology, especially
seen in the following perspective. Even if some mystical experience of shared meaning – by Basset described as the peak of dialogical communication – may be a reality
of such a significance as he maintains, one preparatory question remains to be asked.
Could such a mystical fulfilment of dialogical rapprochement be generally foreseen
and meaningfully programmed in advance? Could it be stated as an aim that must be
accepted by each of the partners before opening the dialogical procedure?

---

[21] Ibid., 29.
[22] Ibid., 313–355
[23] Here, 0.2., note 1.
[24] Op.cit., 354f.
[25] Here 5.1.

As we have observed, BASSET allocates "intrareligious dialogue" on two different steps of a great process: at the beginning and at the end – but does he offer an acceptable justification of this terminological duplicity? As an initial stage he foresees a prestructural experience of shared meaning, which precedes and inspires the subsequent, organized dialogue event. Later, at the final stage, the label "intrareligious dialogue" occurs a second time, attached to a final, supposedly unsurpassable experience of wordless, dialogue-based understanding. Undeniably, it may be meaningful to explain and support organized dialogue by referring to prestructural experience of communication, one's own and that of persons or communities under corresponding observation. Such observations seem to be widespread enough to sustain a general theory of wordless dialogical experience without compromising the convictions of any potential participant. But such a justification does not in itself imply the theory of an all-surpassing wordless stage of final, mystical accomplishment. Can an empirical verification of dialogue as ultimately fulfilled be imagined in this world of ours?

The intriguing problem is that BASSET's theory presents to the partners, as they are passing the gateway to dialogue, a prospect which anticipates agreement on important decisions of faith as already well behind us. In such circumstances, the very option for dialogue may contain violations of positions vital to some partakers. Viewed as an essential element constitutive to dialogue, the theory of a final transverbal, universalized accomplishment does not extend, but narrows the scope of the eventual dialogue to follow.

Encompassing interreligious dialogue in some universal theory of dialogue at large may easily exclude potential, highly desirable exchange partners, and more so the more the construction itself takes on metaphysical garments. When dialogue itself, or a dominant section of it, is proclaimed a priori to possess a conclusive mystical character, it is no longer an unrestricted exchange on religion(s) by religions, it threatens to establish the very process of exchange as a new religion of its own.

Our conclusion on BASSET's methodological approach, then, is less paradoxical than it may sound. His integrative principle seems to be a global theory of dialogue, held together by an impressive vision of a concluding apophatic unification. Expressed as a pious yearning by one dialogue partner in front of the others, this may in itself cause no damage to a mutual dialogical approach. It is, however, a different thing if it gives profile to a theory supposedly to be accepted and applied as heuristic principle by all the dialogue partners in unison. As we understand Basset's theory, it is definitely too narrow to support a non-discriminatory invitation to dialogue – i.e. to an unrestricted exchange of fundamental convictions.

1.5 A World in Need of Dialogue

In his first major contribution to the dialogue debate 'God has Many Names – Britain's New Religious Pluralism', 1980, the sturdy pioneer of a "pluralist" theology of religions JOHN HICK describes his own lane to dialogue. After a captivating description of his personal development from an ardent evangelical to a militant liberal theologian, he proceeds to a description of "The wider context: Christianity and race in Britain today."[26] It is remarkable how ethnic encounter here is made the hermeneutical clue to religious plurality. This may be a meaningful and highly recommendable approach – seen in a predominantly sociological perspective. But a question must be asked about the propriety of making it a supreme principle of theological judgement – even if a robust theological adaptation may have several favorable effects in the actual situation.

Even if problems of racial reconciliation may have different proportions in little Norway compared to those in big Britain, it is clear that a racial aspect of the dialogue challenge is by no means absent in my, or in any other Western European, country. The immigration boom of the last generation has established a substantial presence of non-Christian religions, particularly Islam, in countries which forty years ago were massively monocultural, not least in terms of religious belonging. And certainly the experience of religious difference is but one, even if the most spectacular, expression of cultural differentiation. It must be seen as a part, and as a constituent, of that variety. Westerners tend to oversee that to the majority of non-Western immigrants a deep-rooted consciousness of religious belonging constitutes ethnic, and thus cultural, identity in a way widely unintelligible to the "Christian" Occident.

In Norway the challenge of immigrant religion(s) has since 1991 found an initial, if, so far, quantitatively modest, response from "prevailing" Christianity in the new Emmaus movement: a dialogue-center in Oslo with affiliated groups in major cities around the country. This work is sponsored by the Nordic Christian Buddhist Mission (from March 2000: "Areopagos"), a foundation which, from its start in 1922 by the visionary pioneer KARL LUDVIG REICHELT, specialized in a dialogical approach to Buddhist monks (starting in China). Initiatives similar to the Emmaus project may in the last decade be observed in several countries in the East as well as in the West.

But just as demanding for our existential reflection as mass immigration and crumbling of religious uniformity, is the fact of a world becoming more and more unified and – with all its increasing pluralism – more and more uniformed. The challenge of dialogue is inside as much as it is outside our geographical borders. It transcends borders as much as it challenges borders.

Whatever one may think of JOHN HICK's pluralist theology of religions as guide to the mutual rapprochement needed between cultures – and to this we shall certainly have possibilities to return – his wrestling with irresistible dynamics of social transformation, as presented in 1980, are in themselves equally relevant today, and so is his plea for increased understanding between the world religions.

---

[26] HICK 1980, 10–27.

2. Expectations to Dialogue

The method unfolded in this chapter will be a somewhat unusual one. We don't start our reflection by collecting and arranging facts on dialogue: origin, development, discussion, various evaluations ... We start by stating a series of motivating expectations. The rest with the test will follow in time. It may stimulate reflection to face a series of hypothetical constructions, reviewing critically the hopes and foresights stimulating our research. When handled with care, this method may even provide some help to uncover and to bar lanes of wishful thinking. We would rather give an account of motivations, bringing them out in the open air, than risk them to guide the research – unobserved and uncontrolled.

Certainly, it may also happen that an imaginative recording of desirable aims could exercise an unduly captivating influence on the accommodation of facts to follow. The advantage of complemental procedures is that they allow different possibilities of exercising supplementary as well as corrective influence on each other.

2.1. Options for Peace in Actual Situations of Conflict

"Kein Weltfriede ohne Religionsfriede!" – No world peace without peace of religion! These famous words by HANS KÜNG are not merely a thought-provoking slogan, they are the title of a comprehensive program of international study and conscience-making.[1] The statement sounds immediately convincing, even if some may doubt whether religion plays so influential a part in contemporary life that peaceful relations between the world religions could be among major prerequisites for peace worldwide. For peace in certain regions of the world, it obviously does.

As a whole it is more than difficult to distinguish the precise role of religious disunity as source of political conflict. Nevertheless, in some of the most heart-breaking conflicts of the day it is impossible to shut one's eyes to a spectacular role of religious controversy in the descriptions by the news media, and so, often, in the propaganda of the conflicting partners themselves. – There is the confrontation of Eastern religions – religions with high general reputations of peacefulness: Buddhists and Hindus on Sri Lanka. Behind the latent conflict between India and Pakistan we distinguish dominant majorities of Hindus and Muslims respectively. In the Middle East, Jews and Muslims are facing each other. In the region of Caucasus, Christians (Armenia, Georgia) and Muslims (Azerbaidzhan, Kazakstan) have been in armed confrontations. In former Yugoslavia there is the triangular tension between Catholic

---

[1] KÜNG 1990, cf. 102. – KÜNG & KUSCHEL 1993.

Christians (Croatia and Slovenia), Orthodox Christians (Serbia, Bosnia) and Muslims (Bosnia, Kosovo). In Northern Ireland we have the old struggle between Roman Catholic (Irish) and Protestant(English) Christians. The list could be continued.

Even with the reservation suggested about religion as a pretext for highly secular interests, our case list may be more than enough to give reality to Küng's pathetic appeal. Even if the role of religion in political conflicts were definitely reduced to that of "holy" pretext for unholy assaults, armed or unarmed, this would be enough to recommend serious dialogue as a hopefully efficient instrument for peace. Dismantling arguments which justify conflict, may in turn serve to expose and to neutralize also the real causes of conflict.

For the sake of fairness, cases should also be recorded where religion has undeniably contributed to solve conflicts which might otherwise have taken a rather frightening course. Most impressive among examples from recent years is the racial conflict in South Africa. Also the peaceful transition from communist dictatorship to democratic government in countries like Poland (Catholic majority) and the former GDR (Protestant majority) was to a large extent staged through the respective churches. Even if a similar initiative was scarcely observed from the official churches in the USSR, the presence of organized religion to fill into the spiritual vacuum after disintegrating Marxism, has probably contributed to securing a peaceful political transition.

It must be added, however, that in some of the conflicts listed above, the peacemaking contributions of religious organizations and leaders have been less remarkable than there were reasons to expect. It can be assumed that more has taken place to that end behind the scenes than observed by news media, but the general impression is that religion generally is linked with nationhood, ethnic identity and established power to an extent that makes religious leaders remarkably hesitant to voice opinions differing from those of their constituency. That image is, alas, too familiar to call for concrete exemplification.

Universal peace, as an indisputable good to be pursued by all people(s), is apparently an agreed goal to all religions. Nothing, then, should be more natural than steadfast peace initiatives, be it a single religion acting on its own, or be it in suitable cases two or more religious communities acting in common.

We could imagine such initiatives in cases like the following. (1) In the midst of a concrete crisis, particularly where followers of different faiths stand face-to-face in open confrontation, and the need to speak with each other is urgent. (2) In situations of permanent, often latent, tensions, where the relationship between believers of different faiths in a region are chronically suffering under unresolved conflicts, and where, in the long run, violence may be threatening if issues are left unresolved. (3) In a transregional perspective, where traditional attitudes of suspicion and fear between two religions show an enduring tendency to elicit conflicts around the world, and a transnational, maybe global, rethinking of the relationship between those two may have consequences also for peace and socio-political harmony. (4) Independent of time, place and particular situations, in principle: open conversation between religions on mutual peace responsibility, as a permanent resource to prevent the emergence and spreading of conflicts world-wide.

2.2. Human Survival – Sharing of Socio-Ethical Resources

In our contemporary world there are also, apart from any arms race, permanent, expanding threats to the survival of humankind and of creation, where possibly conflicting interests can hardly be attached to differences of religion. At the same time, it seems obvious that not least the call for cooperation in order to save our planet from environmental destruction should have a particular appeal to organized religion.

What can religions accomplish – if anything – in face of such challenges? Can faith replace science, can prayer do better than innovative research? At least one lesson has been learned by our generation: Science – and her daughter technology – are not alone able to solve the problems of the world, least of all the ones sustained by themselves. Growing knowledge means growing possibilities – for good and for evil. For troublemaking as much as for troubleshooting. Without some unifying vision of world and meaning, how can there be motivating power sufficient to bring the overwhelming potentialities of human know-how under control?

Here a particularly demanding (and promising?) domain of dialogue opens up. Different as religions are in their conception of God and world, they share a common experience of global purpose, of some universal that gives integral meaning even to the most trifling occurrence in the universe. Such an integrative vision is held and interpreted in a variety of languages, but through joint examination apparent differences may turn into complementary expressions of a common truth, indeed, may even throw clarifying light on common positions. How far this may be so in a particular case, can be concluded only through joint, dialogical exploration.

I – and I know, many with me – had a most striking experience of such clarification in observing the impressive and highly challenging presence of Native Americans ("Indians") at the World Council of Churches' Assembly in Vancouver B.C. in 1983. In our contemporary world it is apparent that the "Abrahamic" religions (Mosaic, Christian, Muslim) can be profitably reminded of truths basic to their own traditions, by more environmentally integrated indigenous religion. By this I am referring not only to remnants of traditional, pre-biblical religion, but to Christianity as received and adapted in communities with a strong previous inheritance of veneration for what they sense to be the great mystery of nature. A similar observation may apply to the great civilizations of the East, which to a certain extent still resist the invasion of modern, technologically supported, materialism.

We have already indicated the "green revolution" around 1970 as an important orientative event in the history of theological reflection. It contributed to the rediscovery of "religion" as rooted in creation and therefore as a universal. This again was apt to encourage communication between different religions as pertaining to ecological balance in the widest sense. A similar reinforcement of exchange imposed itself through an observation of the threats to creation in a world of close to universal environmental crisis. The preservation of nature calls for human reflection and initiative on a global scale, which above anything else must imply communicative solidarity.

A particularly critical challenge was directed to the "Abrahamic religions", affiliated as they were and are with the industrialized, supposedly most anti-ecological segments of humanity. This was interpreted as no mere chance, but was given a fundamentally theological explanation. Viewing the Creator as exalted, remote, non-objectifiable – a vision leaving creation itself as void of obliging mystery – this "family" of religions with their joint background in Mosaic creation faith was accused as the main culprit of the environmental catastrophe.[2] Entrusting the earth to a "dominium terrae"[3] exercised more or less arbitrarily by the human species, these religions have allegedly relinquished the earth to exploitation by human inventiveness = greed.

To a large extent, these accusations must be seen as a response to the so-called "secular theology" of the 60's, with HARVEY COX's best-seller 'The Secular City' (1965) as a spectacular highlight. Here the Bible was praised as forerunner of the modern urbanized civilization with its abrogation of all sacred taboos in the name of individual freedom. In a peculiar way this trend continued and sharpened the neo-orthodox denunciation of extra-biblical "religion" and supported the slogan of the late 60-s: "The World Provides the Agenda".[4] In an environmental setting that meant: biblical tradition has set humankind free from traditions and taboos and entrusted the earth to the administration of human rationality.

Neglected were two highly regressive consequences of this so demonstratively "progressive" theology. First, there was the striking absence of ecological awareness. The uncritical acceptance of modern urbanized culture with its consumers' pattern, exempt from any taboo restriction, was more rapidly detected and denounced by sociologists and economists than by theologians. Then, there was the obvious arrogance against religion-based cultures, the great religions of the East as well as the remainders of indigenous religion in various parts of the world. "Ontocratic" was the denunciatory badge proposed by the religionist AREND TH. VAN LEEUWEN to pinpoint the identity of religions yet untouched by the historical flow of "secularization".[5]

---

[2] The most spectacular advocates of this criticism were: Lynn WHITE. 'The Historical Roots of the Ecological Crisis', Science 155 (10 March 1967) and: 'The Environmental Handbook' 1970, further Carl AMERY 'Das Ende der Vorsehung – Die gnadenlosen Folgen des Christentums', 1972. A more comprehensive presentation of the debate is given by LØNNING 1989, 5–24.

[3] Especially "anthropocentric" Old Testament creation texts like Gen 1:28, 9:1ff, Ps 8:6ff came under fire.

[4] Slogan launched in the WCC study report 'The Church for Others' (1967), one of the main inputs for the WCC Assembly in Uppsala 1968, 20ff. – The so-called "secular Theology" of the 1960s leans heavily on Dietrich BONHOEFFER's posthumous prison diary 'Widerstand und Ergebung' 1951, and on Friedrich GOGARTEN: 'Verhängnis und Hoffnung der Neuzeit' 1953. – Among chief contributors are Martin VAN BUREN 'The Secular Meaning of the Gospel' 1963, Thomas J.J. ALTIZER 'The Gospel of Christian Atheism' 1966, and Dorothee SÖLLE: 'Atheistisch an Gott glauben' 1968.

[5] A. VAN LEEUWEN 1964, 331ff.

In the course of a few years this triumphalist proclamation of a Christian, Occidental, technologically secured superiority was brusquely swept away. In view of a forthcoming environmental crisis Western self-exultation was swiftly turned into an accusation. Not the historical denunciation of GALILEO's mechanical universe, a denunciation so passionately condemned by Enlightenment civilization, but three centuries of subsequent prostration for his "knowledge as power of conquest", was now pointed out as the Church's capital failure in face of the modern scientific revolution.

The Church had to admit: we have failed; first, by the voices of ecumenical conferences and church-related study agencies; soon also through more official channels: theological faculties and church synods and even, finally, the Pope. The fault, as confessed, was not one of the biblical authors' of old, but of interpreters' of Scripture through several centuries, not least the 20th. The authors of the Old Testament are now acclaimed as being much closer to the experience of the big chief Seattle than to the theological best-seller of Harvey Cox.

With this historical lesson in mind, it may be quite rewarding to return to our contemporary issue of dialogue. Like few other topics the future of creation needs to be recognized as an item of shared religious concern. Not only is it a matter of survival to us all. It has got to do with a commitment, more or less recognized by all religions, to preserve creation as constitutive and protective of human identity. What humankind needs is not only knowledge of the material consequences of our choices. Factual information is available to a much larger extent than the world seems able to make constructive use of. The major problem is that of motivation, i.e. of willingness to set aside private interests for the benefit of a wider community, including other social groups, other geographical domains, generations to come. The problem in the problem is a fatal lack of a vision universal.

This applies not only to human survival, dependent as it is on environmental protection, but just as much to the unequal distribution of poverty and wealth worldwide. Even the latter is a long-term threat to the survival of humankind, and no less serious than that of environmental destruction. In the world of tomorrow the two may prove more closely related than dreamed of by most people today. That the two, united as well as individually, are also intimately connected with the arms/peace issue, it should probably be unnecessary to prove!

In the perspective of dialogue, it is impressive that the unequal distribution of wealth to such an overwhelming extent follows religion-related ethno-cultural borders. So far, there are few indications that political conferences, plans, and initiatives have brought the world one step toward increased economic equality. Is it possible that joint initiatives by the world religions could help to overcome that stalemate? At the moment, indications in this direction are few, and the issue of economy has been more visible on the agenda of Christian mission and church aid than of interreligious dialogue. At the same time, it is unthinkable that the process of dialogue can prosper unless the vital dimension of distribution really enters the arena.

For one thing, economy has so much to do with the issue of human sharing versus inhuman greed, that in the long run it would compromise the very idea of dialogical fellowship if money were kept consciously out of the agenda. In the perspective of interreligious understanding as motive of joint human action, poverty/wealth may some day become the ultimate test case. Unnecessary to state, it would also compromise dialogue if this issue did turn the whole dialogical exchange into a process of economic bargaining.

In this connection it may also be worthwhile to recall the limited influence of religion on contemporary political decision-making, particularly in the wealthy parts of the world, and of the actual financial problems of churches (probably also of synagogues, mosques and monasteries) in upholding the traditional level of their own activities. In spite of that, the question has to be raised in a not too distant future: can the worldwide dialogue of religions speak to political rulers and inspire them with motivating power in issues of distribution worldwide? Or, is the problem predominantly this: could they agree with each other about what to say?

Religions cannot claim a special competence in technical, economical or political matters. What they share with each other, may, however, be of no lesser importance for humanity's choice of a common future. After all, the essential need relates to ultimate power of motivation, exposed via some unifying vision of reality. The variety of vesture in which such a vision will evidently present itself, may – all available information dialogically compared and combined – add to its potential of global motivation rather than detract from it.

In all their variety, religions could also share with each other some sobering memories from their own history. Not precisely of the same events, but of comparatively equal substance, if courage is there to admit and to share it. They hold a tremendous experience of human nature in its strength and its weakness, and correspondingly of the power – and powerlessness – of enrapturing appeals seizing human minds and transforming vision into practice. For better, for worse.

2.3. Being Human – Revitalizing a Common Base

What does it finally mean to be a human, and which are the forces particularly threatening the humanity of humans in this rapidly changing world of ours? At stake is not some conceptually agreed definition of humanhood, but a shared experience, a consciousness of joint participation in the mystery of human belonging-together.

Obviously, we cannot command such a fellowship experience to transform itself into a philosophical or theological anthropology demanding to be embraced by all. Over the centuries, experience of human value has been expressed in highly different languages of interpretation. Apart from that, and irrespective of accidental historical circumstances, below the surface there may always have been some latent understanding of the sanctity of human life, an understanding frequently suppressed, but always ready to break through and to open up for a new state of affairs.

Even in our contemporary world, there are many indications that conviction of unconditional value, such as represented by the major world religions, is one of the strongest, maybe *the* strongest, warrantor of inviolable humanity. The most conspicuous exception to this assumption may be the menace to human personhood by resurgent fundamentalism[6] in our day, most visibly represented by expanding militant branches of Islam. It may be assumed that in religious communities open for dialogue, there will be common support to some vision of human integrity as the very base of society – irrespective of theoretical adaptations and explanations as represented by each religion as such

In an "Abrahamic" perspective (Judaism, Christianity, Islam) this fellowship may be explained by reference to the biblical creation story. The human person, man and woman alike, is created "in God's image" (Gen 1:27). It would be more than superficial to exclude peoples and communities not believing in a personal creator from such a vision: Buddhists, taoists, animists, atheists, pantheists, deists ...? No one should ever be pressured into believing in the Creator in order to have his or her full human dignity recognized, and no believer ever could or should exclude a non-believing neighbor from creation-based human dignity. Creation, if really believed, ranges wider than belief in creation.

The dehumanizing powers in today's world are not easily recognizable in the marketing profiles of movements and ideologies. Maybe a global diagnosis could most adequately be picked up by the etiquette so much in use in the late 20th century of a "consumers' culture". – In a bold attempt to see the wide variety of menaces to the future of creation and humanity, the Bishop's Conference of the Lutheran Church of Norway in 1992 invited and consecutively recommended and published an experts' report on *The Consumer Society as an Ethical Challenge*, followed by a special appeal to public reflection.[7] A wide range of practical challenges were brought together in a searching question about what this society of ours does to human personhood by forging "consumer souls" – in its own image. This initiative was met with unusual interest and a multitude of interested comments by media and so, it seemed, by the public in general. A promising sign – or a self-contradiction?

The consumer society, as religious surrogate, is characterized by its implicit understanding of consumption as supreme rationale of human existence. The alliance between booming technology and flourishing market psychology has signalized a reification of human identity like never in history: to "have one's life from one's belongings" (Luk 12:15).

If anything is a provocation to religion in all its shades and shapes, this must be it! Particularly the great religions of the East seem ready to identify Western materialism as spiritual enemy No. 1. They see it rapidly spreading also in their part of the world: a disintegration not only of a traditional spiritual universe, but of an integral human society in all its appearances – to the benefit of a conscienceless amassment of material goods.

---

[6] Cf. LØNNING 1997.
[7] Issued in Norwegian. English edition 1993 (Church of Norway Information Center, Oslo).

To a certain extent, the critical attitude in other parts of the world directed against "Western materialism" is combined with a general reproach against Christianity, the religion of "the white man", for insufficient resistance to modern developments, yea, for compromising what should presumably be its own vision of the world. The distance between biblical standards and the economic, political, cultural strategies on display in "the Christian World" is too striking.

Possibly the criticism directed against Christianity in other parts of the world, underrates the repercussions of secularization in 20th century Europe and North America, and seems to overestimate the opinion-shaping potential of the Occidental churches. But such an explanatory apology should definitely not exempt Christians from exploring this criticism in open conversation with their critics.

In the domain of human dignity/human rights, there may also be an additional, apparently opposite perspective: the "Christian" West asking questions of oppressive political systems in other parts of the world, including the role of domestic religion in the countries and regions concerned. The breakdown of communist regimes in extensive parts of the world has – quantitatively, at least – reduced the problem of totalitarian governments systematically exploiting religion(s) for political purposes – a strategy which in modern times has probably hit and hurt Christian churches at a larger scale than any other religious family. That has been a predicament which, for goods reasons, could not be mastered through open dialogue, neither with the regimes nor with the religious communities directly affected.

The major challenge in the area of religion and political oppression today may be that of resurgent politico-religious fundamentalism seizing political power in not unimportant segments of the world. This fact is obviously an obstacle to dialogical exchange, as much as it, at the same time, urges the necessity of it.

In Sudan we have so far probably the only example of an Islamic government organizing interreligious dialogue as an official enterprise. This has led also to the arrangement of official conferences, partly with representative international guests, not least from Christian churches, where issues basic to religious freedom and interfaith cooperation have been on the agenda. Official documents give, however, a somewhat depressing impression of this as an establishment initiative organized in order to quench the international criticism which for years has been voiced against the Sudanese regime for oppression of religious freedom.[8] Undeniably this observation of government-supported interreligious dialogue as political instrument – to which we shall return more extensively in a later context – relates the issue of dialogue to the political and ideological discussion of the comprehensive issue of Human Rights in our contemporary world. Can the world religions contribute to bringing that important exchange out of a contemporary stalemate?

In any case, a profound fellowship must be assumed between spiritual forces searching to protect human identity against political oppression of conscience, as well as against the major threat of our day: the "consumerization" of the human mind as

---

[8] References and further comments are given in our section on Islam, particularly 5.2.1.1.

already suggested. Religions believe in some superior, universally integrative aim of human existence, and see its disintegration into a variety of pettier acquisitions as a lamentable loss of authenticity, even if – to an average Western eye – it may look less alarming than the violations of human dignity affected by government oppression. In other parts of the world, that item may in certain regards look different.

2.4. Mutual Information – Breaking Cultural Barriers

So far, attention has been called to possible joint reaction by religions to challenges from the surrounding world, even if religion-related orientations have in several cases contributed to the conflicts in view and shaped their profile in the worldwide opinion. We are now turning to controversies where differences between one religion and another constitute the very issue. An introductory question may well be this: Do the religions of the world know each other, do they really know each other? If not, how can such knowledge come into existence?

The expansion of insights obviously needed, can hardly be restricted to plain exchange of information about doctrine, organization, practical operations. It will include growing reciprocal acquaintance through communication of whatever kind. Conversation partners present themselves to each other also when, formally speaking, that is not what they are doing, they just engage in exchange on whichever level and whichever topic they find of common interest. Understanding is more than knowledge. Absence of understanding leads to misrepresentation, fear, antagonism, conflict ...

In the realm of religion this general dynamic of acquaintance-making is particularly loaded with consequence, as the constitutive concern of religion claims to be that of ultimate truth. This intensifies the divisive effects if circumstances critically unexplored are taken to signalize more thorough-going oppositions than they really do. In no area of communication is it more important, and more demanding, to distinguish package and content.

Information, the prime element in dialogue, must be discovered as the multiplex matter it really is. (1) It is important to see a religion as it sees itself, i.e. as it is seen by practicing believers. This intent can never be realized 100%, as it is impossible to be an inspecting outsider and an integrated insider at the same time. But it would be shortsighted to abandon it as an aim essential to true dialogue. (2) It is essential that questions from one religion to another are raised, heard and – to the extent possible – answered. (3) It is no less significant that a religion is invited to discover how it looks in the eyes of its conversation partner(-s) – through listening, be it to clarifying questions, to critical remarks, or to constructive suggestions.

As difficult as it is for an outsider to understand how a spiritual movement (including a religion) looks from inside, just as difficult may it be for an undisturbed insider to get an adequate picture of how it looks from outside. The insider usually identifies with his movement/religion as it defines itself, and may not be inclined to discover facts which point in conflicting directions. Thus, the impression "from outside" may, when critically assessed, be just as true as, and no less relevant to face than, the one "from inside". In dialogue, a religion is not exclusively called upon to act out, to present itself and – correspondingly – to listen to the self-presentation of the other. Each partner in dialogue should also be prepared to receive questions and remarks as a call to reexamine own identity and own appearance. Not least: to ponder correspondence and lack of correspondence between intended presentation and actual appearance.

Raising questions for the sake of clarification may be a mediating bridge between active self-presentation and receptive self-criticism. Two kinds of questions should be anticipated. Having heard the partner's self-presentation, I may have questions concerning elements which I still find unclear or incomplete, perhaps even misleading – questions which I am obliged to bring forth, with due respect, in order to sustain communication. Listening to a partner's explicit or implicit criticism of me, I may find it wise to return questions in order to ensure that I have understood the criticism rightly before I eventually respond.

Correspondingly, it may be well worth reminding myself that an insufficient or seemingly irrelevant riposte by my respondent may suggest that he responds not to what I intended to communicate, but to what he – for one reason or another – heard me saying. In dialogue reciprocal observation relates to a good deal more than to successive elements in a verbal exchange. My conversation partners will hold their preconceived images of Christianity (often entangled with their general idea of Western civilization) and will listen to me with such images in mind. In these circumstances it is hardly my task to overcome what to me seem inappropriate ideas of my identity, the sooner the better, but to invite an exchange where the partners inform each other reciprocally. Any misunderstanding has its reasons, which are vital for the conversation partners to discover – jointly.

The outcome of dialogue should be secured by something widely transcending verbal duels. When the hall of history is entered for joint exploration, the problem may uncover itself less as one of lacking information and apologetical explanation than one of lacking credibility. Thus, clarification must aim at something far beyond communication of facts. The need is for no less than a new founding of confidence.

In this perspective it is difficult to avoid the soul-searching question: Is *intra*religious dialogue really the contribution called for today? Aren't a good thirty years of heated exchange between Christians on the prospects of interfaith encounter sufficient? And – for that matter – sufficient warning to other religions that may be about to follow the Christian trail of introspection. If you want business, intrareligious conversation – in our case: represented by Christians discussing Christian premises and Christian prerequisites – can at the best be seen as preparation for the real thing: interreligious dialogue = deepened contact between followers of different faiths. Elaboration of a thorough theology of dialogue may become an alibi just for postponing dialogue!

At the turn of millennium we may well ask: Haven't preparations for dialogue so far taken a good deal more resources than dialogue – is that justifiable? Some would even suggest that the outcome of the preparation so far may have been counterproductive. More than anything, that preparation has been handling – or could we even say: has produced – objections and restrictions suppressing the spontaneity of the dialogical communication called for.

This riposte needs reflective listening. Like any ideal enterprise, intrareligious – and interreligious! – dialogue can be misused and end up as pretext, or at least as a faint excuse, for some accomplishment rather remote from the official purpose. But of what impressive enterprise may not similar things be said? It is important that the partners confront themselves and one another with the pitfalls luring in the enterprise, and that they keep warning inscriptions on the wall under joint inspection.

What dialogue demands above all, is confidence. The actual dialogue adventure must be an authentic expression of own identity, and of confidence in a corresponding authenticity molding the response of one's partner. Such mutual confidence may be efficiently supported by an uninterrupted reflection process in each of the faith communities involved.

Insights acquired in dialogue must be brought back to one's own constituency for subsequent reflection and – hopefully – reception. Intrareligious dialogue, then, will by no means restrict itself to a preparation for some future encounter of faiths. Rightly understood, it should precede as well as accompany and succeed the physical meeting. Interreligious dialogue thus becomes efficient only when surrounded by intrareligious dialogue. None of them can meaningfully subsist without the other!

In addition, another – one might call it: more static – consideration should be noted. A community concerned with dialogue needs to reflect critically not only on the actual process in which it is involved, but on the very nature of dialogue, as relating to its own identity and to its operative commitments in general. Such a reflection must have reached a preliminary conclusion before steps are taken toward an obliging dialogue engagement. The development to follow will depend on a live interaction between the dialogues internal and external.

Even if an impressive segment of a religious constituency reaches agreement on a number of practical steps toward dialogue with neighbors, pragmatic agreement is not sufficient to secure the ambiance of mutual confidence called for, and to give a reasonable assurance of success to a subsequent dialogical adventure.

2.5. Dialogue – An Incentive to Self-Examination

Authentic dialogue does not limit itself to giving the participants a more correct picture of each other, it also offers to every one of them a more complex and searching image of itself. My partner questions my identity through presenting me – hopefully in a manner apt to strengthen further communication rather than to hamper it – not only certain preconceived ideas of my identity, but also immediate expressions of understanding or not-understanding vis-a-vis my actual self-presentation.

At an initial stage, such reciprocal "attacks" will need to be presented in a particularly careful manner. As communication proceeds and mutual confidence confirms itself, it will hopefully be possible to address the issues with growing frankness.

To unpleasant confrontations with one's own image several types of reaction may be imagined. The least constructive – and least dialogical – of all would be to take any inconvenient challenge for an insult and respond with defensive measures or even with a counter-attack. As long as possible, it should be assumed that a dialogue partner does not intend to offend. If that were the case, why does he show up here? It should also be born in mind: coming from culturally disparate backgrounds, we have different ways of expressing ourselves and may easily hear an utterance differently from what was intended.

Paradoxical as it sounds, an essential element in dialogue is bound to be monologue. An individual participant in dialogue will generally be engaged not only in the open, joint discussion, but in an accompanying, hidden exchange with him-/herself. In order to succeed, this monological dynamic presupposes that joint dialogue be supplemented by extensive teamwork in each of the "camps", where individual deliberations are shared with fellow believers, adapted and coordinated, and in due time transported and made profitable for interreligious dialogue. Conversely, challenging assaults from the partner call for constructive processing by joint internal reflection in the recipient camp and, if the reflection so recommends, for corporate responses.

In the rather complex process of self-examination arising from dialogue encounter, it is not only the question of "digesting" immediate messages, to distinguish between appropriate and non-appropriate elements in the criticism explicitly heard, and to ask which initiatives of improvement could immediately be undertaken. There is also a more long-term invitation to continued reflection, not least due to the acknowledgement that even accusations that seem unjust at first, may deserve understanding through further explanation. A portrait,in which we find it hard to recognize ourselves, may reflect observations of appearances and situations where "we" (in the widest sense: including cultural forebears, relatives, allies) have exposed ourselves in ways inconsistent with what we like to think of as our own precious identity.

2.6. Joint Self-Examination in Face of Common Temptations

Again, a different orientation. We turn to dialogue partners speaking not about differences and confrontation of distinctive identities, but about shared exposure to common temptations: partners questioning themselves and each other in a "we" apt to promote solidarity. The actual supposition is that a religion commonly will be exposed not only to temptations shaped by its peculiar historic and geographical situation, temptations often most easily arrested by observers from outside. It is also faced with some – rather massive – temptations residing in all religion, on which dialogue can shed light through an exchange of experiences common to the participants in the midst of their differences. These are challenges connected with the global role of religion, independent of time and place, but are usually discovered and unveiled as attached to circumstances typical of a certain age, or fixed to some geographical or socio-cultural segment of the world.

In this perspective there may be reason to assume that religions can render important service to each other, probing into shared weaknesses and failures by learning in dialogue to distinguish between content and package. This service will be a mutual give-and-take, where the common point of departure is awareness of, and readiness to admit, own strain and struggle, including failures in past and present. Such a face-to-face would also, in all meekness, include readiness to review the shortcomings of one's partner(s) in light of one's own. The conversation partners could reciprocally learn from each other's experience and take inspiration from each other's honesty, serving each other as mirrors for new insight into dynamics of corresponding challenge to both.

Of what could such panreligious temptations consist? Organized religion stands in the danger of compromising its identity, and thus its integrity, in a manner more flagrant than maybe any other movement. Religions profess relationship with ultimacy as their specific orientation: fundamental truth, unlimited wisdom, uncompromised goodness. Such a relationship, however, is realized within the framework of a world, which, in all observable regards, is relative and restricted, with no other indisputable manifestation of perfection than unblended human nostalgia. The life of single believers as well as that of religious communities manifest an overwhelming amount of imperfection not only in their immediate appearance, they are inclined to legitimate nearsighted human claims in the name of the Absolute. Again and again in history crusaders' ambitions have been defended with a loud "Deus lo vult" – "Gott mit uns" – "God with us!"

Even if such a faux-pas will be differently styled from one religious culture to another, the temptation to confuse divine and human horizon, heavenly and earthly ambition, seems inseparable from the very vision of Ultimate Truth – as represented among, in and by humans in a world of apparently universal imperfection. Under such circumstances, religions have ample reason to listen to criticism from outside, not least from non-religious critics questioning their lack of consistency – consistency not with the demands of some alien "world", but consistency between own claims and own manifestation (in words as in deeds). But the advantage of listening to each other could be just as great to sisters somehow caught in a common trap. An honest "family talk" about common entanglement in the complex interrelatedness between ultimate truth and penultimate promotion of truths, based on joint existential struggle with own identity, might certainly be no minor achievement – especially as a riposte to the overwhelming contemporary challenge of fundamentalism.[9]

---

[9] Cf. 1.3., note 17.

2.7. Facing the Intellectual Challenge of Today

"The intellectual challenge of today" may point in two directions. There is the conscious, explicit attack on religion launched in the name of some "scientific world view". Then, there is the unreflected, largely non-verbalized, challenge to faith and traditional culture through a transcultural process of secularization, notoriously a transformative social event. Whether intended rebellion against religion or not, these are profound strains in the contemporary world, which may invite a sharing of reflections and reactions within the family of world religions.

We make this supposition, without neglecting the fact that secularization, especially as reflected in public legislation, is today most differently orchestrated in different cultures! In some countries – most of them with a Muslim majority – the legal trend during several years now has been that of, sometimes rather obstinate, desecularisation. But first of all, this does not mean that the issue of secularization/secularity has come to a final settlement even in the social and intellectual process in those countries. Second, it does not mean that the peoples of these countries are not affected – consciously and unconsciously – by dominant trends in the worldwide formation of the human mind.

"Secular theology" of the 1960's vehemently rejected such a fellowship-in-fate and corresponding fellowship-in-arms of the world religions, lodging, as it did, Christianity itself as the standard bearer of contemporary secularization, with other world religions unwillingly lagging miles behind.[10] Undeniably, Christianity, in several regards, is linked with modernity in a way different than other world religions. Regardless how one thinks of the thesis from the 1960's about the Bible as source of secularization, it cannot be denied that socio-geographically, modernity did emerge as a child of Christendom. This has marked Christian theology like no other world religion. The most visible trends are in this regard the acceptance of historical criticism and a wide-ranging acceptance of religious freedom. Even if the general thesis quoted should be amply modified, this peculiarity must, for better or for worse, be born in mind. The facts observed make it, however, urgent for Christianity and for its conversation partners, the other religions, to pursue a dialogue on joint vis-a-vis split strategies for religion facing modernity.

In wide segments of the world today the most conspicuous trend is not antireligious propaganda, but various kinds of spiritual rebirth through new religious movements, a "New Age" with as little respect for established religion as for what is considered a positivistic adoration of purely material values. Should these new movements be considered as potential partners in interreligious dialogue or rather be confronted as destructive enemies to established religion?

Necessary as it may be to suggest some reflective distinction between authentic and inauthentic religion – notably in view of the phenomenon commercialized religion as a growing, highly spectacular part of the consumers' market of the day – it

---

[10] Cf. notes 4 and 5.

may be impossible to answer our question with a simple *yes* or *no*. The scenario before us is a good deal too complex to allow a general judgement: religious movements emerging after that or that date cannot be taken seriously as conversation partners. Up to now, this is a puzzlement which has played a remarkably anonymous role in the official dialogue debate.

For good reasons, the remarkable resurgence of "new religion" worldwide, is felt as a not trifling problem in the everyday life of the historical religions, and this topic may certainly deserve a place on the agenda of contemporary dialogue. The same can be said of the more philosophically oriented modern-esoteric world-view reflecting itself in a number of the new movements. The most forward-looking question to discuss for the traditional religions, each individually and together, is hardly: How to stop new rivals, but: what conclusions may established faith draw from this new scenario? Are the innovators primarily challenging neglects on our part, or are they predominantly reflecting general errors of our time ... or perhaps, even of human-kind at all times? A simple either-or would hardly invite a viable answer to this dilemma.[11]

Invitations to general reflection which the religions need to meet together, do not limit themselves to those thrown upon them from outside a supposed circle of "established religion", be it from challengers who believe "too little" or "too much". A more constructive approach than just common defense against common enemies, may result from joint (self-examinatory) discussion of problems linked with the "establishment" position of enculturated religion in its variety of formats, challenged as such positions actually are in a world of incessant departure.

What can religions teach each other about general strategy in issues of faith difficult to handle, and in questions of structures difficult to adjust in our common world of today? This could be a particularly delicate domain of dialogue, since it questions the identity of each single religion vis-a-vis its environments as well as vis-a-vis fellow faiths. How much of such "cooperatio in sacris" will the authenticity of each single religion, according to its own understanding, allow? Most likely that answer will vary quite a bit from one religion to another.

Let us suggest a few challenges facing religious thought in our contemporary world. How can we fancy divine sovereignty in a world fenced in by science and technology like ours? How does that same sovereignty allow human freedom and responsibility –

---

[11] A remarkable apropos to this aspect of the dialogical challenge is the existence, and the work, of Dialogcenteret in Århus, Denmark. This is founded and directed by professor Johannes AAGAARD at Århus University. For more than twenty years it has directed its attention to trends in contemporary spirituality, particularly the new religions of our time. It has assiduously challenged manipulative and commercialized religious movements of the day, and focused a major part of its efforts on surveying and spreading information about, their activities around the globe. At the same time it has shown openness to "classical" religion of whatever extraction, even if it has not seen it as its task to place "big" dialogue between the world religions on its agenda. The most informative presentation of this institute, which also suggests its network around the world, may be the festschrift issued by the Dialogcenter for Aagaaard's 70th birthday in 1998: 'Identity in Conflict: Classical Christian Faith and Religio Occulta'.

and conversely? How does divine providence relate to seemingly meaningless suffering – or to the obvious power of evil on our globe? Such problems traditionally present themselves with different emphasis from culture to culture and from one religion to another. But our common frame of reference is today a world communicatively unified like never in history. And the place and role of different religions in the over-all image show enough of structural resemblance to make comparison and consultation between religions a pledge of vital concern.

This may be particularly visible in the case of the three Abrahamic religions. That Jews, Christians and Muslims all recognize the Hebrew Bible (The Old Testament) as holy scripture is important enough, even if this common collection of writings is overshadowed, in Christianity by the Greek New Testament, and in Islam by the Arab Qur'an. Basic orientations shared by the three religions, are: belief in a transcendent God, creator and ruler of the universe, history moving towards an aim set by the Creator, ethics framed by divine commandments conducive to that aim, a final judgement to confirm the full dominion of the Creator over his creation.

It is clear that such a far-reaching correspondence of beliefs opens up a wide ground for common reflection and for mutual intellectual stimulation. At the same time the three religions of Semite origin are, through historical circumstance, separated by hardening confrontations more than any other "family" of religions. In the eyes of Judaism and of Islam, the Christian proclamation of Jesus as Son of God and participant in a trinitarian mystery is a violation of the most sacred principle of monotheism, whereas Christianity has seen her two sisters as legalistic structures insensitive to the unifying mystery of saving grace. Are such judgements of old premature, as several within each of the camps have indicated in recent years?[12] May a joint confrontation with the modern world and its challenges to traditional religious thinking, be the incentive needed to push these religions not only to respond jointly to that world, but to approach each other in working out, if possible, convergent premises for such answers?

2.8. Contradictions – A Call to Authentic Tolerance

More than one controversy stems from the fact that each religion regards itself differently from how other religions (and "outsiders" in general) regard it. Adequate pictures of each other can only be obtained by two religions through a trustful and at the same time critical confrontation of their respective self-images with observations made by the colloquial partner. Such dialogue-based pictures allow religions to get beyond unessential disagreements, caused by socio-cultural patterns of secondary religious

---

[12] From the Christian side one of the most impressive spokespersons of this understanding has been Hans KÜNG, who sees the distances within the Abrahamic family as widely conditioned by an exaggerated hellenization of Christian thought in the early centuries, cfr. his analysis of "Das ökumenisch-hellenistische Paradigma des christlichen Altertums" (KÜNG 1994, 145–335).

relevance or by confrontative events of the past, more meaningfully seen as accidental historical circumstances. Lack of cultural synchronization must be discovered in its fundamental difference from religious disunity.

Indeed, it is easier to handle this distinction in principle than in practice. In actuality, faith and societal adaptation of faith are so intertwined that a reaction to the one may more or less automatically be taken to hit the other. The fundamental distinction we have called for, will need time and patience in order to be turned into practice. Also for that reason, it would be meaningless to postpone dialogue on burdensome items of disagreement until a viable method of distinguishing culturally conditioned and religiously motivated disunity is established – provided that the issue of distinction is kept constantly in mind.

At the same time, straight confrontation, if combined with respectful listening, may in several cases open up lanes precisely to the kind of distinction we are seeking and so, in its turn, also a more meaningful circumscription of "the matter". Two stages of confrontation – localizing a disagreement and discussing a disagreement first identified – tend, in matters of discernment, to be explored not consecutively, but through repeated intersections. A question points in the direction of an answer, and progress towards an answer invites adjustment of the question.

What finally produces the experience of "distance" between two religions, are scarcely a series of single issues – some regarded by the discussion partners as minor, others as major (sometimes with considerable disagreement within each of the camps as to which is which) – but the way each of them demonstrates its identity and expresses its main concern(s). The dynamics of exchange may to a large extent be the same as have for generations been observed at work in the ecumenical movement within Christendom – only that divisive questions may be still more demanding to overcome. And, reciprocally: that integrative factors will be still more difficult to explore.

Can interreligious rapprochement be generally foreseen through a discursive downgrading of doctrinal differences? Could such exchange, as a logical end, lead to some proclamation of an overarching common understanding? Even if it may be good to start with expectations considerably more modest than that, nothing may be healthier for a reciprocal relationship than an open exchange on divisive issues. As a matter of fact, the prospects of dialogue will be quite restricted if the really "tough" issues of division are pushed under the table. What seems immediately clear, is that open exchange may lead to a segregation of non-essential controversies, and thus, obviously to an improved insight into the thoughts of the other part. This, in its turn, may prepare for a growing understanding, and a growing joint control, of what have so far been unconquerable differences. This will open up for increased tolerance: insight into, and respect for, the integrity of a conversation partner with opinions differing from my own. Seeing the basic motifs and the inner logic of their orientations makes it easier to experience solidarity with those who hold opinions different from mine.

2.9. Agreeing to Disagree?

Is it probable that a clarification of doctrinal disagreements – even where it does not result in a rapprochement of opinions – may accomplish more in direction of fellowship than just an improvement of the psychological climate?

It seems important that dialogue doesn't start with a fixed, final aim: such and such quantities of agreement, or such and such manifestations of mutual togetherness to be achieved. It may turn utterly deceptive to anticipate an ultimate solution to the core issue: what, when, how, where? Where dialogue may take us, can be decided through the progress of dialogue alone.

An aim which could, and should, be declared at an early stage of a dialogue procedure, is to achieve some explicit agreement on the principal importance of unresolved disagreement. In which sense and to what extent does the subsistence of yet unappropriated opinions demand to be respected. If true desire is there to wipe out more or less established caricatures and ill-founded accusations, dialogue has to be entered as a risky enterprise with no advance guarantee of a mutually consolatory *quantum satis*.

The accomplishment thus suggested may seem modest in face of the tremendous task of unrestricted understanding. But it is definitely an essential step in that direction. To be envisaged is a mutual purification of the images which the world religions hold and propagate of each other. In concreto: a common critical review, discussion and hopefully overcoming of touchy topics, stemming historical inaccuracies, obvious misinterpretations, inappropriate vocabulary ...

It must be possible to identify, and to ban, notoriously superficial accusations and clichés. Likewise to exchange assistance to self-examination: why has just our religion become an object of such or such – in our own eyes, undeserved – slander? Prejudices serving to hamper conversation between the world religions seem to be globally spread and fairly divided between different camps. A reciprocal purification process like the one we have suggested, must certainly be worth aspiring after, a necessary condition as it seems to be for improved interreligious relations.

This is an agenda a good deal more concise than just to meet and forward good will and friendly conversation. Besides, it seeks substantial results apt for conference partners to take home, not mere subjective moods and general impressions. Many of the prejudices referred to, are widespread, particularly among "common people", and can hardly be invalidated without some kind of steadfast discourse, based on mutual trust.

2.10. Communicative Openness – Confidence-Building

As a whole, it is easier to fix the destructive aim of dialogue – a disappearance of suspicion built on misunderstanding – than to fix a constructive correspondent. A maximal amount of agreement would hardly be meaningful as an overarching purpose in itself. Agreement just for the sake of agreement may too easily compromise deep-rooted convictions, in a way that most likely will provoke unforeseen strike-backs in posterity. A mutual idea of direction has to be there in order to make dialogue a meaningful enterprise. More concise accomplishments to be pursued by dialogue will have to be discovered and phrased *en route*. How far the enterprise is going to take us in terms of common thinking can hardly be stipulated in advance without doing violence to dialogue as a live event of human rapprochement, as much as to the religions involved, viewed as live communities with their consciousness of identity.

"Progress" in dialogue is not demonstrated by a bunch of more or less grudging concessions. Bold advances in corporate statements and in joint worship experiments may give an immediate impression that "forward we go". But as common experience and numerous comments from recent years show, the fruits do not always match with the promise. What one part offers as an obliging generosity, the other may observe as a manipulative invitation to give up own integrity. Not least do Western standards of tolerance frequently remind people in the East of bad old-fashioned colonialism: the Occident, having lost faith in its own religious doctrines, consistently invites the rest of the world to give up theirs – as a suitable compensation.

Different standards of inclusive- or exclusiveness respectively may reflect deep-going differences of orientation in general: between religions linked with different cultures, but also between discrepant traditions within the same religion. Tension between competing currents may be a distinctive phenomenon within most religions. Modifications of this overall picture may be of a proportional more than of a principal character.

In this perspective it is necessary once more to recall our important distinction between *intra-* and *inter*religious. Inward- and outward-directed conversation must be carried on more or less simultaneously. Dialogue is nurtured by dialogue on dialogue, and the latter takes orientation from its mission to serve the former. *Inward* and *outward* in this context refer not only to alternating communicative orientations of a religious community speaking soon to itself, soon to a partner. They even apply to dialogue as a process, reflecting now on itself as destined for a general commitment, now on topics essential in, and to, a concrete, transsubjective relationship towards which it is called to direct its attention.

Neither of the two is primarily a dialogue between single individuals. Interreligious dialogue is an exchange between religions as integral communities, even if its most widespread scenario is that of a daily symbiosis between single persons sharing geographical and social space with each other. Intrareligious dialogue, then, is an exchange within each of these communities, dedicated to the relationship of one's own community to the others. An organized procedure of dialogue between religions will have to be prepared, accompanied, critically evaluated and finally accepted and integrated within each of the participating communities. The same dynamic interaction of inter and intra will apply on an international, a regional, and a national as well as on a local level.

Methodologically, the decisive thing is that interreligious dialogue is a new and ambiguous enterprise, so that a guiding theology of dialogue has itself to be shaped through a dialogue not only on, but with, dialogue. This means: it must be adapted and adjusted as part of a constant interaction between the two. That opens up for a true dialectic: a stepwise process with give-and-take between dialogue and dialogue-on-dialogue.

We distinguish a dynamic of complex interaction, where progress is not synonymous with quick and uncomplicated acceptance of foreign opinions and traditions – be it in the intra- or in the inter-sphere of dialogue, and be it on whatever level of socio-geographical organization. It is an exercise in common openness to common problems, with an accent on everybody's readiness to take his proportional share of self-examinatory responsibility. Moving forward, then, does not necessarily mean a continuous progress from glory to glory, but a realistic presentation of alternatives and correctives, at every point carefully adjusted to the receptive capacities of the respective communities of believers.

After these a priori reflections on possibilities and expectations, we are ready to inspect and reflect on events of actual development.

3. Dialogue on Dialogue – How It Started

Most of the dialogue which has caught the eyes and ears of the world so far has actually taken place as dialogue on dialogue: exchange on the meaning, justification, presuppositions, aims and methods of dialogue.

Actual programmation of dialogue may, in a wider perspective, be seen as an integral part of dialogue. Without methodological planning, dialogue on dialogue may end up with talk taking the place of the real thing.

A good deal more analytical preparation for bi- and multi-lateral dialogue has probably taken place in "the Christian world" than in the other "worlds" of the world put together – a fact to which there may be explanations not primarily of a theological kind, but in terms of structural and economic resources, as well as of socio-cultural factors.

Considering events in a historical retrospect, this is precisely what could have been expected. And for a good time yet, extended dialogue on dialogue may probably dominate the picture of interreligious relations. It is likely that at the middle of the new century plain dialogue may have conquered the ground: the *what* of interreligious exchange will have overshadowed the *why* and the *how*, hopefully without having completely replaced them. The dialogue partners should not be deprived of a constant possibility to revaluate own premises and identity, as dialogue proceeds and experience multiplies.

A short description of how things took their present direction may be an adequate background for entering into the discussion of principles.

3.1. The Roman-Catholic Take-off

Why review the Roman Catholic and the Orthodox / Protestant developments as two separate stories? Primarily for reasons of structure. The Catholic start came first and was intimately linked with the Second Vatican Council (1962–65). The extra-Roman start of a developing dialogue program is linked with the World Council of Churches (WCC), of which the Roman Catholic Church was not and is not a member. But, important enough, the two separate starts took place around the same time and as responses to a common challenge.[1]

---

[1] When reviewing dialogue between different religions as an event of the last third of the 20. century, events connected with the World Parliament of Religions in Chicago in 1893 (and 1993) and the remarkable network of private organizations to which it gave impulse world-wide, should not be forgotten. See: BAYBROOKE 1980, 1992 and 1996. The flow of dialogue events up to the official initiatives around 1970 was, however, limited, compared to the successive development.

Two explanatory circumstances should be born in mind. First, the close to total lack of contact between the theological development in the Catholic and Protestant segments of Christendom up to Vatican II is hard to fancy today. The Council meant a historic break-through, first in inviting a more than symbolic presence of observers from other churches, and next in making a series of remarkable decisions initiating future rapprochements – to other Christian denominations – and to other world religions.

However, the said distance in the mid-sixties was still such, that a common program of interreligious dialogue would have been theologically unthinkable and structurally impracticable as well. The churches certainly needed a wide-ranged dialogue with each other in order to prepare for a unified Christian dialogue with other faiths in the future.

Another important factor is this. As to theology of religions, the Roman Catholic Church has an impressive record of its own, going back to the first great period of world mission in modern times, the late 16th and early 17th centuries. At that time, the two great schisms of Christendom – the East/West of the 11th and the North/South of the 16th century – were already established facts, and Catholic reflection was not only territorially separated from other Christian churches, in addition it was very much directed by the spirit of the Counter-Reformation: geared among other things to counterbalance what was regarded as an illegitimate depreciation of human nature by the Reformers.

As to overseas orientation and world wide missionary responsibility – two vital conditions for interreligious involvement – the Protestant churches at that time lagged far behind the "Mother Church". Dialogue and debate on dialogue anno 1600 were predestined to become a purely Roman Catholic enterprise. In the 1960's it still seemed a utopia to synchronize a Roman and a Protestant theology of religions. And with the ecumenical awakening already well on the way, seeing the reestablishment of Christian unity as issue Number 1, there were enough separating issues to be tackled before the relationship with extra-Christian religions could demand a paragraph of its own on an ecumenical agenda. In more than one regard, *intra*-religious relations at that time definitely demanded priority over *inter*-religious.

It gives sense, then, to commence with the most decisive ecumenical milestone of the twentieth century: The Second Vatican Council. *Nostra Aetate – Declaration on the Relationship of the Church to Non-Christian Religions* was promulgated on Oct. 28, 1965. The Secretariat for Developing Relations with Non-Christian Religions[2] had been established already the year before.

'Nostra Aetate' was a remarkable document for its time, describing non-Christian religions with an amiable openness till then unmatched in the history of Christendom. Already style and structure are impressive. The declaration starts with (1) a general exhortation motivating a new era of contact with the world religions. Follo-

---

[2] Restructured 1989 and renamed from Secretariatus pro non-Christianis to Pontificium Consilium pro Dialogo inter Religiones.

wing are (2) a statement on religions in general, including a word of appreciation on Buddhism and Hinduism, (3) a word on Islam with an appeal to Christians to leave the hostilities of old behind in favor of practical cooperation for peace and justice, (4) the longest passage, the one on relationships with Judaism, passionately dedicated to the theme of atonement, reconciliation and new fellowship. Just a few of the most captivating passages will be quoted:

"In our times, when every day men are being drawn closer together and the ties between various peoples are being multiplied, the church is giving deeper study to her relationship with non-Christian religions. In her task of fostering unity and love between all men, and even among nations, she gives primary consideration in this document to what human beings have in common and to what promotes fellowship among them". (As biblical arguments are accentuated: creation faith, eschatological finality.)

"The Catholic Church rejects nothing which is true and holy in these religions. She looks with sincere respect upon those ways of conduct and of life, those rules and teachings which, though differing in many particulars from what she holds and sets forth, nevertheless often reflect a ray of that Truth which enlightens all men. Indeed, she proclaims and must ever proclaim Christ, "the way, the truth and the life" (John 14:6), in whom men find the fulness of religious life and in whom God has reconciled all things to himself (cf. 2 Cor.5:18–19). The Church therefore has this exhortation for her sons: prudently and lovingly, through dialogue and collaborations with the followers of other religions, and in witness of Christian faith and life, acknowledge, preserve, and promote the spiritual and moral goods found among these men, as well as the values in their society and culture.

Although in the course of centuries many quarrels and hostilities have arisen between Christians and Moslems, this most sacred Synod urges all to forget the past and to strive sincerely for mutual understanding. On behalf of all mankind, let them make common cause of safeguarding and fostering social justice, moral values, peace and freedom.

Since the spiritual patrimony common to Christians and Jews is thus so great, this sacred Synod wishes to foster and recommend that mutual understanding and respect which is the fruit above all of biblical and theological studies, and of brotherly dialogues ..."

The most surprising statements here are found in (2). There are elements "true and holy" reflecting "rays of that Truth that enlightens all men" in other faiths. This statement is not restricted to the religions reviewed by name. The range and consequences of these fairly open-ended formulations may be characterized as somewhat puzzling. Nor is their connectedness with the christological quotations from the New Testament, so emphatically emphasized in the following development, evident. But that hardly diminishes the historical importance of the document. In general, the presentation supports what has later been frequently referred to as an "inclusivist" theology of religions,[3] a basic attitude not uncommonly referred to as 'typically catholic'.[4]

Already a year before 'Nostra Aetate' an international Catholic conference on theology of religions had been held in Bombay, and an official Imprimatur given to the

---

[3] Cf. RUOKANEN 1992.
[4] KNITTER 1985, 120–144; HILLMAN 1989, 45–65; SULLIVAN 1992.

conference report. The latter contains papers by four prominent Catholic scholars. Considering their names, this must have served as a major preparatory input for the Council, even if the official edition only appeared in print after the important Declaration by the Council.[5] The language in the official "Conclusions of the Conference" is less poetic and more conceptually concise than that of the following Council:

> "I.1. The meaning of the world religions in the plan of salvation cannot be fully understood by considering them from an ecclesiocentric point of view ... They have to be considered from a theocentric point of view: the whole of mankind is embraced by the one salvific plan of God which includes all the world religions. – I.2. These religions are ... sharply ambiguous: on the one hand embraced, upheld and penetrated by God's grace, on the other hand held fast in the bonds of man's weakness and sinfulness. What truth they teach is from God, but this truth needs to be liberated by Christ from entanglement in error and sin. For a man who is not confronted in an existential way with the Gospel of Jesus Christ they can be the channel of Christ's saving grace. – I.3. Christian faith represents radical universalism. Every human being and every world religion is under God's grace. But Christian universalism is grounded and centered in Christ; it is equally far removed from narrow intolerant particularism and from an enfeebling agnostic indifferentism.– I.4. The Church will not conquer but serve the world religions ... not in passive coexistence, but in active proexistence ...
> II.1. Assuming the fact that non-Christians can be saved in their own non-Christian religions – a fact which has been explicitly declared in the Constitution on the Church – we shall now examine the way ..."[6]

Even if not formally authorized by the Roman Catholic Church, this report was officially accepted for study and reflection. Several provocative themes are suggested. We observe: An "ecclesio-centric point of view" dismissed to the advantage of a "theocentric" – the religions of the world evaluated as "sharply ambiguous": "upheld and penetrated by God's grace ... not just natural piety", but "held fast in the bonds of man's weakness and sinfulness"; under certain conditions, though, "the channel of Christ's saving grace" – in a sum: "radical universalism centered in Christ".

The report was daring for its time, and was largely disavowed by official Catholicism in the subsequent development, but was certainly not unimportant for the (after all) amazingly brave advances by the Council! At the same time it is worth noticing – in face of the staunch confrontation of "christocentric" and "theocentric" theology of dialogue in the discussions of the eighties [7] – that the contrast to "theocentricity" here is rather "ecclesiocentricity". Not the uniqueness of Christ is questioned by this "theocentric" approach, just that of the church! And where a saving power of non-Christian religions is suggested, this is attributed to some hidden presence of

---

[5] Cf. NEUNER 1967. The speakers were: Hans KÜNG, Piet FRANSEN S.J., Joseph MASSON S.J., and Raimundo PANIKKAR. Küng and Panikkar have in the meantime placed themselves among the most influential theologians of religions on a world level, but none of them would be considered as typical "main streamers" in Catholic theology.

[6] NEUNER 1967, 21–24.

[7] See particularly the description of "pluralist" theologies of religion(s), our section 4.1.

Christ and of grace – not to some "natural" power of religion in general, nor to some virtue of this or that religion in particular.

Already here we can distinguish the profile of what has later been referred to as an "inclusivist" position, not unrelated to the much debated idea of "anonymous Christians" presented by KARL RAHNER.[8] The Bombay characteristic of the world religions as "sharply ambiguous" has definitely elicited two critical questions. (1) Doesn't this universal "ambiguity" apply also to Christianity, and is it fair – as Bombay definitely does – to leave that circumstance beyond consideration? (2) Must a suggestion of God as acting in various religions, necessarily attribute this to some hidden presence of Christ, thus excluding the possibility for God to act through other religions as they understand themselves? But much water from Ganges has poured into the ocean since 1964. From other rivers to.

In 1970 the Roman Secretariat published a 600 page collection of papers,[9] which is, by definition, considerably less obliging than 'Nostra Aetate', but with a more official status than the Bombay report. In a drawing of the "Premise" (by P. ROSSANO) the following remark may be worth observing:

> "It should also be expressedly noted that if attention is continually drawn in these pages to the deep solidarity in the religious nature of man, which in fact is shown in history, and the fundamental analogy of its expressions, it is not therefore intended to favour nor open the door to relativism, nor to syncretism, nor to agnosticism not even to an alleged Panchristianity which does not take into account the specific differences of the individual religions, but we wish solely to elucidate the religious nature of man, just as it appears in the historic and psychological analysis."[10]

This may be read in a certain contrast to the Bombay statement six years earlier, and meets to a certain extent care of our second question to that conference. The "alleged Panchristianity" under attack may be an echo of the Rahner-discussion. But is it meant as a blow against the "anonymous Christian" theory or against critics exaggerating and fighting (im-)possible consequences of RAHNER's proposal?

The most remarkable thing, however, is that attention is turned away from the doctrine of the "universality of grace in Christ" and directed to a general view of the religious nature of man, seen as a psychological and historical given with analogous expressions in various religious cultures. The renunciation of relativism in various shapes shows consciousness of, and readiness to challenge, such a possibility. Maybe even awareness that the main concern is stated in a way lending itself to different interpretations. Indirectly, that may also testify to the difficulty of finding a dialectically balanced expression of the "inclusivist" concern. It is difficult to see that this has become easier in the time to follow.

---

[8] See our section 4.2.
[9] 'Fundamental Themes for a Dialogistic Understanding', Rome 1970.
[10] Op.cit., 10. To the immediately following development, see SHEARD 1987.

3.2. The World Council of Churches (WCC) Take-off

We are coming to the other great dialogue take-off in contemporary Christianity. As a matter of fact, scattered initiatives and a variety of organizations for interreligious cooperation have emerged ever since the first World Congress of Faiths in Chicago 1893. It might, however, be somewhat misleading to see this rather tumultuous history as a straight prelude to "dialogue" in the stringent sense which took shape in the last third of the 20th century.[11] It is fair to say that the WCC, beside the Roman Catholic Church, has been the great promoter of dialogue initiatives as well as of reflection on dialogue, even if a variety of organizations have contributed – and still do contribute.

The WCC working group on Dialogue with People of Living Faiths and Ideologies came into existence at the meeting of the Central Committee in Addis Ababa in 1971, as part of a comprehensive restructuring of the council. The event came almost six years later than the organization of the Roman Catholic Secretariat, and WCC *Interim Policy Statement on Guidelines* can hardly be called a historical document of lasting importance like *Nostra Aetate*. The – extremely turbulent – baptismal event of the WCC dialogue program was the Assembly of the Council in Nairobi 1975, and the confirmation took place at a far more conciliatory consultation in Chiang Mai, Thailand, in 1977, followed by the lasting *Guidelines on Dialogue*.

As a participant on both occasions I can testify that the difference in mood was remarkable. One reason may be that Chiang Mai, with a limited number of participants and with just one great assignment, much more easily took the track of a dialogue event in itself than Nairobi, where the first report on the new dialogue program was brought before the governing WCC body as a limited part of a rather stressed agenda, and many delegates voiced fear that a new program with a wide range of consequences was taking shape with minimal opportunities for the member churches to ask questions and formulate proposals.

In the alphabetical Index to the vast report from the WCC Assembly in Uppsala 1968 he word "Dialogue" had occurred several times, but applied then to contacts not between different religions, but between persons, groups, peoples and churches in general. Only in the section on "Renewal in Mission" was there found a programmatic, but, in terms of structure, rather unobliging indication of the new issue to expand: "The meeting with men of other faiths or of no faith must lead to dialogue."[12]

The inter-assembly period Uppsala/Nairobi (1968–75) is summed up in an official report, where also the first review of the emerging dialogue program occurs.[13] Special attention is given to the naming of the project, not least to the programmatic

---

[11] Cf. BAYBROOKE, references here note 1.

[12] Norman GOODALL (ed.): 'The Uppsala Report 1968', Geneva 1968, 29. – Important preparations had been done by three meetings at Kandy, Ceylon, in 1967, cf. the report from the WCC Central Committee 'New Delhi to Uppsala 1961–1968', 74f.

[13] David JOHNSON (ed.) 'Uppsala to Nairobi', Geneva 1975, 98–108.

decision not to refer to other religions as "non-Christian". The report volume also contains a review of the first contacts and experiences of dialogue with the other world religions. Steps in that direction had been taken by ecumenical study centers and agencies on a regional level, particularly in Asia, bilaterally and multi-laterally as well. From 1969 single initiatives had been taken on an international level by several agencies within the WCC. The preliminary conclusion is that multilateral dialogues may be especially useful in confronting the three great religions of semitic background together with the contrasting religious experiences of the great religions of the East. Apart from this, the most promising advance of the next years is prophesied to be of a bilateral kind: the face-to-face encounter of single religions.[14]

This report, presented to the Nairobi Assembly, anticipates "different and even conflicting views on dialogue", due to the fact that "The churches that constitute the fellowship of the World Council come from a plurality of cultural situations, reflect different historical backgrounds and hold a variety of confessional beliefs."[15] The fulfilment of just this prophecy in Nairobi went far beyond expectation. After a heated plenary discussion with a rejection of the first draft of a report, the final version came out with considerable emphasis on divergence of opinions. Even if clearly stated disagreements may in ecumenical reports as elsewhere have their clear advantages over vague language burying unresolved issues in compromise, the assembly left a strong impression of unresolved tensions in need of immediate relief. With no solution the new program might have been paralyzed, and fellowship and cooperation within the Council might have suffered immensely.[16]

This resulted in the Chiang Mai consultation barely 1 1/2 year later (1977), with representation from the member churches worldwide. There an agreed statement was obtained, which came to serve as foundation of the WCC *Guidelines on Dialogue*, accepted by the Central Committee in 1979.[17]

The famous Nairobi discussion had gravitated less around a theology of religions than around its practical applications. "We are only at the very beginning of our reflection; it is not yet time to crystallize a theology of dialogue." So the moderator of the WCC Central Committee M.M.THOMAS from India had put it in his opening address.[18] Much of the discussion centered around a not too sharply clarified concept of "syncretism", feared by the critics of the program. Another hot potato was the appropriation of "shared spirituality": the inclusion of holy readings and prayers in the procedure of dialogue itself. A good deal of tension seemed due to the feeling of the assembly to be overrun by the very flux of events. The Working Group for the

[14] JOHNSON, ibid., 103f, 108.

[15] Ibid. p. 100.

[16] A condensed minute of the proceedings is found in David M. PATON (ed.): 'Breaking Barriers – Nairobi 1975', 70–73. The full text of the section report 'Seeking Community: The Common Search of People of Various Faiths, Cultures and Ideologies' as adopted by the Assembly, is found pp. 73–85.

[17] WCC: 'Dialogue in Community' 1977, and: 'Guidelines on Dialogue with People of Living Faiths' 1979. Cf. SAMARTHA 1977.

[18] PATON, op.cit., 235.

dialogue enterprise had come into existence by a vote of the Central Committee in 1971.

This vote was part of a comprehensive revision of the whole structure of the council, and the Committee meeting did not give much opportunity for working out a rationale of the decision on dialogue as such. The new program was forwarded by an obviously very enthusiastic leadership, and many missed a preparatory dialogue within the ranks and files of the ecclesial world community itself. The official start of a dialogue program within the WCC with its combined Orthodox-Protestant membership was, indeed, much different from the start made by the Second Vatican Council a few years earlier.

The role of the provocative item "syncretism" in Nairobi may not least have been caused by the plea for a "Christ-centered syncretism" in the opening speech of Mr. Thomas.[19] In order to calm the discussion on this point, the following entry was added in the assembly report at the last minute:

> "We are all opposed to any form of syncretism, incipient, nascent or developed, if we mean by syncretism conscious or unconscious human attempts to create a new religion composed of elements taken from different religions."[20]

As may easily be seen a quarter of a century later, this is a statement which, in the midst of a heated confrontation, could have comforting effects a good deal beyond its worth. Not even the most radical of declared "pluralist" theologians of religions would declare him or herself in favor of the syntheticizing brand of "syncretism" here defined! In recent years it seems to be more and more accepted that "syncretism" – mixing of religions – is not a very enlightening category to describe pluralistic theories or practices in interreligious dialogue, since the survival of a religion with a non-interrupted consciousness of identity seems to depend less on its faculty to keep itself "clean" from alien impulses than on its capacity critically to assort, to absorb and eventually to integrate such impulses.

Seemingly, the Chiang Mai consultation was a most necessary, and remarkably successful, cleaning-up after Nairobi, a fact hardly touched upon in the (very diplomatic) official report of the event *Dialogue in Community*. The most captivating

---

[19] "Is it not legitimate to welcome a Christ-centered process of interreligious and intercultural penetration through dialogue? If you will permit the use of the word "syncretism" to denote all processes of interpenetration between cultures and religions, the only answer to a wrong syncretism which means the uncritical, superficial, normless mixing of basically incompatible religious conceptions and cultural attitudes is a Christ-centered syncretism which grapples with and evaluates all concepts and attitudes critically in the light of Jesus Christ and converts them into vehicles for communicating the truth of the gospel and for expressing the meaning of life." (M.M. Thomas, quoted by Paton, op.cit., 236)

[20] Paton, op.cit. 73. – In order to understand the rather frightening sound of the word "syncretism" in the ears of many Western delegates in Nairobi, observe the declinatory use of the word by the first WCC general secretary, W.A. Visser't Hooft: 'No Other Name – The Choice Between Syncretism and Christian Universalism' 1962. His puristic approach may be seen as typical of the Barth/Kraemer school. – A dialectically rather subtle comment to the concept 'syncretism', with the Nairobi discussion explicitly in mind, was given by the Chiang Mai consultation, cf. 'Dialogue in Community' §§ 25–30.

element in that report may be the general orientation drawn from the very "Community" aspect referred to in its title.[21] – "Dialogue in Community" develops a vision of togetherness (community) as the integrative expression of the Creator's purpose for humankind. Thus an all-encompassing quest for community must be the basic orientation of dialogue. The concept of community is here oriented by close neighborliness as experienced in our everyday world. Interreligious dialogue in a wider geographical setting is just a magnifying transfer of that neighborly experience, the dynamics of face-to-face community, reflected on a scale complying with the dynamics of our contemporary world. The most challenging single statement may be that on the duplex character of Christian community as such:

> "As Christians, therefore, we are conscious of a tension between the Christian community as we experience it to be in the world of human communities, and as we believe it in essence to be in the promise of God. The tension is fundamental to our Christian identity ... In the heart of this tension we discover the character of the Christian Church as a sign at once of people's need for a fuller and deeper community, and of God's promise of a restored human community in Christ. Our consciousness of the tension must preclude any trace of triumphalism in the life of the Christian Church in the communities of humankind ... Rather it should invoke in us an attitude of real humility towards all peoples since we know that we together with all our brothers and sisters have fallen short of the community which God intends."[22]

This is remarkable in its dialectical portrait of the Church – and, let us surmise, of its official advocates – as trendsetters in dialogue. As the passage reads, particular advantages of a Christian community will strike back as disadvantages in the very moment they are appropriated by self-satisfied Christians. The greater the vision, the heavier the deficit where the vision is not brought to adequate expression.

In the *Guidelines* from 1979 this is further elaborated as follows:

> "It is Christian faith in the Triune God ... which calls us Christians to human relationship with our many neighbours. Such relationship includes dialogue: witnessing to our deepest convictions and listening to those of our neighbours. It is Christian faith which sets us free to be vulnerable. In dialogue, conviction and openness are kept in balance.
>
> In a world where Christians have many neighbours, dialogue is not only an activity of meetings and conferences, it is also a way of living out Christian faith in relationship and commitment to those neighbours with whom Christians share town, cities, nations, and the earth as a whole. Dialogue is a style of living in relationship with neighbours. This in no way replaces or limits our Christian obligation to witness, as partners enter into dialogue with their respective commitments."[23]

---

[21] Cf. MULDER (in SID 2/1, 1992, 136–151) 147: "The Chiang Mai statement was a remarkable achievement. It certainly helped to alleviate criticism of the idea or program of interreligious dialogue and was a milestone after the Kandi consultation in 1967." Mulder had himself served as moderator of the sub-unit under review. – The post-Nairobi context of Chiang Mai is strongly underscored by the same author in his Preface to SAMARTHA 1977.

[22] 'Dialogue in Community' § 15.

[23] 'Guidelines', 16.

Again, we are struck by the strength of the community perspective. Even formal dialogue carried out by professors and religious leaders on an international stage is basically seen as an extension of what is supposed constantly to take place in everyday life, where people of different faiths mix with each other in a shared neighbourhood. We also observe an almost emphatic connectedness of dialogue and witness.

Against this background, it is of a certain interest to observe that the word "mission" does not occur. It seems clear that "witness" here is not primarily thought of as an evangelizing effort to convince the partner, but as a basic need of self-expression, a plea for person-to-person understanding, by giving voice to what is there in the deep of the heart. That kind of motivation should never be difficult to recognize for a dialogue partner. But at the same time, it may be seen as an easy escape from an intriguing question: has dialogue a purpose in communicating my conviction in such a way that my partner in dialogue may come to share it? Is it acceptable to affect, or even to try to change, the convictions of one with whom I am (officially) in dialogue?

The community approach contains another important aspect, namely a clear "awareness of the great diversity of situations" in which congregations and member churches addressed by the Guidelines find themselves. There may be disparity in numerical strength, in resources and in the social and political involvement of the respective dialogue partners, shifting from one to another. Formal dialogue is not equally possible in all places, and congregations are not equally equipped to take initiatives in that direction. The concluding advice should therefore be read in light of that understanding:

> "Churches should seek ways in which Christian communities can enter into dialogue with their neighbours of different faiths and ideologies.
> Dialogues should normally be planned together.
> Partners in dialogue should take stock of the religious, cultural and ideological diversity of their local situations.
> Partners in dialogue should be free to "define themselves".
> Dialogue should generate educational efforts in the community.
> Dialogue is most vital when the participants actually share their lives together.
> Dialogue should be pursued by sharing in common enterprises in community.
> Partners in dialogue should be aware of their ideological commitments.
> Partners in dialogue should be aware of cultural loyalties.
> Dialogue will raise the question of sharing in celebrations, rituals, worship and meditation.
> Dialogue should be planned and undertaken ecumenically, wherever possible.
> Planning for dialogue will necessitate regional and local guidelines.
> Dialogue can be helped by selective participation in world interreligious meetings and organizations."[24]

To participants familiar with the history so far, it may be no surprise that the statement requiring most explanation is number 10, the one about what is usually referred to as "shared spirituality". For good reasons, this is the only non-normative thesis

---

[24] Ibid., 17–22. To each thesis is added a short, paraphrastic comment.

on the list. As could be expected in light of the solid community orientation of the basis document from Chiang Mai, dialogue as located in daily life, is seen as opening up the possibility that presence as "guests and observers in family and community rituals, ceremonies and festivals" may provide "excellent opportunities to enhance the mutual understanding of neighbours".

On a level of more conscious reflection, however, we meet with "the very difficult and important question of fuller sharing in common prayer, worship and meditation." Here the *Guidelines* provide no general rule, but limit their scope to observing this as "one of the areas of dialogue which is most controversial and most in need of further exploration ... sensitive to one another's integrity and fully realizing the assumptions and implications of what is done or not done."[25]

[25] Ibid., 21.

4. Dialogue on Dialogue – Actual Positions

For years actual theologies of religions would, without further discussion, be classified within a triple framework of competing positions: exclusivist – inclusivist – pluralist. This scheme had become common-place after it, in the mid-eighties, had been powerfully proclaimed by fervent advocates of the "pluralist" approach, with *John Hick* and *Paul F. Knitter* as the most audible.[1]

In the nineties this scheme was increasingly criticized for oversimplification. Already in 1990 J.A. DINOIA O.P., in a thought-provoking essay, formulates his objection in a headline: "Varieties of Religious Aims: Beyond Exclusivism, Inclusivism, and Pluralism." Main objection: the triple scheme presupposes three different, conflicting lanes to a common aim – salvation – but such a comparison must be of limited interest, since it tends to camouflage the core issue: salvation – what is that?[2]

At a WCC consultation held at Baar, Switzerland, in 1993, JANE SMITH proposed a scheme of six competing alternatives, but it is difficult to see her key words as sufficiently synchronized to offer increased clarity.[3] In a balanced assessment at a LWF (Lutheran World Federation) conference in Bangkok in 1996 ISRAEL SELVANAYAGAM, without making an alternative proposal, complains about the lack of flexibility in the customary use of the "old" scheme: it tends to camouflage the complexity of the actual positions.[4] He pleads for an increased awareness of the reservations necessary to all schematization, an awareness lacking in the theological discussion so far.

A comparison of these comments sustains a double observation: (1) The triple division: exclusive – inclusive – plural – may give as good a preliminary over-all view

---

[1] HICK 1980, 28–42, and: 1985, 28–45. – In 'No Other Name?' 1985, 73–167, KNITTER still offered a four-focal model: "The Conservative Evangelical Model: One True Religion ... The Mainline Protestant Model: Salvation Only in Christ ... The Catholic Model: Many Ways, One Norm ... The Theocentric Model: Many Ways to the Center ...". In the meantime he adopted Hick's tri-focal scheme as heuristic principle, cf. particularly his contribution: 'Hans Küng's Theological Rubicon', in SWIDLER 1987, 224–230. Here the two first categories from 1985 ("Conservative" and "Mainline") have coalesced under the headline "Exclusivist", the "Catholic Model" has been rebaptized to "Inclusivist", and the "Theocentric Model" (with a slightly new description) to "Pluralist".

[2] DINOIA(in: Marshall 1990) 249–274.

[3] CD 26, June 1994, 34–42.

[4] 'Theological Perspectives on Other Faiths' (LWFD 41/1997), 181–201. SELVANAYGAM gives a more comprehensive development of his position in his own book 'A Dialogue on Dialogue' 1995. His comprehensive idea of "a Dialogical approach to Reality and Religion" opens for "Dialogue ... as a mode of existence ... applied to all areas of life ... There is no place either for fanaticism and/or for indifference" (14). This may to some extent explain his disapproval of the customary confrontative triple model as oversimplified.

as any. (2) The complexity of the arena demands great care as to the use of classificatory terminology. The etiquettes used should be constantly reexamined, and the following born in mind. Some kind of classification is necessary in order to survey,
compare and evaluate competing interpretations, but any classificatory model is, in
one way or another, a simplification, and has to be constantly questioned about
presuppositions, advantages and limitations.

It should be remembered that the given trichotomy – terminology as well as definitions – was proposed by those who refer to themselves as "pluralists", and manifestly served to sustain their image of themselves as well as of their rivals. "Exclusivist" in
their language tended to evoke the idea of a square exclusion of other than Christians
from any hope of future "salvation", thus associating Christians of a missionary orientation with the most provocative brands of "fundamentalism". It thus had its immediate flavor of monologism and negativity. Quite opposite, "Pluralist" is used as a
prestigious word in contemporary society and acquires the meaning: someone ready
to take the multiplex spiritual situation of the day seriously, and to show timely tolerance. "Inclusivism" may indicate a relaxed conviction of own identity combined
with considerable willingness to share one's prerogatives with "outsiders". This may
sound as the least prejudiced position, but fenced in as the middle term of the three,
it lacks dynamic elan in either direction, and may be taken to cover any in-between
position.

We will not advance, then, by constructing three systematically coherent, alternative doctrines: pluralism – inclusivism – exclusivism, as the architects of that model
have actually done. We are not exploring the three as presumably consistent doctrines, but as rather multiplex clusters of authors, each cluster to describe itself through
a maximally representative selection of informants. For that purpose we need a simple system of survey so we can relate conversation partners to each other as meaningfully as possible – without doing conceptual violence to any of them. For the sake of
survey some elementary organization of our observations will be needed, and for
practical reasons it may be useful to keep in critical contact with the scheme so widely
used in previous discussion. So, nomenclature must be practiced with restricted ambitions, attention constantly paid to the danger of an overstrained conceptualism.

A particular accent to this preliminary conclusion we find in the neat polarization
of the "Christian Uniqueness" debate 1988–90. We refer to the two contrasting
volumes (anthologies) *The Myth of Christian Uniqueness*[5] and, as a critical response,
Christian Uniqueness Reconsidered – The Myth of a Pluralistic Theology of Religions.[6]
Neither of the two confronting groups of commentators stands for a strictly unified
opinion or – even – an emphatically unified specter of opinions. With regard to the
traditional triple classification, one could say that the former advocates various
shades of "pluralism", the latter an entente cordiale of "exclusivists" and "inclusivists".

---

[5] HICK & KNITTER 1987/1988.
[6] D'COSTA 1990.

The distance between the most "moderate" contribution in *The Myth* ... and the most "progressive" in *Christian Uniqueness* ... is not overwhelming, but the average difference of orientation in the two volumes is impressive enough. Here and there one may think that the dividing factor has been polity as much as theology. Langdon Gilkey on the "mythologist" side voices reluctance toward "the imperialistic effort to take over, absorb and dominate" inherent in the universal "theocentric" approach of his brother-in-arms John Hick,[7] and in the "uniqueness" camp JOHN B. COBB JR. finds it "odd" that for once he should be fighting against eager promoters of dialogue, being himself so definitely one of them. As reason he gives "the very narrow way ... in which pluralism has come to be defined."[8]

The confrontative emergence of the two anthologies, the one presenting itself as a direct riposte to the other, could make it rewarding to start just with a reflective comparison between the two. Multiplex as each of them is, it would, however, be ill counseled to try to extrapolate from each of them some profile of a unified theology of religions. Besides, we may register many of the contributors as frequent travelers, whom we shall meet again in the dialogue debate – several of them with more extensive arguments in writings strictly of their own.

4.1. "Pluralist" Approaches

Under this headline I am looking for influential authors who – accepting for themselves the etiquette "pluralist" or, at least, manifesting fellowship-of-arms with the camp which associates itself with that standard – in principle grant all religions equal access to truth, and consequently favor a theology of religions ready to offer equal recognition to each one of them.

4.1.1. John Hick: Theocentric Universalism

The Anglo-American theologian JOHN HICK has gained his fame not least as editor – and spiritual promoter – of two controversial anthologies: *The Myth of the God Incarnate* in 1977 and (together with PAUL F. KNITTER) *The Myth of Christian Uniqueness* ten years later. It may be worthwhile to observe the two book titles together. In his presentation – as in that of several contemporary authors – there is a clear link between a critical approach to the christological dogma of the Ancient Church and his rejection of Christian uniqueness of whatever kind. The greatest shock was undoubtedly caused in 1977. The inner connection between the two anthologies is strongly supported by his own books explicitly dedicated to dialogue: *God Has Many Names,* 1980, and *Problems of Religious Pluralism,* 1985.

---

[7] 'The Myth ...', 41.
[8] 'Christian Uniqueness ...', 81.

The latter of these volumes opens with a self-biographical sketch reviewing the growth of controversies between HICK and conservative churchmanship over the years. This refers in particular to his own Presbyterian/Reformed church, conflicts caused by his personal development over years from a fairly conventional to an outspoken liberal stand on theological core issues.[9] That discussion has more or less centered around christology, starting with his attack on the virgin birth as far back as 1962, and culminating in his polemical rejection of the "God incarnate" in 1977. As constructive correlate he offers his developing understanding of salvation as founded exclusively in the One God, creator and sustainer of life, equally present to earnest worshipers, irrespective of creed.

God Has Many Names may be seen as the first consistent attempt by a Christian theologian of religions in our time to develop a theology based on a concept of full, equal value of faiths. He accords to Christianity just one major advantage: Christendom is

> "the civilisation within which the transformation of medieval into modern man first took place and through whose influence it is therefore taking place elsewhere. This is Christianity's unique historical role."[10]

The book seems determinately inspired by the author's observation of "Christianity and Race in Britain today", combined with his more general reflections on "The New Religious Pluralism".[11] His actual theory of religious truth is comprehended as follows:

> "I am making the very major assumption ... that man's religiousness is innate and that religion will continue in some form so long as human nature remains essentially the same ... The broad trend of the present century is ecumenical ... Projecting this trend into the future we may suppose that the ecumenical spirit which has already so largely transformed Christianity will increasingly affect the relationships between the world faiths ... The relation between them may thus become somewhat like that between the Christian denominations in this country ... A single world religion is, I would think, never likely, and not a consummation to be desired. For so long as there is a variety of human types there will be a variety of kinds of worship and a variety of theological emphases and approaches ..."[12]

On this background HICK repeats his attack from 1977 on the Christian core dogma of divine incarnation, an attack based on the presupposition that such a dogma inevitably leads to a horrid consequence: the exclusion of the rest of humankind from the hope of eternal salvation.

> "The specifically Christian gift to the world is that men should come to know Jesus and take him into their religious life – not to displace but to deepen and enlarge the relationship

[9] HICK 1985, 1–15. Cf. elements of a theological autobiography in: HICK, 1980, 1–9, and in: WALL 1981, 60–66.
[10] HICK 1980, 95f.
[11] HICK, ibid. 10–27, 28–42.
[12] HICK, ibid. 57f.

with God to which they have already come within their own tradition. And we too, in turn, can be spiritually enriched by God's gifts mediated through other faiths. For we must not think of the religions as monolithic entities each with its own unchanging character. They are complex streams of human life ..."[13]

HICK's position thus seems to be a somewhat modernized version of the theory dominant in the 18th century Enlightenment, of religion as a natural phenomenon geared towards an ever more "purified" realization in the future, liberated from the limiting self-consciousness of historically conditioned religions. If each of these religions may claim a specific value of its own, such value is only of a relative kind, circumscribed by geographical and historical circumstances. Any attempt to make such specifics essential for human salvation, would betray the most basic of all theological assumptions: that of universality.

HICK's own contribution to *The Myth of Christian Uniqueness* is dedicated to *The Non-Absoluteness of Christianity* and represents no essential revision of the position described.[14] Hick finds his view basically anticipated by ERNST TROELTSCH in his famous lecture on the "absoluteness" of Christianity in Oxford in 1923. Hick attacks that concept through reference to the ways in which it has been – and always will be – exploited by greed and arbitrariness, "human nature" being as it actually is. The history of Western imperialism is here the main witness and, thus, the chief argument against a claim of "absolute" truth. Hick's exposition ends up, however, in a remarkably balanced statement on the common fate of the world religions:

> "... each tradition has constituted its own unique mixture of good and evil. Each is a long-lived social reality that has gone through times of flourishing and times of decline ... In face of these complexities it seems impossible to make the global judgement that any one religious tradition has contributed more good and less evil ... than the others."[15]

It should not cause surprise that JOHN HICK has been a particularly beloved target by authors of a more "moderate" – be it "exclusivist" or "inclusivist" – observance. As already mentioned, even a fellow-contributor in Hick's and Knitter's 1987 anthology, LANGDON GILKEY, makes him addressee of a close to crushing remark: his "classic theism" seems as excluding against non-theist Hindu, Buddhist and Confucian orientations as does any theological orthodoxy. To replace faith in Christ with confidence in a universally available godhead must be of little comfort to religious practitioners who by conviction relate to no godhead at all![16]

This objection seems particularly important while it obviously hits not only Hick, but also the "classic" Enlightenment position, as most brilliantly presented by G.E. LESSING's *Nathan der Weise* (1779), where the three monotheistic religions (Judaism,

---

[13] HICK, ibid. 75.

[14] HICK & KNITTER 1987, 16–36.

[15] Ibid. (1987), 30.

[16] Ibid., 41. – It may be a question whether "classic theism" is the most appropriate label to Hick's position (and not "deism"), considering his emphasis on an a-historical "natural" orientation of religion. A discussion of terminology would, however, in this case be of minimal interest.

Christianity, Islam) are encouraged to mutual tolerance, believing in the same sovereign God – but with the rest of the world of religion evidently excluded from the vision. This observation may in itself be sufficient to establish that HICK, through his elimination of the specifics of Christianity, does not succeed in establishing the solid foundation of universal tolerance which he claims.

As one might expect, it is in the opposing volume *Christian Uniqueness Reconsidered* (1990) that Hick comes really under fire. WOLFHART PANNENBERG accuses his concept of "salvation" for lacking any synchronization with the New Testament,[17] PAUL J. GRIFFITHS attacks his ideas about "the nature of doctrine" for a priori excluding cognitive incompatibility from the world of religions,[18] and KENNETH SURIN rejects his "modernistic space of discourse" as out of contact with a postmodern philosophy of culture.[19]

In the same volume LESLIE NEWBIGIN holds five main accusations against HICK's position. It is (1) logically self-defeating, pretending to know the existence of a Reality in itself unknown, (2) lacking ontological foundation for its judgements, (3) performing an "anti-Copernican revolution": a turn from facts ("the reality of the man Jesus Christ") to a view centered in a purely subjective understanding of ultimate reality, (4) presupposing an omnipresent quest for own salvation, overlooking that such a quest, emancipated from the question of truth, is identical with self-assertion, the very destructive drive in human history, and (5) signalizing the "approaching death of a culture" (the Western) which lacks vitality to stand for a convincing truth in face of other cultures which evidently possess such vitality.[20]

In PANNENBERG's view, HICK succeeds in demonstrating the presence of "salvation" in various cultures and in different kinds of religious experience, only because he starts with a superficial definition of salvation as "actual transformation of human life from self-centredness to Reality-centredness." In this way he screens the fundamental New Testament reference to the eschatological judgement of God and to participation in God's kingdom as the final human destination. These observations lead Pannenberg to challenge the general tendency of modernity to "evade or play down the conflict of truth claims" between the religions.[21]

A critic still more occupied by the principal importance of truth claims is PAUL J. GRIFFITHS, who makes this the capital issue in his assessment of "John Hick's View of the Nature of Doctrine", a constitutive element in a more comprehensive essay on

---

[17] PANNENBERG (in: D'Costa 1990) 97–104.

[18] GRIFFITHS, ibid. 159–162.

[19] SURIN, ibid. p. 209.

[20] Ibid., 141–143. – NEWBIGIN as an old missionary, formerly bishop in the Church of South-India, and a leading ecumenical figure for decades, is a particularly interesting witness in this connection, cf. also his book 'The Gospel in a Pluralist Society' 1989, particularly the chapters 'No Other Name', 155–170, and 'The Gospel and the Religions', 171–183. As they stand, some of his accusations against Hick may, however, need more scrupulous precision before they present themselves for unambiguous judgement by the reader.

[21] Ibid., 101f.

The Uniqueness of Christian Doctrine Defended.[22] Griffiths sees HICK as the typical exponent of the main weakness of religious pluralism: actually it represents precisely the "traditional Christian imperialism" which it pretends to do away with, only "with a new twist: ... they require of their dialogue partners an identical rejection and identical reinterpretation" of own positions, similar to those already presented with regard to Christianity.[23]

HICK's and his consorts' principal denial of conflicting truth claims can thus only be taken as a "no" to truth claims in general. An observation which – so GRIFFITHS – does not prevent pluralists from discussing and rejecting particular truth claims in concreto. Their rejection, then, does not take place by facing the claims as they present themselves, but by reviewing what the critics see as rejectable practical (ethical, political) consequences. That judgement, however, takes place by the standards of the judges, not that of those under judgement.

> "... HICK does not allow the possibility that there are genuine, deep-going, cognitively significant incompatibilities among the doctrines expounded by religious communities ... this he knows a priori on the basis of the functionalist criteria already adverted to, and the example he takes is that of the traditional Christian Christological dogma ... The power of Hick's pluralist convictions here becomes evident. These convictions enable him to do ... what only the most assured of traditionally exclusivist apologists is able to; that is, to judge that certain key doctrines of major religious communities are clearly false, and to do so without engaging them upon their own terms ..."[24]

From a logical point of view GRIFFITHS' double remark to Hick makes the most serious objection set forth against the pluralists by an opponent. It is – as also the worldwide discussion so far has shown – utmost difficult to deny the observation that HICK's pluralism is heard by other cultures as an "imperialist" voice of modern Western standards of truth. It may be somewhat easier for the "pluralists" to tackle objections against pragmatic criteria for evaluation of debatable consequences of religious dogmas – provided that these are not proposed as sheer substitutes to a confrontation of truth claims, and thus, as a dogmatization of pure epistemological pragmatism. In that connection later attempts to couple a pluralist theology of religion with socio-ethical liberation theology – as they are presented a.o. in *The Myth* ... – may be of a certain interest,[25] even if "Liberation theology" in general seems more reluctant to mixing social ethics with doctrinal truth controversies.

Through comparing different "discursive spaces", and defining distinctive cultures as separate rooms of identity, SURIN intends to show how unconscious intrusion from one "space" into another violates human integrity:

---

[22] Ibid., 159–162, cf. 157–173. The over-all perspective of Griffiths' criticism is developed and defended in his book 'An Apology of Apologetics – A Study in the Logic of Interreligious Dialogue' 1991.

[23] Ibid., 158.

[24] Ibid., 161.

[25] 'The Myth of Christian Uniqueness', particularly Knitter's contribution 'Toward a Liberation Theology of Religions', 178–200, and the feminist contributions by RUETHER, 137–148, and SUCHOKI, 149–161.

"... HICK's discursive space is the space typical of an educated liberal Western. The occupant of this space is someone who – like Hick – ceaselessly dissolves the dense particularities of any struggles against dominion and injustice ... he is totally resolved to maintain the abstract equivalence of all such spaces. The result is a complete occlusion of the always contingent forces ... which destroy, reconfigure, and realign these spaces ... This traditional intellectual has been demystified in other intellectual disciplines, but not, alas, in the philosophy and theology of religions ... I am convinced that the time of this modernist general intellectual is over ..."[26]

Without commenting on this model of "discursive spaces" in itself, we note a fundamental consonance between the core observations of SURIN and GRIFFITHS. They both want to arrest what they see as a paternalistic use of (an abstract idea of) plurality as a refusal to take the specificness of one's conversation partner seriously. They both claim to have shown how HICK, as chief spokesman of religious pluralism, unconsciously dismantles a great paradox: how professed liberalism by the "pluralist" school is transformed into a pretext for ideological oppression. Could a similar criticism be sustained also in confrontation with other influential pluralists?

4.1.2. Paul F. Knitter: Pluralism – Liberation

The main speaker for a pluralist theory of interreligious dialogue has, beside of John Hick, been his fellow editor of *The Myth of Christian Uniqueness,* PAUL F. KNITTER. Knitter makes no secret of being a Roman Catholic and of seeing a deep consonance between his "pluralist" concern and the theological tradition of his church. – He is also chief editor of the much observed book series *Faith meets Faith* published by Orbis Books (Maryknoll, New York, 1987ff), a series including also several works critical of his own standpoint.[27]

Knitter's *No Other Name? – A Critical Survey of Christian Attitudes Toward the World Religions* from 1985 is – however one may judge of its sharp critical profile – a remarkable over-all view of the *status questionis* in the mid-eighties. No one can describe his project at that stage of events better than he does himself:

"The structure of the book reflects the path I have followed in confronting and trying to resolve the question of Christ/Christianity and other religions. Chapter 1 sets the problem: the new experience of religious pluralism in the world of today, the vision many persons have of a new kind of unity and dialogue among religions, and the perplexing questions Christians encounter when they feel themselves drawn toward such a unity and dialogue ... I review the different Christian models for understanding and approaching other religions: the conservative Evangelical, the mainline Protestant, and the Catholic. Each is helpful in that each stresses central Christian beliefs that must be brought to interreligious dialogue. Yet none of these confessional models seems really able to listen to what followers of other ways have to say. The problem, in all of them, appears to hinge on the traditional Christian

---

[26] 'Christian Uniqueness ...', 209f.
[27] Cf. the general review by James H. KROEGER, SID 3/3 1993, 71–92.

claim to the superiority and normativity of Jesus Christ ... a new, "theocentric" model for Christian encounter with other faiths is taking shape ... I try to confirm the validity of this theocentric model by showing how a theocentric christology is consistent with the witness of scripture and with much of contemporary mainline Christian theology ... A theocentric view of religions and of Christ allows Christians to be fully committed to Jesus and fully open to other ways."[28]

KNITTER's vision, thus, comes close to that of JOHN HICK, and so do the – many would say: reductive – christological assumptions underlying it. Hick is also the first fellow author whom he turns to for a joint development of the new "theocentric" model. He quotes each of his main allies by some programmatic formula: "*John Hick*: The Myth of the Incarnation – *Raimundo Panikkar*: The Universal Christ vis-a-vis the Particular Jesus – *Stanley Samartha*: The Relativity of All Revelations – *Jewish-Christian Dialogue*: Jesus Not the Final Messiah – *Liberation / Political Theologies*: Absolute Norms Unethical."[29]

It is worth noting that the pan-religious universe of KNITTER is subject to precisely the same limitation as that of HICK: in its "theocentricity" it seems remarkably linked up with the monotheistic religions of biblical extraction. Or, one could equally well say: with the tradition of Western Enlightenment. The Jewish-Christian dialogue becomes a normative model for interreligious dialogue as a whole. Knitter's two main "supporters" from India (PANIKKAR and SAMARTHA) are not allowed to disturb this impression, both being quoted as unhesitant supporters of a general "theocentric" framework – an interpretation surprisingly narrow, as we will see when these names show up for a closer review.

KNITTER (as a declared Catholic) differs from (the definitely Protestant) HICK in his explicit attempt to come to terms with the flow of Christian tradition. He sees the various attitudes to dialogue in contemporary Christendom as basically related to confessional patterns. Not least is he – in spite of his cordial fellowship-at-arms with Hick – keen to observe a general difference between Catholic and Protestant types of approach, and to reassure us of his solidarity with a Catholic way of thinking. At the same time he regrets a general unwillingness in dominant Catholic theology so far to embrace his own full-blooded "pluralist" orientation.

The denominational aspect of his orientation is brought still more eloquently to the fore in his subsequent contribution to the renowned international Catholic periodical Concilium, which dedicated an issue in 1986 to *Christianity between the World Religions*.[30] Here KNITTER maintains that the "exclusivist" rejection of non-Christian religions championed by Augustine and, in his succession, by Medieval Catholicism in general, was overcome by the "inclusivism" of post-Reformation Jesuits, who opened up for a more comprehensive orientation of Catholic theology as a whole.

He discovers the same trend in the revitalization of Catholic theology of religions following the Second Vatican Council (1962–65). Contemporary developments

[28] KNITTER 1985, xi-xii.
[29] Ibid., 145–167.
[30] 'Katholische Religionstheologie am Scheideweg' (C 1/8, 1993) 63–68).

show, however, that these initiatives have been insufficient to secure a consistent Catholic understanding of Christian relations with other faiths in the world of to-day.[31] Most of KNITTER's essay is dedicated to a critical review of what he sees as compromising "inclusivist" positions and, may better be dealt with in our analysis of that general trend in 4.2. One senses already the profile of Knitter's favorite anta-gonist looming in the background: HANS KÜNG.

Already in this article KNITTER seems to have after-thoughts with regard to a nominal "theocentric" approach, which his book one year earlier had supported so eloquently. His main accusation is now that dominant Catholic theology of religions has come into a certain contradiction with basic ethical demands.[32] A much needed exchange between Liberation Theology and theology of religions must lead to a prag-matic reorientation of the latter. The final aim must be the well-being of humans. Not ecclesiocentricity, not christocentricity, not even theocentricity can be the ulti-mate point of reference, but soteriocentricity – focus on "salvation" as supreme human concern.[33]

Later, this idea – making theology of religions a most important branch of a uni-versal Liberation Theology – has established itself as a cornerstone in the thinking of PAUL KNITTER.[34] This can be taken as an attempt to secure that family of theologies as a powerful and prestigious ally for a pluralist theology of religions in its struggle for worldwide acceptance. But there may be more to it than that. It is hardly coincidental that Knitter, as one of the two editors of the programmatic 1987/88 symposium *The Myth of Christian Uniqueness*, besides writing the preface to that volume, has chosen to contribute with the longest single exposé in the book: *Toward a Liberation Theolo-gy of Religions*.

This essay starts by reciting two "signs of the time", with two particularly deman-ding challenges to contemporary Christians: that of the numerous poor, and that of the many religions. The corresponding replies in contemporary Christian thinking to the two challenges: Theology of Liberation and Theology of Religions, are en-couraging signs of a church alert and open to renewal. A purely Christian liberation theology, however, fails to observe a lot of resources and potentials, which are there on a world-scale. In order to accomplish its aim, any liberation appeal needs the support of a broadminded theology of religions:

"...a preferential option for the poor and the nonperson constitutes both the necessity and the primary purpose of interreligious dialogue."[35]

It is noteworthy that Knitter here indicates some hesitation even about the program-

---

[31] "Die römisch-katholische Religionstheologie sieht sich in diesen Tagen an einem verwirrenden und herausfordernden Scheideweg ... Was wir brauchen ist, so denke ich, eine Befreiungstheologie der Reli-gionen." KNITTER, ibid., 63.

[32] Ibid., 65.

[33] Ibid., 67.

[34] 'Toward a Liberation Theology of Religions' (in: HICK & KNITTER 1987/88) 178–200

[35] 1987/88, 180f.

matic word "pluralist", of which he has himself been so hardy a supporter. It is precisely in the Preface to this book that he most programmatically, on behalf of the contributors, proclaims "Religious pluralism" as the great and inescapable "paradigm shift"![36]

When in the essay quoted he also proclaims "The basic liberationist maxim that orthopraxis holds a primacy over orthodoxy" as "a workable pastoral tool for mediating the new nonabsolutist christologies",[37] that "tool" could easily be understood as a means to distract attention from notorious doctrinal objections and to replace one kind of theological absoluteness by another.

It may be just as surprising that virtually, if not verbally, in one major domain he has done completely away with the constituent idea of "pluralism", namely in social ethics. It is not easy to see how the rigidity of the "orthopraxis" proclaimed could allow him to accept, or even to dialogue with, communities that do not cope with his definition of (politico-)ethical standards. This must evidently also prescribe: unwillingness to dialogue with religious doctrines which seem to hinder or hamper "correct" patterns of political action.

Where do his fellow fighters in *The Myth* ... stand on this issue? Are they as ready as their ensign to compromise the banner of "pluralism" – thus restricting the arena of dialogue in the domain of socio-ethical orientation – and still face the world as champions of a "pluralist theology of religions"? In this setting it may be appropriate to recall the criticism directed against the other editor of the book, JOHN HICK, notably by PAUL J. GRIFFITHS and KENNETH SURIN, for combining doctrinal indifferentism with what they see as socio-cultural imperialism.[38]

The three contributions in *The Myth* ... which, beside that of Paul F. Knitter, represent a pronounced liberationist approach to dialogue, move in somewhat disparate directions. ROSEMARY RADFORD RUETHER in her 'Feminism and Jewish-Christian Dialogue' is looking for the prophetic criticism of religion in the Bible to include also religious oppression of women, but must regretfully admit that what she looks for, is not there.[39] More successful seems MARJORIE HEWITT SUCHOCKI: 'In Search of Justice – Religious Pluralism from a Feminist Perspective'.[40] She sees in "an exclusivist attitude toward other religions" an echo of "the exclusivist attitude toward women".[41]

"I reject, however, the possibility of entering into dialogue with no judgements whatsoever ... in light of the relativism of belief systems, but a shift of judgement from ideological ground to ethical ground, along with an open recognition of the conditioned nature of the norm of justice we bring ...[42]

[36] Ibid., vii.
[37] Ibid., 195.
[38] Cf. our notes 18–20.
[39] Ibid., 137–148.
[40] Ibid., 149–161.
[41] Ibid., 153.
[42] Ibid., 150.

Affirming religious pluralism within the context of justice shifts the focus of dialogue to the concreteness of human well-being ... Interreligious dialogue focused on justice promotes intrareligious dialogue concerning ultimate and penultimate values. The pluralism among religions then finds its calling attentive to the pluralism within each religion; dialogue engenders dialogues."[43]

Strangely enough, SUCHOCKI takes HANS KÜNG as typical spokesperson of a theology which – approaching non-Christian religions with a norm intrinsically foreign to them: the absoluteness of Christ – acts in precisely the same way as conventional masculinism trying to impose its own repressive norms on the opposite sex.[44]

We shall refrain from commenting on SUCHOCKI's unspecified analogy between interreligious and intergeneric dialogue, and on her unexpectedly unfriendly predilection for HANS KÜNG in that setting. The interesting observation is her blunt proclamation of "a shift of judgement from ideological ground to ethical ground", the issue of inter- as well as of intra-religious dialogue being changed to "human well-being", i.e. an unconditioned transfer of attention from truth to value. Not a "theocentric", but an emphatically anthropocentric orientation is declared dominant of a religious "pluralism" with no urge in the direction of reciprocal doctrinal understanding, but with very concise socio-ethical demands.

SUSHOCKI's remark about "the conditioned nature" of our norms of justice seems, however, to lack both in precision and in argumentative integration. Structurally her "shift" reflects the same pragmatic reorientation which we have just observed with KNITTER, only in a less sophisticated form. The concept of "human well-being" more or less corresponds with KNITTER's "liberation". It is, of course, not to be understood as a sheer reference to what may at any time be felt most pleasing to someone concerned. It implies a very definite idea of values, but a reflective basis for establishing them is not secured.

The last contribution in *The Myth* ... which concentrates on a liberation aspect, is ALOYSIUS PIERIS S.J.: 'The Buddha and the Christ – Mediators of Liberation'.[45] Here the liberation aspect is not primarily geared to political change: "The 'core' of any religion is the liberative experience that gave birth to that religion."[46] Pieris moves in the opposite direction of the pluralist tradition so far: he sees Pauline christology in its presumably hellenistic adaptation as essential to a Christian liberative experience, and his concern is to show its similarity with influential Buddhist interpretations of soteriology. A fundamental equality of the two religions is established, not by reducing the christological ambitions of primeval Christianity, but by elevating those of the partner to a corresponding level. The unifying factor is not a theocentric idea of a common godhead – which would in any case be irreconcilable with a non-theistic Buddhist orientation – but the liberative dynamic of buddhology and christology respectively.

[43] Ibid., 160.
[44] Ibid., 152ff.
[45] Ibid., 162–177.
[46] Ibid., 162.

In our later visitation of the world religions one by one, we shall see how precisely Buddhism as dialogue partner explicitly elicits a non-political soteriocentric criteriology. This is, however, a kind of pragmatism which replaces *orthodoxia* not by *orthopraxis*, but by some unspecified *orthospirituality*.

In any case: this is also a pluralistic approach that manifestly relocates the premises of established theocentric pluralism. Not some common – however vague – idea of a universal godhead revealed in differing historical disguise, but a universal human experience of the liberating power of religious integration is invoked as basis of mutual interreligious acceptance. This is a model which can be launched with more or less socio-political programming, or with more or less socio-psychological introspection. But in any case it turns attention away from the arena of conflicting truth claims to that of a prospective sharing of liberative resources – be it conceived in a more political or a more spiritualized direction.

PAUL F. KNITTER can, probably more than any one else, be said to have opened up for a development of contemporary "pluralism" in a pragmatic direction. As far as we have been able to survey the sources, he has not succeeded, however, to lead that development to an acceptable level of logical consistency. Nor can that be maintained of his followers whom we have quoted, so far.

4.1.3. The Circle of "Mythologists"

Our attention is still geared to the *The Myth of Christian Uniqueness* and to some of the more challenging authors contributing to it. As we shall see, this volume is not the exponent of some massive ideological unity, but a fairly representative symposium of authors eager to forward the development of interreligious dialogue by rejecting the traditional claim of "Christian uniqueness". Among these authors several have made remarkable contributions in the same direction also before and after the appearance of that volume, contributions which in several cases also will be observed in the progress of our study.

The Myth ... was prepared by a consultation at Claremont Graduate School in March 1986.[47] It is worth observing that some of those invited to take part, they themselves well-known advocates of liberal attitudes to, apologized, expressing disagreement with the project as such.[48] The image of a well organized international "pluralist" phalanx behind the publication is, however, impressive enough, an observation which could also be made on another "Pluralist" anthology published around the same time: *Toward a Universal Theology of Religion* from 1987.[49]

---

[47] 'The Myth ...', viii-ix.

[48] KNITTER mentions the apologies of three Process theologians: COBB, OGDEN and TRACY, ibid., viii. This is confirmed by John B. COBB Jr. in 'Christian Uniqueness ...', 81. Cf. the review of the Claremont conference by DRIVER, in: 'The Myth ...', 203–218.

[49] (Ed.) SWIDLER, 1987.

The 1987 volume contained papers presented at a conference at Temple University in October 1984 and a follow-up seminar at the University of Tübingen in the summer of 1985. Two out of four main presentations on the first occasion were given by prominent lecturers later taking distance from the "Mythologists": JOHN B. COBB JR. and HANS KÜNG. To each of the four presentations three responses from people of various religions are included. In addition to this, a comprehensive preconference paper by the editor LEONARD SWIDLER and a second presentation by Küng (opening address in Tübingen) make up the publication.

"The Rubicon conference"– that is what HANS KÜNG humoristically called the Temple consultation,[50] namely because PAUL F. KNITTER in his response 'Hans Küngs Theological Rubicon', after having accused Küng and Cobb of lacking clarity, makes a straight appeal to Hans Küng:

> "... a number of Christian theologians ... have more recently shifted from an inclusivist Christocentrism to a pluralist theocentrism ...: RAIMUNDO PANIKKAR, STANLEY SAMARTHA, JOHN HICK, ROSEMARY RUETHER, TOM DRIVER, ALOYSIUS PIERIS ... But I ask you, HANS KÜNG, do you think such a new direction in Christian attitudes toward other religions,such a crossing of the Rubicon, is possible? And would it be productive of greater Christian faith and dialogue"?[51]

The anthology contains no direct answer, in spite of KÜNG's additional contribution at the follow-up consultation in Tübingen. Also Küng's later publications show that he, in spite of his ardent dialogue engagement, never had in mind to accept Knitter's rhetorically brilliant invitation.

The two "Mythologists" who participated with main contributions already at the Temple consultation, were WILLIAM CANTWELL SMITH and RAIMUNDO PANIKKAR. Together with Hick and Knitter they have been the voices most listened to in the "pluralist" camp, and it may be worthwhile to observe their positions.

Smith's contributions in the field of dialogue so far are well summed up in the *Festschrift* issued in his honor *The World's Religious Traditions*[52] from 1984, particularly in the panegyric contribution by JOHN HICK.[53] Here is Hick's judgement:

> "WILFRED CANTWELL SMITH ... has been responsible, more than any other individual, for the change which has taken place within a single generation ... Seen through pre-Cantwell Smith eyes there are a number of vast, long-lived historical entities or organisms known as Christianity, Hinduism, Islam, Buddhism ... contraposed socio-religious entities ... bearers of distinctive creeds; and every religious individual is a member of one or other of these mutually exclusive groups ... And so the proper question ... is, which is the true religion? Cantwell Smith has offered an alternative vision. He shows first that the presently dominant conceptuality can be traced back to the European Renaissance ... having reified their

---

[50] In a lecture at Chr. Michelsen Institute in Bergen, Norway, August 1995 – observed by P.L.

[51] 'Toward a Universal ...', 229 (224–230).

[52] Ed. Frank WHALING, 1984.

[53] 'A Philosophy of Religious Pluralism', recorded also in: John Hick 'Problems of Religious Pluralism' (1985) 28–45.

own faith in this way Westerners have then exported the notion of 'a religion' to the rest of the world, causing others to think of themselves as belonging to the Hindu, or the Confucian, or the Buddhist religion ... over against the others. But an alternative perception can divide the scene differently ... something of vital religious importance ... within the contexts of the different historical traditions. This ... Cantwell Smith calls faith ... a positive openness to the Divine which gradually transforms us ... essentially the same within the different religious contexts ... the transformation of human existence from self-centredness to Reality-centredness".[54]

Particular to the approach of CANTWELL SMITH is his – philosophically as much as empirically founded – footing in a comprehensive study of the history of religions. He insists on seeing this history as a unity, and all authentic theology as directed to, and by, that common history. This leads him to reject any concept of conflicting religious identities as a misleading historical novelty of Western production.

This orientation is spelt out with lucidity in his Temple Conference paper "Theology and the World's Religious History",[55] evidently a compendium to his book *Toward a World Theology*. The term "Christian Theology" he calls "a contradiction in terms ... virtually unknown before the nineteenth and rare before the twentieth century."[56] What he fails to note, however, is that the reason for that rareness scarcely can be the kind of universalism which he advocates, it is rather the opposite: a massive unawareness that something like "theology" could take place outside the premises of Christendom.

One of SMITH's respondents, a Hindu, seems also to make a just observation, seeing practical difficulties not only in the immensity of such a universal theology, but still more in the fact that, if loyal to history, it would be obliged to make room for conflicting truth claims.[57] What could it, finally, propose as a criterion of judgement? How could Smith's universal theology integrate systems which, in their basic self-understanding, manifestly reject his pretended all-encompassing orientation? Could his integration be experienced as anything but a violation of the integrity of the one as well as the other?

SMITH's contribution to *The Myth* ... carries the title "Idolatry – In Comparative Perspective" and elaborates on the phrase that "Exclusive claims for one's own (religion) is idolatry ... Christianity – for some Christian theologians – has been our idol."[58] This provocative statement becomes more than understandable in light of his definitions of "religion" and of "theology". Smith has contributed to "pluralism" not only as an impatient precursor of unrestricted dialogue, but as an original thinker combining history and philosophy of religion into a unified model, independent of political and ecclesio-political considerations. Unlike Hick and Knitter, who, with all their interreligious broadmindedness, speak in a Christian family setting, where they speak

---

[54] HICK, op.cit., 28f.
[55] 'Toward a Universal ...', 51–72.
[56] Ibid., 70.
[57] MITRA, ibid., 81.
[58] 'The Myth ...', 60f (cf. 53–68).

as constant militants in an intrareligious warfare, the old missionary Smith has argued from a consistently cross-religious platform.

The other name which plays a capital role both in *Toward a Universal ...* and in *The Myth ...* is that of RAIMUNDO PANIKKAR. Panikkar, an Indian, who is professing to be a Roman Catholic and a Hindu at the same time, has been one of the most fascinating characters in the worldwide dialogue debate of the last generation. His contribution has in more than one regard rendered piloting service to the growing "pluralist" movement.

Besides the two essays already announced, we find a particularly lucid introduction to his style of thought in his contribution to the opening issue of the new periodical *Dialog der Religionen* in 1991: "Begegnung der Religionen: Das unvermediliche Gespräch".[59] In this exposé he gives to dialogue a metaphysical motivation, as "a religious act" founded in the very fact that "human nature is dialogical".[60] PANIKKAR loves imagery. On that occasion he calls for

> "a middle road between firm castles on always higher hills in war with one another –
> because every castle will preserve salvation for itself – and a flat, dull remaining in the
> valleys of human indiscrimination, where each religion has lost its identity and characteristic
> qualities."[61]

So, as it appears, he is most determined to combine historically founded identity with unrestricted openness.

In the 1987 Temple symposium his contribution – one of four main lectures – carries the title 'The Invisible Harmony – A Universal Theology of Religion or a Cosmic Confidence in Reality?'[62] The polemical thrust indicated in the either-or, is consciously directed against the tendency of "modern Western scholarship to search in the direction of a universal theory of religion ... this thrust is not universal ... no theory is universal."

> "My thesis is clear: a universal theory of whatever kind denies pluralism. Any alleged uni-
> versal theory is a particular theory, besides many others, that claims universal validity, thus
> trespassing the limits of its own legitimacy ... theory, the contemplation of truth, is neither
> a universal contemplation, nor is (theoretical) "truth" all that there is to Reality."[63]

PANIKKAR remarks that after this rejection of universal theories he must be utterly careful not to establish one himself. Instead he suggests a three step reorientation: to "put our house in order", to "open ourselves to others" and to "rely on the overall thrust of human experience".[64] It is not difficult to distinguish his implicit reservations against generalizing theories as they seem to underlie even the constructs of

[59] DdR 1/91, 9–39.
[60] Ibid., 3f, 38f. – English translation by P.L.
[61] Ibid., 32.
[62] 'Toward a Universal ...', 118–153.
[63] Ibid., 132.
[64] Ibid., 137.

other pluralist theologies of religions (Hick, Knitter?). Nor to sense the influence of a traditional Indian mystical approach in his reluctance to what he sees as a "Western" tendency to capture "Reality" in conceptualized theories.

The reactions of the respondents to his approach are interesting. As a Taoist/Zen reactor, CHARLES WEI-HSUN FU greets Panikkar's expression of the "Asian ... mentality of dialogical openness".[65] The Buddhist BIBHUTI S. YADAV, on the contrary, accuses him of violating history and producing an unfounded idea of some universalized spirituality.[66]

Do their split reactions question the common idea of a unified "Eastern" attitude to religious pluralism? From a Western point of view THOMAS DEAN opposes the disjunction at the base of Panikkar's argument and sees it founded in an equivocal notion of "universal theology", lacking in conceptual distinction and confusing universality of objective observation with some universality of subjective orientation.

In *The Myth* ... PANIKKAR chooses as headline "The Jordan, the Tiber and the Ganges".[67] The three famous rivers are taken as respective symbols (1) of the Palestinian origin, (2) of the European development and (3) of the universal realization of the "christic principle", which he defines as the real root of historic Christianity.

> "We should not identify the christic fact of Christianness with Christianity as Religion, and much less with Christendom as civilization ... There is no need for one single view of Christ, however broadly it may be conceived ... the christic principle ... can be experienced as a dimension at least potentially present in any human being, as long as no absolute interpretation is given. This could equally be said of a similar principle in other traditions (Buddhahood for instance) ... Christians may find in this christic principle the point of union, understanding and love with all humankind and the whole of cosmos ..."[68]

Doesn't PANIKKAR here come close to what he has earlier denounced as a "universal theory"? But without such a theory isn't it difficult to arrive at a coherent universe of understanding at all? Wouldn't the only consistent alternative be unrestricted "pluralism", not only as acceptance of various, competing truth claims in the world of religions, but of various, mutually non-integrative patterns of understanding in the mind of the interpreter? Dean's criticism at the Temple symposium is rather understandable.

It is clear, however, that among contemporary declared "pluralists", PANIKKAR – together with ALOYSIUS PIERIS[69] – is the one closest to an "inclusivist" position: an orientation which, starting from the blessings of one particular religion, tries to show how the same blessing can be shared by followers of other faiths without a change of religious allegiance.

Much, then, depends on the historic distinctiveness of his "christic principle". Does "principle" stand for some pattern of religious behavior which can be communicated

---

[65] Ibid., 154–161.
[66] Ibid., 175–191.
[67] 'The Myth ...', 89–116.
[68] Ibid., 112.
[69] Ibid., 162–177.

to posterity by an indiscriminate number of mediators, independent of each other, and independent of common historical roots? Is the "christic principle" a potential latent in the human nature, just waiting for some adequate impulse to wake it up – or is it, maybe, a new dynamic once implanted in human history and thereafter accessible through some experience of contact with that implantation event? If the latter be the case, the borderlines of religious pluralism would certainly be pierced. But here we are touching on problems which may be more fruitfully elucidated in the following conversation with "inclusivist" thinkers.

A compatriot of PANIKKAR, who has given an extraordinary contribution to the discussion on dialogue, and who for several years has presented himself as a declared pluralist, is STANLEY J. SAMARTHA, 1970–1981 director of the World Council of Churches Dialogue program. Many would identify him as the chief architect behind the ambitious start of this program, which caused so much confrontation around and in between the WCC Assemblies in Nairobi (1975) and Vancouver B.C. (1983). At the same time he administered the reconciliatory WCC consultation in Chiang Mai(1977) and contributed actively to the balanced "Guidelines on Dialogue" which issued from that event.[70] A more confrontative profile in recent years may reflect his more independent position after having laid the WCC position well behind, but also the general shift of ecumenical tides during the 1980s.

In *The Myth* ... SAMARTHA[71] is fighting what he calls "normative exclusiveness" and "the stranglehold of propositional theology": "Christocentrism without theocentrism leads to idolatry ..."[72] Nothing of this sounds new compared to what we have heard from others. Especially his reluctance to "propositional theology" and his predilection for an Indian mystical orientation will indicate consensus between the Protestant SAMARTHA and his Catholic countryman PANIKKAR. But his appraisal of theocentrism at the cost of christocentrism brings him closer to Western debaters like HICK and KNITTER. Indeed, his theocentric emphasis runs rather contrary to a Hindu/Buddhist vision of the Divine – and brings him at a solid distance from Panikkar's explicitly Indian approach.

Of special interest is SAMARTHA's historical sketch, not primarily of the genesis of contemporary dialogue, but of what he sees as the development of dialogue in India already from the day of the Jesuit mission in the late 16th century up to our time and to a contemporary readiness to integrate Christ as a source of mystical inspiration in Hindu reflection.[73] This is how he sums up his theological conclusion:

"Through the incarnation in Jesus Christ, God has relativized God's self in history. Christian theologians should therefore ask themselves whether they are justified in absolutizing in doctrine him whom God has relativized in history ... Christians are moving toward a

---

[70] See particularly SAMARTHA 1977, and the WCC 'Guidelines...' 1979. Some supplementary observations are presented by Michael MILDENBERGER (ed.) 'Denkpause im Dialog', 1978.
[71] 'The Cross and the Rainbow', in: 'The Myth ...', 69–88.
[72] Ibid., 70, 82, 81.
[73] Ibid., 72–75, 81–84.

position of 'relational distinctiveness' of Christ, relational because Christ does not remain unrelated to neighbors of other faiths, and distinctive because, without recognizing the distinctiveness of the great religious traditions as different responses to the Mystery of God, no mutual enrichment is possible."[74]

An immediate question to this may have logical as much as theological repercussions: Are the concepts of "relativizing" and "absolutizing" sufficiently unambiguous to carry the load of his argument? If God's self-relativization in Christ is thought of as an act in history – which is undoubtedly the case in Christian tradition – the believer must relate to it as a dynamic event and not as a static, timeless condition. That fundamental distinction is too easily camouflaged by a rhetorical disjunction of "absolutizing" and "relativizing" theology.

In the meantime, has SAMARTHA's monography *One Christ – Many Religions – Toward a Revised Christology* 1991 shed more of light on his basic (theo-)logical assumptions? This book deserves attention as probably the most circumspective review of the dialogue arena in a "pluralist" perspective since PAUL J.KNITTER's *No Other Name* in 1985, and the author has an exceptional background for viewing the field. His longtime WCC responsibility with worldwide experience of practicing combines with his profound identification with his ecumenically challenging environments on the Indian continent, of which he is so brilliant an informant.

In this book SAMARTHA presents a multiplex observation of "New Perceptions of Religious Pluralism". This observation is partly founded in historical orientation: the aftermaths of the second world war with the collapse of colonialism, political and cultural – a mitigation of truth claims in science, including theology – a worldwide transfer of theological interest from biblical Salvation History ("Heilsgeschichte") to a religious interpretation of indigenous identity. But his concern also rests on ontological assumptions:

> "Religious Pluralism is part of the larger plurality of races, peoples, and cultures ... Plurality ... belongs to the very structure of reality."[75]

It would not be difficult to affirm the last statement – in general. The logical problem is that without a clarifying definition of "plurality" the extent of possible consequences remains undecided. This term may be extended ad infinitum: to an unlimited differentiation of everything imaginable. The unspecified principle resulting from this may exclude conceptual distinctiveness in whatever direction. Argumentative use of unspecified principles may open for consequences unintended by everybody. This observation makes SAMARTHA's reference to "plurality" equally unprotected as his use of "absolutizing"/"relativizing" already observed.

"What do neighbors of other faiths think of Christian initiatives in dialogue?" SAMARTHA raises the question, and his observations are most informative.[76] He ad-

---

[74] Ibid., 69f.
[75] 'One Christ ...', 4 (1–12).
[76] Ibid., 13–31.

mits the difficulty of a general answer. The dialogue initiatives of the last generation have to an overwhelming extent been taken by Christians, and a fear has naturally installed itself in other communities that some Western imperialist motive – if ever so unconsciously – may be lying behind.

SAMARTHA recalls the scandal it caused to participants at the international Prayer Day in Assisi, to which the Pope summoned different communities of faith in October 1986, when they were told to split up for the real, concluding prayer session. – He goes on reviewing the general responses to interreligious dialogue in Judaism, Islam, Hinduism and Buddhism and dwells on encouraging signs of responsive openness, without hiding certain, generally explicable, hesitations which have come to the fore. On this background he underscores the importance of Christians finding a reliable balance between the roles of teachers and learners in the further development of dialogue.

His following reflections on "Religions, Cultures, and the Struggle for Justice"[77] are less concerned with the task of religion(s) to question the actual state of economic and social justice than with the opposite orientation: the question of justice to turn its face and examine the religions themselves. He sees it as important to expose and to refute the "aggressive religious militancy" and "the crypto-colonialist theology of religions and cultures that lies hidden in the heart of the North". Such an attitude repels people of other faiths, also from cooperating with Christians in concrete issues of social justice. In addition to this, new North-South relations must invite more equally proportioned study of reciprocal spiritual inheritances. Likewise, a more extensive spread of information on accomplishments of dialogue, observing academic as well as practical consequences.

SAMARTHA's comments on "Scripture and Scriptures"[78] follow more or less directly from the same approach. Reviewing the world of religions, he sees "a plurality of scriptures" which in principle demand the same unconditional respect from all faiths, exploring the fact that "Scriptures function differently in the life of different religious communities". It is difficult to relate simultaneously to "certain exclusive elements within each scripture leading to truth claims by each community of faith", he observes. In addition to written texts, each religion contains "symbols pointing to something beyond that is deeper". Therefore devotional use of each other's scriptures can be encouraged, at the same time as the "pilgrim character" of religious life warns us against an idea of "petrified texts written once for all".

Four of the ten chapters in SAMARTHA's study are thematically geared to issues of christology.[79] His demand for a revision of the historical Christian doctrine of Christ is partly pragmatically, partly religiously motivated. Exclusive claims "make it difficult, if not impossible, for persons belonging to different religious traditions to live

---

[77] Ibid., 32–44.
[78] Ibid., 58–75.
[79] Ibid., 76–91, 92–111, 112–131, 132–141.

together in harmony and cooperate for common purposes in society."[80] "Exclusiveness puts fences around the Mystery."[81]

"In moving beyond exclusiveness and inclusiveness, Christians must come to a clearer grasp of the uniqueness of Jesus ... Elevating Jesus to the status of God or limiting Christ to Jesus of Nazareth are both temptations to be avoided. The former (?) runs the risk of an impoverished "Jesuology" and the latter(?) of becoming a narrow "Christomonism". A theocentric christology avoids these dangers and becomes more helpful in establishing new relationships with neighbors of other faiths."[82]

Two, obviously not coordinated, principles at work make the reader a little confused: "... both historical pressure and theological imperatives demand a reexamination of all exclusivist claims."[83] It can hardly be neglected that, in a theological perspective (in other religions as in Christianity), there is more of discrepancy between these two dynamics: "historical pressure" and "theological imperatives", than Samartha seems willing to admit. This tension should scarcely be left unconsidered in an intrareligious – nor even in an interreligious – perspective of dialogue.

It is also a question whether those defending a traditional christology against his attack, would quite recognize their position in the rather simplified alternative presented. An option between one of the two opposite aberrations ("impoverished Jesuology" and "Christomonism") and his own "theocentric christology" cannot be handled as logically obligatory – like he does it – before reasons are given to assume that no fourth option could exist.

According to SAMARTHA: "Any exclusive claim leads to four negative consequences in a multireligious society."[84] (1) Splitting people in religious "we"-s and "they"-s, (2) Preventing cooperation between religious communities for solution of social problems, (3) Creating tensions and conflicts in society, eventually in infiltration with economic and military power, (4) Raising serious theological issues about the fate of people who died before Christ and the "right" of Christians "to limit God's freedom to intervene in history at more than one point." To these general accusations is added a more casual list of social complaints.

Two questions to Samartha's critical assertions may be indicated. Is it certain that "any exclusive claim" leads to one or more of the consequences listed? – And: will SAMARTHA insinuate that his opponents, such as e.g. JÜRGEN MOLTMANN and WOLF-HART PANNENBERG with their support to what he evidently declines as "exclusivist" christological claims, would endorse the consequences he puts into their mouths: "Everybody deceased before the birth of Jesus is excluded from eternal salvation" or "God is not free to intervene in history except ..."? Could it be suggested that Samartha in this regard is founding a substantial part of his argument on unverifiable construction?

[80] Ibid., 76.
[81] Ibid., 85.
[82] Ibid., 86.
[83] Ibid., 76.
[84] Ibid., 102.

4.1.4. David J. Krieger

The same year as Samartha's book was published, 1991, another pluralist over-all approach appeared in the same *Faith meets Faith-* series, DAVID J. KRIEGER's *The New Universalism – Foundations for a Global Theology.* The author had been in charge of a research program on dialogue conducted by the *Evangelische Studiengemeinschaft an der Zürcher Hochschule*, where he had published a preliminary study on interreligious exchange.[85] It may be particularly interesting to see what, at that time, divided a Swiss from an Indian plea for "pluralism".

The project of KRIEGER is, from a philosophical point of view, a remarkably unified one. Arguing "within the framework of PAUL TILLICH", he advocates an abandoning of the traditional "horizon" of established Christianity – defined as "apologetical universalism", a general orientation which Christianity, in his view, shares with its main enemy "secularism":

"... constituted by the presupposition of its own absolute totality and the denial of the validity and truth of other world-views ... The fact that neither Christianity nor Secular Humanism ... could fully neutralize and incorporate the other into its views may seem to have undermined the credibility of the entire apologetical project and thus to have opened up the question of ... whether a non-apologetical universalism is possible."[86]

But the contemporary collapse of "apologetic universalism" may just as much be due to the fall of colonialism and, with it, to the relativization of Western culture as a whole.

"It became apparent that no one, neither Christian nor secularist, stands on solid neutral ground. Everyone has the same access to truth; which can only mean that every world-view is as true as every other. The truth, if there is still "one", is that truth is many and not one."[87]

This reorientation, however, does not favor a simple shift to "relativism", since that would only end up in nihilistic skepticism, by the simple move of subjectivizing what was previously held for objective.[88] The duplex orientation needed can be provided through WITTGENSTEIN's "discovery of 'other-rationality'" which makes a claim of universality possible in today's global situation. For this situation accepts neither "an imperialistic objectivism" nor "a skeptical and finally self-contradictory relativism".

"My thesis is that this can only be found if philosophical hermeneutics, the theory of communicative action and the ethics of discourse are incorporated into a pragmatics of non-violence ... which itself is grounded in transcendence, that is, in a cosmotheandric solidarity."[89]

---

[85] 'Das Interreligiöse Gespräch: Methodologische Grundlagen der Theologie der Religionen', Zürich 1986.

[86] KRIEGER 1991, 4.

[87] Ibid., 4.

[88] Ibid., 5.

[89] Ibid, 7.

This is rather heavily loaded rhetoric, from which it is anything but easy to derive one logically unified "thesis", and much will depend on how his subsequent procedure succeeds in giving recognizable substance to the fundamental categories quoted.

Krieger's reflection moves forward in four main steps: "Opening the Horizon for a Global Theology", "Method", "Foundations" and "The New Universalism",[90] each section presented with one intellectual predecessor as chief guide: PAUL TILLICH, RAIMUNDU PANIKKAR, LUDWIG WITTGENSTEIN and MAHATMA GANDHI, respectively.

In the work of TILLICH, Krieger is particularly fascinated by his early "Philosophy of Religion" from 1925 and his last public lecture "The Significance of the History of Religions for a Systematic Theologian" from 1966, thus viewing Tillich's intermediary production as a parenthesis, yea, almost as an apostasy from his more comprehensive, encompassing vision. Through his final two years of seminars, in cooperation with MIRCEA ELIADE, Tillich is brought back to his primeval vision with the global horizon of religious cultures. In this vision also secularism is being explored for what it is: a religion among religions with a revelatory experience in its own right. This opens up for a new and relaxed theology of religions, where any kind of apologetical self-assertion is abandoned as meaningless. To Tillich five conclusions emerge, to which KRIEGER expresses full support:

"(1) Revelatory experiences are given to all peoples. They are universal. (2) No revelation is fully transparent and comprehensible. Revelation is symbolic. (3) Critique prevents these symbols from becoming closed up in fixed and unquestionable interpretations. (4) Critique transcends the given borders of any particular tradition and aims at an absolute truth. (5) The sacred is not a separate realm alongside the secular, but the ground of the secular. Secularism is, therefore, itself a religion with sacred and profane elements of its own."[91]

Surprisingly enough, KRIEGER next, in his look for a methodology to fit the "new universalism", turns to PANIKKAR, whom we have met as a great challenger of any "universal theory of religion".[92] His main point of reference is Panikkar's "Diatopical hermeneutics" in *The Unknown Christ of Hinduism* (1981). It turns out, however, that what Krieger seeks for here is mainly a mental preparation for dialogue, a "genuine conversion" through personal experience of "truth" as present in traditions other than one's own. But to an observer, that kind of exercise may seem rather irrelevant to the strictly philosophical project of "Universalism" already heralded by Krieger.

With his third adviser WITTGENSTEIN, Krieger is particularly impressed by his progress from the closed rationality of *Tractatus* (1921) to the open language-game theory of *Philosophische Untersuchungen* (1953). KRIEGER here finds a logical legitimation of the principle of "other-rationality". This opens up an approach to diffe-

[90] Ibid., 9–44, 45–76, 77–123, 124–162.
[91] Ibid., 44.
[92] Cf. the description supported by our notes 59–69!

ring, non-competitive systems of truth, which can all claim universal validity without rejecting each other and without offending against their reciprocal integrity.[93]

Finally, taking GANDHI's principle of "Satyagraha" as his model, KRIEGER spells out his new non-apologetic universalism as "not only the pious wish of a few special disciplines, but the inner need of thought itself."[94] Here we may observe that among the "pluralists" so far inspected, Krieger is the one who proceeds furthest in the direction of a rational construction, not only of religion, but of culture and of human cognition in general. In his vision dialogue is founded neither in religious urge nor in political utility, but in an anticipated structure of human thought, which is seen as revealing itself in the interaction of dominant trends in contemporary culture.

The main question which is left unanswered in this construction, is: what kind of exchange would eventually be possible with, and between, dialogue partners reluctant to base their discourse on such a theory? Is it sure that they are able to accept "the new universalism" as speaking on their behalf just as much as on that of its proponents or, for that sake, of everybody in the world? Can a particular theory of "universalism" be proclaimed as the basic foundation of intercultural (including interreligious) exchange, without *eo ipso* abrogating the universality of its own claim? How can theories of dialogue with specific claims to universality escape the accusation of inconsistency?

4.1.5. German "Pluralism": von Brück, Bernhardt

Apart from the pioneering signals of KARL RAHNER a generation ago and the comprehensive efforts of HANS KÜNG to follow and to improve his tracks – initiatives to which we shall return in the context of "inclusivism" – we can observe that on the German speaking arena a full-scale discussion on dialogue has developed a little decade later than on the Anglo-American. A programmatic vehicle like the (half-yearly) periodical *Dialog der Religionen* came into existence in 1991.

The first signal of a new challenge emerging in the midst of German Protestant theology was the comprehensive study by MICHAEL V.BRÜCK: *Einheit der Wirklichkeit* from 1986. v.Brück has been a dynamic power behind the periodical *Dialog der Religionen* and also behind the "Tübinger Dialoggespräch" in 1991 and the "Siegen Symposium" in 1993.[95] His competence on Eastern religions gives very much profile also to his determined reflections on principles. This is a fact he is himself aware of – at the same time as he assures us of his awareness with regard to the significance of other world religions.[96] For the observer there can, however, be little doubt about the

---

[93] Section: 'The New Universalism', 120–127.

[94] Ibid., 162.

[95] v.BRÜCK 1986, and DdR 2-91 (130–178). – The papers of the Siegen symposium are published by: v.BRÜCK & WERBICK 1993.

[96] DdR 1–93, 4f (3–20), cf. also his 'Heil und Heilswege im Hinduismus und Buddhismus ...', in: v.BRÜCK & WERBICK, 62–106.

orientative influence of his Hindu studies on his theory of dialogue in general. His record of Hindu-Christian exchange is less a description of events and of strategy, than an attempt to spell out a common foundation: "The Unity of Reality" as a mystico-philosophical concept, extrapolated from a comparison of basic concepts in the two religions, with the notions of Holy Trinity and of Advaita as the two illuminating discoveries.

The fundamental idea of his study can be expressed as follows:

"Der Dialogpartner ist ein Spiegel, in dem eigene Schwächen und Stärken erscheinen. Die gegenseitige Spiegelung ist ein Weg, zur vertieften Selbsterkenntnis zu finden. Der Höhepunkt des Dialogs liegt dort, wo der andere zur Quelle des Selbstverständnisses wird. Dieses Geschehen ist gleichzeitig der Inbegriff personaler Gemeinschaft, um die Menschen verschiedenen Glaubens ringen. Auf unsere Studie angewandt heißt dies, dass Advaita zur Quelle des Selbstverständnisses der Trinität werden kann."[97]

The meaning seems clear: in listening to a reciprocal profession of faith, Hindus and Christians arrive at a deeper understanding of their own beliefs, and their respective insights about godhead and mystery will serve to illuminate each other.

The three main steps in v.Brück's study are: (1) Non-Duality in Hinduism, (2) Non-Duality in the trinitarian doctrine, (3) Unity of reality. Of particular interest to our research is the section in the third part which bears the title "Heilswirken Christi und die Einheit der Wirlichkeit."[98] The base of Hindu ontology is apparent enough:

"Die nicht-dualistische (advaitische) Polarität von Konkretheit und Universalität ist eine Applikation der generellen Polarität von Vielheit und Einheit, die wir im Symbol der Trinität dargestellt haben. Diese Polarität ist der Horizont für unsere Interpretation der Tragweite des Christusereignisses. Christus ist der konkrete Name für das Liebeshandeln Gottes. Das Heil ist vollkommen immanent, wo immer die Tiefendimension der Wirklichkeit aufbricht und die vollkommene Transzendenz durchscheint. *Jede authentische religiöse Tradition reflektiert einen solchen Aufbruch in der Geschichte.* Jeder derartige Aufbruch ist eine Reflektion der ewigen innertrinitarischen Perichorese."[99]

The ontological implications of this are far-reaching. v.Brück visualizes a global unification of reality. The specific appearance of each particular religion reflects a breakthrough of timeless universality.

An idea of one all-comprehensive mystery in diversified socio-cultural shapes is by no means new and by no means limited to Hinduism. For those seeking undelayed mutual understanding and recognition between the world religions it seems to offer the most available pattern of solution. But such a solution can be hammered out on differing ontological premises. There is a rather broad gulf between a traditional Western approach of cool, distinctively deistic "natural religion" and a mystical "advaitic" approach of pantheistic character, and there are many shades of color in-

---

[97] 'Einheit der Wirklichkeit ...' p. 3.
[98] 'The salvific work of Christ and the Unity of Reality', ibid. 224–253.
[99] Ibid., s. 234.

between. While the dogma of Christ as "God incarnate" by John Hick and his school is seen as a Christian particular to be abandoned in the name of a universal godhead present in all religions, to v.Brück universality is organically interwoven with the authentic particularity of specific traditions. Thus the vision of Trinitarian godhead, to which traditional christology relates, claims the status of absolute truth to Christian believers, without violating the principle of cultural pluralism or of rejecting a corresponding absoluteness of belief within other traditions. v.BRÜCK, then, does not share the need of more regular "pluralists" to undo the doctrinal process of the Early Church to the benefit of some assumedly pre-dogmatic version of historic Christianity. On the contrary, he greets the truth of dogmatic expressions domestic to different religions, provided that none of them objectifies truth and claims universal validity for itself alone.

> "Der Messias (Christus) ist die Erfüllung der Geschichte Israels. In diesem Bezugsrahmen verkündigt er nicht nur absolute Wahrheit, sondern verkörpert sie. Außerhalb dieses kulturell-geschichtlichen Rahmens wird das konkrete Symbol aber bedeutungslos. Es wird ein relatives Absolutes."[100]

This shows Biblical truth interpreted in the framework of an ontology as remote from ancient Hebrew as from later Roman thinking. Reconciliation between Hinduism and Christianity is evidently achieved by wholeheartedly adopting the ontology of the former, and silencing the question of how this ontology fits to the historically given self-understanding of the latter. An irreducible specificity of Christianity is accepted as idea, but is submitted to a vision of reality with no visible exposure to the test of history.

In order to fertilize the encounter of religions in the contemporary world, v.BRÜCK recommends "creative integration". He warns against the traditional fear of "syncretism", but declines to include that concept in his own vocabulary, in order to avoid the accusations of selectiveness and opportunism attached to it in twentieth century discussion. As a desirable achievement of authentic dialogue, he foresees "no superreligion which integrates all others, but each religion winning its proper identity more deeply, exposing itself to the theme of its own specific history."[101] But what if that "theme" turns out to be inseparably linked with a claim to universal validity?

Following his lane of thought, v.BRÜCK concludes by summing up four main consequences of dialogue for the self-understanding of the Christian church. (1) Experiencing through dialogue itself as committed to a process of *kenosis*,[102] it discovers, existentially, the "ontological value" of humility. (2) Further, it discovers how Christ as "the second Person of the Trinity" is no possession of the church alone: the presence of that Christ is shared with people of different creeds, who, consciously or unconsciously, partake of a common inspiration. Correspondingly, Christians have to accept the idea of the presence of – say – a "Buddha implicit" in Christianity. (3)

---

[100] Ibid., same page.
[101] Ibid., 242.
[102] Greek: "self-emptying", cf. Phil 2:7.

As to Jesus Christ, the incarnation of God in history, distinction needs to be made between a particular and a universal meaning, between Jesus as the "fulfilment of all promises in the history of Israel" – a vision indispensible to Christians – and the "universal meaning which cannot be confined to this manifestation". In this sequence of thought v.Brück sees the Trinitarian mystery reflected also in the advaitic experience of Hinduism and in similar experiences of other religions. Even without a historical tie, these religions are intrinsically linked with Christianity – through a "transhistoric interrelatedness". (4) The legacy of Christ is not to make people around the world localize his presence doctrinally, but to have them experience it in a way which delivers from concentration on dogmatic issues and a "Vergötzung des Endlichen" – an idolization of finitude, a rule of "the Law", not of "the Gospel". Seen in the proposed perspective, dialogue involves no surrender of the missionary calling of the Christian, but the opportunity of conversion, not, in principle, from one religious incorporation to another, but from objectifying narrowness to "the realization of the Advaita of God and humanity, up to the universal integration which we signify by the concept of 'Unity of Reality'."[103]

The merit of v.Brück's study is, as observed, less the picture which he presents of the actual state of affairs in Hindu-Christian dialogue, than his systematic reflection on the encounter of spiritual traditions in general. For that purpose he presents a characteristic, deeply rooted, Hindu pattern of reflection, trying to make it compatible with Western theological thinking. So doing, he also conveys a mystical orientation – a trend which in varying historical garments has been powerfully present also in the quest for Christian identity through the centuries – to which he gives new shape in a conversation between two great world traditions. This project is consistently related to dialogue, which, seen in such perspective, becomes the main theological and cultural challenge of the day.

Attempts to make Christian and Hindu spirituality accessible to each other on a level of practical experience have been numerous in this century, but hardly anyone has penetrated so deep into the epistemological requirements of such rapprochement as v.Brück. Thus he has also added to pluralist non-discrimination a combined theory of universalism and particularism which differs not only from the Western rationality of Hick and Knitter, but also from the anti-intellectualism of Indian Christian theologians, like the farewell to "universal theories of religion" of Panikkar or the "revised christology" of Samartha. When comparing v. Brück with the latter, one is immediately struck by their different emotional attitudes toward the historic Christian dogma (incarnation, trinity). But there is ample reason to ask whether the implicit (ontological) reinterpretation by v.Brück, functionally, involves less deconstruction than the explicit (theological) break-up of Samartha.

Starting his study from a different platform, REINHOLD BERNHARDT, as a more polemical profile, focuses attention around the determinant concept of "absoluteness", but ends up by sketching a position not unlike that of the more conservative-

[103] Ibid., 248–253.

sounding v.Brück. Over the years he has written enthusiastic essays in support of Knitter as well as of Hick, and of other contributors to *The Myth* ...[104] Major contributions from Bernhardt are a study in the historical prelude to contemporary theological pluralism, and a fervid systematical plea in favor of a reorientation of the "absoluteness" problematic. He is also the editor of a trans-Atlantic anthology from 1991 with an overall presentation of contemporary theological pluralism to a German audience.[105]

Even if Bernhardt's exposé of history proclaims to start just with the Enlightenment, it actually surveys and arranges typologically the stands towards non-Christian religions taken during the whole history of Christianity. Different from the anglophone pluralist tradition, he reviews three main models of absoluteness claims, all to be overcome and absorbed by pluralism: "Das Modell dualistisch-exklusiver Alleingeltung ... Das Modell hierarchischer Superiorität ... Das Modell inklusiver Dualität ..."[106]

The first of these can have as its central orientation: objectified revelation, institutionalized church, or monolithic Christianity, and it extends from Old Testament monotheism over Early Christianity, authoritarian Fathers and Reformers – up to Barth, Bonhoeffer and Kraemer towards the middle of the twentieth century. The second is represented by the Enlightenment, the 19. century liberal tradition, and, in our own day, Wolfhart Pannenberg. The third, foreshadowed by the "logos spermatikos" of the Alexandrian Fathers, had its great break-through in our century, with the Catholic Karl Rahner and the Protestant Paul Tillich as its most illustrative voices. But intellectually as well as religiously Bernhardt finds only the "fourth alternative", theological pluralism, apt to serve as integrating principle.

> "Die ... vier grundsätzlichen Möglichkeiten ... Abwehr ... Überbietung ... Zuordnung ... Gleichstellung ... behalten ihre Berechtigung ...; doch werden sie sich nicht einlinig auf die Beurteilung ganzer Religionen anwenden lassen, sondern eher auf einzelne ihrer Erscheinungen und Überzeugungen. Ein Christ wird in allen Religionen Elemente entdecken, die er kompromisslos verwirft, andere, die er in einer Wertskala positiv würdigen, aber doch als überholt ablehnen wird, wieder andere, die er als erfüllungsfähige Bewegungen in die richtige Richtung anerkennen kann, und schließlich solche, die neben seiner eigenen Glaubenseinstellung zu bestehen vermögen und diese sogar gleichwertig bereichern. Gleiches gilt für die Anhänger anderer Religionen."[107]

This is a remarkable construction. The three models, even if regarded as voices from the past, are not only allowed, but required to survive, however, in a different and more humble function than was their traditional claim. Repulsion, Surpassing,and Coordination are all legitimate attitudes, not with regard to a religion as a total, but to particular aspects, here observed as "appearances and convictions".

---

[104] Bernhardt, ETh 49/6 1989, and ÖR 43/2 1994.
[105] Idem: 'Von der Aufklärung zur Pluralistischen Religionstheologie' 1990, 'Zwischen Größenwahn, Fanatismus und Bekennermut ...' 1994, and (ed.): 'Horizontüberschreitung ...' 1991.
[106] Bernhardt 1991, 58–71, 71–94, 94–124.
[107] Ibid., 233f.

To what extent is it possible to approach a religion as a multiple compound, with the purpose of rejecting or accepting single "elements" with various degrees of reservation/ confirmation? Such a piecemeal procedure is reduced to second rank importance if religion is discovered as a unifying vision of divine-human relationship. There are certainly contexts where critical attention can meaningfully be focused on single convictions or practices. And analyses with assessment of social complexities may in themselves be important contributions to dialogue. But such research will in no case get to the heart of interreligious exchange.

The impression should by no means pass on that BERNHARDT, by his dialectical adoption of "all the other models" – restrictive and affirmative as it claims to be at the same time – has integrated the chief orientations in history Christian and non-Christian, into a new and unquestionable system of pluralist allegiance. The restricted critical function of single orientations, as he describes it, becomes clearly subordinate to his main, allegedly non-discriminatory, thesis. Finally, in his model of interpretation, there exists no conflict of truth claims.

His second, explicitly polemical, book, takes as orientative departure "Theology in the Service of Religious Peace".[108] Because Christian theologians "at all times" have seen it as their task to prove the "Uniqueness and superiority" of Christianity, they have frequently "prepared a spiritual ground for hostility, particularly against Jews and Muslims." Today it is up to the same theologians to "yield a most actual and important service to peace", exploring self-critically "the sources of own tradition" in search for new ways to deal with the others.

On this background BERNHARDT discusses FEUERBACH's accusation against the Church: "Verdammen liegt im Wesen des Glaubens."[109] He admits, and illustrates through examples – with that of the conquistadores in Latin-America as the most striking – the bloody track of religious oppression in history. The source of the tragedy he sees, however, not in the essential character of faith, but in a "religious self-glorification and self-righteousness that takes God's truth in own custody", attitudes which "find their concentrated expression in the claim of absoluteness by Christianity".[110] One striking distinction is immediately added:

> "Es gibt Ausnahmesituationen, in denen ein Absolutheitsanspruch nicht nur ein legitimer, sondern sogar ein notwendiger Ausdruck des wehrhaften Bekennens ist. Situationen, in denen Christen um ihres Glaubens willen unterdrückt werden. Oder Situationen, in denen eindeutig und unbedingt Stellungnahmen von ihnen gefordert sind, etwa gegen totalitäre Regime ... Zwischen diesen Extremen ... und dem anderen des 'Herrschaftsabsolutismus' ... liegt eine weite Bandbreite von Erscheinungsformen des christlichen Absolutheitsanspruchs. Im weiten Bereich zwischen Größenwahn, Fanatismus und Bekennermut sind die Glaubensauffassungen angesiedelt, die uns in den folgenden Kapiteln begegnen werden."[111]

---

[108] BERNHARDT 1994, 8–12.
[109] "Condemning lies in the essence of faith", 'Das Wesen des Christentums', Gesammelte Werke V, 1984, 417f.
[110] Ibid. 18.
[111] Ibid. 19.

This is, indeed, a remarkable allowance. The experience of an absolute commitment attached to religious faith is authorized, at the same time as the main battle is directed against Christian "claims of absoluteness". Stimulating dialectical tension – or sheer, confusing contradiction?

Through a comparative analysis of Christian conservatism in contemporary Germany Bernhardt states the core of the problem as "die 'absolutistische' Haltung" – the attitude of absolutism, a way of domesticating convictions which is equally present in other religions and in non-religious world views: "a whole syndrome of religious and ideological self-absolutization."[112]

Bernhardt sums up his conclusions with reference to, and in general accordance with, John Hick's thesis about a corresponding tension between self-assertion and salvific liberation in all religions. "It makes a great difference if one says: the religions are ways of salvation, or: there are ways of salvation in the religions."[113] But more explicitly than Hick, Bernhardt is anxious to spell out the limited, but at the same time vital, importance of absoluteness – and this in a rather paradoxical-sounding way.

Two convictions seem fundamental to BERNHARDT's reflection. (1) Faith in Jesus Christ as the exclusive way to God has its fundamental importance and validity – *within* Christianity. (2) The claim of universality is not limited to the historical appearance of Jesus Christ; it refers to "God's way with humanity", i.e. to divine promise as a global vision.

"So verstanden kann der Anspruch auf Universalität und Endgültigkeit und sogar ... auf Exklusivität der christlichen Wahrheitsgewissheit beibehalten werden, ohne in die "absolutistische" Haltung zu verfallen. Er trägt dann dazu bei, die Besonderheit des christlichen Glaubens zum Ausdruck zu bringen, ohne die Besonderheiten anderer Glaubensformen abwehren zu müssen. Seinen eigentlichen Ort aber hat der Absolutheitsanspruch ... nicht im Dialog, sondern im Gotteslob, in der Doxologie. Um das Unsagbare anzudeuten, muss die Sprache an ihre Grenzen gehen – und auch einmal darüber hinaus."[114]

The difference between JOHN HICK and REINHOLD BERHARDT, a difference which the latter seems by no means eager to emphasize, may be one of pedagogy more than

[112] Ibid. 45f.

[113] Ibid., 229–231, cf. particularly Hick 1989, 36ff. – In his essay 'Deabsolutierung der Christologie?' (in: v.BRÜCK & WERBICK 1993) Bernhardt gives the following reasons in favour of "deabsolutization": (a) God deabsolutizing himself in his revelation ... (b) The Christ event deabsolutizing ... (c) Historicity deabsolutizing ... (d) The plurality of biblical interpretations deabsolutizing ... (e) Christologies "from above" and "from below" reciprocally deabsolutizing ... (f) The "openness of fulfilment of the Christ event" deabsolutizing ... (g) Global aspects of religious encounter deabsolutizing ..., 196–200. This leads him on to "an inclusive Spirit-christology", which again tries to show how the principle "Christ alone" in its strict sense speaks to Christians alone, but just – through that very discovery – sets free and becomes a potential of cross-religious openness, without bleaching the enthusiasm of one's personal testimony of faith.

[114] Ibid., 231. – Cf. already HICK 1980, 78: "But there will be a growing awareness of the mythological character of this language, as the hyperbole of the heart, most naturally at home in hymns and anthems and oratorios and other expressions of the poetry of devotion."

of principle. Bernhardt sees more clearly an urgency to keep the commitments of religious worship and everyday witness vibrant through elements of a traditional "absolutist" language. This lays the question close at hand: Could Bernhardt's remarkable yes-and-no to absoluteness be reinterpreted in a way acceptable to the considerable number of critics who protest what they see as the "relativism" of the "pluralist" school?

Our immediate answer would be: no – particularly as BERNHARDT, in a later review of the *status discussionis,* so emphatically, without the least reservation, associates himself with "the Pluralist Theology of Religions" against its critics.[115]

4.1.6. At the Borders of "Pluralism"

In contemporary use "pluralism" may signify two fundamentally different things. We can refer to a highly advanced state of cultural differentiation, characteristic of our time, as an indisputable fact to be taken into account, irrespective of likes and dislikes. In this sense all reflective observers of our time are more or less "pluralists". We live under a given state of affairs, and we have to get reconciled with these circumstances, and we have to communicate with our surrounding world accordingly.

But it is not in this observers' meaning we use "pluralism" to designate the least traditional of contemporary approaches to the theology of interreligious dialogue. We use it to signify – as it does in the discussion worldwide – the proclamation of plurality as a value in itself. In principle, this means equal appreciation of all, not only with regard to their personal integrity, but to their participation in truth as truth. This means: "pluralism" is not merely a sociological fact to be recognized as a base of politics and of public demeanor, but as a constructive trend to be sustained and encouraged. Indeed, as a genuine invitation to a deeper understanding of our common human identity.

At the same time religious "pluralism" generally differs from unmodified relativism in maintaining the indispensible value of a personal belonging to, and identification with, the live religious/cultural tradition of one's belonging. Correspondingly, missionary activities with the purpose of transporting people from one type of doctrinal and/or institutional commitment to another are generally judged as destructive.

In order to survey, and to conclude, our reported excursion in contemporary "pluralism", it can be useful to return to REINHOLD BERNHARDT and review an essay already mentioned, which – for strictly apologetical reasons – gives an illustrative bird's view of the landscape.[116] As a verification of pluralist genealogy he calls attention to the two "myth debates" caused by JOHN HICK in 1977 and in 1986,[117] and at the same time he identifies Hick as the one who has been the chief target of antipluralist strike-backs.

[115] ÖR 43/2 – 1994, 172–189.
[116] Cf. here, note 104.
[117] Cf. 4.1.1.

BERNHARDT does not visit the critics one by one, but arranges their objections to pluralism systematically. All together he sees six of them, each focused on one particular concept, and he brings a quick riposte to each one. The advantage of his method may be that of a clear and well-systematized overall view. The weakness may be an oversimplification which too easily pretends to bring the challengers to silence Here are the general objections to pluralism as identified – and allegedly defeated – by Bernhardt.

(1) *"Reductionism"*: the rich variety of religious concepts reduced (literal meaning: led back) to some unifying idea of transcendence, from where all actual religion is relativized as culturally conditioned reflexes.

(2) *"Relativism"*: the issue of truth pushed aside and replaced by a specific concept of value ("salvation"), making it possible to lodge different faiths alongside – crushing the heart of Christianity: confession of Christ, the living Lord.

BERNHARD responds to these two objections in one: he sees HICK recommending "reduction" only as a "lead-back (re-ductio) to a more fundamental and universal level of truth, not as loss of substance and as depreciation". So Hick's pragmatic concept of truth rejects an identification of truth with this or that single religion, but not a distinction between truth and lie within each religion respectively. A danger may be there, however, that a certain pluralist wing reluctant to any explicit frame of universal conceptuality in the name of some unqualified open-mindedness,[118] may fall prey to a certain relativism. But dialogue based on reciprocal "questioning and criticizing", cannot be threatened by the same danger.[119]

From our discussion with these "pluralist" authors, however, is it evident that we are facing two distinctive pluralist "wings", of which BERNHARDT can so easily acquit the one of "relativism" simply by passing the accusation on to the other?[120] As it looks, he invalidates the relativism accusation through pragmatic standards of truth. But the critics are raising a question of truth substantial, including that of authority and Holy Writ! With Bernhardt and his hero HICK, that orientation seems replaced by a purely pragmatic standard of discernment. So, basically his critique of the critics seems geared to vocabulary, not to contents.

(3) *"Apriorism"*: This is how BERNHARDT perceives KNITTER's critics at this point. Truth being a priori allocated in everybody's possession, the partners in dialogue are virtually protected against reciprocal truth claims. – Bernhardt responds that precisely unprejudiced listening is the purpose of the pluralists. Predetermined are only the formal conditions of dialogue, no issue concerning the truth claims of the partners. The declared equality of the dialogue partners is no more, no less than "equal right according to the model of non-dominant (herrschaftsfreien) discourse". So, even this remark by the critics is pushed aside as having "extremely conditional (nur sehr bedingt)" validity.

---

[118] Cf. here, notes 113–114.

[119] BERNHARDT 1994, 175–178.

[120] SWIDLER 1987, particularly the summarizing comments of Thomas Dean to the Swidler-Panikkar confrontation, 162–174.

On this point a remark may be made to BERNHARDT that statements of purpose are not frequently testimonies of accomplishment. So, accusations or denials of "apriorism" should rather be based on factual observation. "Equal right to open exchange on equal terms", is hardly what the critics of "apriorism" contest. Such a general statement would probably be sustained by all convinced supporters of dialogue – be they of whatever observance with regard to exclusivism, inclusivism, pluralism ...[121]

(4) *"Essentialism"*: An abstract idea of some transhistorical "essence of religion", used as a criterion to curtail living faith. – BERNHARDT declines this attack, maintaining that HICK, and still more Knitter, seek a common ground not *in*, but *behind* the religions, "a ground of transcendence ... observable in compatible fundamental experiences". Religions don't share elements of substance, but are jointly based on "an eschatological hypothesis by religious reason," which signalizes one ultimate source of revelation, and motivates one common effort toward universal transformation.

Our comment would be that in this construction the border between "essential" and "non-essential" seems rather indistinct. Several of the critics would see BERNHARDT's "common ground of transcendence" as a confirmation more than a refutation of the essentialism complaint.[122]

(5) *"Speculative monism"*: An evaporation of the Judeo-Christian concept of God as the God of history, to the benefit of some time- and place-less divine presence. This means a reorientation which may even lead to the replacement of theocentricity with egocentricity.

Precisely the contrary – so BERNHARDT – is the purpose of the pluralists, namely to realize the immanence of God as an empirical foundation of the idea of godhead. Unwilling are the pluralists to accept only one history, the Judeo-Christian, as medium of divine revelation. Their aim is a wider horizon of God in history and environment. Bernhardt, however, is ready to accept the objection of monism with regard to "their attempts to found (zurückführen) the different concepts of God on an underlying principle of unity", as "there is no cognitive standpoint from where such a postulate could be argued."

This remark should undoubtedly be taken in account, even if the question arises whether the standards applied are not considerably stricter this time than in BERNHARDT's evaluation of the "apriorism" and "essentialism" complaints. Again we must recall our distinction between declared purpose and observable result. But it is equally important to warn against the terminological confusion so incumbent in an argument for or against abstracts. The statements: "The argument X lacks the dimension of history" and "The argument X is through-and-through historical" can both be conceptually defended – as long as the key concept "historical" remains hazy.[123]

---

[121] Ibid., 178–179.
[122] Ibid., 179–180.
[123] Ibid., 180–182.

(6) *"Theological imperialism"*: A global theology encompassing the entire world of religions, and claiming to be built on a fundamental experience shared by all faiths, but actually based on an arbitrary selection of observations – this seems, according to BERNHARDT, to be the apex of all accusations against a pluralist theology of religions. His riposte is that many pluralists, with KNITTER as the most representative, see the dangers of such an imperialism and take sufficient precautions. Bernhardt also avows some actual difference among leading pluralists, as far as awareness of the contextual restrictedness of their own theological horizon is concerned. But, as he observes, none of them wants to "leave his own Christian tradition behind", nor to "displace the specific religious perspectives of the other dialogue participants." Only if a denial of their own traditions had been demanded of the conversation partners, would the reproach of imperialism have been justified.

The power of this argument again depends on terms which are but too easily caught up in verbal ambiguity. Assurance of neither abandoning own tradition nor demanding others to abandon theirs, is subject to interpretation. This applies to content as well as to extent. A hermeneutical framework presented by the one part as a basic presupposition of dialogue – as it is offered by BERNHARDT – may, when demanding a certain amount of mutuality, easily be understood by the other part as an attempt to circumscribe his own spiritual identity, irrespective of comforting, general declarations to the contrary.[124]

In his summary BERNHARDT characterizes a suspected tendency attributed to "pluralism" to "examine the gods of the religions in search of some underlying ground of transcendence" as an undesirable "speculative monism, which runs contrary to all religions". But this, in his view, is no typical trend of the pluralism he is defending. Its chief concern should be greeted without reservation:

> "In der Polarität von Universalität und Partikularität lässt sich das Charakteristikum der pluralistischen Sichtweise nicht beschreiben. Es liegt viel mehr in der Anerkennung der Tatsache, dass es neben der christlichen andere religiöse Global-Weltsichten gibt, die der christlichen funktional vergleichbar sind. Die Anerkennung dieser Tatsache führt unmittelbar zum Protest gegen die Tendenz, die eigene Religionsperspektive zu verabsolutieren und gegen andere zu isolieren."[125]

Does one really have to be a "pluralist" in order to accept this general statement including the "fact" – the "Tatsache" – which it proclaims? Would I be in full understanding with the author if I accept them? And do the premises coextend with the rather provocative presentation which Bernhardt has given of his own orientation in *Zwischen Grössenwahn, Fanatismus und Bekennermut* – a study appearing precisely the same year as the essay under review? The answer seems by no means evident.

In sum: I find it rather difficult to accept BERNHARDT's dismissal of any one of the six points against pluralism, as fully convincing.

---

[124] Ibid., 182–185.
[125] Ibid., 186.

4.2. "Inclusivist" Approaches

4.2.1. Karl Rahner

The history of an "inclusivist" theology of religions could be said to start with the much observed Jesuit theologian KARL RAHNER's challenge *Das Christentum und die nicht-christlichen Religionen*.[126] Rahner's comments were, for good reasons, interpreted by many as the voice of the Second Vatican Council (1962–65). His four concluding Theses were taken for the authentic interpretation of the encyclical *Nostra Aetate* and as an unofficial guideline for the new Roman *Secretariat for Non-Christians*. Rahner's position at the Council laid such a supposition close.[127]

Reviewed in a more comprehensive historical perspective, RAHNER's draft will today be read as a summary of four centuries Catholic missiological thinking and at the same time as the prelude to a new era of inter-religious rapprochement.[128] But in our day he is still more remembered as proponent of the term "anonymous Christians", a concept which has been subject to much, and close to unanimous, criticism during the rest of the century. He sums up his theology of religions in four concluding theses:

"(1) ... Das Christentum versteht sich als die für alle Menschen bestimmte, absolute Religion, die keine andere neben sich anerkennen kann ...

(2) Bis zu jenem Augenblick, in dem das Evangelium wirklich in die geschichtliche Situation eines bestimmten Menschen eintritt, enthält eine nicht-christliche Religion ... nicht nur Elemente einer natürlichen Gotteserkenntnis ... sondern auch übernatürliche Elemente aus der Gnade, die dem Menschen wegen Christus von Gott geschenkt wird ...

(3) Wenn die zweite These richtig ist, dann tritt das Christentum dem Menschen außerchristlicher Religionen nicht einfach als dem bloßen und schlechthinigen Nichtchristen gegenüber, sondern als einem, der durchaus schon als ein anonymer Christ in dieser oder jener Hinsicht betrachtet werden kann und muss ... dann ist ihm ... in einem wahren Sinn schon Offenbarung geschehen, weil diese Gnade als apriorischer Horizont ... zwar nicht gegenständlich gewusst, aber subjektiv mitbewusst ist ...

(4) ... dann wird sich die Kirche heute nicht so sehr als die exklusive Gemeinschaft der Heilsanwärter betrachten, sondern vielmehr als der geschichtlich greifbare Vortrupp ... dessen, was der Christ als verborgene Wirklichkeit auch außerhalb der Sichtbarkeit der Kirche gegeben erhofft ..."[129]

---

[126] Karl RAHNER: Schriften zur Theologie, V, 136–158.

[127] About the Roman Catholic roots of the inclusivist development, see KNITTER, 1985, particularly the chapter on 'The Catholic Model: Many Ways, One Norm', 120–144. Here the role of Rahner in connection with the Council is also observed and reflected upon.

[128] A strongly committed introduction to the history of Roman Catholic theology of religion(s) as a history of growing "openness" – from the Jesuit missionaries Matteo Ricci (in China) and Roberto di Nobili (in India) around 1600 to the official document 'The Attitude of the Church Toward the Followers of Other Religions', 1984 – is given by HILLMAN 1989. Hillman wants to show a dynamic gravitation in direction of pluralism. But what he really documents, is rather varieties of "inclusivist" thinking (and dominance) in Catholic missiology through 400 years.

[129] Ibid., 154–156.

Can anything meaningfully be labeled "inclusivism" – this must be it! RAHNER is aware that it may sound presumptuous to a non-Christian if Christians in this way should try to define his spiritual identity, and thus make of him a Christian not yet arrived to full self-awareness. But he stands firm on his vision: a Christian can never refrain from this "presumptuousness", which rightly understood signalizes the highest humility on behalf of the Church, confirming God as infinitely much greater than humans, including: greater than the Church.[130]

In spite of this, the objection foreboded by himself has been massively directed against his argument. Not only by non-Christians who feel offended by the offer of an unrequested Christian identity, but also by Christian "pluralists", who reject the theological validity of RAHNER's Thesis no.1. Even a considerable number who share his principal orientation if not his terminology, see the badge "anonymous Christians" as an unnecessary insult to those concerned.

That HICK and KNITTER bluntly reject not only RAHNER's terminology but also the balanced concern behind, will surprise nobody.[131] Nor that some Protestant critics have accused Rahner's theory of unduly interlacing Christian soteriology and transcendental philosophy.[132] More unexpected is the criticism by HANS KÜNG, the most powerful promoter of the Catholic inclusivist tradition in the last generation, and by many regarded as the most prominent successor of Rahner, not at least in the domain of interreligious dialogue. Küng himself denies being an "inclusivist" in the sense established in the discussions of the 1980s – another apropos to our observations about the limited value of terminological classification.

In a special issue of *Evangelische Theologie* in 1989, dedicated to "Dialog der Religionen?", KÜNG treats the theme "Dialogfähigkeit und Standfestigkeit".[133] He starts by criticizing four "unsatisfactory" standpoints: Atheism, Absolutism, Relativism and Inclusivism. The fourth he describes as follows:

> "Eine einzige Religion ist die wahre. Oder alle Religionen haben auf ihre Weise Teil an der Wahrheit der einen Religion! Doch auch hier wäre eine Rückfrage zu stellen, und zwar sowie im Blick auf die indische Variante (alle Religionen repräsentieren nur verschiedene Ebenen der einen universellen Wahrheit) oder auch an die christliche Variante (alle gutwilligen und wohlmeinende religiöse Menschen sind 'anonyme Christen'): werden die anderen Religionen so nicht faktisch zu einer niederen und partiellen Erkenntnis von Wahrheit herabgesetzt? Wird die eigene Religion nicht zu einem Supersystem erhoben ... Nein, was als Toleranz aussieht, erweist sich in der Praxis als eine Art Eroberung durch Umarmung, eine Integration der Relativierung und Identitätsverlust."[134]

---

[130] Ibid., 158.

[131] HICK 1985, 53–58; KNITTER 1985, 125. – The whole "anonymous Christian" controversy is broadly reported by SULLIVAN 1992, 162–181.

[132] 'Religionen, Religiösität und christlicher Glaube' (VELKD & Arnoldshainer Konferenz), Gütersloh 1991, 122f.

[133] ETh 1989, 492–504.

[134] KÜNG, op.cit., 498. Approximately the same text: C 1986, 76.

Küng's criticism of the "anonymous Christian" concept reflects a widespread reaction. His conclusion as quoted seems more or less to have established itself as "the judgement of history". It is not difficult to see that the concept of "anonymous Christians" may lend itself to an interpretation which undergirds such an objection. It must be observed, however, that such a judgement is badly geared to Karl Rahner's theological attitude in general. There may be good reason to ask if the debated concept should not be understood in a more sophisticated way, and if a reflected interpretation might not be in good harmony with the determinant vision, if not of Hick and Knitter, so at least of Küng and other travellers along "the middle of the road".

The "anonymous Christian" concept can be most adequately evaluated in the framework of reflection in which it was presented. Reviewing it as an isolated slogan – as there has been a certain tendency to do – may too easily invite subjective remarks and ill-founded judgements.

A helpful comment may be to ask: How would I – as a Christian – react if, after a constructive experience of dialogue, a Muslim partner would say to me: "Brother, I am so impressed with what I hear you say, that I will call you an anonymous Muslim, truly confident that we are once going to meet in heaven. I hear you confirming what to me are essentials in my Muslim conviction, even if you dress them in words different from mine."

Apart from my opinion on the matter, and thus on the character and extension of our agreement, my reaction to "anonymous Muslimship" could well be as follows: My partner in his conversation with me has obviously experienced what to him is a significant concord between different human relationships with God. But according to his habit of thinking, such a relationship is inseparably linked with what he feels as his Muslim identity. He may be surprised to meet so much of a kindred engagement with me, a Christian. But he does not intend to designate me as an apostate from Christianity, nor to declare me as a prospective convert to Islam. He is not willing to relativize his own Muslim identity and declare one religion just as conclusive as the other. In this perspective, the expression "anonymous Muslim" could well be an expression of respectful recognition, if not of a foreign religion (mine), so at least of the spiritual authenticity of some one professing it. Neither my personal self-esteem nor my Christian integrity would suffer from my partner's remark if understood in this manner. Could corresponding observations apply to Rahner's "anonymous Christians"?

As members of two mutually isolated faith communities my Muslim conversation partner and I may be insufficiently informed about each other's communities. But regardless of that, my partner wants – and I may want it too – to express appraisal of what we have recognized to have in common. Eventually, this may raise some reciprocal assurance that the hope of "salvation" offered to "me" in "my" faith, may be available also to "you", even if this in my reflection implies no doctrine of a salvific power of your religion as such. Neither of us may for that reason be ready to proclaim regular channels of divine grace as alternatives to that of our own religious communities.

Our apology for RAHNER is not an argument in favor of the attitude thus described. Nor is the purpose to promote the "anonymous Christian" terminology as the most adequate to clarify the inclusivist concern. Sketching my interpretation of his "anonymous Christians", I hesitate to believe that his main point is hit by the big chorus of critics. It seems as if Rahner's vision has been pushed aside on too quick assumptions, and that his concern should not be seen as finally dismissed, even if, evidently, it could have been expressed in a language exposing itself to less misunderstanding.

RAHNER's sketch as we have presented it, implies no discrimination of one religion or the other, since it does not invite anybody to redefine own identity or force him to adopt some – eventually modified – version of the partner's. The possibility would be there for you to designate me as an "anonymous" (= honorary?) follower of your faith, and for me to understand this as a legitimate attempt from your side to combine your own identity with a maximum expression of brotherly or sisterly openness. For that sake, Rahner should not be regarded some prejudiced voice of the past.

4.2.2. Hans Küng

Nobody has given a more comprehensive and a more challenging contribution to the discussion over the years than the controversial Swiss-German professor HANS KÜNG. Küng is famous as the theology professor in Tübingen who (in 1979) by papal decree was deprived of his authorization as teacher of Catholic theology. This papal initiative, however, had no immediate reference to his theology of religions, which was at that time only in bud. His doctrine of the Church and particularly his questioning of papal infallibility may have played a major role, although christology has been the overshadowing theme in the official Roman procedure against him.[135]

Significant and thought-provoking observations to the theme of interreligious dialogue can be found in his writings over more than thirty years, but for many reasons it is practical to focus attention on his explicit efforts in the field starting with *Christentum und Weltreligionen* from 1984. Here Küng as chief editor involves himself in discussions on Islam, Hinduism and Buddhism with three historians of religion, experts on each of the three religions respectively.[136] Other major works are a study on Christianity and Chinese religion, and one on contemporary Judaism.[137] In a voluminous festschrift to his 65. birthday in 1993, one of the main sections is dedicated to "Dialogue with Judaism" and one to "World Religions".[138]

---

[135] H. KÜNG 'Unfehlbar? Eine Anfrage', 1970. – To the "Küng Case" in general, see Walter JENS (ed.): 'Um nichts als die Wahrheit – Deutsche Bischofskonferenz contra Hans Küng', München/Zürich 1978.

[136] The three co-authors were Josef van Ess, Heinrich v. Stietencron, Heinz Bechert (1984).

[137] KÜNG & CHING 'Christentum und chinesische Religion', 1988. – KÜNG 'Das Judentum', 1991.

[138] HÄRING & KUSCHEL (ed.): 'Hans Küng – Neue Horizonte des Glaubens und Denkens' 1993, particularly 520–586, 589–672.

In his following great exposé on the essence and history of Christianity, KÜNG pays extensive attention to historical relations with Judaism and Islam, anxious to show the importance of these relations for an authentic Christian self-understanding.[139] Küng does signalize a corresponding monography on Islam to appear in the same series as the volumes on Judaism and on Christianity – *Die religiöse Situation der Zeit*.[140] A major part of Küng's dialogue engagement in the 90's is linked with the "Projekt Weltethos", which more than any other initiative so far raises the issue of interreligious dialogue as one with immediate implications for the survival of humankind.[141]

In addition to this, an impressive amount of contributions by KÜNG in anthologies and periodicals are dedicated to aspects of dialogue. Not only the quantity of his contributions and their wide variety of topics, but just as much his provocative dialectical method combined with unique rhetorical performance makes it little meaningful to review his contributions separately one by one. We shall rather look for texts demonstrating the dialectical watershed between his two reciprocally challenging concerns, that of courageous departure and that of faithful preservation. During the 90's we also have to see his ever stronger engagement for world peace as the paramount aim of dialogue, in a politico-ethical perspective.

Next to JOHN HICK, Küng may in recent years have been the most beloved target of critique in the dialogue debate. Hick is attacked by conservative and moderate observers as chief exponent of expanding relativism. KÜNG is attacked by the "left" as lukewarm in his rapprochement to other religions and as too simplistic about the political accomplishments of his own contribution, and by the "right" for being to eager to manifest top trendiness.

In spite of our methodological reservations, let us start with a quick glace at HANS KÜNG's impressive prelude to the interreligious-dialogue-geared phase of his production! *Christentum und Weltreligionen*, 1984, contains a series of exchanges at a summer-school in 1982 at the University of Tübingen. Main agents were Küng and three German Religionswissenschaftler, each of them an expert on "his own" particular religion. Küng, besides writing the introduction and an epilogue to the volume as a whole, acts as respondent to 4 x 3 lectures by his fellow editors, his responses being, however, revised and extended before literary publication. Most interesting for our purpose is Küng's preface "Zum Dialog" and the epilogue, where his later so famous slogan appears as headline: "Kein Weltfrieden ohne Religionsfrieden!"[142]

Küng's preface starts with two observations: Today, as to interreligious dialogue, we stand approximately where we stood fifty years ago with regard to interchurch

---

[139] 'Das Christentum – Wesen und Geschichte', 1994.

[140] Op.cit., 1056.

[141] KÜNG 'Projekt Weltethos', 1990. KÜNG & KUSCHEL (ed.) 'Erklärung zum Weltethos – Die Deklaration des Parlamentes der Weltreligionen', 1993, and (ed.) 'Weltfrieden durch Religionsfrieden – Antworten aus den Weltreligionen', 1993.

[142] 1984, 15–23 and 617–621. "No world peace without peace of religion!"

fellowship. And: "*Oikumene*" means: the whole inhabited world, i.e. an arena of human cooperation breaking all barriers.

> "Ökumene darf deshalb heute weniger denn je eng, verengt, ekklesiozentrisch verstanden werden ... sie muss die Gemeinschaft der großen Religionen einbeziehen, wenn Ökumene – nach dem ursprünglichen Wortsinn verstanden – den gesamten bewohnten Erdkreis meint."[143]

Some may ask how an *argumentum ex etymologia* may possess such a monarchial power to decide an issue of today. Doesn't such a transfer of vocabulary inevitably imply a transfer of meaning which must be tested out for what it is worth in itself? For more than three generations the word 'ecumenical' with its correlates has acquired a concise meaning and come in common use as reference to a distinctive challenge: the unity of the Christian Church. Can meaning and use of such a crucial term be changed without critical semantic examination? No manipulation of language may be less convincing than undigested etymology!

But let us proceed to the substance of KÜNG's concern! The most important section of his quoted preface may be the final one: "Jenseits von Absolutismus und Relativismus", where Küng sums up his position.[144]

> "So versuche ich den schwierigen Mittelweg zwischen zwei Extremen zu gehen. Einerseits möchte ich einen borniertene, eingebildeten Absolutismus (christlicher oder islamischer Provenienz) vermeiden ... Es soll hier weder ein *Exklusivitätsstandpunkt* verteidigt werden, der die nicht-christlichen Religionen und ihre Wahrheit global verurteilt, noch auch ein *Superioritätsstandpunkt*, der die eigene Religion als die von vornherein bessere ... ansetzt ... Zugleich aber wird von mir als christlichem Theologen auch niemand einen oberflächlichen und unverantwortlichen Relativismus (christlicher, hinduistischer oder buddhistischer Provenienz) erwarten ... Unhaltbar scheint mir ein *Beliebigkeitspluralismus*, der undifferenziert die eigene und die anderen Religionen billigt und bestätigt ..., ohne auf die Unwahrheit trotz aller Wahrheit aufmerksam zu machen; unhaltbar ... ein *Indifferentismus*, der bestimmte religiöse Positionen und Entscheidungen von der Kritik ausnimmt. Ein solcher Standpunkt führt nur zu billiger Toleranz ...
> ... die Grenze zwischen wahr und falsch verläuft heute auch nach christlichem Verständnis nicht mehr einfach zwischen Christentum und den anderen Religionen, sondern, zum Teil mindestens, innerhalb der jeweiligen Religionen ..."[145]

The rhetoric of this passage calls for particular attention. When drawing his demarcation lines against an absolutizing "right" and a relativizing "left", KÜNG mentions two traps, one on each side of the track. On the one side: staunch *exclusiveness*, or, as a smoother version: *superiority*: to possess truth alone, or to possess it in a more perfect way than the others. On the other side: arbitrary *pluralism* or a selective *indifferentism*: to accept this and that according to unclarified preferences.

Two observations make our image more concrete.

---

[143] Ibid., 16.
[144] Ibid., 20–23.
[145] Ibid., 21f.

(1) The cutting edge between false and true is, according to KÜNG, "no longer simply" (nicht mehr einfach) one *between* Christianity and other religions, but "partly, at least" (zum Teil mindestens) *within* each religion. The two idioms are particularly worth noticing in their semantic openness. "No longer" – how much adaptation of truth to historical change could that indicate? "No longer, simply" obviously indicates: "but still, to some unspecified extent." "Partly, at least" – calls for a corresponding remark. A more precise criterion is needed.

(2) Truth must finally be one:

> "Die Wahrheit kann in verschiedenen Religionen keine verschiedene, sondern nur die eine sein; durch alle Kontradiktionen hindurch haben wir das Komplementäre zu suchen: durch alles Exklusive hindurch das Inklusive".[146]

KÜNG's aim is "a presentation of Christianity in the mirror of the world religions:"

> "Wechselseitige Information, wechselseitige Diskussion und wechselseitige Tranformation: So wird es langsam nicht zur unkritischen Vermischung, wohl aber zur gegenseitigen kritischen Erhellung, Anregung, Durchdringung und Bereicherung der verschiedenen religiösen Traditionen kommen, wie sich dies zwischen den verschiedenen konfessionellen Traditionen im Christentum selbst schon seit längerem abzeichnet ... Ja, dies dürfte der Weg sein, der zu jener Verständigung zwischen den Religionen führt, die keine Welteinheitsreligion kreieren, wohl aber – nach so vielen heißen und kalten Kriegen ... – die eine echte Befriedigung herbeiführen will."

In this sequence – as so often in the dialectical yes-and-no's of KÜNG – it is not immediately easy for the reader to translate rhetorical impressiveness into a precise argument, and thus to format a straight dialogue with his three selected partners.

With regard to *Islam*, KÜNG has little difficulty in seeing Muhammed as "a prophetic corrective for Christians in the name of one and the same God",[147] not least as a counterbalance to a remaining hellenistic influence in traditional christology. At the same time he sees Islam open for a less biased rapprochement to the Jesus of the New Testament and to the revelation of God's love in Christ, than overtly manifested by Muslims so far.[148]

The exchange with *Hinduism* becomes more complex, since prophetical and mystical religion are structurally different and at the same time supplementary types of approaches to the divine. The "tension-filled synthesis" to be looked for, is no external harmonization with mixing of single elements, but a

> "mediation that includes acceptance, rejection and transcendence at the same time. Should religions, which have so much in common, in the future not be able to have still more in common"[149]

---

[146] Ibid., 22.
[147] Ibid., 200.
[148] The section on Islam: Ibid., 31–204.
[149] Ibid., 269.

KÜNG sees striking parallels between the function of folk religion in Hinduism and Roman Catholicism. Further, a mystical experience of ineffable ultimate reality underlies also the Christian concept of godhead, and, from a Christian point of view, Hindu mythology cannot simply be done away with as superstition or as unbelief. From his Christian standpoint, however, he writes off the Hindu concept of history as circular and the corresponding idea of reincarnation. Nor can he see belief in the historical person Jesus Christ, image and incarnation of God, as coalescing with a Hindu relationship with Krishna, synthesis of various mythological and historical characters.[150]

Similar distinctions between prophetic and mystical religion are applied to the dialogue with *Buddhism*. In concreto KÜNG sees that dialogue focusing on main themes like: (1) the historical Buddha as a teacher to be compared with the historical Jesus. He sees many common features, but at the same time a distinctive difference between "the Illuminated" and "the Crucified" – (2) the character of Buddhist world-denial vis-a-vis a Christian vision of creation/nature, (3) the meaning of being and non-being, and (4) not least: how "personal" and "absolute" relate to each other as ontological fundamentals.

To KÜNG it is important to observe how this type of dialogical exchange all the time hinges on the border of language. In a wider perspective this means that the West must offer "more respect for the ineffable, more pious awe for the secret, more reverence for that absolute, which Christians, Jews and Muslims call the one true God", whereas the East should realize that the absolute is not separated from the world and humanity, and discover how relationship with the godhead as a "transpersonal" Thou opens up a new experience of dignity to our "interpersonal" human I.[151]

The impressions we get from KÜNG in dialogue with other religions must evidently be supplemented with his contributions to the (controversial) dialogue on dialogue within the Christian constituency. Only in this way will we get a full impression of his dialogical profile.

As his most polemical contribution to the intrareligious discussion, I have found an article which in slightly different versions appeared first in an issue of the international Catholic review *Concilium* dedicated to 'Christentum zwischen den Weltreligionen' (1986): *"Einige Thesen zur Klärung"*. A few years later it was republished in an issue on interreligious dialogue of the *Evangelische Theologie*, but with a new and programmatical headline to expose the interaction between "readiness for dialogue" and "steadiness", as two supplementary virtues.[152] The first version is more or less a response to the attack on KÜNG's position by PAUL F. KNITTER in the same issue of Concilium.[153] It may be observed that the captivating word "Standfestigkeit" (steadiness) in the second version appears as a replacement of "Glaubensüberzeugung" (conviction of faith) in the first.

---

[150] The section on Hinduism: Ibid., 207–410.
[151] The section on Buddhism: Ibid., 415–616.
[152] C 1986, 76–80; ETh 1989, 491–504.
[153] KNITTER, ibid., 63–68, particularly the section 'Christus über anderen Religionen stehend', 64f.

The disagreement between KÜNG and KNITTER, the two most influential spokespersons of contemporary Catholic theology of religions, where is that lodged? In his Concilium article, reviewing actual divergences among Catholic theologians in this domain, Knitter criticizes what he finds as commonplace among progressive Catholics at that time: a lack of consistency between their recognition of other religions as legitimate paths to salvation, and their remaining claim of "Christ above the religions" as the ultimate fulfilment of religious ambition. In that connection he mentions the name of Hans Küng as the first in a row of six.[154]

In his *No Other Name?* from the previous year, KNITTER had, in a more comprehensive treatment of "Recent Developments – Beyond Rahner"[155] offered an explicit attack on KÜNG. He had rebuked him for ending up "with much of the same ambiguity that he criticized in RAHNER's theory of anonymous Christianity", namely by moving the traditional Catholic model from ecclesio-centricity (church-centredness), not to theocentricity (god-centredness), but to christocentricity (christ-centredness). This is a contemporary accent which Knitter sees as symptomatic not only of Küng and of a considerable group of Roman Catholics, but of Anglicans, Eastern Orthodox and Third World Protestants as well.[156] To Knitter this is logical inconsistency. Pretending to do away with earlier discrimination of other religions, it succeeds only halfway – and halfheartedly.

How does this criticism apply to KÜNG? In his two-version article under consideration, the latter lists, as we have seen, four "insufficient basic positions": atheism, absolutism, relativism, and inclusivism.[157] Atheism and absolutism are of little interest in our present setting. We have already seen how Küng, in his remark to KARL RAHNER, relates critically to what he, at that time, calls "inclusivism". We have seen how KNITTER accuses Küng of sticking precisely to the prejudice for which he himself reproached Rahner, i.e. for being an "inclusivist", in the sense of making faith in Christ focal not only to a Christian self-understanding, but even to his theological interpretation of the world of religions.

KÜNG, as we observe, elaborates his "critical ecumenical position" in confrontations both to the right and to the left. Finally he proceeds to developing a "criteriology", distinguishing between constructive and destructive elements not primarily *between* but *within* each single religion: one criterion "general ethical" (humaneness), one "general religious" (fidelity to own origin and canon) one "specifically Christian". The latter is so described:

"Nach dem spezifisch christlichen Kriterium ist eine Religion wahr und gut, wenn und insofern sie in ihrer Theorie und Praxis den Geist Jesu Christi spüren lässt. Direkt kann dies

---

[154] Ibid., 64f. The other names are: H.R.Schlette, M.Hellwig, W.Bühlmann, A.Caps, and P. Schonenberg.

[155] KNITTER, op.cit., 130–135.

[156] Ibid., 137.

[157] KÜNG: 'Vier ungenügende Grundpositionen', C 1986, 76, and: 'Vier unbefriedigende Standpunkte', ETh 1989, 497f. In the following we shall stick to the 1986 version, as the polemical orientation here is the sharper of the two.

Kriterium nur auf das Christentum angewandt werden ... Indirekt ... lässt sich dasselbe Kriterium gewiss auch auf die anderen Religionen anwenden ..."[158]

This third criterion, vague as it may sound, is finally hammered out in confrontative distinction from overtly relativizing positions. That which in our days is advertised as "brand new" (pluralist) doctrine, reveals itself, by more thorough inspection, to be "the spirit of liberal Protestantism" with its surrender of "the finality and normativity of Jesus Christ", and has lost "all criteria for distinguishing the spirits".

This rejectable liberalism, according to KÜNG, was already refuted by the Neo-orthodox challenge of KARL BARTH (and PAUL TILLICH and RUDOLF BULTMANN). "Going back beyond them is no progress... For the whole N.T. – convenient or not – Jesus is normative and definitive: he alone is the Christ of God." Sticking to this ground conviction of Christianity – like the other religions stick to theirs – is not theological "imperialism" or "neocolonialism", since it does not deny the truth or reject the prophets and illuminati of other religions. Here comes the concluding statement:

> "Es muss hier – will man den Grundmangel sowohl absolutistisch-exklusivistischer als rela-tivistisch-inklusivistischer Positionen vermeiden – zwischen der Sicht der Religionen von außen und der Sicht von innen (...) unterschieden werden. Nur so ist eine differenzierte Antwort auf die Frage nach der Wahrheit der Religionen möglich".[159]

This formula is said to open up for a possible – and necessary – combination of unrestricted fidelity and unrestricted openness: the distinction between a "view from outside" and a "view from inside". This vision grants the right to a corresponding distinction from the side of other beliefs. Committed, uncompromised fidelity to truth as experienced in one's own faith, involves, in face of dialogue partners, an attitude of solidarity with them in their corresponding allegiance to own heritage. The final delineation of truth, then, will read like this:

> "Von innen gesehen, vom Standpunkt des am Neuen Testament orientierten gläubigen Christen ... gibt es die *wahre Religion*: das Christentum, insofern es den einen wahren Gott, wie er sich in Jesus Christus kundgetan hat, bezeugt. Die eine wahre Religion schließt Wahrheit in anderen Religionen keineswegs aus, sondern kann andere gelten lassen: als *mit Vorbehalt wahre* (...) Religionen. Diese können, sofern sie der christlichen Botschaft nicht direkt widersprechen, die christliche Religion durchaus ergänzen, korrigieren und vertie-fen."[160]

Universal criteria of religious truth deserve to be upheld in front of absolutizing ex-clusiveness. The triple distinction: what is (unconditionally) true to me within my tradition/community – what is even so true to my neighbor within his or hers – what is universally (and, thus, equally) true to us all – seems to appeal to a number of theologians of religions, within several religions, in our day.

---

[158] KÜNG, 1986, p.77.
[159] Ibid., 78.
[160] Ibid., 78.

But is this distinction between truth "from inside" and truth "from outside" tenable: logically and theologically? Logically, the distinction should be defendable if "truth" is understood not as conflicting (objective) truth claims, but: truth as a personal or communitarian experience of meaning. Theologically, the issue seems more complex. Can unconditional loyalty to the New Testament, as verbally proclaimed by Küng, coexist with an unspecified admittance of (equal?) salvific power in a plurality of religions?

PAUL F. KNITTER's attacks on KÜNG's position had already culminated at the Temple University conference in 1984, where he had faced him with a most personal challenge.[161]

> 'From recent conversations and from his conference paper, I think that he is not so sure about these earlier christocentric, inclusivist claims that insist on Jesus as the final norm for all. I suspect that, like many Christians today, he stands before a theological Rubicon. To cross it means to recognize clearly, unambiguously, the possibility that other religions exercise a role in salvation history that is not only valuable and salvific but perhaps equal to that of Christianity; it is to affirm that there may be other saviors and revealers besides Jesus Christ ... I ask you, Hans Küng, do you think such a new direction in Christian attitudes toward other religions, such a crossing of the Rubicon, is possible? And would it be productive of greater Christian faith and dialogue?"[162]

The public edition of the conference papers suggest no reply from HANS KÜNG, not even in his contribution at the follow-up seminary in Tübingen the following year.[163] His most immediate response to the challenge may be the one in the Concilium 1986, which we have already reviewed. In a lecture at the Christian Michelsen's Institute in Bergen as late as August 1995 Küng referred with a certain humor to "The Rubicon Consultation" and – directly asked from his audience – confirmed that still he had found no satisfactory reason for complying with the demand of Knitter.[164]

An assessment of the theological consistency in KÜNG's rather duplex position will also have to bring to attention a later major accomplishment, his 1039 page observation of *Das Christentum – Wesen und Geschichte.*[165]

Our observation does not primarily relate to the attention actually paid by KÜNG to the role of other religions – mainly Judaism and Islam – as reference partners in the historical formation process of Christian self-understanding, but to the scheme of changing historical paradigms which frames his understanding of history in general and of Christianity in particular. What he is advocating here, is an adaptation of THOMAS S. KUHN's concept of scientific revolutions as a shift of structural paradigms.[166]

---

[161] 'Hans Küng's Theological Rubicon', in SWIDLER 1987, 224–230.
[162] Ibid., 225, 229.
[163] Ibid., 231–250.
[164] Observed by the author.
[165] München 1994.
[166] Op.cit., 88, 622f, cf. T.S. KUHN: The Structure of Scientific Revolution, Chicago 1962.

Applied to the arena of world religions, the import of this theory is that mutual relationships may change. A pattern of mutual distance, ignorance, uncertainty, may (hopefully) yield to one of contact, information, confidence – in correspondence, and in interaction, with the global shift of orientations in the midst of which we stand today.

In Küng's ecumenical vision this means not least that contemporary Christianity, in recalling its pre-hellenistic, semitic genesis – to which genuine dialogue with Judaism and Islam may give vigorous stimulants – will acquire a more balanced image of its own identity and, thus, a more unrestrained communication with the surrounding world.

On this background one may ask if Küng's adaptation of shifting historical paradigms may suggest a relativizing historization of truth itself. Certainly, in frequent statements of principle he boldly resists any (uncatholic) temptation to abandon the continuity of tradition as a fundamental criterion of Christian authenticity.[167] There is no reason to see Küng's distinction between truth "from inside" and truth "from outside" as simply derived from an interpretation of history (presumably inspired by HEGEL's dialectic and by KUHN's theory of paradigm shifts), but at the same time his interaction of "history" and "truth" has an overtly deabsolutizing effect: Christianity to be confirmed as truth unique – to Christians only.

The said interaction is intended to restrict objective claims without compromising the pledge to unconditional commitment – not to timeless principles, but – for Christians – to Jesus the Christ as the focal reference of divine presence in history. Even if the "truth from inside/ truth from outside" distinction holds much in common with certain "pluralist" orientations of the day – one may sometimes wonder whether the collision between Küng and them is not mainly one of vocabulary – the distinction between his christological approach to history and the a-historical "theocentricity" of HICK and KNITTER seems manifest enough.

A quite special contribution to the history of dialogue is HANS KÜNG's *Projekt Weltethos*, prepared in cooperation with the World Congress of Faiths and forwarded at the *World Parliament of Religions*, Chicago 1993.[168] Küng's attempt to formulate a global ethic, acceptable to all faiths, has as ultimate aim to secure world peace by securing peace between the religions of the world: "Kein Weltfriede ohne Religionsfriede!"[169]

This frank initiative has been met with a good deal of appreciation world wide, both in, through and outside of the (unofficial) world conference mentioned, but has also received a good deal of critique for being too vague or too self-evident and thus

---

[167] In order to understand the historicizing orientation of Küng's concept of truth, it may be important to bear in mind not only his declared dependence on T.S. Kuhn, but also his old preoccupation with Hegelian philosophy. His 'Menschwerdung Gottes' from 1970 wears the subtitle 'Eine Einführung in Hegels theologisches Denken als Prolegomena zu einer künftigen Christologie'. See also the comments on Küng's "Hegelianism" in: LØNNING 1986, 190–197.

[168] Cf. note 141 and, additionally, BAYBROOKE 1996.

[169] "No world peace without peace of religion!", KÜNG & KUSCHEL, 1993, 21.

of limited practical value. The sharpest and theologically the most provocative exchange on Küng's "global ethic" may be the one which took place between Michael Welker and HANS KÜNG in Evangelische Kommentare the same year.[170]

Discussions around the "Projekt Weltethos", interesting as they are in themselves, are not directed to the foundations of interreligious dialogue as such, and in our present context it may therefore suffice to refer to them summarily.

4.2.3. The Process Orientation: John B. Cobb Jr.

A characteristic and much observed contribution to the discussion stems from the increasingly influential Process school of theology, with JOHN B. COBB JR. as its most observed spokesperson. Process theology has as its background the philosophy of A.N. WHITEHEAD, translated into theological language by CHARLES HARTSHORNE.[171]

Its main thrust is on ontological premises. "Becoming" is defined as prior to, and thus as constitutive of, "being". In such a vision God cannot be fancied as some constitutive behind the all-embracing process of reality. God is partner in, and at the same time the integrative aim of, universal becoming. This pushes towards a unified image of reality, where everything becomes part of everything else, and any distinction between good and evil elements in the process of actuality is basically relativized. "Evil" stands for our experience of a world yet unfinished, and thus incomplete.

It would be expected that the unconventional (if by no means unprecedented!) understanding of reality as process would have determinant consequences also for religion and for interreligious relations. And, indeed, it had. As to practical conclusions, the dialogue theology of COBB and other process theologians may come close to that of KÜNG, but ontological presuppositions are remarkably different. At the same time it is worth to observing how process theologians generally tend to hold a quite unified vision of inter-religious rapprochement.[172]

In order to assess COBB's approach to non-Christian religions rightly, it is helpful to start with a book thematically dedicated to a different topic. In *The Liberation of Life*, written together with the Australian biologist CHARLES BIRCH,[173] Cobb develops the process understanding of "Life" (= ecological totality), starting with its biological and continuing with its social and cultural expressions, up to the highest:

---

[170] Michael WELKER: 'Gut gemeint – aber ein Fehlschlag. Hans Küngs "Projekt Weltethos" ', and: 'Autoritäre Religion – Replik auf Hans Küng', EK 1993, 354–356 & 528f. – KÜNG: 'Nicht gut gemeint – deshalb ein Fehlschlag. Zu Michael Welkers Reaktion auf "Projekt Weltethos" ', ibid., 486–489.

[171] Cf. John B. COBB Jr & Franklin J. GAMWELL (ed.): Existence and Actuality: Conversations with Charles Hartshorne, Chicago/London 1984.

[172] This fact is offered particular attention by KNITTER who (1985, 137f) offers a special passage to "Process theology". Together with the name of John Cobb Jr. he mentions particularly those of Schubert OGDEN and Norman PITTENGER.

[173] Charles BIRCH & John B. COBB Jr.: The Liberation of Life: From the Cell to the Community, Cambridge 1981.

"Life as the central religious symbol is God".[174] "The greatest power in the world ... comes from faith in Life and the ideas this faith brings."[175] This suggests a contour of religion as a universal occurrence, where historical patterns of realization – religions in plural – are secondary to trust in Life as an event making its presence felt always and everywhere.

As we are soon going to see, however, COBB is far from following the example of HICK and KNITTER, advocating "natural religion" more or less in the 18th century deist sense. In his vision of religion as "becoming", and thus as an undetachable determinant in the process total, he pays principal attention to the importance of diversified historical strains, and to what he sees as a constructive tension between reciprocal independence and interdependence of existing faiths.

COBB's first major contribution to a theology of dialogue was a discussion of, and, at the same time, a contribution to, dialogue intrareligious as well as interreligious : *Beyond Dialogue – Toward a Mutual Transformation of Christianity and Buddhism.*[176] His point of departure was clear:

> "Unfortunately, there is now a widespread sense that our choice is either to continue our belief in Christian superiority ... or to see Jesus as one savior among others. The former choice turns Christ into an instrument of our arrogance. The latter abandons the universal meaning and truth of Christ so central to our historic faith. Is there no other option? Certainly there must be."[177]

Some might call this a *petitio principii*, unintentionally inviting examinatory questions. "Christian superiority" could have the two rather different meaning of: "being better than ..." and of "being entrusted with more to account for than ..." In the latter case it could be presumed to inspire self-examination and humility rather than arrogance. And is it granted that "historic faith" – in whatever meaning – may be preserved as an unambiguous criterion, once the decision is made to resign any claim of "superiority"? What COBB obviously has in mind, is to overcome the ugly option between indifference and arrogance. For that purpose he ponders what a third and more desirable alternative could possibly look like.

COBB starts with a general reflection on interreligious dialogue, reviewing the development of Christian theology of religions so far, with a major critical reservation against the kind of theist imperialism which he senses in the more or less united approach of W.C. SMITH, HICK and KNITTER. He recommends the dialogue initiatives taken by the Vatican Council and by the World Council of Churches, but finds them lacking in clarity and in ultimate goal and orientation as well, although he commends them for not being linked up with some rigid concept of religion as are the authors mentioned.

---

[174] Op.cit., 195.
[175] Ibid., 330.
[176] Philadelphia 1982.
[177] Op.cit., vii f.

His main thesis is that dialogue should be approached in full openness without a preestablished model of the consensus to be obtained. Each one of the dialogue partners should bring along to the symposium the most valuable in his/her own historical inheritance. Unprejudiced listening and mutual openness for transformation will hinder a face-to-face encounter from ending up as a sterile confrontation.

In an extensive introductory polemic against JOHN HICK, COBB makes a point of methodology. His own method is basically oriented by an openness for mutual transformation. Hick's orientation, on the contrary, is a preconceived idea of such and such a common ground of all faiths to be jointly explored. A corresponding doctrinal difference between the two inevitably follows: christology (as a historic doctrine vital to one particular religion) is opposed to "a purely transcendent God as the common ground of religion".[178] Cobb has no difficulty in showing how the universalist criterion of Hick (and other "theists", as he calls them), just in face of Buddhism unveils a fundamental lack of universality. Their theocentric approach – a blunt defiance of Buddhist non-theism – proclaimed as the chief prerequisite of dialogue, abolishes precisely the dialogue that it claims to establish. So, we don't move closer to our dialogue partners if we "downplay in advance our most precious beliefs."

Right here we shall refrain from a description of how COBB *in concreto* foresees what he calls a "mutually transformatory dialogue" between Buddhism and Christianity, but it may be of interest to throw a glance at his final "Conclusions":

> "A Buddhisized Christianity and a Christianized Buddhism may continue to enrich each other and human culture generally through their differences ... it is the mission of Christianity to become a universal faith in the sense of taking into itself the alien truths that others have realized. This is no mere matter of addition. It is instead a matter of creative transformation. An untransformed Christianity, that is, a Christianity limited to its own parochial traditions, cannot fulfill its mission of realizing the universal meaning of Jesus Christ. It can only continue to offer its fragment alongside the offerings of other traditions. When it appeals for total commitment to so fragmentary a realization of Christ, it is idolatrous. When, to avoid idolatry, it asks for only fragmentary commitment to the fragment of truth it offers, it ceases to express the ultimacy of the claim of Christ and continues its inevitable decay ...".[179]

We observe COBB's strong stance against the two opposite, logically simplex answers. By "total commitment to a fragmentary realization of Christ" he challenges "exclusivist" claims of truth in its totality as expressed in, and limited to, Christianity. He maintains the "universal" Christ not only as one addressing himself to all, but as the One integrating truth universal. Christ is seen as global depositary of truth present in the faiths of humanity, even those historically unrelated to Christianity. When Cobb rejects "fragmentary commitment to the fragment of truth it offers", he denounces "pluralism": be it for devaluating ultimate truth to a number of independent claims entitled to coexist side by side, or for dogmatizing some readily presentable "common

---

[178] Ibid., 44, cf. 36–38, 41–46.
[179] Ibid., 142, ('Conclusion', 140–143).

core", defining – and delimiting – truth without respecting its vast variety of existing shapes.

This indicates a dialectical solution not unlike that of HANS KÜNG's combined vision of a "truth from inside" and "truth from outside", but with a different ontological foundation. To Küng the task is to combine his vision of the faithful believer with that of the unprejudiced observer, both of vital importance for true dialogue, i.e. for human understanding across cultural borders, and thus – finally – for world peace. The ontological stress, however, is on what is already given, on *being*. To COBB, with his process model of reality, the question is one of dynamic rapprochement through openness for mutual transformation. Here the meaning of dialogue (as of everything else) is visualized as *becoming*. Difference of ontology, however, turns out to be of secondary importance when we try to list practical consequences.

A particularly thought-provoking element in COBB's presentation is his "Postscript", where he frankly confesses that "as a Whiteheadian I have found myself changed in my encounter with Buddhism."[180] This change, according to his description, consists least of all in a critical modification, but in a confirmative deepening of WHITEHEAD's process ontology. A comparison of their practical conclusions does not, however, exclude that the non-Whiteheadian KÜNG could have spoken of change in a close to similar way. Indirectly this is powerfully confirmed by Cobb himself in his eulogistic contribution to the festschrift for Küng's 65th birthday, a contribution to which we will soon return.[181]

From a logical, and also a theological, point of view there remain basic questions attached to COBB's combination of universality and reciprocal transformation. *Logically*: the mutual, transformative enrichment by historically divided "truths" must either discharge any idea of conflicting truth claims, or it must include some principle for distinguishing particular claims from truth itself. But where could such a distinctive principle be found within a Process horizon? – *Theologically*: If Christ is figured as the fulness of truth (= the integrating principle for all truths at all times and in all places), where do we stand in relation to the much debated discovery of "others" as "anonymous Christians"? Could not the Process version of a Christ Universal be seen as a back street to Christian "imperialism"? Other faiths are accepted, but principally as branches of the one universal stream of truth: Christ!? Isn't this contrary to Cobb's own purposes when he declares his emphatic *no* to any shade of "Christian arrogance"?

One answer might be that if Christianity is visualized and emphasized as one historical current alongside others – as done by Cobb – it claims no moral prerogative for itself. To a believing Christian such a model of thought must command a fundamental distinction between Christ-relatedness in an ultimate sense and institutional belonging to a Christian community. Believing in the uniqueness of Christ neither requires nor allows belief in a corresponding uniqueness of the Christian Church as

---

[180] Ibid., 145, ('Postscript', 145–150).
[181] Cf. our notes 135, 187.

empirical institution. This might be a dialectic worth further contemplation. But, in any case, this is not what Cobb explicitly says.

Another valid riposte would be for COBB, like KARL RAHNER, to save his consistency through accentuating that the universality of his claim implies no demand that dialogue partners should accept in advance one limited agenda or one unified language for their common adventure. He might argue so even more successfully than Rahner, since in a process ontology the integration envisaged is one of, and in, becoming. That suggests: confluence in a – maybe – distant, non-prefigurable future, whereas in conventional transcendental thought integration depends on something extant: a permanent commonality as coordinating key to the historic variety of human responses. In any case, a process model of thought seems more open to imagination and, in its consequences, more acceptant of a variety of religious commitments, than a static transcendental interpretation.

It may be a good deal more difficult to absolve the question we have suggested to Cobb's idea of a final unification of truth(s) across religious and cultural borders. If, as it looks, his theory really excludes (finally) conflicting truth claims, this lays in the first place a rather heavy restriction on dialogue. Then, if colloquial partners disagree on whatever issue of truth, this means that at least one of them must have misunderstood what the exchange finally is about. Worse still, if we decline the possibility of authentic disagreement, we implicitly deny the use of critical standards: the possibility of challenging and being challenged face-to-face.

This may sound contrary to what COBB himself says, in his rather optimistic designation of dialogue as a way to reciprocal change. But for his argument to convince, his provisions are hardly sufficient. The idea of Christ integrating the full universe of truth (claims), obviously demands that dialogue as a process of change does not – in principle – correct, but complete. Each of us is in advance pledged to sustain a reciprocal claim: "I am alright, you are alright."

At an immediate glance, this may seem an ideal basis of any dialogue. But, upon further reflection, doesn't it restrict communicative openness if, in principle, we exclude the possibility of mutual understanding growing through joint wrestling with conflicting truth claims? And doesn't it exclude dialogue partners who insist on an unprejudiced confrontation of such claims? If we answer that such a dilemma would hardly arise within a Whiteheadian process horizon that obviously unveils the process vision as too narrow to lodge the fulness of orientations essential to a universal fellowship of dialogue.

In the meantime COBB has shown, however, that it is really possible for different religions to present radical challenges to each other. Given the respondent's own vision of reality, it may sometimes be justified to ask about conformity between ambition and practice.[182]

But COBB goes further than that. It is of interest to observe his position in the "Myth of Uniqueness" controversy. At a conference in March 1986 preparing that

---

[182] Cobb & Ives 1990, particularly 91–101.

provocative anthology, Cobb together with his Process comrades in arms SCHUBERT OGDEN and DAVID TRACY was among the invited participants who chose not to participate in the project. Even if presenting themselves as "ardent advocates of interreligious dialogue", they feel "that the pluralist move is either unwarranted, unnecessary or illegitimate".[183] Cobb explains why in the contrasting volume *Christian Uniqueness Reconsidered.*[184]

Here COBB opposes "pluralism as it has come to be defined", in the name of "a fuller and more genuine pluralism". Instead of attacking "the uniqueness of Christianity" he wants to defend the "uniqueness" of all religions. Each one possesses "a unique superiority, namely, the ability to achieve what by its own historic norms is most important."

> "The implication of ... what happens in dialogue, then is that the one norm that can be applied with relative objectivity to the great religious traditions has to do with their ability, in faithfulness to their heritage, to expand their understanding of reality and its normative implications ..."[185]

This is the reason why COBB wants dialogue to be hampered by no predetermined idea of "religion", but to let "the great religious traditions" meet, everyone of them restricted only by its awareness of own identity.

By this "open" orientation he presents himself as an ally of HANS KÜNG. In the huge festschrift for Küng's 65th birthday 1993 COBB has, as mentioned, a contribution on interreligious dialogue, world ethos and the problematic of humaneness (das Humanum).[186] Here he recommends Küng for having contributed more than any other Christian theologian to the building up of an interreligious dialogue, and also for the attention he has given to the world religions in his powerful campaign for a contemporary world ethos. He also expresses full support to Küng's protection of dialogue and of the ethos project against two opposite "groups". Against one – the seemingly progressive – by never leaving his Christian identity out of consideration in dialogue, and by resisting all constructions of some definable essence common to all religions. Against the other – the seemingly conservative – by insisting on humaneness as a common ground of ethical orientation and resisting any diastatic idea of an exclusively Christian contribution.

COBB has, however, one critical remark to KÜNG's Humanum concept: it may too easily lend itself to a traditional anthropocentric interpretation, and an articulation of present day environmental awareness is needed. An emphasis not unexpected from the side of Process theology! The most interesting aspects of Cobb's respectful critique of Küng are, however, his remarks concerning Küng's distinction between an

---

[183] KNITTER, in the preface to 'The Myth ...', viii.
[184] Cobb, op.cit., 81–95.
[185] Ibid., 87.
[186] 'Interreligiöser Dialog, Weltethos und die Problematik des Humanum' in: HÄRING & KUSCHEL 1993, 589–606.

external and an internal perspective. Küng's dialectical leaps from uncommitted critical observer to committed Christian advocate are not always equally convincing.

> "Meines Erachtens ist die sogenannte externe Perspektive KÜNGS ständig von der internen
> durchdrungen, während umgekehrt die sogenannte interne Perspektive ständig von der
> externen durchdrungen wird. Genauso, wie er aus christlichen Gründen ganz bestimmte
> Aspekte der globalen Situation hervorhebt, lässt sich umgekehrt aus äußeren Gründen im
> christlichen Glauben Wahrheit finden. Deshalb wäre es wohl besser, nicht von zwei Pers-
> pektiven, sondern von zwei Polen in einer durchgängigen Denkart zu sprechen."[187]

COBB and KÜNG, allies in a two-front war against non-committed pluralism on one
side and partisan exclusivism on the other – both committed to indiscriminate openness toward faiths in the plural *and* to integral identification with Christian faith in
its singularity. What may be the deepest difference between the two comrades in
arms? It has obviously to do with ontology and – consequently – with style of thinking. Küng's double approach to the truth of religion, external and internal, reflects
a pattern of dialectical thinking which – as we have seen – may have certain, not
unimportant roots in HEGEL.[188] The movement: thesis – antithesis – synthesis involves a particular reconciliatory dynamic.

The consequences of COBB's Whiteheadian Process thought have been observed
on several occasions, and the mitigating influence of its unifying vision is easily recognized. Process means constant movement in a unificatory direction. Cobb's fri-
endly-critical review of Küng is anything but surprising. KÜNG's reply to Cobb might
have been a corresponding: Yes, but ... On the contemporary arena and in face of
powerful critics to the left as well as to the right, they have both been obliged to
emphasize fellowship in practical conclusions instead of exploring the their profound
epistemological incongruence.

4.2.4. *"Inclusivists" for "Christian Uniqueness"*

A search for a wider specter of intermediary positions could profitably pick out certain contributors from the anthology *Christian Uniqueness Reconsidered* (1990*)*, to
which several references have already been made. This collection covers a variety of
approaches. The only common denominator is an emphatic reservation against *The
Myth of Christian Uniqueness* (1987/88).[189]

What we immediately observe, are more or less Janus-faced orientations: convinced advocates of dialogue, and at the same time critical to pluralist dialogue-at-any-
price demands. This means that some of the more conservative "uniqueness"-suppor-
ters present at the party (JÜRGEN MOLTMANN, LESLIE NEWBIGIN, and WOLFHART
PANNENBERG) will not be presented right here. They will appear in our next section

---

[187] Ibid., 600.
[188] Cf. our observations in note 165.
[189] Cf. the editor D'Costa's general presentation in: ' Christian Uniqueness ...', x.

(4.3) – "Identity-first / dialogue-next!" as their catchword definitely is. Nor will we pay broad attention to declared "Process" participants. Their characteristic contribution has just been presented in our conversation with their most influential advocate COBB. More than any other on the stage, they make up a phalanx distinctive in its principal approach and solidly unified in its overarching conclusions.

A contribution from the anthology under review, which wholeheartedly accepts the terminological distinction between "pluralist" and "inclusivist" theologies of religion, and which, in addition to this, undertakes a comparison resulting in a total triumph of the latter, is FRANCIS X. CLOONEY, S.J.: *Reading the World in Christ. From Comparison to Inclusivism.*[190] The orientative focus of Father Clooney is how "comparative theology as the dialectical activity of reading and rereading the Bible and other Christian texts in a new context formed by non-Christian texts" – in his case the context of the Tamil-Sanscrit Shrivaishnava tradition – lays the foundation of "an inclusivist theology of religions".[191]

> "Inclusivism's insistence that salvation is in Christ alone and yet is universally available is a perplexing double claim The inclusivist insists on both salvation in Christ alone and the true universality of salvation, just as the comparative theologian insists on reading back and forth from text to context, in the act of creative amplification of what has already been "written" from the start."[192]

In this light the author spells out his dialectical difficulties with *The Myth* ... It "seems to assume a number of things that require demonstration", for example its polemical insistence on linking inclusiveness intrinsically with attitudes of domination, and pluralism with seriousness about contemporary problems of social justice. Further, he observes a general "pluralist ambivalence about the value of language and ... about the function of texts", taking words simply for secondary in relation to world and to human experience.[193] In his opinion, the difference between pluralism and inclusivism may be argued on a variety of levels. But if we take as criterion "how well either position functions in taking other religions seriously, inclusivism appears the more successful position, at least for those who ... read texts."[194]

Unlike his Indian compatriots PANIKKAR and SAMARTHA on the pluralist team, M.M.THOMAS (moderator of the World Council of Churches' Central Committee 1968–1975) sees the Mythology approach as a failure, in spite of his wholehearted commitment to the cause of dialogue. In their attempt to construct a common ground for an East-West dialogue, the adversaries of "Christian Uniqueness" have only succeeded in showing the impossibility of their enterprise in our contemporary world. "Religious ultimates like God or Reality or Faith, the Transcendent Mystery, The Spirit, the Kingdom, or their metaphysical or historical equivalents like Being and

---

[190] Ibid., 63–79.
[191] Ibid., 64.
[192] Ibid., 73.
[193] Ibid., 75.
[194] Ibid., 79.

Justice" – are all derived from the modern West and turn out to be essentially foreign to the spirit of Hindu religiosity. The criterion which experience has shown as most naturally adopted by people in India, is the person of Jesus Christ himself. In him they find a critical standard which they can easily make their own and even summon against the West. True universality, thus, speaks in favor of Christocentrism as the orientative principle of dialogue.[195]

It may look striking that another Indian in the group (living in Britain) GAVIN D'COSTA, editor of the volume, finds the decisive clue in "an appropriate doctrine of the Trinity": how does that relate to the simple christological proposal of his compatriot THOMAS? Part of the answer is that the two authors deal with different issues, so that by comparing them we illuminate the ambiguity of the general dialogue debate as such. Thomas responds to the question: which criterion of dialogue should Christians propose to their non-Christian conversation partners? D'Costa asks a different question, namely: how should Christians, arguing with Christians, motivate their common obligation to dialogue with others? Thomas sees the portrait of Jesus Christ as the mediating event to be presented to Hindu partners (interreligious dialogue). D'Costa does not present the Trinity on identical terms. He argues with Christian believers (intrareligious dialogue). Besides, the Catholic theologian D'Costa is obviously more preoccupied with dogmatical thinking than the layman Thomas (of the Syrian St.Thomas Church).

D'COSTA like CLOONEY finds it meaningful to characterize his position as "inclusivist", transcending "pluralism" as well as "exclusivism" in combining dialectically what he sees as the decisive issue to them both.[196] He suggests that "at the heart of a trinitarian doctrine of God, the multiplicity of religions takes on a special theological significance". A trinitarian christology reconciles "the exclusivist emphasis on the particularity of Christ and the pluralist emphasis on God's universal activity in history". It is "open" to the world religions, in the sense of refusing to make either critical judgements or positive affirmations a priori, but looks forward to "hearing the voice of God, through the Spirit, in the testimonies of people from other faiths."[197]

"Openness" is the key word of his trinitarian construction, at the same time as D'Costa emphasizes the necessity – for Christians – to have the rationale of their dialogue commitment anchored in the heart of Christian faith, without expecting this motivation as such to be shared by dialogue partners of other faiths. As he states it in his preface to the volume, Knitter's boasted "crossing of Rubicon", the particular landmark of a good pluralist, like the crossing by Caesar, in whom it glories, is "a forceful attempt to encompass the 'other' within the assailant's framework.[198]

Hesitant as to the clarificative value of the exclusivist-inclusivist-pluralist confrontation is J.A.DiNOIA, O.P., who raises the issue: *Pluralist Theologies of Religions: Plu-*

---

[195] M.M. THOMAS: Ibid., 49–62.
[196] D'COSTA: Ibid., 16–29.
[197] Ibid., 26f.
[198] Ibid., ix.

ralistic or Non-Pluralistic?[199] Above all, he accuses the pluralists of importing a religious value of their own under the guise of a general theory of religions. "Distinctively conceived religious objects" in different religions are substituted by religiously indeterminate concepts, pluralism thus giving name to a comprehensive spiritual transformation. The final expression of this he finds in the subsumption of "the varieties of distinctive aims pursued by religious communities" under some diffuse terminological shelter of "salvation", supposed to be a common good naturally recognizable to and by all.

Let us throw a glance at another contribution by DiNoia from approximately the same time,[200] which can profitably be read as a further explicative development of his argument. In the discussion about "salvation" of non-Christians, inclusivism and pluralism both take a liberal stand, although inclusivism, in DiNoia's judgement, has the advantage of "combining a favorable account of other religious communities with a strong avowal of the universal scope of salvation in Christ". Pluralism, on the contrary, homogenizes cross-religious varieties, particularly various concepts of salvation, "in the direction of an indeterminate common goal". One accusation seems to hit them both, however: they do injustice to dialogue partners, paying insufficient attention to what "others" understand as "salvation" (under whatever term).

The fundamental question, according to DiNoia, must be asked in a more reflective manner. The issue of future "salvation" cannot be separated from the notion of a final, overall goal which each particular religion proposes for human life. Christian theology, then, cannot meaningfully start by asking whether adherents of other religions can obtain "salvation" (= ultimate fulfilment, as Christians understand it: eternal fellowship with God and with fellow human beings), without paying attention to what these religions themselves see as the meaning of life and, thus, as the kind of human fulfilment worth pursuing. Are their aspirations really compatible with a Christian vision of "salvation"? What could be the meaning of promising someone a "salvation" he or she never asked for? Do we have the right to force our hopes upon him?

The Dominican DiNoia recurs to the classical Catholic doctrine of Purgatory in a slightly modernized version, seeing the possible eternal salvation of non-Christians, as of Christians, warranted by the hope that imperfect human ambitions through God's grace be transformed to perfection in an existence hereafter. This cannot be visualized as a process of temporal duration and attached to some particular location. The supposition is, however, today as in Medieval times, that Purgatory never changes the fundamental orientation of a human life.

A human person, according to DiNoia, gives the decisive Yes or No to universal integration ("salvation"), through his or her decisions in this life. But Purgatory overcomes imperfection, lacking information, and inadequate expectations of the salvati-

[199] Ibid., 119–134.

[200] DiNoia: Varieties of Religious Aims: Beyond Exclusivism, Inclusivism, and Pluralism, in: Bruce D. Marshall (ed.): Theology and Dialogue – Essays in Conversation with George Lindbeck, Notre Dame, Indiana 1990, 249–274.

on to come. Given that perfection is not achieved in this life – be it by Christians or non-Christians – this prevision opens up for salvation to all who, with their variety of backgrounds, welcome the perfective orientation toward universal fulfilment finally offered by divine grace. Through this vision DiNoia hopes to safeguard the synthesis of universal openness (advertised, but not realized by the pluralists) and an organic liaison with historic Christianity (sought, but not brought home by the inclusivists).

> "Thus, Muslims or Buddhists could be said to develop dispositions conducive to the enjoyment of the true aim of life – fellowship with the blessed Trinity – even if they did so in the light of conceptions which ruled out personal relation either in God himself or in the ultimate state of enlightenment ... such persons could reach to the threshold of the enjoyment of the true aim of life not only despite but also because of dispositions fostered in their communities, even though some of their doctrines are regarded as mistaken or incomplete from the Christian point of view."[201]

This is probably as close as an argument today can come in accommodating an inclusive-oriented understanding of non-Christian religions in a classical Thomist framework. We are here at a considerable distance from the premises observed with contemporary "progressive" Catholic theologians of religions like PAUL F. KNITTER, RAIMUNDO PANIKKAR and even HANS KÜNG – in itself a testimony of the restricted role played by scholastic tradition in post-Vatican-II catholic theology. The difference is, however, one of methodological approach as much as one of theological consequence.

DiNoia develops his Thomist reflections on the issue in an anthology in honour of the influential Lutheran theologian GEORGE LINDBECK, thus signalizing a certain fellowship of arms, without reflecting explicitly on possible overlappings of thought. As DiNoia, at the same time, pays so much attention to Catholic and scholastic roots – which are certainly not those of Lindbeck's – it may, however, be meaningful to compare his position on non-Christian religion to that indicated by Lindbeck in *The Nature of Doctrine*, 1984.[202]

This author resolutely does away with what he sees as two opposite and equally destructive uses of language in theology: the "cognitive propositional" (orthodoxy) and the "experimental-expressive" (liberalism). Thereafter he presents his own version of language: the "cultural-linguistic". This results in a "rule theory": doctrines have their most prominent function neither as truth claims nor as expressive symbols, but as "communally authoritative rules of discourse, attitude and action."[203] This has far-reaching consequences with regard to interreligious dialogue.

> "The cultural-linguistic approach can allow a strong case for interreligious dialogue, but not for any single type ... The legitimate reasons for discussion are as varied as in international relations."[204]

---

[201] Op.cit., 266.
[202] LINDBECK 1984.
[203] Op.cit., 16ff.
[204] Ibid., 53f.

"... different religions are likely to have different warrants for interreligious conversation and cooperation. This lack of a common foundation is ... also a strength ... the partners in dialogue do not start with the conviction that they really basically agree ... representing a superior (or an inferior) articulation of a common experience ... while a cultural-linguistic approach does not issue a blanket endorsement of the enthusiasm and warm fellow-feelings ... easily promoted in an experiental-expressive context, it does not exclude the development of powerful theological rationales for ... efficacious commitment to interreligious discussion and cooperation."[205]

For a more extensive comparison DiNoia/Lindbeck it may be relevant to quote also Lindbeck on the issue of final salvation. Here he formulates his "proposal" with particular care and modesty without pretending to offer a final solution:

"The proposal is that dying itself be pictured as the point at which every human being is ultimately and expressedly confronted by the gospel ... It is only then that the final decision is made for or against Christ; and this is true not only of unbelievers but also of believers. All previous decisions, whether for or against faith, are preliminary ... We must trust and hope, although we cannot know, that ... no one will be lost ... Thus it is possible to be hopeful about the salvation of non-Christians no less than Christians even if one does not think in terms of a primordeal, prereflective experience of Christ's grace."[206]

In this perspective Lindbeck speaks most critically of "supposing that Christians know what nonbelievers ... believe in the depths of their being better than they know themselves"[207], so that the task of dialogue or of evangelism should be to sharpen their self-awareness. This remark by Lindbeck sounds as smashing to the "theocentric" approach by the "pluralists" Hick and Knitter as of the "anonymous Christian" proposal by the "inclusivist" Rahner.

In this setting it may be a striking observation that the Catholic DiNoia and the Protestant Lindbeck – so much in agreement about hope for the salvation of non-Christians – differ so much, not only in (onto-)logical foundations, but also in conceptual undergirding of their joint assumptions. To DiNoia, the traditional Catholic doctrine of Purgatory gives substance to the hope – for Christians and non-Christians alike – that present accommodation to God-willed fellowship (irrespective of religious affiliation) may be lead on to perfection in an existence "hereafter". To Lindbeck, classical Protestant reliance on "faith alone ... Christ alone" forbids that a foreseeable process of human development, in this life or the next, could be a determining vehicle of ultimate salvation. In order to maintain "salvation" as pure gift, the final response of faith must be deferred to a situation beyond human control, the final edge of imaginable existence, death.

Returning to *Christian Uniqueness*, still a couple of observations remain to be made. The Reformation accent just mentioned, very much underlies Christoph Schwöbel's *Particularity, Universality and the Religions.*[208] Schwöbel states "the uni-

---

[205] Ibid., 55.
[206] Ibid., 59.
[207] Ibid., 61.
[208] 'Christian Uniqueness..', 30–46.

versality of God's presence in the particularity of religions" as a principle which demands general recognition by Christians, in their dealing with other faiths as much
as in their understanding of their own. When, at the same time, he refuses to speak of
"revelation" in other religions, this is not grounded in a claim of religious superiority,
but in the impossibility to fancy how "salvation" is understood in faiths other than
one's own. This is due to the observer's outside position, and – consistently – to a
refusal to reinterpret other faiths in order to make them fit with a Christian understanding, or with some general theory of religion. The universality of God's revelation as an open accessibility to his creative and redemptive action for all creatures
"remains for the Christian something to be hoped for in the *eschaton*" – a statement
which comes close to the final conclusion of Lindbeck. In their common aspiration
the distinction between God's work and human performance, so fundamental to the
Reformation, is recognized as fundamental also to a contemporary theology of religions.

> "While revelation as the condition for the possibility of faith is a divine work and therefore
> lays an absolute claim on the believer, no human form or expression of faith, neither an
> ecclesial institution, nor any form of sacramental action or form of doctrine can claim
> absoluteness."[209]

This may be an important statement, depending on its interpretation. More concise-
ly: depending on how and where the borderline is drawn between "revelation" and
"human form or expression of faith". That issue would demand a good deal of reflection in order to produce a viable criterion. In any case, it is hard to figure "revelation"
as an isolated event. If it contains a real message – as the term itself contends – this
can obviously be neither received nor even fancied, without some kind of human
cooperation. How can we identify a communication as coming from God, without
reviewing critically the human activity implied in the reception process?

As already observed, more than against anyone else the polemical spike of the
Christian Uniqueness ... is directed against JOHN HICK, regarded as the unmatched
high priest of pluralism. Some of the most challenging attacks on him have already
been reviewed in our presentation of his doctrine (4.1.1) and shall not be repeated.
Suffice it to bring to mind the accusation, repeated and seconded in a variety of
versions, that "pluralism" through its generalizing concept of "what religion is about",
in fact exercises a considerable pressure in the direction of uniformity, and that, with
its base in Occidental modernity, its potential influence on non-Western cultures
must be mainly seen as a repressive one.[210]

---

[209] Ibid., 41.

[210] In a socio-cultural setting this is argued with particular emphasis by SURIN, op.cit., 192–210, cf.
our description 4.1.1. – MILBANK (ibid., 174–191) resumes the accusation against pluralism in four
challenging theses: "Religion is not a genus ... Practice is not a foundation ... Pluralism does not serve
justice ... Trinitarian difference is no neo-Vedantic difference". The first of these theses recalls the standard objection against pluralism already frequently referred to, the second and third attack the attempt
most powerfully represented by KNITTER to produce a pluralist "liberation theology of religions", and
the fourth is mainly directed against PANIKKAR's integration of Christian and Hindu principles.

The most vigorous of these attacks on JOHN HICK is one already specifically mentioned,[211] but which still needs more attention in our context. PAUL J. GRIFFITHS has made a particularly striking point out of "the logic of interreligious dialogue": the necessity for religions to keep up their reciprocal identities through presenting and defending their essential truth claims in open exchange. This he maintains not only in *Christian Uniqueness* ..., but in a separate monography on interreligious apologetics published not long after.[212] Having already reviewed his particular issue with Hick, we shall here call attention to the wider expanse of his engagement. Griffiths sees "a certain kind of uniqueness ... that includes both universalism and exclusivism" as constitutive of Christianity, which necessarily must involve readiness to grant other religions a corresponding right to define their own terms:

> "... a frank acknowledgement of universalistic and exclusivistic dimensions of Christian syntax and semantic by Christians committed to interreligious dialogue will lead to the crossing of new frontiers in interreligious dialogue, frontiers inaccessible from within the pluralist paradigm ..."[213]

What GRIFFITHS champions, is the right for every one to define and to defend his own identity. And the "new frontiers" envisaged are obviously those of recognizing one's own demand for integrity in the corresponding demands of the others. Respect for authentic disagreement fosters a new and more authentic experience of fellowship. His more comprehensive study from 1991 expounds the theory of "apologetics as one important component of interreligious dialogue".[214] His concern is to argue in favor of what he calls "the NOIA principle".[215]

GRIFFITHS is aware of a real collision between this classical principle – as he defines it – and dominant currents in contemporary culture, including much of modern theology. That remark applies not only to liberal Protestantism; also Roman Catholic theology after Vatican II has by and large "moved far from the apologetical" orientation to be desired. A clearer understanding, then, must be found of "the significance of religious claims to truth made in a context of radical religious pluralism".[216] A dialogue which does not take truth claims – be they ever so conflicting – for what they are and confront them seriously with each other, is not taking the conversation partners seriously, they are "not even playing the play they think they are playing."[217]

Listening to "inclusivist" voices has confronted us with a remarkable variety of reflectors dedicated to the task of dialogue, but reluctant to "crossing the Rubicon" of

---

[211] Here 4.1.1, cf. particularly references in our notes 16–20.

[212] 'An Apology for Apologetics ...'1991. – It is typical of GRIFFITHS' concern for interreligious distinction that, almost at the same time, he appears as editor of an anthology 'Christianity through Non-Christian Eyes', 1990.

[213] 'The Uniqueness..', 170.

[214] GRIFFITHS 1991, xi.

[215] NOIA = 'Necessity of interreligious apologetics', Ibid., 1. Maybe a playful reference to the Greek διανοια (= intellectual condition, thought).

[216] Ibid., 2.

[217] Ibid., 21.

the declared "pluralists". They are not willing to declare faiths in general as equally valid avenues to "salvation" – or as equally valid vehicles of interpreting such avenues. Some of them bluntly deny this core of the pluralist claim, or they grant it only with stark modifications. Others would refuse to take a comparative stand on truth claims and instead restrain themselves to denying the possibility and/or the admissibility of raising the issue. Together they stand for a variety of arguments, not all immediately unifiable.

The most common accusation against pluralism is that of lacking respect for own religion in its historic authenticity, as entailing a similar lack of respect for the faith of one's dialogue partner. Even if the collision between pluralism and inclusivism may look rather apodictic in light of the rhetorical confrontation of the *Myth...* and the *Uniqueness...* crews: we are not dealing with two neatly segregated armies, but rather with two neighboring camps, each with a complex variety of weapons and equipment, and with a complex line of demarcation between the two, but yet, as shown, with a remarkable awareness of confronting loyalties.

We shall see a similar observation applying to the third family of standpoints, which we will now inspect. As "pluralism" and "inclusivism" are clichés which will always, consciously or not, presuppose a "more or less", so will be the case of (what we – in spite of the logistics of systematized terminology, and in opposition to a custom firmly established by its enemies – shall voice certain objections to calling:) "exclusivism".

4.3. "Christiano-Centric" Approaches

Terminologically, this is the most awkward of our three classification categories. Readers grounded in the customary triad of plural-inclusive-exclusive would expect this section of our study to focus on "exclusivism". As used in modern discussion, this term is, however, so narrow in meaning and so prejudiced in estimate, that it would take extraordinary efforts to clear it for reliable use. In addition, the positions most appropriately characterized as "exclusivist", would be of limited interest in the study of our topic.

The adjective "christiano-centric" is chosen as notoriously different from "christo-centric", although the realities usually covered by the two may largely coincide. By a "christianocentric" theology of interreligious dialogue, we understand a theological approach to religious differentiation which takes its stand in a reference to Jesus, the Christ, as unique conveyor of ultimate truth, and which allocates its understanding of extra-Christian religions accordingly. This by no means excludes dialogue between religions, since it encourages rather than precludes confrontational "islamo-centric", "buddho-centric", or whatever attitudes from prospective dialogue partners. In order to converse fruitfully on faith, we have to take truth, our own and that of the others, dead seriously.

At first glance, then, a "christianocentric" theology of religions distinguishes itself from an "inclusivist" by a more simplex approach. It does not start as a declared attempt to unite historic Christian authenticity *and* universal human openness in one dialectically consolidated theory. Its basis – at least in several cases – may be the simple assumption that an integral self-presentation by each dialogue partner comes first, and that everything else, if not will, then at least may, follow from an uncompromised willingness to face each other in openness.

Massively simplified, we could say that while "pluralism" invites dialogue partners to a full mutual recognition a priori, based on some common ground more fundamental than the legacy of each single religion, and "inclusivism" generally invites a dynamic mutuality based on exchange and sharing of hopes without necessarily seeking one unified theory, so-called "exclusivism" – in its more reflected versions – sets no other formal requirement than full reciprocal loyalty to own identity and full equality of rights and duties in the very process of exchange. "Christiano-centricity" as here defined will greet "Islamo-centricity", "Buddho-centricity" etc. as colloquial partners with exactly the same dialogical obligations as its own.

In the context of a global theology of religions, the most concise name for this could be *"idio-centricity"* – self-centredness (not to be confused with the "ego-centricity" of individuals!). As little as – in the particular case of Christianity – a "christiano-centric" approach necessarily includes an attitude of dominance, do – on the global level – "idio-centric" orientations indicate an attitude of arrogance. Only a religion faithful to its own historical identity is open to converse with followers of other faiths in full recognition of their commitment to theirs! That the perspective may be exploited to forward institutional self-centredness, is apparent enough – as national may be turned to nationalist and confessional to confessionalist. So, precisely here the universal insight has to be remembered: *Non tollit usum abusus* (use is not abolished by abuse).

Our preliminary definition of "christiano-centric" is wide enough to comprehend even orientations which could in a rather literal meaning be labeled as "exclusivist". Most "exclusive" in this regard are "fundamentalist" expressions of Christianity – as of other religions, and ideologies. By "fundamentalism" we understand orientations which identify absolute truth with their own particular message in a way which *a priori* excludes anybody disagreeing with them as "outsiders".[218] In Christendom fundamentalism in a fairly unmodified form may be found in "sects" negative to dialogue not only with non-Christian communities but with Christian churches as well. The circle of inclusion – which automatically also describes the territory of exclusion – may, however, by various groups be drawn with highly different width of radius.

Between exclusivist and non-exclusivist types of christianocentricity there is, as we easily see, a broad zone of more or less oscillating stands: "We are not commissioned by God to proclaim that everybody (fulfilling such or such verifiable conditions) can, or will, be finally saved – nor are we authorized to distinguish people and anticipate some final selection." For our present research an exchange with exclusivist critics

---

[218] Cf. LØNNING 1997, 177–184.

rejecting interreligious dialogue on grounds of principle will not be meaningful. Nor is there reason to occupy ourselves with segments who, without investing principal reflection in the issue, turn their back on dialogue for pragmatic reasons, frequently expressing unwillingness to waste resources on a secondary enterprise and thus detract attention from the authentic (Christian) concern, which is that of mission.

We should, however, abstain from making the somewhat obtuse word "exclusiveness" – as it has been used in international discussion so far – a barrier to conversation, in cases where a challenger declares readiness to accept some project of interreligious exchange, be it on ever so restricted conditions.

In this part of our study, we shall look for conversation partners mainly in two directions, corresponding to a general pattern of division (not necessarily of separation) in contemporary Christendom. On the one side we find the theological world of established "churchmanship", prevailing not only in a majority of "historical churches", but also in the main ecclesial world organizations and at the academically established theological faculties in the Western world. On the other side we observe expanding "evangelicalism", especially in the two Americas and in parts of the "Third World". A dividing line between "evangelicalism" and "fundamentalism" is not always easy to draw, there are an infinity of shades, not least with regard to ecumenical vision and to openness vis-a-vis other religions.

As to Western academical theology, the interest in theology of religions was, as we have already seen, rather restrained, not only in the Barthian period (the second third of the 20th century), but also in the following decade of post-Bonhoefferian "secular theology". This may partly explain why the development of a new theology of religion(-s) from the mid-sixties onward was channeled through international church agencies more than through theological faculties, even if several of the leading exponents, in their daily work, were faculty related.

In an academical setting we shall mainly observe how JÜRGEN MOLTMANN and WOLFHART PANNENBERG cope with the problem. These are two of the leading German Protestant theologians of the last generation, and both – on rather divergent premises – are representatives of what we have proposed to call a "christianocentric" approach. Inspection of the two may give a general idea of how mainline continental Protestant theology, with, and in spite of, some hesitation has accepted the challenge.

4.3.1. "Evangelical" Orientations

In the German review Dialog der Religionen 1–95 there is an instructive review comparing five "evangelical" contributions from the USA, on the theology of religions. The review, by S. MARK HEIM, carries the noteworthy headline *A Wideness in God's Mercy*, the title of one of the five books evaluated.[219] The five volumes were all

---

[219] DdR 1–1995, 67–76.

published in 1992, and according to the reviewer they signalize, if not a shift in general orientation among evangelicals, so at least a new and astonishing openness for discussing questions which up to recently had been taboo in their constituency. Two of the books are monographies which have met a good deal of contradiction in their own spiritual environments. Two are collections of conference papers which reflect a not unimportant variety of opinions. The fifth is a popular instruction for parents: how to bring up their children in a multireligious cultural setting – firm in principal orientation, but amazingly wide-hearted in practical counseling.

The two monographies are both essentially geared to the classical problem of "salvation of the pagans", and generally lead to a common conclusion: Christ is exclusive as ontological, but not as epistemological basis of salvation.[220] In plain words: salvation granted by Christ alone, but possibly in many cases channeled through a faith which is not explicitly directed to Christ. Christ the Savior may be at work in a saving faith which simply, when all inessential circumstances are deleted, limits itself to an attitude of openness to God's generosity. Such an attitude would in each single case be supposed to correspond with the quantity of light which a person has actually received in his/her situation in life.

This is a solution argued not for reasons of equity, but through references to the Bible, from which are quoted not only sequences which speak explicitly to the item, but to theology and soteriology as integrated in a global orientation. And – not to forget – this is done with an impressive material of support collected from the history of the church, to a large extent from teachers with a solid reputation in latter evangelicalism.

One of the two authors is CLARK H. PINNOCK, presenting the "Wideness ..." study already mentioned, and quoted by his reviewer.[221] The other, JOHN SANDERS, explicitly gears his study to "the destiny of the unevangelized",[222] and is able to some extent to take account also of Pinnock's book, which was the first of the two to appear. The one that has caused most commotion among fellow evangelicals is evidently PINNOCK. On the "ontological" level, his resistance to contemporary pluralism is impressive: his orientation is to Jesus Christ, the incarnate, as exclusive vehicle of God's grace. But precisely his strong emphasis on grace turns into an uncompromised universalist claim, in light of Act 10:34f as decisive reference. Faith based on a full biblical observation of Christ, presupposes a comprehensive knowledge which is not present in the majority of biblical authors individually, and certainly not in the heroes of faith appearing all through the Bible, including the pagan Job as the peak. But does that mean that they are excluded from the great manifestation of divine grace: salvation through Christ in faith? Must not the fundamental conclusion be

---

[220] This terminology can actually be misleading, as "ontological", strictly taken, designates what relates to being as being, and not – like here – to an actual event, which should in a corresponding language rather be designated as "ontic".

[221] PINNOCK 1992.

[222] SANDERS 1992.

drawn: saving faith is not identical with "correct" intellectual reproduction of saving events.

The procedure of SANDERS is more analytical. He uses the well known strategy of seeking a "third solution", having shown the insufficiency of the two opposite extremes: a *restrictionism* which bluntly delivers those who die without professed faith in Christ to eternal condemnation, and a *universalism* which – independent of circumstances – accords salvation to all. Between these two extremes Sanders observes from church history several attempts of a "theology of wider hope", generally confirmed by well-reputed defenders of Christian orthodoxy. Some of those referred to stand for a general "evangelization" concept: everybody is to be met with a call to personal conversion, in this life (open or hidden), at the border of death, or in some non-objectifiable "here-after". Others are "inclusivists", endorsing also a response of faith not explicitly geared to a biblically clarified idea of Christ as the ground of salvation. Sanders is rather generous in his selection of historical "inclusivists", counting among others names as IRENAEUS, ZWINGLI, WESLEY, and C.S.LEWIS. He even suggests that such an orientation has been abundantly present among evangelicals also in our time.

Nuances, correctives and objections in various directions are brought to the fore in two conference reports. The anthology *One God, One Lord* echoes a conference at Oak Hill Theological College in England in 1991. And the first annual Wheaton Theology Conference had as topic "The Challenge of Religious Pluralism: An Evangelical Analysis and Reply" – published in the proceedings of that conference.[223] The Theological Commission of the World Evangelical Fellowship dedicated a good deal of its meeting in Manila in 1992 to the issue of "Confessing Christ in a Religiously Pluralist World".[224] Considerable attention is paid by these conferences to the fact of foreign (?) fire being brought into the camp. Different shades of opinion are accentuated, showing that the plain soteriological optimism of PINNOCK and SANDERS is by no means dominant in evangelical theology so far. But nor is it generally banned or universally questioned.

HEIM may be right, both in observing an emerging rethinking among "evangelicals" – however representative or non-representative his examples may be – and in pointing out the logical possibility of uniting ontic particularity (Christ-centredness) with epistemological universality. But spelling out a logical possibility is not the same as presenting a coherent theological justification. It may also be a question whether the solution of SANDERS – and still more that of PINNOCK – would not adjust more easily to the main-line "inclusivist" presentation of, say, COBB or KÜNG, than to the "evangelical" tradition of which they claim to be the consistent promoters.

Searching for a heavyweight contribution from recent years which clearly continues the evangelical tradition – without being particularly occupied with a formal clas-

---

[223] CLARKE & WINTER 1992. – CLARK a.o. 1992.

[224] Planned to appear with Paternoster Press under the title 'The Unique Christ in Our Pluralistic World', cf. HEIM, DdR 95, 72.

sification of that fact in itself – we could mention LESLIE NEWBIGIN's *The Gospel in a Pluralist Society*.[225] His book is an emphatic attack on the HICK / KNITTER position and its unmistakable influence on the dialogue concept of the ecumenical establishment. The following year he offered an extract of his reflections, in *Christian Uniqueness ...*[226]

His main objection against pluralism concerns separation of a universal human quest for "salvation" from the question of truth. This, in his opinion, means an indiscriminate endorsement of conflicting human aspirations. This objection of his consecutively opens up for the following constructive vision:

> "It is a fact that the cross is the very center of the Christian proclamation that drastically relativizes every Christian claim to embody the full truth of God in any intellectual system ... Every specific claim, intellectually or politically, made by the Christian church is relativized not by invoking the 'rough parity of all religions' ... It is relativized by invoking the name of Jesus. Everything is held *sub specie crucis*."[227]

The provocative question which immediately sprouts from this statement, concerns the concept of relativization. Where does NEWBIGIN draw the real borderline between relativizable and non-relativizable aspects/elements in his own theological project? He refers to the cross of Christ as unique reference point, not – like some might have expected – in the sense of a protective wall resisting the contemporary afflux of relativizing powers, but as the challenging edge of radical relativization itself.

Behind this language we surmise Pauline assumptions like Rom 3:22ff and 1 Cor 1:18ff: The cross confirms the inadequacy of any human enterprise – Christian or non-Christian – to cope with divine standards, and total human dependence on the sovereignty of God's grace. Any religious accomplishment is, at the best, of relative value. Every religion, so far, is set on equal terms, including established Christianity. The cross of Christ is different, not only as the steadfast accomplishment – of God – which brings all other accomplishments – by humans – to falter, but it has become the basic reference point of human existence as such.

Our first question to this construction is, of course, whether it can be maintained without contradicting itself. If all human theories are relativized by the cross, this must certainly also include theories, statements, and proclamations about the cross. How can we escape the following syllogism: (1) The cross relativizes all human achievements, (2) Any concept of the cross must be understood as a human achievement, (3) The cross relativizes any concept about the cross – including the idea of the cross relativizing all human achievements ...?

This dilemma could obviously be attacked also from the opposite side: NEWBIGIN seems to be as eager as his opponents to state a basic equality of all people, and of all religions, in face of a final divine judgement. But isn't that equality brought to a

[225] Grand Rapids / Geneva (WCC Publications), 1989.
[226] NEWBIGIN's contribution 'Religion for the Marketplace', Op.cit., 135–148. Cf. our comment 4.1.1., note 20.
[227] Ibid., 145.

manifest end if we suppose God's saving grace to be present in a way sustained by one religion, but not given appropriate attention by the others?

These questions are not enough, however, to describe NEWBIGIN as trapped in his own argument. There would be no logical inconsistency in pointing to a historic event as ultimate point of communicative reference and to combine this observation with a clear understanding that my attempts of explaining that event and of relating it conceptually to other events, are imperfect and can claim only relative validity. Even if I insist on "God's revelation in Holy Scripture," I have to admit that my use of Scripture is not identical with Scripture per se, but undoubtedly implies an element of my own (if ever so imperfect) activity.

The really difficult issue might rather be the second of the two suggested, that of equality. Will NEWBIGIN succeed in convincing – say – a Hindu, that he is claiming no human superiority over him when proclaiming the cross of Christ as the matchless event of human history, and consequently as the authentic meeting place of all the religions of the earth? This may be uncontroversial if that cross is interpreted as historic expression of some timeless truth, of which other faiths may be invited to propose their corresponding, alternative images. But that is precisely what Newbigin will not allow.

The critical question will then be whether the Calvary event can be visualized as separate from, and as judicial of, institutionalized Christianity. This must eventually imply that what was immediately a Christian prerogative (first to know of the mystery), at closer observation is outbalanced by a load of guilt (neglectful or even distorted communication of the same mystery). This counterbalance, then, could be thought of as straightening out what might elsewise turn into an undue, immitigable claim of superiority. This may be a crucial question to keep in mind when finally summing up the conclusions of our study.

4.3.2. German "Mainline" Protestantism

We have had ample occasion to commemorate the negative attitude of dominant Continental Protestantism to religion in the second third of our century. This was an attitude not directed against non-Christian religions in the name of "superior" Christian spirituality. The enemy was not the religions – in plural – but religion, primarily as residing within Christendom itself. Intended was a break-up from liberal theology, so closely linked with the self-complacent optimism of modern Western society, an alliance said to have started with the Romantic contemplation of an anthropocentric universe in SCHLEIERMACHER's *Reden über die Religion* (1799) and ending up with the mythologized ethnocentricity of the "Deutsche Christen" in the Nazi era.

The most influential theologian of the following era – with a name still of tremendous programmatic significance – was KARL BARTH (1886–1968). His vision can hardly be brought into the formula of a simple No-to-religion, although it is obvious that his general influence went very much in that direction. His judgement about religion seems to have followed a curve with an absolute low during the German ideological crisis under the Hitler regime. WOLFHART PANNENBERG calls attention to the impressive distance between statements in Barth's *Römerbrief²*, 1922, and his *Kirchliche Dogmatik 1/2*, 1938.[228] HANS KÜNG calls attention to the striking imagery of the one light and the many in the last completed volume (*KD IV/3*) of that *chef-d'oeuvre*, 1959: a turn that may indicate that Barth in the last stage of his reflection has abandoned the confrontative attitude and expresses a new will to accord to religion a role in God's universal plan for humanity.[229]

Similar observations have been made with regard to the leading historian of religion of the "Barthian school": HENDRIK KRAEMER (1888–1965), whose most famous and most influential contribution to that discussion was undoubtedly *The Christian Message in a Non-Christian World*, prepared for the International Missionary Conference in Tambaram, India, 1938. Here religious orientation is interpreted as something fundamentally ambiguous: by fallen man even religion, the most eloquent evidence of being created in God's image, is perverted and exploited as an escape from God. Also in Kraemer's case a subsequent development in a more "open" direction has been observed by critics.[230]

In his survey of various theological approaches to the world of religion(s) PAUL F. KNITTER lists "The Mainline Protestant Model" as a position between "The Conservative Evangelical Model" and "The Catholic Model".[231] As programmatic headlines he proposes the "Salvation only in Christ" of mainline Protestantism, as mediating between the "One True Religion" of conservative Evangelicalism, and the "Many Ways, One Norm" of official Catholicism.[232]

From this synchronization of formulae one easily fancies the profile of such an in-between position. The Protestant "mainliners" claim Christ as the only authentic savior of humankind, without claiming a unique position for Christianity as established religion. For that reason it lacks the need – and also the readiness – of Roman Catholic thought to deal integrally with other faiths in their concreteness.

From the generation of Barth and Kraemer, KNITTER high-lights two names to suggest an orientation rather different from the two – and from the majority of their

---

[228] Compare the positive evaluation: Religion represents "das Göttliche ... ausserhalb des Göttlichen selbst" (= the divine ... outside the divine itself) 1922: 226, n.11, with the absolute negative statement: Religion is "Götzendienst und Werkgerechtigkeit" (= idolatry and justification by works) 1938: 343, n. 7. – "Die spätere Verschärfung der Kritik an der Religion entspricht offensichtlich der Konzentration Barths auf den Begriff der Offenbarung als Gegeninstanz – nicht etwa als Bestandteil – der Religion" (PANNENBERG, in: Bsteh 1987, 184.) – "In the last volume of the 'Church Dogmatics' ... the harsh judgements of the early Barth are mostly missing. One does not need to hypothesize that Barth has changed his mind or contradicted himself, only that he is looking more at the positive side of the dialectic." (Carl E. BRAATHEN 'No Other Gospel!' 1992, 56.)

[229] KÜNG, C 1/1986, 3. – A striking attempt to enroll Barth as a constructive forerunner of a contemporary theology of religions is presented in BERNHARDT 1990, 149–173.

[230] In 'Christian Uniqueness ...', 195, SURIN observes the "liberal exclusivism" – funny expression! – of "the later Kraemer".

[231] KNITTER 1985, 97–119.

[232] Ibid., 97, cf. 75. 120.

day – PAUL ALTHAUS (German Lutheran) and EMIL BRUNNER (Swiss Reformed), whom he sees as chief architects behind the increased openness to religion, which has in the meantime broken through in the subsequent generation of Protestantism, where all the leading names seem to "build on the foundations laid by Althaus and Brunner".[233]

Be this as it may – the positions of these teachers were, as was the period between the two world wars in general – more directed to the problem of religion than to that of religions, and more dedicated to the issue of revelation than to that of communication. The whole challenge of interreligious dialogue had not yet appeared on the theological firmament, and there is no indication that BRUNNER, ALTHAUS or anyone else of the interwar generation hailed, or even foresaw, its coming. The new orientation described, was to proceed from a new generation.

4.3.2.1. Jürgen Moltmann

It may be appropriate to see how the Protestant "mainline" tradition has been carried on and adjusted by two of the most influential Protestant theologians in Germany in the last generation, JÜRGEN MOLTMANN (b. 1926) and WOLFHART PANNENBERG (b. 1928), the former to some extent an offshoot of the Barthian religio-critical tradition, the latter rather an heir to Paul Althaus. They have both been among the chief architects of Protestant theology in their generation, and their attitudes toward interreligious dialogue are solidly rooted in their global theological visions. Also for that reason it may be worthwhile to explore their evaluations of other religions with particular attention to their general orientations.

The fame of JÜRGEN MOLTMANN has been intimately connected with his *Theologie der Hoffnung*, 1964, and with his later series of challenging dogmatical monographies (1980ff) under the joint concept of a "Messianische Theologie".[234] The backbone of Moltmann's theological construction is the Barthian concept of "Heilsgeschichte" (history of salvation): God generating salvation in and through the history of a particular people (Israel). This was utterly accentuated through Moltmann's meeting with ERNST BLOCH's Neo-Marxist *Das Prinzip Hoffnung*, 1954–59: the development of a forward-looking, utopian vision of the world, inspired by the biblical vision "Behold, I make all things new"(Rev 21:5). Moltmann's theological readaptation of Bloch's Bible-related utopianism seems to be the immediate impulse behind the irruption of Latin-American Liberation Theology in the years around 1970, even if Moltmann in posterity has taken clear distance from an indiscriminate identification of political and religious liberation, and few would see him as typical exponent of "Liberation Theology" today.

How does MOLTMANN's "Messianic" vision of history affect his observation of non-Christian religions? There is a remarkable width and at the same time a distinctive narrowness in Moltmann's dialogical horizon. His trinitarian reflections echo a strong

---

[233] Ibid., 97.
[234] A more comprehensive discussion of these basic orientations in Moltmann's theology may be found in LØNNING 1989, 92–99, 102–112, and: KuD 1987/3, 207–223.

appeal for reconciliation between Eastern and Western Christianity, widely accepting the presuppositions of the former.[235] His theology of creation comes close to an identification of Jewish and Christian premises, but gives no sign of a rapprochement to religions other than Judaism, nor of reflection on religion in general.[236] This is particularly remarkable in a theology of creation, supposedly geared to a vision embracing peoples (and creation) in a perspective prior to all history-based commitments. But this is precisely where a "messianic" theology of creation departs from a more conventional creation theology, excluding in principle also the traditional idea of "natural" (= creation-based) religion.

That MOLTMANN, at the same time, lays great stress on presenting his vision as an "ecological doctrine of creation" (subtitle of his "Theology of Creation") reflects a great openness for dialogue with natural science, just like the primary liberation/salvation perspective has left his vision remarkably open for dialogue with historians and social scientists. Precisely on this background, his christianocentric attitude to the world of religions may cause surprise, particularly when dealing with creation faith.

The exceptional status he accords to Judaism may be taken as an expression of the same: the status of this religion is grounded less on a universal vision of nature and of the human species as created in the image of God (Gen 1:27), than on biblical "Heilsgeschichte". In that regard, MOLTMANN's theology has a striking similarity with that of right wing "evangelical" segments, not least certain "fundamentalist" orientations world wide: Judaism makes a case of its own totally independent of (a Christian observation of) other religions. It represents biblical history of salvation as a perspective where all religions – including "Abrahamic" Islam – are viewed as foreigners.

On the other hand, MOLTMANN's "utopian" vision of hope creates a horizon of eschatological openness which prevents him from passing a definitely excluding judgement on people of other faiths, only that the same orientation makes him utterly reticent to penetrating further into that topic.

In spite (or maybe: because?) of his somewhat reserved attitude to the official dialogue polity of the day, MOLTMANN has frequently participated in intrareligious discussions, and his challenging and often stimulating contributions deserve observation. "Only a sharp profile is worthy of dialogue," he proclaims in a discussion of scientists of religion in Tübingen, and he goes on to state that a proclaimed "plurality of religions" is less likely to foster awareness and personal decision than to procreate agnosticism. "The closer you come to the actual depth dimension of a religion, the more difficult becomes the issue of dialogue."[237]

---

[235] 'Trinität und Reich Gottes – Die Lehre von Gott', 1980.

[236] 'Gott in der Schöpfung – Ökologische Schöpfungslehre', 1985. To the (not explicitly restricted) support on Jewish sources (including the Kabbala) for the construction of a Christian theology of creation, see particularly ibid., 13! The striking difference between the positive attitude to Judaism and the remarkable absence of other religions in Moltmann's theology of creation is particularly observed by LØNNING 1987, 215–219.

[237] DdR 2–91, 133.

As might be expected, the domain where Moltmann sees the most constructive possibilities of interreligious dialogue are those not immediately linked with variety of faith, but with questions of peace and practical cooperation. In an issue of *Evangelische Theologie* dedicated to "Dialog der Religionen?" from 1989 he raises the question "Dient die 'pluralistische Theologie' dem Dialog der Weltreligionen?"[238] His contribution is heavily polemical against the repressive tolerance (Herbert Marcuse's expression) of contemporary Western consumers' society. He frankly states:

> "Es gibt solche Formen von religiösem Pluralismus, die nicht der Anfang, sondern das Ende jedes Dialogs sind, weil es sich über solche private Religionen so wenig zu streiten lohnt wie über den persönlichen Geschmack ... Eine 'pluralistische Theologie der Religionen' ist nicht weniger imperialistisch als jene christlichen 'Theologien der Religion', die Knitter überwinden will."[239]

In spite of this, Moltmann suggests a constructive role for a dialogue of mainly practical orientation:

> "Ohne die Rettung der gemeinsamen Welt wird es auch keine Religionen mehr geben. Im Forum der bedrohten Welt werden darum diese Dialoge die Form der Disputation annehmen, die auf Entscheidung und reale Veränderung angelegt sind. Es ist nicht von Ungefähr, dass die meisten Dialoge der Weltreligionen heute auf Friedenskonferenzen stattfinden. Das kann aber nur ein Anfang sein, denn es stehen nicht nur die verschiedenen Auffassungen der Religionen zu Frieden und Gerechtigkeit zur Diskussion, sondern diese selbst mit ihrem Wesen und ihren Funktionen ... dann muss es in den Dialogen um die Herausstellung des Lebensförderlichen in den Religionen gehen."[240]

After all, Moltmann and Küng have lived a long life in the same city (Tübingen), as professors of the same academical discipline (systematical theology), at the Protestant and the Catholic theological faculties respectively.

In *Christian Uniqueness* ... Moltmann again attacks the basic presuppositions of pluralism,[241] even if he makes one pragmatic concession: A "relativistic theory of religion" may be necessary for the USA, given its wide diversity of faiths, but whether this might be a suitable model for the rest of the world, should be a matter of debate rather than a claim of self-evidence.[242] The burden of his contribution this time, however, focuses on four "Lessons from Christian-Marxist dialogue in Europe" to be applied to dialogue in general. These are the following:

> "A life-threatening conflict must be present, a solution to which a dialogue offers hope ...

---

[238] ETh 49/6 1989, 528–536.
[239] Ibid., 531, 535.
[240] Ibid., 536.
[241] 'Is "Pluralist Theology" Useful for the Dialogue of World Religions?', 'Christian Uniqueness ...', 149–156.
[242] Ibid., 155.

All participants must engage in the dialogue from within the context of their own faith or worldview. A dialogue that does not revolve around the question of truth remains irrelevant.

All participants must remain conscious of those for whom they and their inter-locutors speak. If people deviate too far from their roots ... they will eventually end up with being isolated ...

Dialogue should not be carried on 'for the sake of dialogue'. Rather, its motivation should be to change conditions which are life threatening ..."[243]

These statements, kept together with each other and with MOLTMANN's theological outlook at large, should give a rather precise theory of dialogue as issuing less from a theological need for different religions to understand reciprocal ideas of faith in detail, but for taking care of a joint, basic human concern, that of keeping the world (including one's conversation partners) alive.

There is, however, at least one contribution by MOLTMANN which prevents us from interpreting this orientation too simplistically. It is worth observing, that this intervention was launched not in an intrareligious setting of Christian theologians (and/or Occidental scholars of religion) researching joint premises for (Christian) participation in interreligious dialogue, but at an interreligious dialogue event of the most genuine interfaith exchange imaginable. His challenge is a lecture given by the outstanding Buddhist scholar MASAO ABE at the Second Conference on East-West Religious Encounter, in Honolulu, January 1984, where comments to his presentation on "Kenotic God and Dynamic Sunyata" were given by five Christian and one Jewish respondents, one of them being Moltmann himself. The papers of that conference, including a rejoinder by Abe, were published as a book 6 years later.[244]

ABE's concern is to show that "without eliminating the distinctiveness of each religion but rather by deepening their respective unique characters – we find a significant common basis at a deeper dimension." He sees a new possibility for creative dialogue and for the overcoming of antireligious ideologies in today's world through the joint discovery suggested. His observations apply to the motif of *sunyata* in Buddhism and of *kenosis* in Christianity. The former is defined as "a pure and unceasing function of self-emptying, making self and others manifest their suchness", a motif which, as soon as it is understood in its dynamic character, may give new life to Buddhism in the contemporary world. The latter, a Greek word used about the self-emptying of Christ in Phil 2:7, must, in order to maintain consistency, apply also to God-self, and then warrants correspondence on a deeper level between the Buddhist denial of an objectifiable godhead and the Christian understanding of godhead as perceptible only in the mystery of divine self-sacrifice.

Obviously, this reflection by a Buddhist has made a real impression on MOLTMANN. He recommends Abe for an interpretation of the biblical kenosis motif more profound and precise than found in most Christian comments. But he refuses ABE's

[243] Ibid., 154.
[244] COBB & IVES 1990. Abe's paper is found 3–65.

interpretation of Christian doctrine in general as monolithically monotheistic and as stuck in a metaphysical concept of the Trinity – an image of Christianity very much contrary to that championed by Moltmann. But he is thrilled by Abe's sunyatic/kenotic approach, and sees in that a platform of deeper reciprocal understanding by, and of, the two religions, yea, of joint resistance to "the modern mechanical world-view", a distorted view made possible above all by monotheism as championed in traditional Christendom. Even beyond the borders of sunyatic-kenotic understanding outlined by Abe, Moltmann discovers a consonance of the two concepts which to his ear may echo the biblical concepts of Trinity and of Creator/creation.[245]

Immediately one sees, and one does not see, the consistency between MOLTMANN's remarkable utterance here and his positions as already explored. The enthusiastic expression of discovering conformity with an extra-biblical religion in fundamental motifs of faith, seems to burst borders he has otherwise so consistently and confirmatively advocated. On the other hand, Moltmann's concept of godhead is in itself bifrontal. On the one hand, marked by the Barthian tradition, it insists on turning its back to all "natural theology" and observing God from biblical "Heilsgeschichte" alone. On the other hand, rejecting a traditional monotheistic model of thought to the advantage of a "perichoretic" (mutually pervasive) model of trinitarian interrelatedness,[246] what it does, is really to propose a new ontology. But who would accuse Moltmann of inconsistency for expressing joy when he discovers traces of that same ontology in other religions?

The only issue on which an accusation of inconsistency could be raised against Moltmann, would probably relate to his declared attitude to interreligious dialogue in general. Magnifying a particular non-Christian concept so unambiguously as Moltmann at this occasion does with the Buddhist sunyata – as it seems, a rather unique happening in his career – may be consistent with the Messianic orientation of his Creation study: it definitely supports his No to a timeless, monolithic Creator. But it is difficult to see how it fits with the role he has accorded – and predominantly: refused to accord – to the universality of religion, for example in his interpretation of creation in general.

4.3.2.2. Wolfhart Pannenberg

WOLFHART PANNENBERG is definitely not a follower of KARL BARTH; he might sooner be seen as a promoter of what we have seen KNITTER refer to as the ALTHAUS-BRUN-NER tradition. One could say that to him HEGEL's concept of "Freiheit" plays an equally important role as BLOCH's concept of "Befreiung" to MOLTMANN. These are mutually rivaling concepts, not as philologically differing designations of a common

---

[245] MOLTMANN: op.cit. 116–124.

[246] Greek περιχωρεσις = mutual permeation, description of the intratrinitarian relationship, dating back to Johannes Damascenus (ca. 700), and traditionally lodged in Greek Orthodox theology. Taken up by MOLTMANN 1980, 168, 178–194). His purpose is to confront traditional Western monotheism with a social image of God, prefiguring, and reflecting itself in, the structure of the created universe. – Cf. 5.2.2.1. our note 64.

item, but as agents of rivaling enterprises, one of a predominantly anthropological (Pannenberg), the other of a sociological, character (Moltmann).

MOLTMANN's "liberation" can, as expression of a "heilsgeschichtlich"-messianic universe – with all its sociological implications – be adequately observed only from within a biblical horizon. PANNENBERG's "freedom", on the other side, is an anthropological category verifiable by all, offering a criterion which can allegedly be tested out in the light of (global) history. The role of religion is namely to open up the future as the space of human authenticity = freedom, and it is oriented not toward specific social or political circumstances, but toward nothing less than the very realization of humanhood. The truth of Christianity may be observed from the constitutive importance of the gospel for human freedom over the centuries, although an irrefutable proof, in compliance with the very nature of the issue, can be expected only as, and in, the final eschatological realization.

How does this relate to the world of religion(s) and to dialogue? We may start our observations with PANNENBERG's "Erwägungen zu einer Theologie der Religionsgeschichte", contained in his *Grundfragen systematischer Theologie*, published in 1967. This is an essay, previously unpublished, from 1962, but revised and further developed in the meantime. In its original version it thus stems from the pre-dialogue period of European theology, and has received its final form in response, and in challenge, to an era still dominated by the religio-phobia of Neo-Orthodoxy and of its immediate heir: post-Barthian and post-Bonhoefferian secular theology. At the same time the essay is most relevant to – and in more than one way even proleptic of – a subsequent, and essentially changing, epoch.

In its 1967 version the essay opens with a fresh observation of PAUL TILLICH's (1886–1965) posthumous *The Future of Religion*, published 1966. What PANNENBERG finds particularly stimulating about the surprising signals from Tillich at the end of his career, is the demonstration of the disastrous consequences of a proclamatory kerygmatic theology (Neo-orthodoxy, above all in its Barth- and Bultmann-ian versions), which refuses to present Christianity as a religion among religions and, thus, to defend its truth claims in exchange with competitive claims, be it by religions or by secular ideologies.

PANNENBERG's approach to the history of religions is at this stage of events – what many would find hard to imagine today – at the same time comprehensive and outspokenly competitive.

"Die Endgültigkeit der christlichen Offenbarung kann nicht als supranaturale Voraussetzung einleuchten, sondern nur dann, wenn sie sich im Rahmen eines unbefangenen Verständnisses des Gesamtprozesses der allgemeinen Religionsgeschichte ergibt."[247]

"Erst durch die Konkurrenz der verschiedenen Religionen ... erwächst eine gemeinsame Geschichte der Religionen."[248]

---

[247] PANNENBERG 1967, 255.
[248] Ibid., 274.

In this perspective PANNENBERG declares, and claims to demonstrate, "the God prea-ched by Jesus" as "the power of future", far "ahead of" all epochs in the history of the Church and of extra-Christian ("ausserchristliche") religions as well. Thus, the histo-ry of religions, beyond all single events, presents itself as "history of the appearance of the God who has revealed himself through Jesus."[249] – Already here, it is adequate to observe the combination of a universal claim attached to one particular occurrence – God revealing himself "through Jesus" – and a non-discriminatory equality attribut-ed to "the history of the church" and to that of religions in general. Obviously, a full congruence is not claimed between divine "revelation" in Christ and divine "appea-rance" in history, nor is an – obviously genuine – appearance of God in the religions simply to be measured and interpreted by established Christian standards. The bea-ring of this is more precisely stated as follows:

> "... ein unvermitteltes Geltendmachen der ... Beziehung einer Religion zum Christentum
> würde der spezifischen Situation jener anderen Religion ... gar nicht gerecht werden kön-
> nen. Ihre Unmittelbarkeit zum göttlichen Geheimnis zu respektieren, ist auch von der
> christlichen Offenbarung her geboten ... der charakteristische Beitrag christlicher Theolo-
> gie zur Religionswissenschaft (besteht) ... darin, einer unvoreingenommenen Aufgeschlos-
> senheit für das Erscheinen des göttlichen Geheimnisses ... in der Geschichte der Religionen
> Raum zu schaffen ... in jedem Fall zu prüfen, inwieweit die einem religiösen Phänomen
> zugrundeliegende ... Erfahrung des göttlichen Geheimnisses die Daseinswirklichkeit, wie
> sie *damals* erfahren wurde und wie sie sich heutiger Erfahrung darstellt, zu erhellen vermag
> und damit ihren Anspruch bewährt, einen Zugang zum göttlichen Geheimnis selbst zu
> eröffnen." [250]

What is remarkable in this statement – particularly for its time – is that it takes no dogmatic stand on the truth claims of various religions, but refers these to be tested, compared and discussed in the light of common standards, standards not to be prescribed (but certainly to be supported) by Christianity. Such standards are actual-ly proposed by PANNENBERG through his anthropological approach. The discussion between the religions, the ultimate test of their taking each other seriously, will focus on the contribution – and non-contribution – of every one of them to authentic humanhood (= "freedom") in the past, as well as in the present, where people find themselves here now.

To a superficial reader this may sound like the political criteria proposed by some of the "pluralists" we have already visited. But with PANNENBERG's anthropological orientation of "freedom", his research is directed not to some historical appearance, but to the essential truth claims of religions in their eye-to-eye confrontation. How do the focal ambitions of these religions coincide or collide, and how do they finally correspond and not correspond with fundamental criteria of reality? Truth itself is at stake, not only patterns of "right" or "wrong" societal adaptation.

---

[249] "Erscheinungsgeschichte des Gottes ... der sich durch Jesus offenbart hat", Ibid., 292.
[250] Ibid., 294f.

On this background it is most interesting to see how PANNENBERG, looking backward, reacts to the following epoch of interreligious dialogue (and the way in which the dialogue on dialogue has developed). At a first glance a certain discrepancy may suggest itself between his seemingly liberal stand in the 1960's and his overtly conservative position in the 1980's and 90's. But at a second glance an unmistakable continuity manifests itself.

Pannenberg strongly favors a face-to-face encounter of religions in order to confront their truth claims with each other and with anthropological criteria to be jointly explored. Therefore, at a second stage of discussion, he attacks a relativizing "tolerance" which does not find the truth claims of a religion worth discussing – just like he has previously attacked an absolutizing "arrogance" for its escape from discussion via a self-confident No to apologetics.

We shall look at four minor writings, where PANNENBERG in a condensed but explicit format deals with the recent dialogue discussion. His contribution in the frequently quoted *Christian Uniqueness* ...[251] is polemically directed against "a pluralist theology of the world religions", an occurrence which he judges as reflecting "a process of erosion of the confidence of the theologians in the truth of the Christian faith ... a symptom of crisis within the modern Christian mind".[252]

Faithful to his apologetical orientation he sees it, however, essential to clarify the issues raised by the pluralists. In a heated argument with JOHN HICK, PANNENBERG repeats his principal concern: to take any religion seriously is to relate to its own truth claim – this he exemplifies with the Christian understanding of salvation, which he finds distorted in Hick's inoffensive pan-religious talk of a changed life-style.

"Human experiences of salvation are as ambiguous as other human experiences ... communion with God, the God of Israel and of Jesus ... is promised to Christians, provided they do not desert their faith ... communion in Christ in whom they trust, not in themselves as they can be looked upon in abstraction from Christ ... how could it be less ambiguous in the case of the non-Christians? We may hope that God will look graciously upon them as we hope for ourselves. But one difference remains: the Christian has the promise of God in Christ. The other religious traditions do not provide that particular promise ..."[253]

This is a vision which comes close to the distinction recently voiced by evangelicals in the USA between ontic universalism and epistemological particularism. We can put no limit to God's saving grace – neither in order to reserve it for ourselves nor to deprive it from others – but recognition of God as the God of saving grace is unseparably linked with proclamation of the gospel. The sharp profile of this message is not drawn by PANNENBERG in order to seclude religions other than Christianity, but to seclude what he sees as the pluralist surrender of religious authenticity, that of Christians and of non-Christians alike.

---

[251] 'Religious Pluralism and Conflicting Truth Claims – The Problem of a Theology of the World Religions", op.cit., 96–106.

[252] Ibid., 97.

[253] Ibid., 104.

'Gott eint – trennt Christus? – Die Einmaligkeit und Universalität Jesu Christi als Grundlage einer Theologie der Religionen ausgehend vom Ansatz Wolfhart Pannenbergs' is the title of a dissertation from the University of Tübingen by the Indian Catholic Theologian GEORG AUGUSTIN.[254] This study is remarkable in several ways. Its orientation is essentially different from the liberal attitude of several Indian theologians of religion and also distinguishes itself from what is commonly seen as a Catholic ("inclusivist") tradition.[255] It explicitly refers to the Lutheran PANNENBERG as its guide in the contemporary landscape, and Pannenberg's "Geleitwort" (preface) indirectly confirms an acceptance of his image as presented by the study. Augustin intends to get beyond the "negative theology" of our day, stuck as it is with the memory of ancient colonialism in the consciences of super-progressive Westerners or in the minds of complex-ridden Easterners. He wishes also to avoid "the Enlightenment fundamentalism" of pluralism, as much as the plain fundamentalism of outdated exclusivism.[256] Evidently in the spirit of Pannenberg, the following program is announced, although, may we remark, with a certain rhetorical ornamentation:

> "... eine 'positive' Theologie der Religionen, die aus dem Geist des christlichen Realismus entsteht, die Sinntotalität der Wirklichkeit darstellt, das Wesentliche im Christentum vom Unwesentlichen unterscheidet, die Tiefe und Breite, die inneren Zusammenhänge und die Schönheit des christlichen Glaubens im Dialog mit den anderen Religionen und den Wissenschaften aufzeigt, den Menschen befreiend begeistert."[257]

A further precision by PANNENBERG himself could be brought in by an essay in Theologische Quartalschrift in 1989, where he asks about the importance of other religions for the self-understanding of Christian theology.[258] Attention is called to "the claim of eschatological finality attached to the figure of Jesus" as indispensible to Christian theology and, at the same time, as destructive of all dogmatic intolerance. It (dis-)qualifies all theological accomplishments as preliminary and as directed toward a fulfilment beyond human control.

In PANNENBERG's perspective this adds an argument to the ones in favor of Christian doctrine, since it restricts theological truth ambitions to the level of human cognition in general. This very orientation keeps the possibility open of other religions as vehicles of truth, even if it must be asserted that the ultimate salvation also of non-Christians is effected through Christ and "not through the institutions of their own religions", even if they may have experienced the theme of salvation as actualized in their own contexts of worship. Pannenberg sees the word Luk 13:29 about people coming to the feast of the Kingdom from all the corners of the earth, as an assurance that "belonging to Jesus is not limited to those explicitly confessing him", but

---

[254] Paderborn 1993.
[255] HILLMAN 1989. – Cf. KNITTER 1985, 120–44, and: C 1986, 63–68.
[256] AUGUSTIN 1993, 9, 369.
[257] Ibid., 10.
[258] 'Die Religionen als Thema der Theologie', ThQ 1989/2, 99–110.

"even in such statements Jesus and his message make the criterion for sharing salvation".[259]

One can say that here the dialectic of "ontic universality / epistemological particularity" is further elaborated. The vision of eschatological finality relativizes any dimension of religious performance. This has, at the same time, a constructive, unifying consequence: other religions can be accorded (preliminary) cultic and doctrinal truth as activating the same horizon of unmanipulable ultimacy as does Christianity.

Aspects of this orientation are further elaborated in a contribution at the Religionstheologische Studientagung St.Gabriel, April 1986.[260] PANNENBERG's paper on that occasion carries the character of a compendium of a theology of interreligious dialogue. But particularly striking in our context are two features: his explanation of "Jesus and his message" as the final eschatological criterion for salvation of all people, and certain concrete observations on possibilities of dialogue with the major world religions. After having confirmed and somewhat elaborated the dialectical universality/ particularity aspect already mentioned, he goes on:

> "Wie im Endgericht die Botschaft Jesu das Kriterium für die Heilsteilhabe jedes einzelnen Menschen sein wird, so wird auch der Christ die außerchristlichen Religionen auf ihre Nähe oder Ferne zur Botschaft Jesu zu befragen haben, und die Urteilsbildung darüber wird in jedem Einzelfall anders ausfallen. Der sachlich naheliegendste Ausgangspunkt für eine solche Urteilsbildung ist zweifellos Jesu Botschaft von Gott ... Eng damit verbunden ist freilich die Zuwendung zum Mit-Menschen, die der in der Sendung Jesu offenbaren Zuwendung Gottes selbst zu den Menschen entspricht und im Gleichnis vom Weltgericht in Mt 25 das Kriterium bildet für das Urteil ..."[261]

One may ask if this isn't just too much and too little at the same time. Too much in terms of knowing and asserting. Too little in terms of clarifying the soteriological assumptions behind. Ultimate criterion for an answer would be PANNENBERG's own claim of authentic self-presentation by each religion to meet in honest and respectful dialogue, with no particular privileges to Christianity.

The first concretizing subquestion would then be whether a horizon of eschatological finality, as the one drawn by PANNENBERG, permits a doctrine concerning the eternal fate of people of other faiths, i.e. of someone not immediately addressed by, and thus actually unable to respond to, the message of salvation which you preach. Can final salvation be proclaimed as anything but a promise, offered to one actually listening, i.e. as an existential communication to a potential receiver? For those not yet reached by the gospel, the ones conveying it can express hope and eventually search for patterns of fulfilment in a biblical perspective in general. But neither personal hopes nor arbitrary guesses can be incorporated in the Creed. Doesn't Pannen-

---

[259] Ibid., particularly 108–110.

[260] 'Religion und Religionen – Theologische Erwägungen zu den Prinzipien eines Dialogs mit den Weltreligionen', in: BSTEH 1987, 179–196.

[261] Op.cit., 190.

berg in the text we now consider go further in that direction than his declared premises permit?

The second subquestion would be whether the role attributed to Jesus in PANNENBERG's eschatological scenario is in full consistency with the christological orientation of his own theology, and – not to forget – with the general biblical and confessional standards which he usually pleads. As we have seen, "Jesus and his message" presented as the criterion of eschatological judgement, do not presuppose explicit knowledge of Jesus, nor a conscious decision to act in accordance with his teaching. What matters is practical conformity with the attitude toward God and neighbor taught by Jesus, whichever may be one's source of information. Jesus is here the one informing us of the standards of judgement – but is he anything in addition to that? To us and/or to those not informed of his teachings?

Let us go back to the way in which PANNENBERG phrases his equal hope for Christians and non-Christians in *The Uniqueness ...!*[262] Seeing the essence of Christianity as a communion with God "in Christ in whom they trust, not in themselves ... in abstraction from Christ ...," he goes on by asking: "... how could it be less ambiguous in the case of the non-Christians?" Here Christ is presented as something far more than a teacher of moral standards or a judge to appear on the last day, but how was that reflected in his use of Mt 25 in the St. Gabriel paper? How does the proclamation a few years later of God's saving grace as equally available to Christians and non-Christians fit with a reflection which leaves the latter group to a judgement according to "works" – the person of Christ being present to Non-Christians only as a nameless authority, the one to reveal himself on the last day and assess their deeds, and pronouncing a final judgement accordingly?

Probably one is closer to PANNENBERG's idea of interreligious relationships in his quick but lucid remarks (1987) on the prospects of exchange with regard to the most visible contemporary dialogue partners of Christianity. He starts with observing a restricted group of religions which immediately articulates itself by "worshiping and believing the same God as the message of Jesus, the God of Israel, being also the God of the Muslims". Even if the understanding of God is different in Judaism, Christianity and Islam, they have a common historic root in the biblical tradition. As far as they are conscious of this fact, they will also be conscious of worshiping one and the same God. The classical controversy on Trinitarian belief versus monotheism is dealt with in the following way:

"Der Monotheismus des Alten Testaments ist für den Christen unaufgebbare gemeinsame Basis mit dem Glauben der Juden und der Muslime. Aber er wird doch nicht als trinitarischer Monotheismus erfasst, weil er nicht vom Primat der Eschatologie her verstanden wird, die in der Verkündigung Jesu zu einem Verständnis des Gottes Israels und zur Neubegründung der Situation des Menschen vor Gott im Lichte des ersten Gebotes führte. Die christliche Theologie hat im Dialog mit den Juden (und auch gegenüber dem Islam) zu zeigen, dass gerade das trinitarische Gottesverständnis erst wirklich konsequent monotheis-

---

[262] 'Christian Uniqueness ...', 104, cf. our quotation, note 253!

tisch ist, weil es Gott nicht einseitig in seiner Transzendenz ... denkt, sondern als ... zugleich auch immanent und daher als umgreifend."[263]

For conversation partners not particularly versed in PANNENBERG's eschatological ontology – as may easily be the case with partners in an interreligious conversation, at least – it is probably easier to understand the second argument (Trinitarian faith challenging an exclusively transcendent concept of God) than the first (Trinitarian consequences of the primacy of eschatology).

PANNENBERG sees the relationship with Jews and that with Muslims as similar and as different at the same time.[264] He finds "a comparatively larger openness" in the dialogue between Jews and Christians, while the message of Jesus started as "a Jewish possibility, emerged from Jewish traditions". So, Jews can concern themselves about "bringing Jesus home to Judaism" and Christians may hope that the Jewish people will finally recognize its own Messiah in Jesus from Nazareth. With Muslims, however, after the clearing away of mutual misunderstandings, there will still remain the opposition of "the eschatological claim of Jesus" and "the prophecy of Mohammed". There may be no other way of getting beyond that stalemate than the one or the other part giving up its claim of "eschatological liability" (Verbindlichkeit). But – Pannenberg asks – would that be possible without the one, the other, or both renouncing their identity?

The relationship with "the great religions of the East" PANNENBERG sees as, not only practically but also theologically, less confusing than that with Islam, even if it can be historically asserted that Christians and Muslims "worship the same God". For the prospects of dialogue, clear-cut differences are not always the most difficult to assess. Christians and Buddhist are in dispute as to whether there is a God at all, and Christians and Hindus discuss, whether the one God is identical with the God of the Old Testament. Even if dialogue does not open up for unity in the sense of ecumenical dialogue between churches, Pannenberg is ready to admit that:

> "Auch der interreligiöse Dialog eröffnet die Chance gegenseitiger Bereicherung der großen religiösen Traditionen der Menschheit. Aber Einheit wäre hier nur erreichbar durch eine Veränderung der Identität hindurch ... so ist es auch schwer, sich vorzustellen, dass Hindus und Buddhisten die Einmaligkeit, Unwiederholbarkeit und absolute Bedeutung des geschichtlich Besonderen überhaupt und darum auch ganz bestimmte geschichtliche Ereignisse und Personen ihrem Denken einordnen könnten ..."[265]

The interesting thing for us here is to observe a statement like this as part of PANNENBERG's theological orientation at large. To trifle away the seemingly irreconcilable truth claims of various religions is least of all what he wants. Therefore dialogue, in his opinion, should consist in confronting, not circumventing, competing claims. So

---

[263] Op.cit., 191f.

[264] We have already seen that two compatriots of his own generation regard it either as moreover similar (Hans Küng) or as principally different (Jürgen Moltmann).

[265] Ibid., 196.

he resists any theological theory based on the assumption that the religions of the world, if only rightly understood, "speak about the same thing". He further insists that the relativizing tolerance of contemporary pluralism represents a disintegrating Christian identity as well as a repressive Western attitude toward other cultures.

In spite of these observations, however, he voices confidence not only in the possible salvation of people outside the rank and file of professing Christians. He also accepts a possible mediating role of other faiths in waking to life in their followers volitions and attitudes corresponding to those intended by the preaching of Jesus. These religions, thus, to a certain extent, comply to the standards of ultimate judgement. His seemingly well-balanced solution to the underlying dilemma, by means of "eschatological finality", may make his combination of contrasting concerns sound less paradoxical than it may appear through the simple juxtaposition of single elements. But what may we, finally, conclude from that? The answer seems by no means unambiguous.

5. Dialogue: Religion and Religions

The importance of locating *inter*religious dialogue in a setting of *intra*religious reflection has been – indirectly, but strongly – confirmed by our review of contemporary
Christian discussion on the relationship with non-Christian faiths. Our assumption
is that a similar distinction must be equally relevant within other faith communities.
To every community concerned with dialogue, the former will, in principle, have to
be preceded, encompassed, and succeeded by the latter.

In order to exemplify this assumption, the following part of our study will visit
major faith communities particularly involved in the dialogue process, for concrete
observations. We shall listen to voices from within as well as to informed observers
from outside the communities concerned. Viewing the magnitude and the complexity of the scene, it is evident that such a review will present itself as limited and to
a certain extent casual. But on the present stage of events circumspections of a
seemingly arbitrary kind may be necessary as preparations for the progress toward a
common survey – provided that the limitations of each project are kept in mind, and
that the incompleteness of one's observations may serve as supplementary to that of
several others.

Before envisaging that task, it may, however, be useful to view more explicitly a
dimension of dialogue which, for at least two hundred years, has been particularly
conducive to a Christian understanding of 'we and the others': the use of the term
"religion". In general this has been a vehicle to confirm and/or delimit Christian
identity in relation to other (similar, comparable, competing) identities. In the history of theological (and philosophical) reflection it has also to a not unimportant extent
served as a universal designation of fundamental commitment. 'Religion' as a universal has generally signalized a common human disposition and/or attitude in relation
to ultimate truth. Commonly it will, especially when unmodifed by some critical
reflection, exercise directive influence both on the general orientation toward an ultimate goal and on the appreciation of corresponding orientations of others. Some
indication of such a reflection ought definitely to be offered.

5.1. "Religion": A Concept Relevant?

We have seen that the World Council of Churches did not follow the language of the
Roman Catholic Church, extending its invitation to "Non-Christian Religions"
(1965, official English translation),[1] but chose to stretch forward the hand to "people

---

[1] Latin: Secretariatus pro Non-Christianis, 1989 changed to: Consilium pro Dialogo inter Religiones.

of living faiths and ideologies" (1971). In the meantime the terminologies have been changed to "... Dialogue between religions" (Rome, 1989) and "... Interreligious relations" (WCC, 1991) respectively. The differences of language between the two segments of Christianity may indicate not only slightly divergent orientations of polity, but a partly differing concept of living faiths as established entities. The latest change of terminology within the WCC may suggest two things: the necessity of a less lyrical vocabulary than 20 years before with a more down-to-earth naming of actual development, and "inter-religious" may advocate a less biased attitude to "religion"/"religious" in Protestant theological language than in the first round.

The word "religio" has a rather complex history in Western Christianity, as it has in relevant disciplines of academical studies. Discussion on the suitability of the term for an understanding of relationships between differing faith traditions may be of importance for: history, phenomenology, philosophy, psychology and sociology of religion(s), and equally for theology understood as the self-interpretation of any such tradition.

Early Christianity was not inclined to speak of itself as a "religio", but rather preferred terms like "fides", "secta", "lex", "via".[2] In the further history of Latin-based European civilization "religio" turned its back to the etymological speculations of Roman Antiquity and was gradually adopted by Medieval Christian philosophy – rather than by practical devotion – and then for a more or less explicit underscoring of the universal validity of Christianity. The Renaissance adds to the term an aroma of individual, subjective choice, whereas the Enlightenment in its more consistent form ends up with a construct of dehistoricized "natural" religion as superior to any historical revelation, including Christianity.

A distinctive turn takes place with Romanticism (HERDER, SCHLEIERMACHER, COLERIDGE), where the predominance of historical religion and its integrative role in cultural formation are again brought to the fore. In the Neo-protestant development, which came to an eventual collapse with World War I, Christianity was finally seen as the (hitherto?) supreme actualization of religion, which actually meant: of the essential human quest for universal integration.[3] It should be noticed, however, that through its integration in pre-war Western culture, the liberal theology of the age, in its optimistic, humanistic outlook, undeniably combined religious tolerance as a much cherished ideal with a massive socio-cultural condescendence, domestically and not less worldwide. In the world of post-darwinian evolutionism, it was granted that some civilizations – their religious orientations included – resided on a higher level of development than others. "Primitive religion" was a beloved term characteristic of the feeling of scientific, cultural and missionary superiority in Europe (and North-America) anno 1900.

A shift of paradigm no less dramatic than that of Romanticism a good hundred

---

[2] To this and the following, see: RATSCHOW 1979, further: FEIL 1986, and WAARDENBURG 1986.
[3] As the most consistent expression is usually regarded Ernst TROELTSCH's refusal of Christian "absoluteness", 'Der Historismus und seine Überwindung', Tübingen 1924.

years earlier, was intoned by dialectical theology around 1920. The post-war reaction to Occidental evolutionary optimism, for good reasons, started in war-broken Germany. Nowhere was the experience of "crisis" more eloquently expressed than in OSWALD SPENGLER's *Untergang des Abendlandes* (1918–22).[4] The Dialectical theology (or: Theology of Crisis, as it was commonly called in the beginning) of KARL BARTH, EMIL BRUNNER, FRIEDRICH GOGARTEN a.o. could in several regards be seen as a preparation for, and as an equivalent of, the break-through of existential philosophy a few years later: MARTIN HEIDEGGER, KARL JASPERS, EBERHARD GRISEBACH a.o.

In Dialectical theology the reaction to "religion" had little to do with Occidental arrogance and denigration of Non-Western cultures. On the contrary, that reaction must be seen as an expression of an extreme self-criticism on behalf of the Occident – with Christendom and its self-asserting theology as culprit no. 1. The attack on religion aimed primarily at human confidence in own religious possession, now attacked as an landmark of dominant Occidental preaching for generations.

For the sake of survey it should also be kept in mind that the epoch between the two World wars viewed other impressive critical approaches to 'religion' than Continental-based Dialectical theology. A remarkable Yes-and-No to religion emerged with the Swedish Lundensian school of theology ("Lundateologien": AULÉN, NYGREN, BRING a.o.). Here post-Kantian philosophy with its affirmative construction of 'religion' was further developed and – in a certain, not unimportant, sense – overcome. What remained, was KANT's confirmation of human cognition as structured by a series of unmistakable a priori's.

In the Lundensian adaptation 'religion' was, as in KANT, developed as the final expression of ethical rationality, not as the fundamental human experience of universal belonging ("schlechthinige Abhängigkeit": Schleiermacher), but as a basal category of 'eternity', initiating the unity of all cognitive categories. The question thus underlying all our questions is then seen as the one which all historical religions try to respond to, and their competing answers may be synchronized through a "motif research". The answers are many – the question is one![5]

The categorical answer of Christianity, its "ground motif", turns out to be "Agape", divine love as unmotivated generosity. The name of ANDERS NYGREN is above all connected with his impressive study 'Eros and Agape', which in its comparison between the Greek "Eros" (love as human desire for ultimate perfection) and the Christian "Agape" (love as unlimited generosity) shows how Christianity during the centuries, starting with Augustine, has been deprofiled through compromises with Hellenic Platonism.[6]

---

[4] The official English translation 'The Decline of the West' sounds weaker than the German original. The semantic specter of "Untergang" stretches from an ordinary sunset to ruin = full destruction, with a strong bend toward the latter. But, as one may see it: Britain, at that time, had lost no world war, Germany had!

[5] Anders NYGREN: Religiöst apriori, Lund 1921.

[6] Classical monument, Anders NYGREN: Den kristna kärlekstanken I-II, Stockholm 1930/36.

The most challenging thing about the Lundensian approach, in our present context, is how a consistently deductive application of the concept "religion" can be used to explore and give profile to the distinctive character of one particular religion. NYGREN's historical analysis, which, in a solid Kantian succession, pretends to be purely descriptive and to speak no value judgement, takes no formal stand on the right of certain Christian emphases against others, nor on the truth of Christianity versus that of other religions.

The message of NYGREN's "motif research", then, may be simplified as follows: Religion is basic to all human orientation, posing, as it does, the very integrating question of human culture. More than any other item, it therefore deserves to be explored. Religion, at the same time, can only be realized in the plurality of historical entities, i.e. in the shape of living faiths. And such faiths actually give different, mutually exclusive answers to the one, common question. Thus, they face us with another question, which cannot be decided by research, but requires a decision of faith: Which of these answers, if any, may be the authentic one? In a nutshell: All religion is solidly unified – as far as the basic, transcendental question is concerned. Historical religion is diversified and cannot be synthesized – actuality means confrontation.

Even if interreligious dialogue was not on the agenda in the period of Lundensian triumph (the second third of the 20th century), a further conclusion could easily be drawn: scholarly based dialogue may be an important vehicle to remind the contemporary world of the indispensability of religion, and to clarify the differences of character of existing religions as seen by each one of them. How such dialogue may affect the further relationship between them, is a different issue, and was not really up for discussion at that stage of events.

When the Lundensian theology of religion(s) has not much of a bearing on contemporary intrareligious dialogue, it may be due to the fact that it – with all its fame in the years around World War II – was more or less out of the arena when the challenge of dialogue was launched a good generation later. At that time the reputation of "motif research", after its initial triumph as an unmatchable clue to Christian self-understanding, was rather an accusation of fostering unduly simplified comparisons. Its strictly theoretical approach likewise gave little promise of rapid practical accomplishments. – But a fundamental question was raised, which has not been answered by posterity: could a dialectic combining religion (in singular) and religions (in plural) be fruitful: an analytical avenue to a universal question, eventually inviting a systematical comparison of actually available answers? Could such a synchronization open up a new perspective for meaningful dialogue, or would it just present another opportunity for advocates of one tradition to silence those of another?

Different from the instant spiritual upheaval following World War I, it took around twenty years for the wide-ranging cultural consequences of World War II to become visible. In theology, the single impulse which came most deeply to affect the climate in the mid 1960's was, however, definitely one dating back to the wartime. DIETRICH BONHOEFFER (1906–45), the much celebrated German martyr theologian, had written his explosive collection of notes, posthumously published under the title *Widerstand und Ergebung*,[7] while waiting for his final fate in a prison cell in Berlin.

BONHOEFFER's shocking question was this: "We are proceeding toward a time of no religion at all ... How do we speak of God without religion ... How do we speak in a secular fashion of God?"[8] It is not easy to interpret his surprising statements about secularity, a "world come of age", and faith in Christ "without religion". In its historical setting, though, it is less important what Bonhoeffer meant, than how his challenge was understood and responded to in aftermath, not least by the "Secular theology" wave of the mid and late 60-s, which so expressively declared itself the authentic heir to his legacy.

Two, in format very different, monuments of this theology may serve as particularly illuminating. The theological bestseller, HARVEY COX: *The Secular City* gives a systematized and popularized elaboration of the general theory most comprehensively elaborated by the Dutch religionist AREND TH. VAN LEEUWEN: *Christianity in World History – The Meeting of the Faiths of East and West.*[9] The main thesis is that of the Bible as the great source of secularization, which liberates its believers from the tyranny of a sacralized world with its infinity of irrational taboos. Biblical faith in a truly transcendent God leaves the earth open to the rule of human rationality. Biblical revelation liberates humanity from religion, understood as an obsolete vehicle of divine statutes and regulations.

This vision implicitly defines extra-biblical religion as inferior and makes it dependent on biblical instruction for discovering the secular meaning of created life. Cox sees this glorious liberation as fulfilled in the emerging contemporary urban society, liberated from the chains of oppressive neighborhoods. In the modern metropolis a world is taking shape where the pressure of village expectation exists no more, and individual self-determination is unrestricted. To Cox, who makes an amazingly literalistic use of biblical quotations, the apocalyptic image of the Sacred City, the New Jerusalem descending from heaven (Rev 21), is seen as realized in the rapidly expanding metropolis of the 1960's.

It is unnecessary now to describe how and why this vision, widely observed and acclaimed as it was for a handful of years, did not live long into the 1970's. This had, among other things, to do with the "Green wave" as a reaction against Occidental self-admiration. A new veneration for "religion" and "religions" emerged from a discovery contrary to that of VAN LEEUWEN and COX: a rediscovery of the role of the "taboo" for preserving creation in its integrity. "The secular city" was suddenly discovered as the domicile, not of unlimited freedom and undisturbed self-realization, but of unlimited waste, pollution and inhumanity.

Now the turn had come for the great religions of the East to be exalted for their reverential attitude toward the universe and its mystery as expressed in symbolic ter-

---

[7] 1951. British edition: Letters and Papers from Prison, 1953 – American: Prisoner for God, 1959.
[8] (30.4.1944), ed. 1959, 123
[9] VAN LEEUWEN 1964. Cox: The Secular City, 1965.

restrial elements (taboos). A similar elevation took place of indigenous religion worldwide, with particular reverence to North American native culture and its heroic cen-
tury-long resistance to "White" exploitation. Now, as Secular theology was turned
upside down and its colorful theses reversed, the fall gave rise to heavy accusations
against the biblically rooted faiths: Judaism, Christianity, Islam. The three "Abrahamic religions" – with their square distinction between Creator and creature, and with
their joint maxim "Subdue the earth" (Gen 1:28) – were once more confirmed as the
sources of "secularity", but this time not as laudation for their heroic liberation of
humankind, but for their treason to what should have been the very vision of religion: that of sacred awe in face of creation – and, no less, for their contempt of sister
religions sensitive to that responsibility.[10]

The remarkable return of a religious universe in the 1970's must be seen as a
cultural no less than a theological event, even if the reorientation initially was only to
a minor extent instructed, or even accompanied, by a fundamental reexamination of
'religion'. An interaction between theology in specific and culture at large became
conspicuous in these events, as it had been at the previous stages reported: in the pre-
World-War-I era of humanist religiosity, in the existentialist break-up of the 1920's,
and in the post-bonhoefferian celebration of secularity in the 1960's. Even if the
trend-setting role of theology has been massively reduced in Western society from the
13th to the 20th century ...

In English-speaking Christianity, as in the Roman Catholic world, the No-to-
religion had never been as emphatic as in Continental Protestantism. The American
explosion of "secular theology" in the 1960's rather makes an exception in that regard. German-American PAUL TILLICH (1886–1965) with his orientative focus on
religion as "ultimate concern", invited a more dialectical evaluation of religion as
category than Continental theology had done, and, much observed as he was, he
provided a bridge between the continents. In his later years he showed growing interest for adapting the empirical world of religions into his theological vision, and
developed this in practical cooperation with the influential and enthusiastic Chicago
historian of religion MIRCEA ELIADE (1907–1886), of Romanian Orthodox background, who had formed a school by his fundamental plea for congenial penetration
into the world of faiths.

The most controversial contribution to a reassessment of the notion of 'religion',
was probably the one by WILFRIED CANTWELL SMITH (b. 1916), a historian and a
philosopher of religion at the Center for the Study of World Religions at Harvard.
We have already met Smith as active in the interreligious dialogue controversy, boldly
lodged in the camp of "pluralists" (4.1.3). At the same time his profile in a noteworthy way distinguishes itself from that of HICK/KNITTER, namely through his
more thorough, critical preoccupation with the determinant concept: religion. In

---

[10] For elucidation of this problematic and of the "turn of tides": secularity / religion around 1970, see
also LØNNING 1989, particularly the chapter 'Culture speaks on Creation', 45–55, and the wider section
'Creation – Actuall Theological Confrontations', 89–164.

The Meaning and End of Religion (1962) he comments on four different senses of this word:

"First, there is the sense of a personal piety ... Secondly and thirdly, there is the usage that refers to an overt system, whether of beliefs, practices, values, or whatever ... (with) an extension in time, some relation to an area ... related to a particular community ... specific. In this sense, the word has a plural and in English the singular has an article. In each case, however, there are two contrasting meanings: one of the system as an ideal, the other, of it as an empirical phenomenon, historical and sociological ... Hence insiders and outsiders use the same word while talking of different things. Finally ... 'religion' as a generic summation, 'religion in general' ... The first sense discriminates religion in a man's life from indifference (or rebellion). The second and third (possibly intermingled) discriminate one religion from another. The fourth discriminates religion from other aspects of human life ..."[11]

This linguistic analysis, uncontroversial as it may be in itself, is not presented by SMITH for a purely descriptive purpose. He wants to show that the word 'religion' is one that scientific research – and every-day life as well – may fare better without.

"My own suggestion is that the word, and the concepts, should be dropped ... the term 'religion' is confusing, unnecessary and distorting ... the vitality of personal faith ... and ... progress in understanding ... of the traditions of other people throughout history and throughout the world, are both seriously blocked by our attempt to conceptualize what is involved in each case in the terms of (a) religion.

The proposal ... is that what men have tended to conceive as religion and more especially as a religion, can more rewardingly, more truly, be conceived in terms of two factors ...: an historical 'cumulative tradition', and the personal faith of men and women."[12]

Let us raise the question equally simply and direct it to SMITH himself: where does this proposal take us? Does the author limit himself to saying that keeping track of his four meanings is so confusing a task that it would be wise to stick with a more differential vocabulary? That could be a minor issue in itself, and we need not spend much time arguing for or against his thesis, not even to dispute whether an expression like "an historical 'cumulative tradition'" may be just as clarifying a tool for our common purpose. But from the argumentative setting of his argument – more than from the statements quoted – we get an impression that something more is intended.

The issue seems finally to be one of terminology less than one of substance. He obviously sees no complications with the word as applied to the spiritual experience of individuals (his sense no. 1) or to the universal dimension of orientation open to all (sense no. 4). SMITH may get in certain difficulties if challenged to clarify the senses 2 and 3, which relate to particular "religions". Certainly, he is ready to admit that religious life – be it as distinctive experience by individuals, or be it as universal dimension equally accessible to all – is commonly related to the existence of specific faith communities, the images of which reflect the tension between their own vision

---

[11] Ed. 1978 (paperback), 48f.
[12] Ibid., 50, 194.

of an ideal identity and an appearance immediately visible to outsiders. But the importance of such observations seems rather difficult to assess.

The pivotal point is that SMITH seems reluctant to give "religions" in concreto a validity of their own. The dignity of religion belongs exclusively to "religious life", understood, in all its differentiations, as a universal occurrence. Thus actual religions remain subordinate to 'religion', as does (social) incorporation to (psychological) individuation. Would it be unjust to infer: concreteness yields to abstraction?

Whether this understanding of SMITH's *no* to 'religion' is right, must be tested by the general rule: 'proof of the pudding is the eating'. We have already seen his particular contribution so eloquently summarized by JOHN HICK, who describes it as rejection of Renaissance reification of faith, a reification obtained by inventing the terms 'a religion'/'different religions' to provide a verbal sacralization of institutionalized human divisions.[13]

We have earlier seen SMITH's criticism of 'religion' exemplified in two of his own texts, which may be of interest to recall also in the present setting. First: his crushing criticism of the term 'Christian Theology', which he calls 'a contradiction in terms'.[14] As logical accomplishment this statement is conclusive only if 'theology' has as object an unambiguously circumscribable research object: "theos" = God, accessible to exploration irrespective of faith commitments. But this is a difficult claim to sustain. Even if it might be possible to fancy the profile of such a universalized objective theology, it would be an unhistorical construct. And, what is equally obvious: its claim of universal validity would be far from compelling in the way his claim goes. Contrary to all assertions, HICK's applause as expressed in the depreciative term 'reification' strikes backward: only a massive reification of the 'Theos', the focal object of 'theology', could possibly motivate the claim of one single, universally valid and cross-culturally integrable theology.

The other text already visited was SMITH's contribution in *The Myth of Christian Uniqueness*, focusing on "Idolatry" and the idolatrous consequences of relating religious faith to single 'religions' and/or to historically limited elements of faith.

> "Each 'religion' is an 'idol' in the best sense of the word, if one were going to use these words at all. Exclusive claims for one's own is idolatry in the pejorative sense ... Christianity – for some, Christian theology – has been our idol."[15]

That the question of idolatry is raised in such a provocative way, may stimulate self-critical reflection in all camps. The problem is, however, that without a more precise delimitation of the terms 'idol' and 'idolatry' any claim by a particular religion to point out authentic truth in a distinctive message may be judged as idolatrous. In the wide world of faiths, SMITH's attack on idolatry may easily be observed as another expression, not of alleged pre-renaissance religious innocence, but of 20th century relativism.

[13] HICK 1985, 28f.
[14] SMITH (in: Swidler 1987), 224–230.
[15] Idem (in: HICK & KNITTER 1987), 60f.

With regard to SMITH's proposed restrictions on the use of the term 'religion', the question arises whether they do not, at the same time, place intolerable restrictions on the matter at hand: abolishing the right of a religion to define its own identity and thus even to invite dialogue. His denial of "religions" in the plural, limits the freedom of a faith community to speak out what its believers perceive as their common identity. What does his rapid recurrence to 'idolatry' as critical principle confirm if not the same?

Characteristic as SMITH's obviously unrestricted recommendation of interreligious exchange may be of the contemporary pluralist camp, his reflections on the key term 'religion' in part move in a direction opposite to solidly established opinions in contemporary studies. Consciously, these normally present themselves not as pertaining to "religion" in the singular – a universal – but to "religions" in the plural, the wide variety of distinctive specimens. This linguistic practice underscores the empirical character of religious studies, geared to the world of faiths as it presents itself in actuality, not to some universal construct.

In the Kantian approach, further developed, as described, by the Lundensian school, the situation is different. Here "religion" as a transcendental category is not an abstract intended to squeeze a common essence out of a number of different-looking phenomena. It is a formative principle observing the space of various phenomena in a preestablished cognitive universe. So, thus, we discern two irreconcilable epistemologies. A world of different "religions" is as absent in a trancendentalist's outlook as is "religion", as a universal, in that of an empiricist. Like NYGREN, SMITH may appear as a transcendentalist rooted in the Kantian tradition, but from there he refuses to proceed. Unlike Nygren, he halts and regards his general concept of religion not as a fundamental question inviting a variety of – maybe contradicting – answers, but as containing the answer in itself, thus prescribing definite borders to what can be allowed of actual variety.

In this way SMITH turns his back on the actuality of mutually challenging religions, allowing concrete observations only to confirm a universality already defined.

SMITH's highly debatable observation of the Renaissance as refashioning the term "religion" fits well into that construction, and so does the alleged simultaneous transformation of 'theology' from a global to a one-faith enterprise. But both these changes are – to the extent that traces of them can really be identified – better explained by an extended world image in the age of the great explorations and beginning colonial expansion, than by some sudden restriction of Medieval openness. That a general narrowing of a multi-religious horizon should take place precisely in the Renaissance, is in itself an assumption which would demand a good deal of elaboration in order to gain credibility.

To a remarkable extent SMITH's thesis, if taken seriously, will curtail dialogue between religions, even if the pronounced purpose of his theory is to forward dialogue. His thesis will demand even of non-occidental religions that they subject to the (Western) Enlightenment theory of 'religion' (in singular, without article) as a normative universal. Whether one adopts one terminology or another, such a unifying theory precedes any historical differentiation of self-defining faith communities. From the other side, the identity of such communities is attacked by the spiritual demands of individual believers. The meaningful existence of "a religion" – be it Buddhism, Christianity, Islam or whichever – thus falls between two chairs: that of 'Faith' personal and that of 'Faith' universal – the two of them supposed to support each other reciprocally, to the exclusion of religions as conversing corporate bodies.

It is not easy to see how this scenario could lead to expanding dialogue in the world of today. Nor in that of tomorrow. SMITH invites faiths to overcome their divisions, not by bringing them together for unrestricted communicative information, but to persuade them away from such confrontation, each of them invited to recognize its acclamation of own historical identity as idolatry. But does that lane lead forward?

What about renewing the Lundensian understanding of 'Religion' as a unifying question eliciting answers open for comparative juxtaposition by the dialogue partners?

5.2. Partners for Dialogue

An overall review of contemporary dialogue would, besides inflating the volume, certainly dislocate the purpose of our study. A maximal accumulation of actual events would in itself be of minor importance for a fundamental analysis of the promotive dynamics of interreligious dialogue.

Certainly, discrepant expectations and initiatives do arise from the variety of actual situations of the dialogue partners, and from varieties in historically "established" patterns of faith and worship. Any dialogue requires understanding by the partners of the specific dialogical constellation into which they step – the particularities of the partners definitely contribute to conditioning their encounter with each other – a situation which, to some extent, must be observed in order for the dialogue to start, and which will inevitably grow in the process of dialogue – if dialogue there be. But this knowledge of particularity can only become an incentive of dialogue in dialectical correspondence with an implicit understanding – acquiring more and more explicitness – of universal rules of exchange. Rules which – to put it extremely simplistically – serve one end: to safeguard the equality of humans without founding it on some indifference of truth.

It is probable that various religions – through an interaction of each one's historic continuity and what may be seen as its actual presence – will be differently disposed towards the challenge of dialogue. In this perspective, glimpses which may be observed of an intrareligious exchange within each particular community, may be more interesting than its deliberate exposure on the interreligious arena so far.

Our aim, then, is to observe single religions in relation to others, in their mutual similarity as well as in their distinctiveness, with the final purpose of detecting, not specifics of each community, but common dynamics characteristic of interreligious encounter – as far as such dynamics there be. For that purpose, some exhaustive review of world religions might be a little rewarding enterprise. Our prospect will more profitably be of a heuristic-exemplificatory kind.

We shall look not only for the visible variety more or less observed by everybody: various religions with different history, different beliefs, different cultural presuppositions, different cultic expressions etc. We shall look for various shapes of dialogability: dynamics conditioning different dispositions for, and different expectations to, dialogue.

Manifest and latent factors may be intertwined or entangled in different ways, one factor to some extent keeping control of another. In live encounter it is also imaginable that, for "strategic reasons", substitutive arguments, dictated by actual circumstances, take control and camouflage dynamics of real interconnectedness. The well-known temptation of an *argumentum ad hominem* may be active in religion as anywhere else: to take advantage of the argument most likely to impress the dialogue partner – and, not to forget, to impress the dialogue public.

For the purpose described, we shall select for review a limited number of conversation partners, namely five: Islam, Buddhism, Hinduism, Judaism and Indigenous Religion. These have been chosen, partly for the place and space they occupy "on the map", partly for their visibility on the actual stage of dialogue. But they are also chosen to provide a variety sufficient to reflect the complexity of the topic.

As supplements to this quintuple circumspection I have pondered the utility of making one or two safaris outside the precinct of traditionally established religions. Visible and audible as well on the scene of religions are two sets of challengers to the historically founded "family of faiths".

First, I refer to the colorful variety of – internationally spreading – cults, which roundly emerged in the 19th and the first half of the 20th centuries. Between these, there is little traceable mutual influence, except for the fact that they all more or less are products of a changing world with a growing urge to infringe on old borders. To a large extent they draw on impulses from old religions (Christianity and Hinduism in particular), and in more than one case they claim to restore these religions to their original authenticity after centuries of apostasy. As the best-known examples of such cults could be mentioned the following. From America: Mormonism, Watchtower Corporation, Christian Science, Scientology, Moonism, Children of God – From Asia: Bahai, Theosophy, Hare-Krishna – From Europe: Anthroposophy.

Next I refer, in more general terms, to what is commonly labeled "New Age". Institutionally, this is an extremely diffuse entity, with an almost insurveyable multitude of organizations, incorporations, publishing agencies, "alternative" markets. Ideologically it is, however, much easier to distinguish a unity in diversity in latter day "alternative" religiosity than in the firmly "established" world of cults. In "New Age" there is a definite concentration on human spirituality as a resource in itself, in various types of mystical contact with the physical universe, and independent of established worship.

It could be interesting to discuss the possibilities, present or non-present, of dialogue, in relation to each of these two quantitatively not unimportant groups of new challengers on the international arena. No doubt, such extensions of the dialogue debate will have to come. Maybe in a not too distant future. But as things actually look, it may still take a decade or two to get the one or the other of the boats afloat. When we have decided to include neither the one nor the other in our analysis, ample reasons are there, in addition to that of volume.

Now, it may be confusing to talk of "cults" and of "New Age" as two more or less unified groups. The "cults", in their more or less monolithic self-understanding, show a variegated tableau of appearances. Differing as they do in claims and ambitions, it would be close to impossible to fancy a multilateral dialogue, i.e. a conversation where more than one of them could meet more than one of the traditional religions in anything resembling a meaningful exchange. So far, an interest for dialogue seems to be absent – and massively so – in most of the communities referred to in this group. Not only do many of the cults combine their exclusivistic self-consciousness with claim to a rightful take-over of the legacy of some historic religion. This may easily raise a confusing question in the opposite camp: should this community be regarded as a different branch of ours, as a falsification, or simply as a new religion unwilling to explore its own identity? In any case, it is obvious that this confrontative situation raises fundamental issues – to various degrees from one case to another – in addition to those of interreligious dialogue in general.

A particularly interesting case in the future development of this issue may be the role of Bahai, which proclaims to present a synthesis of all true religions in the world, representing, thus, in principle an equal challenge to them all. Therefore, it is also imaginable that some day Bahai – different from, say, the Jehovah Witnesses or Christian Science, could be invited to defend its great ambition in face of a truly multireligious panel. A discussion of that ambition would be interesting, and essential, in itself. But it would hardly infringe on the presuppositions of our present research in a way as to include it in our present reflections.

As to "New Age", it would theoretically at least, be a challenge which could also call on multilateral exchange. Its fundamental claim of spiritual independence seems to challenge all organized religions on equal premises. Even if the phenomenological diversity of the "family" at the same time implies that currents of the wide flood has currents which here or there flow closer to one bank or to another. But also in this case, a more detailed collection of, and comments on, concrete details would hardly influence our reflection on the interplay of intra- and inter-religious exchange.

It is not necessary to state how useful it would be to carry on our comparative study on a wider scale, especially with a substantial review of what is taking place of intrareligious dialogue in each religious community separately. Such expansion – and, above all, coordination – of the study is bound to follow, and will prospectively be undertaken by many, if probably not by this author. So much material is already available, even in literature existing. It only calls for additional, complementary interpretation.

Future studies will have to include: direct listening to a good deal more spokespersons coming from the midst of the communities under observation, above all: repor-

ting overtly what is going on in their own intrareligious room. When, in the following, we must restrain ourselves to relatively limited observations – some readers
may even call our selection arbitrary – and when we, to a considerable extent, have to
rely on other and occasionally better informed observers, this is partly due to resources and format, partly also to barriers of language. Most activities of intrareligious
dialogue, not least the more tension-filled, are – unlike most of interreligious dialogue – carried out in languages closed to a majority of European observers, including the present author.

5.2.1. Islam

Starting with Islam we confirm that our research does not proceed chronologically.
Among our religions to be visited, Islam is definitely the youngest. It is natural to
start with it because, next to Christianity, it is the most widespread and – much may
indicate – the fastest growing of world religions today. Besides, our study is taking
place and will, at least initially, be spread in a part of the world where the presence of
Islam, even if new, is quite explosive, and where in many eyes it is becoming the chief
manifestation of challenging religious otherness.

5.2.1.1. Islam and the Contemporary Stage of Dialogue
In the world of today Islam unfolds an impressive vitality, manifested not least as
eagerness to blot out the last footprints of what could be seen as Western colonialism.
Besides, more than any other of the great religions, it exposes a remarkable absence of
distinction between religion and politics, an absence commonly characteristic of what
is referred to as 'fundamentalism' – in this case more and more frequently translated
as 'islamism'.[16]

The common image of Islam may be one of militancy and intransigence, at least
when seen at news media distance. Can the religion of monarchical sultans, oppressive ayatollahs and islamizing revolutionists be fancied as reasonably prepared for
dialogue? Here, as everywhere in the world of religious encounter, reality is more
complex than simple clichés and formulae. Around the world, Muslims have been,
and are, to a considerable extent involved in enterprises of interreligious dialogue, in
more than one case with remarkable fervor. It is important to see "The Muslim
World" as characterized by great varieties, not least in its normative exposition of
holy writ, the Qu'ran.

Language bars most Muslim "intra-" debate to a majority of Western commentators, including the author of this volume. The most representative glimpses of contemporary tensions within the Muslim world are probably those available in French,
partly through the strong Arab community in France, partly in the ancient French

---

[16] See also the chapter on Islam in Lønning 'Fundamentalisme...' 1997, 65–96.

colonies in the Maghreb region (Morocco, Algeria, Tunisia). A remarkable pioneer of dialogue was the Muslim-Christian Research Group in France.[17]

The most energetic and reflective critic of recent islamist reaction, visible to the Western world, may be ABDERRAHIM LAMCHICHI at the University of Picardie.[18] He attacks contemporary islamism for its eagerness to adopt modern Western technology, but lacking all understanding of the profound epistemological changes which prepared and conditioned the scientific revolution in the West. With its fancy for modern technology combined with a "résistance atavique" to the philosophical presuppositions of modernity, islamism, according to Lamchichi, is consistently preparing for itself an immense cultural disintegration.[19]

5.2.1.2. Hans Küng: 'Aye' to "the Prophet"

With few exceptions Muslim contributions to dialogical symposia and anthologies are apologetical with a limited margin for self-critical reflection. At Christian-Muslim encounters this may from time to time condition a certain dialogical unbalance.

Among Christian champions of dialogue, no one may have done more for a reconciliation with Islam than HANS KÜNG. Already in the voluminous *Christentum und Weltreligionen* from 1984 he raises the key issue of the prophetic vocation of MUHAMMED and suggests a brave step of Christian recognition.

> "Ist also vielleicht auch MUHAMMED nicht mehr von vornherein ein falscher, lügnerischer Pseudoprophet ... sondern ein echter, etwa gar ein wahrer Prophet? ... in bezug auf die Figur des Propheten ist zuzugeben: dass die Menschen im Arabien des 7. Jahrhunderts zurecht auf die Stimme Muhammeds gehört haben; dass sie – gemessen am sehr disseitigen Polytheismus der altarabischen Stammesreligionen – auf ein ganz anderes religiöses Niveau, eben das einer monotheistischen Hochreligion, erhoben wurden; dass sie allesamt von Muhammed ... unendlich viel Inspiration, Mut und Kraft zu einem religiösen Neuaufbruch empfangen haben ...
>
> ... müssten Christen, die ja dem Neuen Testament zufolge weiterhin Propheten kennen, diesen Muhammed nicht ernster nehmen? Müssten sie die Warnungen des Koran nicht ernst nehmen: dass der eine unvergleichliche Gott ganz und gar im Zentrum des Glaubens zu stehen hat; dass eine Beigesellung irgendwelcher Götter oder Göttinnen nicht in Frage kommt; dass Glaube und Leben, Orthodoxie und Orthopraxis bis in die Politik hinein zusammengehören? MUHAMMED wäre so immer wieder *prophetisches Korrektiv* für Christen im Namen des einen und gleichen Gottes, wäre ein prophetischer Warner."[20]

---

[17] Groupe de Recherche Islamo-Chrétien (GRIC 1978–82). Cf. its report: 'Ces écritures qui nousquestionnent', Paris 1987, English translation: 'The Challenge of the Scriptures', New York 1989: "A testimony of our reflection and referred to as such, the text that follows does not claim to provide the general or official thinking of our faith communities ... Simply, we have tried to go as far as the current state of our reflection and the capacities of the participants would permit." p. 7.

[18] A. LAMCHICHI: Islam et contestation au Maghreb 1989, and: Islam, Islamisme et Modernité 1994.

[19] Op.cit., 32f.

[20] KÜNG (a.o.) 1984, 59f, 200. Still more emphatically he raises the question: "Muhammed – a Prophet?" in his contribution 'Christianity and World Religions: Dialogue with Islam' (in: SWIDLER 1987, 192–209), 196–198. – A more dialectical approach to the same issue is that of the respected

It is clear that Küng here steps a good foot ahead not only of most colleagues sharing his "inclusivist" dialogue orientation in general, but ahead also of what he himself is actually avowing in face of other faiths. There is, however, a long step from his pragmatic allowances in the first of these quotations – statements of which scarcely many Christian students of Islam would disagree – to the unrestricted concession of Muhammed's "prophetic" legitimacy. His admittance of Muslim monotheism as a valid warning to supposedly more compromise-ready Christians may be of considerable theological significance. Does it refer to the veneration of saints in his own Catholic branch of Christianity, or does it pertain to the trinitarian faith accepted by the ecumenical family of churches in its entirety?

The latter might resound his admiration of a certain non-authorized Christology in the early Church, supposedly presented to Jews and to Arabs by "scattered Jewish-Christian congregations in Eastern Jordania". On this background he suggests the possibility also in our time of "categories that make Jesus as God's revelation more understandable to Jews and Muslims than the hellenistic doctrine of his Two Natures."[21]

Küng's suggestion of a less "metaphysical" Christology as key to a more open interfaith dialogue may recall pluralist advocates of dialogue, particularly Hick and Samartha.[22] Their departure from classical Christology did, however, less seek support in the history of Christianity, and sought more of its motivation in a general universalist orientation. Küng, on his side, draws arguments from a particular image of early Christian relations with Judaism and with nascent Islam.

This advance of his is, and has been, in conflict with most of dominant Christian thinking of the day. Not only did the *Congregatio pro Doctrina Fidei* in Rome 1979 declare Christology a main point when depriving Küng of his authorization as catholic theological teacher. The Commission on *Faith and Order*, the most representative forum for common theological reflection in Christendom – with official representation by Catholic, Orthodox and Protestant churches – conducted 1982–1990 a stu-

---

Protestant Islam expert Kenneth Cragg: 'Muhammed and the Christian – A Question of Response, 1984, 1ff, 126f. Cragg urges an answer to the Muslim plea for a Christian acceptance of "the Prophet", but maintains that this cannot be given as a simple yes or no without a foregoing clarification of the term "prophet", particularly with reference to the Messianic "more than a prophet" (Mt 11:18). – It is worth noticing that Kate Zebiri in her remarkable confrontation of 'Christians and Muslims Face to Face' 1997, 126, finds an unspecified Christian approval of "the Prophet" just confusing, and among contemporary Christian interpreters of Islam sees Küng as "the most eminent theologian and possibly the least qualified as an Islamist." Ibid.,176.

[21] Ibid., p. 197. – The closeness of Islam to an early Jewish-oriented version of Christianity, and its corresponding distance to a subsequent Hellenistic one, is a topic more comprehensively developed and sustained in Küng's 'Das Christentum – Wesen und Geschichte' 1994, especially the sections 'Judenchristentum und Koran', 138–144, and 'Paradigmenwechsel in der Christologie', 203–217. – Khalid Duran (in: Swidler 1987), 210–217, contrary to radical Islamism strongly underscores the historical continuity Judaism-Christianity-Islam, but reproaches Küng for exaggerating the distance between the dogmatical tradition of the Church and the Jesus image of the Qur'an. Ibid., 213f.

[22] Here 4.1.1, and 4.1.3.

dy project '*Towards a Common Expression of the Apostolic Faith Today*', where focus was on the old Nicene Creed. One may say that the exposition of Christology (the Second Article) through this study definitely moves in a direction contrary to Küng's.[23]

A remarkable sign of the times is also the energetic – to a large extent, successful – rehabilitation of the old Christian doctrine of the Trinity by JÜRGEN MOLTMANN, colleague of KÜNG at the University of Tübingen.[24] Like KÜNG, Moltmann is eager to explore the Jewish (Old Testament) roots of Christianity, but in a perspective of Biblical "Salvation History" rather than of methodologically unbiased historical observation (Küng's supposition). This gives Moltmann little occasion for exploring and authorizing some extra-testamental Judaeo-Muslim continuation of biblical tradition, in the strictly monotheizing direction advocated by Küng. Moltmann conjures Holy Trinity – as he sees it: unmatched social model of godhead – against the principle of abstract, authoritarian monotheism. The latter he sees represented not only by Islam, but by a dominant bulk of Christian thinking during the last couple of centuries. To him "monotheistic Christianity in its pure form is ... Arianism".[25] The orientation is diametrically opposite of Küng's, and is thus an emphatic rejection of the main argument for offering MUHAMMED the status of a prophet in Christian "salvation history"!

Precisely this issue: acknowledgement of "the Prophet", as we have seen it wholeheartedly supported by HANS KÜNG, seems to be a main demand from Muslims to Christian participants in dialogue. This demand is sustained by the general observation that Muslims recognize the prophetic vocation and thus a divine legacy of Jesus. This, in conversations with Westerners, they often underscore as an expression of profound tolerance with a moral claim to a corresponding attitude from the Christian side.

Of particular interest is the contribution by ELSAYED ELSHAHED (Riyadh, Saudi-Arabia) in the festschrift for HANS KÜNG's 65. birthday, 1993: *Die Problematik des interreligiösen Dialogs aus islamischer Sicht*[26]:

> "An erster Stelle erwarten die Muslime von den anderen die Anerkennung der Authentizität des Islams, seiner Propheten und des Korans. Die Muslime erkennen nämlich ihrerseits bereits die Authentizität des Judentums und Christentums an, entsprechend dem Koran-Vers: 'Sagt: wir glauben an das, was uns geoffenbart wurde, sowie an das was euch (Juden und Christen) geoffenbart wurde, unser Gott ist mit euerem identisch, wir sind Ihm ergebene Diener.'[27]"

---

[23] Cf. 'Confessing the One Faith', Faith and Order Paper No. 153 (1991), particularly 43–72. "... the eternal Son and Word of God was one with the human reality of Jesus from its beginning, although the explicit formulations of this fact developed in the course of the Christological tradition" (§ 109, p. 48).

[24] MOLTMANN: Trinität und Reich Gottes, 1980. English: The Trinity and the Kingdom of God, 1981.

[25] MOLTMANN, 1980, 149.

[26] HÄRING & KUSCHEL 1993, 663–672.

[27] Ibid., 667. Quoted from the Qur'an: Sure 49/13. As further documentation is offered Sure 2/85. –

This plea for equal terms sounds fair, but reference to a Muslim lead in tolerance invites a few remarks. After all, isn't there a considerable distance between the JESUS of the New Testament and the Isa recognized as prophet by the Qur'an a good half millennium later? Virgin birth and ascension to heaven are definitely underscored, but there is place for no cross and no resurrection. That there is no indication of divine sonship was, of course, to be expected, but in addition to that, his teaching and moral authority are unequivocally seen as less important than that of MUHAMMED.[28] Plainly observed, the Muslim acclamation of Jesus the prophet implies an explicit subordination of the New Testament Gospel to the teachings of the Qur'an.

What then is the precise meaning of "recognizing the authority" of a religion, as requested by ELSHAHED? Different possibilities could be pondered: (1) declaring respect for the moral and intellectual integrity of its founder and its believers, (2) ascribing value of a certain significance to the influence it has exercised in past and present, (3) granting the truth claims of its believers (or at least the claims most important to them).

The suggestions no. 1 and 2 must be seen as indispensible prerequisites of authentic dialogue, and should need no further discussion. But no. 3 – reconciliation of conflicting truth claims – is in itself the issue of dialogical encounter and can scarcely be presented as a condition in advance. What ELSHAHED generously declares on behalf of Muslims and what he, in the name of fairness, demands from Christians, he evidently sees as the two sides of the same coin. But what is apparent, is just a verbal correspondence!

The most exposing and explosive question seems to be precisely this: can or cannot Christians recognize MUHAMMED as a prophet – as proposed by Küng? Obviously no answer can be given before the question in the question is more closely clarified. As Islam is the one of the two religions arriving last on the stage, it commonly insists on a confrontation of the main characters JESUS and Muhammed as they are presented by and in the Qur'an. When Islam gives to Jesus the (subordinate) prophetic state granted to him by the Qur'an, Christians must – in order to live up to a formal equality of tolerance – accord to Muhammed the prophetic status which is granted to him by the same Qur'an. As can easily be seen: Due to the chronological constellation of the two religious founders, as well as to terminological differentiations among their followers, an unreflected honoring of the Muslim claim would immediately endorse essential inequality – in the name of nominal equality.

The most urgent task for creating methodological balance between Muslims and Christians in dialogue, may be to secure equal standards for approach to historical criticism and thus to history-based claims – one's own as well as those of the partner.

Polemical remarks are made to those who think they promote dialogue by "die Selbstverständlichkeit der religiösen Grundprinzipien in Zweifel zu ziehen." This must first of all refer to 'pluralist' participants in dialogue. As an example is mentioned Hans ZIRKER: Christentum und Islam, 1989.

[28] To these suggestions, cf. LEIRVIK: Images of Jesus Christ in Islam, 1999.

The first consequence of this would hopefully be some agreement on the argumentative use of the respective holy scriptures – Bible and Qur'an.

5.2.1.3. Muslim Apologetics: A Case Observation

The following is reported not for polemical reasons, but as an exemplification of difficulties implied in dialogical encounter – in this case between Occidental Christianity and the non-Western religion by far most massively represented in this region of Europe. Unless these difficulties are faced, awkward as they will appear, it is hard to see how steps in the direction of authentic dialogue can be made.[29]

At a public consultation on 'Fundamentalism' in Oslo in 1995 – where, in the discussion, Muslim participants had strongly underscored Muslim tolerance as superior even to that of Christianity – the argument which we have just seen sustained by ELSHAHED – some of these participants presented me with two booklets by the Pakistani professor MUHAMMAD TAHIR-UL-QADRI, founder and spiritual leader of the widespread international network Idara-Minhaj-ul-Quran, and official visitor also of its center in Oslo.

One of the booklets was a presentation named *Islam and Christianity*.[30] As it turned out, QADRI's comparison of the two religions is based on a dogmatical reading of the Qur'an as inerrant divine communication, whereas in the case of Christianity he makes the utmost out of partly diffuse references to Western biblical criticism.[31] Islam is presented as historically infallible, Christianity as utterly unreliable. No concern about equal standards of judgement is expressed. Where the Qur'an image of Christianity and that of the New Testament collide, insistence is made that the holy writ of Christians, as we know it today, must be seen as a falsification of the original.

Admittedly, professor QADRI neither inspires nor aspires to, dialogue, and some might see it unfair to evaluate his contribution in the context of Muslim-Christian conversation. Certainly Christian communities around the world could be quoted which seem equally prejudiced in their references to Islam. The particular thing about the Idara type of apologetic is, however, that it emerges on a high level of politico-

---

[29] As a general comment to the following section we may refer to the critical analysis of reciprocal Christian-Muslim critique in ZEBIRI: Muslims and Christians Face to Face, 1997, particularly the observations of 'Muslim Popular Literature on Christianity', 44–93, and 'The Study of Christianity by Muslim Intellectuals', 137–182. More about Zebiri's study, cf. our notes 20, 48 and 50.

[30] Lahore, without date (evidently, after 1987). The author is presented as influential member of the Federal Shariat Court of Pakistan, 17. Besides, he is the founder of an international network of Mosques with particular information centers: Idara-Minhaj-ul-Quran. "The Muslims in foreign countries regularly receive his books, pamphlets and video-cassetts of his addresses and are constantly in touch with the Institute which serves as a light house of inspiration for them.", 25. – Already in 1993 Idara had organised branches in 40 countries. At a personal visit by the present author to the Idara mosque in Oslo December 1997, the leaders confirmed their close association with professor Qadri. – The booklet seems written for "ordinary readers", but the formal authority of the author together with his official position makes it most interesting as documentation, both of Muslim apologetics on an authorative level, and of the interreligious instruction offered "from back home" to Muslim settlers in Christian environments.

[31] Professor QADRI's criticism is more thoroughly reported and analyzed in LØNNING 1997, 84–96.

religious (and academical) establishment in the home country, and is spread internationally through a network, protected by the legislation on religious freedom in the receiving countries. The effect of such information may be to fill emigrants with a prejudiced image of their new religious environments, apt to shield them against possible observations of their own. In Christendom a similar type of apologetical argument may, on a comparative level of academical theology and religious leadership, have been next to absent for several generations.

"Regarding the view of scripture, even the most moderate Muslims are far more fundamentalist than any Christian can be with support in the Bible." This characteristic by the Norwegian Islam expert JAN OPSAL[32] refers to a circumstance of fundamental importance to Islamo-Christian dialogue. This becomes even more striking, as Opsal elsewise sees a distinctive specter of varieties as to Muslim strategies in face of modernity.[33]

Roughly described, the situation may be as follows. Islam as a worldwide community has never, like Christendom, been struck and shaken by the ordeal of Enlightenment. Whereas Islam in the glorious days of the caliphates in Baghdad (around 800) or in Córdoba (around 1000) was at the incontestable world peak of science, its cultural potentials seemed remarkably exhausted after the expulsion of the Arabs from Spain (shortly before 1500), even if the political elan survived for still a couple of centuries in the Ottoman empire. Epistemology, philosophy and studies in the humanities – the disciplines which particularly relate to historical perspective and methodology – have for centuries shown little development observable to the surrounding world.

To Christianity the shock of Enlightenment, sharpened *in*, *by* and *as* biblical criticism, had complex – in the long run also stimulating – effects. Above all it reinforced the importance of a clear distinction between historical information, based on an unprejudiced evaluation of commonly accessible material, and faith as confirmation of truth claims connected with a particular history.

Of equal practical, if not principal, importance, seems the following. In academical theology – and still more in the wider ecclesial constituency – it took time to bring reflection into an approximative balance after the first, anesthetizing shock of Enlightenment criticism. A close to unmitigated prostration to critical simplicity on the left wing of the Church had been encountered by an equally unmitigated dogmaticism on the right. After more than 200 years the distance between these extremes may be much diminished, but so has the proportional number of extremists on both sides. A huge spectrum of nuances has developed and may in several regards have bridged the gulf of contrasting opinions. Viewed from this platform, the Muslim

---

[32] Opsal 1994, 209.

[33] Opsal counts four main types: (1) single samples of "secularism", craving religious neutrality by political society, (2) "modernism" requesting a certain liberty to adjust regulations of the Qur'an to contemporary culture, (3) "traditionalism" seeking organic continuity, thus resisting nostalgic return to a distant past as much as a modernistic reorientation of the present, (4) "islamism" demanding uncompromising return to what it steadfastly takes for primeval Islam.

world may stand approximately where Christendom stood before the French Revolution.

As the confrontation of skepticism and dogmaticism in Christianity started to smoothen out, a generally accepted "biblical criticism", which remained as an inescapable product, could start to state an approximatively agreed distinction between historical and non-historical elements in the biblical tradition. In the 20th century this combined with a general acceptance of the Kierkegaardian maxim that: "... with regard to the historical the greatest certainty is only an *approximation*, and an approximation is ... so unlike an eternal happiness that no result can ensue",[34] a conviction which has evidently contributed to giving 20th century theology a certain inward balance, leaving a considerable margin for the discussion of historical details.

Important in an interreligious dialogue it must be, however, that after the ordeal of historical criticism – including explicitly anti-church types of radicalism (D.F. STRAUSS, L. FEUERBACH, E. RENAN a.o.) – widespread agreement has developed on the right and the limits of historical criticism. Historical studies effectively prohibit the use of sectarian writings from 2.–4. centuries for refashioning the four gospels, and for disclosing some subsequent manipulation of the original New Testament writings by ecclesial posterity.

A substantial part of conventional Muslim critique of the New Testament, still in remarkably official use, must be left aside on strictly scientific grounds before dialogue can become real exchange. If Muslims want to make use of contemporary (Western) biblical criticism, they cannot cite it to discredit the New Testament unless they themselves respect the prerequisites of modern historical research. This again they cannot do without adapting them for a corresponding reexamination of their own historical origin. Rather unusual reasons would be needed to convince a historian that the Qur'an at the distance of 600 years should give a historically more valid presentation of Jesus than the gospels at the distance of 40–70 years. Could such an assumption be sustained unless through some preestablished theory of Qur'anic infallibility? That is: without basing allegedly scientific judgement on the acceptance of a specific religious belief?

As this is now underlined, our purpose is not to score a cheap point in a dialogical competition, but just to remind the reader that no dialogue is possible if the partners are not arguing on equal terms. A common set of rules must be established and set into practice. If, for the sake of confidence building, it may be good to start a first review of "issues" before an agreement on rules is reached, the partners will have to keep in mind that without such agreement they will not be playing the same game, and no conflict will actually be solved.

The actual dilemma is then: how can pre-Enlightenment Islam face post-Enlightenment Christianity? From a Western point of view, the disparity may easily be

---

[34] 'Concluding Unscientific Postscript', Ch. 1 (Kierkegaard's Writings, Princeton 1978ff: XII.1, vol. I, p. 23).

taken to mean – as it was rudely observed by the "secular theology" of the mid 1960s – that Islam remains on a stage of repugnant self-defense which Christianity by and large left behind 200 years ago. This could mean that, in order to face the future, Islam is bound to undergo the same apologetical detente as Christian theology did in the years 1800–2000, and sooner or later to arrive at a stage of methodological reflection similar to that of "main-line" Christianity now. Such a diagnosis would hardly invite communication. Even if the road to dialogue has to be cleared of methodological imbalances in order to prepare for authentic progress, it is therefore important that Christians don't urge such clarification as the initial stage of exchange. A distinction is necessary between the first issue in a logically structured advance and the first step in direction of human confidence building. It is possible, and it may be necessary, to choose a detour, some procedure of confidence building where issue no.1 comes seventh and the process of logical clarification may have to await its turn.

Served as an unprepared provocation, the thesis about a two centuries gap will be met with the objection frequently heard from Islamic communities when faced with a challenge concerning "Human Rights": why should we accept conditions defined by the West, forged to sustain political and ideological interests in conflict with ours. In a contribution to an issue of "Dialog der Religionen" in 1995, dedicated to the main topic "Säkularisierung und religiöse Erneuerung",[35] ABDOLDJAVAD FALATURI places the issue of Western secularity right in the heart of dialogue.

> "Die Frage nach der Beziehung des Islam zum Säkularismus taucht in der letzten Zeit in verschiedenen Zusammenhängen auf, vor allem im Zusammenhang mit den Fragen: Islam und Modernismus, Islam und Demokratie, Islam und Menschenrechte, Integration der Muslime in Europa, Religion und Staat usw. Ausgangspunkt bei diesen Fragestellungen ist eine unkorrekte, aber sehr beliebte Vorstellung. Man geht einfach davon aus, dass mit den heutigen Kriterien und Maßstäben alle anderen Kulturen in der Geschichte und Gegenwart gemessen und bewertet werden können ..."[36]

The core of this argument can hardly be contradicted. Too often the approach of Occidental modernity "geht einfach davon aus" = simply takes something for granted by virtue of its own cultural superiority. But as right as FALATURI and contemporary Muslim apologists may be when refusing the self-assurance of voices which in the name of one culture imposes its values on another, the limitation of the argument is at the same time evident: it tends to exclude a joint foundation of dialogue from the agenda of dialogue! Discrepant value systems are not observed as calling for confrontation. Joint assessment of divergent presuppositions of thought is excluded as part of the exchange desired! Such an attitude may easily bar the access not only to an unprejudiced comparison of conflicting – or seemingly conflicting – value structures, but also to a joint exploration of what may be common values. As final consequence it may even shadow a common vision of universal values.

---

[35] FALATURI, DdR 2–95, 122–129.
[36] Ibid., 122.

This may signalize total absence of criteria for handling conflicting truth claims. A concrete example may be the argument of TAHIR-UL-QADRI which has been mentioned. In judging the authority as well as the doctrines of the Qur'an exclusively from (what he sees as) its own, non-discussible premises – and judging the Bible partly on premises of the Qur'an, partly from assorted samples of modern historical criticism, he closes the doors to any meaningful dialogue The more philosophical approach by Falaturi seems to end up with equally ghettoizing consequences. What dialogue between Muslims and Christians more than any other thing seems to need, is agreement on a strategy for joint approach to disagreements.

Does this mean that Muslims, in order to complete their dialogue with Christians, have to accept historical criticism as developed in Western modernity? What is recommended, is not acceptance of a particular critical method, nor abjuration of such or such a self-understanding. The elementary prerequisite of dialogue must be to observe, and to respond constructively to, the demand for methodological equality. For the colloquial partners to cherish an identical method is less essential than for each of them to apply equal standards when examining itself and examining its partner. One method or another may always be a matter of discussion – the principle of equal standards may not!

This is, as may easily be seen, a question to be put before any religion (and any single person) ready to engage in dialogue. But the constellation Islam/Christianity puts it in an extraordinary light, viewing their traditional truth claims in light of the discrepancy between pre- and post-Enlightenment assessments of history. The prime task of dialogue is to search for a common language. Not for a philological blend, say, of Arab and English, but for agreed rules to observe similarities and differences, opening up certain converging lanes in direction of common understanding.

It seems remarkable that HANS KÜNG, who has shown such a particular interest for Islam in the development of his theology of dialogue, so long has failed to discover how contemporary Muslim-Christian controversy hinges on precisely that condition. Like no other dialogue of religions the exchange between these two unveils the omnipresent issue of communication: the disagreement at the root of all disagreements is disagreement on how to handle our disagreements.

To which extent, then, can a methodological deadlock be overcome through some single approach which could be inspiring enough to invite a successful methodological detour? Could common visions be initiated and experiences of growing fellowship be made, captivating enough to screen methodological embarrassments until issues of principle some day can be entered with less prestige than is obviously the case today?

5.2.1.4. An "Abrahamic" Ecumenism?

A rather promising possibility may be the prospect of an Abrahamic ecumenism, launched by KÜNG's younger brother-in-arms KARL-JOSEF KUSCHEL.[37] Kuschel's main

---

[37] KUSCHEL: Streit um Abraham ..., 1994.

proposition is the common, historically justifiable, claim of Jews, Christians and Muslims to be the spiritual descendants of one person: Abraham. He tries to show how the character of Abraham, as drawn in the Old Testament, may confirm the identities of all the three religions, at the same time as it questions their historically conditioned custom of degrading each other. As critical challenges to the narrowness of each one of them Kuschel announces "Salvation for others in the Sign of Noah" (to Judaism), "Possibility of Salvation for Non-Christians" (to Christianity) and "No Compulsion in Matters of Faith" (to Islam).[38] At the same time Kuschel warns against an unwarranted optimism:

> "Die Rede von einer 'abrahamischen Ökumene' darf die strukturellen theologischen Differenzen weder im Binnenverhältnis der drei Religionen zueinander noch in ihrem Außenverhältnis überspielen oder nivellieren. In wesentlichen theologischen wie anthropologischen Fragen sind Juden, Christen und Muslime so weit voneinander entfernt, dass von einer Einheit in Bekenntnis, Praxis und Gemeinschaftsstruktur nicht die Rede sein kann und unter irdischen Bedingungen vermutlich auch nicht sein wird."[39]

In spite of this restriction KUSCHEL is rather optimistic about possible achievements in the name of "Abrahamic ecumenism". (1) Joint discovery of Abraham as common critical figure, (2) Mutual recognition of shared Abrahamic presence, (3) Confidence in God as residing beyond intolerance and idolatry, (4) Peacemaking by sharing and agreement, (5) Joint prayer for peace and reconciliation.[40] In a sum:

> "Nur dann also hat das ökumenische Gespräch zwischen Juden, Christen und Muslimen einen Sinn, wenn nicht die Funktionalisierung ABRAHAMS für den eigenen Wahrheitsanspruch im Vordergrund steht, sondern die Sache Abrahams, zu der alle Glaubenden immer wieder auf dem Weg sind: Abkehr von falschen Idolen (darunter besonders der Selbsterhöhung über andere) und das Vertrauen auf den einen und wahren Gott, der je größer ist als alle von Menschen gemachten religiösen Traditionen und Konventionen ..."[41]

Without questioning KUSCHEL's visionary construction, we must make an observation concerning his own delimitation of it. When he speaks of "structural theological differences" neither to be "overplayed nor leveled down", to which extent may then issues of epistemological orientation (methodology) be included? If the expression "essential theological and anthropological questions" is supposed to cover "the internal as well as the external relation of the three religions", and this is what prohibits unity in "Confession, Practice and Community Structure", the whole reconciliation problem seems to be rooted in matters of belief and religious practice, with no reference to cultural factors with possible epistemological repercussions.

---

[38] Section 'Perspektiven für eine abrahamische Ôkumene', KUSCHEL ibid., 213–306. Noah is here understood as the Biblical representative of universal humanhood, different from Moses, symbol of Judaism as one distinctive strain.

[39] Ibid., 241.

[40] Ibid., 248–306.

[41] Ibid., 306.

The uncomplicated exemplary role of Abraham in Kuschel's sketch may support such an interpretation. So, in that regard his abrahamic vision adds little to the proposals we have already received from his teacher Küng. Certainly, the recourse to Abraham may contribute to an ambiance of togetherness which in itself may be promotive of dialogue, but no epochal result of this initiative will probably appear before the basic problem of methodological equality and its cultural embedment are steadfastly explored in common.

5.2.1.5. "Human Rights" – An Issue of Dialogue?

The challenge of the Enlightenment, as indicated, points in the direction av two major issues. So far we have focused on the issue, which in a systematical context must hold priority, but in actual exchange – strangely enough – has been widely neglected so far: hermeneutics, the quest for standards of argumentative fairness. The other issue has on a much larger scale been under scrutiny, in political discussions maybe even more than in religious: the one of Human Rights. Not at least with regard to freedom of faith.

Even the difference of standards in the Human Rights issue must be understood as part of the Enlightenment challenge, which Christendom claims to have faced and – as far as advisable – included in its legacy, but which the Muslim world so far has recognized only casually and to a minor extent. Even in this domain Christianity may be inclined to think of herself as leader in the champions' league, with a vocation to save fellow religions from common sins of old. Another circumstance attached to Human Rights is that, in our world of today – different from that of Medieval times – the most conspicuous use of coercion in issues of belief is definitely that of Muslims harassing Christians, especially threatening Muslim converts to Christianity, more than the other way around (an exception to be made for the former Yugoslavia?).

Has Muslim-Christian dialogue until now accomplished anything for religious freedom and human rights? It is not easy to point out concrete accomplishments. A noteworthy experiment has been made in the Islamic Republic of Sudan, where in 1994 there was organized a *Sudanese Dialogue Association* initiated through the state sponsored *Council for International Peoples' Friendship*. Oct. 8–10 1994 there was arranged an international conference in Khartoum on 'Interreligious Dialogue – Peace for All' with around 50 participants from more than 20 countries.[42]

The conference, which enjoyed great and supportive attention from the Islamic government, but of which there came no identifiable contribution to settling controversial matters in a country ridden for years by civil war, was evidently differently assessed by participants. Muslim comments for obvious reasons magnified the event as proof of friendly relations between divided religious communities in the Islamic

[42] As member of a Norwegian church delegation to the Sudan in April 1995, the author received a selection of the documents pertaining to the Sudanese Dialogue Association and to the conference, upon a visit to the secretariat of that organization, to which I am indebted for courteous reception and information. Copies of certain conference speeches not available at the secretariat were later passed on to me by other contacts in the country.

Republic. Some Christians, especially those speaking for the official Sudan Council of Churches expressed a careful optimism. But strongly critical remarks were heard from the politically more powerful Roman Catholic Church, by the voices of the leader of the Pontificium Officium Pro Dialogo, Francis Cardinal Arinze, and of the Archbishop of Khartoum, Gabriel Zubeir Wako.

Impressions from personal conversations with religious and other leaders in the Sudan give me reason to believe that the Roman Catholic archbishop pronounced what many would have said in case they had dared:

> "In the Sudanese situation I think it is a ... blind disregard of reality to ... present our 'here' as a peaceful and neutral paradise of religious tolerance, interreligious harmony and peaceful co-existence ... The normal Christians look at this very Conference with skepticism ... One reason is that several attempts in the past have failed. Another is that dialogue in other vital areas has made no headway, e.g. the dialogue for peace and an end to the civil war. Yet another is that real trust has broken down between the two communities, and what looks like trust is a maneuver for survival for both ... The Christian who thinks this way is the one who feels discriminated against at schools, in the work place, in the army and even in housing and social services. He is the one who feels that his right to freedom of worship is curtailed ... At the same time there is the Christian who claims that everything is alright and that what the ordinary Christian fears or complains about is nothing but deliberate anti-sudanese propaganda. For this class of Christians there is not even need for dialogue because dialogue already exists.
>
> Muslims also seem divided on the issue of dialogue. There are those who sincerely feel that things are not all right, those who feel Christians, particularly those from the South, are discriminated against and maltreated on religious grounds, and who even openly express their sympathy. This group of Muslims strongly advocates dialogue ... Some others, those who feel that Sudan is and must remain an islamic country, want to see that everything be Islamic ... This group believes there is no possibility of dialogue ... and even question the morality of the Muslim who engages in such a dialogue. This group has gained some ascendancy of late. The bulk of the Sudanese, tired of living under constant tension, strongly opt for dialogue, not only between Muslims and Christians, but also between the various regions, cultures and ethnic groups in the Sudan."[43]

Interesting in this Sudanese initiative is not only the description of the confusing situation as to freedom of religion under an islamic regime, especially the fear of groups who, for the sake of simple security, must present a happy appearance. Observations of this kind manifestly apply to more countries than Sudan, but not linked with the same joyful proclamation of dialogue. Truly remarkable in the Sudanese situation is a prestigious dialogue involvement of a government programmatically linked with Sharia (Islamic Law).[44]

---

[43] Gabriel Zubeir WAKO: 'Interreligious Dialogue in the Sudan, Can We Sustain It?' Copy of manuscript, received in the Sudan.

[44] For documentations, see Abdel Ghaffar M. AHMED & Gunnar SØRBØ (ed.): Management of the Crisis in the Sudan, 1989. – Cf. on the other side the general remark by a moderate Islamic spokesman much concerned about mutual understanding (cf. our notes 47, 48): "The growing demand of Christian leaders to evoke the UN's Declaration of Human Rights in favor of Christian minorities is increasingly

The ideological profile of Islamic governments must inevitably actualize the question about the purpose of dialogue, as it is clear that the basic orientation of dialogue: recognition, practice and promotion of fundamental equality is intentionally absent in the Sudan. From the suggestions of archbishop WAKO – who in the actual circumstances could hardly afford to formulate accusations not recognizable to his audience – one may distinguish two government purposes: the appeasement of disturbing segments in own population, and: presentation to the world of a favorable picture of religious freedom in the country. The one as well as the other indicates a rather alien use of the prestigious word "dialogue". Is there reason to assume that the Sudanese sample will be both the first and the last? Or is it arbitrary that an ear-deafening monological use of "dialogue" should be launched precisely in an Islamic state?

5.2.1.6 Muslim Readiness for Dialogue
At the same time, archbishop WAKO refers to a – evidently not unimportant – segment of Sudanese Muslims ready to affirm their desire for true dialogue, precisely in a situation of violent confrontation like the one in their home-country. This observation may recall the general observation by JAN OPSAL of strongly disparate attitudes in face of the non-Islamic world: secularism, modernism, traditionalism, islamism. As we may conclude, this scarcely draws borders between neatly distinctive camps. The four badges express tendencies, shades and degrees within a wide specter of transitions, where clear-cut confrontations just come to the daylight here and there, now and then.

Critical observations of Muslim readiness, or lack of readiness, for dialogue are not usual in public reflections by potential conversation partners. Such observations could be undiplomatical and, at least in the first round, counterproductive. But can understanding finally be obtained through a diplomacy that evades questions about the foundations of dialogue for fear of squandering dialogue? In this regard, the best way to forward exchange is not to refrain from raising uncomfortable issues, but that of inviting equality in openness.[45]

It may be no mere coincidence that the first radically promising examples of a Muslim readiness to meet Christians in such an open, methodically equal-based exchange, are offered by scholars in Islamic studies at Western universities, with own roots in a Muslim culture. In 1997 two important studies emerged from British centers of learning, very different in structure, but both of them consciously promoting

seen by Muslims as the Church 'siding with' and in 'favor of' Western secular advancement in the Muslim world. The dialogue of salvation in this context will be meaningless unless the Church clearly states how it defines the concept of human rights and where it stands." (SIDDIQUI 1997, 198).

[45] Obviously, it is not literary comments that Khalid DURAN has in mind: "Among my Jewish and Christian partners in dialogue, however, the impression persists that Muslims, on the whole, are not eager for dialogue, that their reluctance is simply too strong, their resentment too deep. The contrary, in fact, is true, but the historical phase we are passing through is not propitious for such an exercise." (in: SWIDLER 1987), 211. – Maybe a thorough analysis of "the historical phase" might bring to light precisely the pre- / post-Enlightenment syndrome we have tried to call attention to.

a balanced, forward-looking revaluation of contemporary Christian-Muslim exchange. I am referring to a study by ATAULLAH SIDDIQUI, University of Leicester, (published in the USA), and one by KATE ZEBIRI, School of Oriental and African Studies, University of London.[46]

SIDDIQUI's analysis of twentieth century Christian-Muslim exchange is strictly structured from a Muslim point of observation, but has as a principal aim to understand differences of approach not primarily between two closed systems of belief, but of two civilizations, historically differently placed due to circumstances largely beyond the believers' choice. A main thrust thus lies on showing the complications caused by a Muslim feeling of inferiority, political and economic, and by Christian insensitivity to this embarrasment. "Muslims have not developed a coherent position about dialogue. The problems seem to lie within the Muslim community. Though Islam provides an acceptable basis of pluralism and a code of conduct with other religions, this aspect has not been explored and has rarely been debated within the Muslim community."[47]

The approach of ZEBIRI is quite different. Her outlook is of a systematical more than of an historical orientation, and her keen analysis, just as critical in one direction as in the other, is widely based on logical reflection. From her strictly balanced critiques it is impossible to conclude whether she identifies herself with one of the two religions or with the other. Her impatience with the clumsiness of contemporary dialogue endeavors hits propulsive liberals as much as reserved conservatives. She especially holds a clear view of the dialogical imbalance caused by post-Enlightenment historical criticism as taken for granted by Christians (even of deep-rooted ecclesiastical commitments), and uncritical pre-Enlightenment handling of history so dominant on the Muslim side. Muslim apologets today to a large extent use arbitrarily collected statements from Western scholars to discredit Christianity as a religion not even worth the confidence of its own believers, and at the same time reserve Islam and Qur'an as a sacred area inaccessible to critical research. Such an application of double standards is obviously lethal to any attempt at dialogue. Zebiri's main concern is to show "why Muslims and Christians often talk past each other" [48] and thus to clear the ground for more authentic exchange.

[46] SIDDIQUI 1997. ZEBIRI 1997.

[47] SIDDIQUI, 195. The word "pluralism" here is hardly meant in the Western sense of: recognizing a plurality of truths – but in the wider meaning of openness to conversation with partners of differing truth claims. – Of particular value in Siddiqui's book are the analysis of 6 Muslim thinkers (born 1921 – 1935) with various approaches to dialogue, 81–169, and his review of international Muslim organizations with regard to dialogical concerns, 173–200.

[48] ZEBIRI, 230, cf. 'Conclusion', 230–234. The following keen observationn is worth observing: "Christian thinkers have sometimes drawn a contrast between religion and revelation, the latter being God's downward initiative towards humans while the former is humans' necessarily imperfect upward search for God. On this understanding, Christianity as a social and historical phenomenon is flawed, as are other religions, and to be distinguished from the gospel ... which God revealed in Christ. For Muslims, religion incorporates not just faith, ritual and ethics, but also culture, government and law ... By Islamic standards, Christianity seems rather inadequate as a religion; by Christian standards, Islam over-prescribes for its followers, and may seem regimented." ibid., 231.

Certainly KÜNG is right in naming godhead (including christology) together with prophet and prophethood as key issues in a Muslim-Christian dialogue. A question is, however, how meaningfully these (and other) issues of content can be raised prior to a joint examination of hermeneutical presuppositions. A question which inevitably follows, is whether the Muslim image of godhead, with its monotheistic-authoritarian emphasis, should be faced primarily as an attack on Nicene trinitarianism or on a widespread tendency in contemporary Christianity: emancipation from established theistic pretensions to the benefit of socially more functional models of godhead.[49]

In the critique of monotheism by MOLTMANN already referred to, the possibility of a politically derived image of Godhead is kept in check by a fervid involvement with classical trinitarian theology.[50] This balance is not equally present with the "theologians of the death of God" of the 1960's. Nor, generally, with their more moderate heirs: "Liberation theologians", "Theological feminists" and others with main accent on the political function of theological concepts – divinity included. There can hardly be doubt that a reflective confrontation of the Allah of Islam with the "a-theistic God" of Western modernity[51] would be no less dramatic and no less thought-provoking than the one with Nicene orthodoxy recommended by KÜNG.

This would to some extent reshape KÜNG's argument for a recognition of MUHAMMED as prophet, drawing attention from the ardent spokesman of monotheism against (real or imagined) polytheism, to the valiant defender of divine transcendence against integration of God in a preconceived social universe. Rather than the use and non-use of the title "prophet" – which in any case has different implications in the two religions – it must be more clarifying also to Muslims that Christians state precisely which functions they may attribute or not attribute to Muhammed in their own religious universe. As to God, politics and integration, this will in any case be a two-sided issue. It does not only raise the question of politics manipulating God, but of God – or rather: an established image of God – manipulating politics. If the former is a temptation typical of modern Christianity, the latter may not be an uncommon temptation to Islam.

5.2.2. Buddhism

Moving from Islam to Buddhism takes us into a different world. Not only did GAUTAMA BUDDHA live approximately 1000 years earlier than MUHAMMED, on a continent – India – where spirituality had already for centuries distinguished itself from anything elsewhere in human history: the Veda tradition. His position is definitely

---

[49] To this problematic, cf. LØNNING 1986, and 1989, especially the section 'Actual theological confrontations", 1989, 89–164.

[50] Cf. ch. 4. our note 236.

[51] Cf. Dorothee SÖLLE: 'Atheistisch an Gott glauben' 1968, a book title rather characteristic of the late sixties!

not that of a prophet proclaiming an authoritative message from a transcendent God, but that of a compassionate teacher, guide to a contemplative life with liberation from the illusions of our finite world as its ultimate prospect. To advocates of dialogue who have proclaimed a universal deity as unifying common denominator (HICK, the early KNITTER a.o.), the a-theistic orientation of classical Buddhism has proven to be a real crux. If fundamental understanding among religions is to be reached by reduction of theology to one common assumption, belief in a Creator God definitely isn't it.

In the following we shall not explore the history of Buddhism or survey the differences of its various branches – a scenario of differentiation not unlike that of Christianity. Our task is to reflect on the role of Buddhism on the contemporary arena of inter-religious exchange by focusing on three persons with particular contributions to a Buddhist-Christian conversation: the Buddhist MASAO ABE, the Christian JOHN B. COBB JR. and the "Christian Buddhist" KATSUMI TAKIZAWA.

This means that, geographically, our observations will be as good as completely limited to Japan and to contemporary trends within the Mahayana tradition, interest and involvement in interreligious dialogue being a good deal more developed there than in South-Asian Hinayana Buddhism. For good reasons it is also ahead of present developments in culturally more isolated countries like Tibet and China.

5.2.2.1. Masao Abe on the Arena of International Dialogue

Internationally, MASAO ABE has been the most influential voice of the so-called Kyoto-school in 20th century Buddhist theology. The very focus of Abe's Buddhist involvement with Christianity is the Pauline statement in Phil 2:6f: *"... though he* (Christ Jesus) *was in the form of God, he did not count equality with God a thing to be grasped, but emptied himself taking the form of a servant."* The crucial word according to Abe is "emptied" – Greek εκενωσεν, corresponding noun: κενωσις.

At the Second Conference of East-West Religious Encounter in Honolulu, Jan. 3–11, 1984, ABE presented a paper on *Kenotic God and Dynamic Sunyata*. The attention aroused by his presentation was great, and six years later a volume resulted with a series of responses by prominent theologians and thereafter an adjacent "Rejoinder" by Abe himself.[52]

In the similarity between the Buddhist concept of Sunyata and the Christian understanding of self-emptying, ABE sees a depth which unites the two religions without extinguishing the identity of either of them. This is how he sums up his discovery:

> "... the true Sunyata is not static but dynamic – it is a pure and unceasing function of self-emptying, making self and others manifest their suchness ... In this paper I have suggested that in Christianity, the notion of the kenotic God is essential as the root-source of the kenotic Christ, if God is truly the God of love ... And when we clearly realize the notion of

---

[52] COBB & IVES 1990. – A comprehensive presentation of ABE, Japanese philosopher and pioneer of dialogue is given by the editor Ives, XIII–XIX.

the kenotic God in Christianity and the dynamic Sunyata in Buddhism – then without eliminating the distinctiveness of each religion – we find a significant common basis at a deeper dimension. In this way, I believe, Christianity and Buddhism can enter into a much more profound and creative dialogue and overcome antireligious ideologies ..." [53]

An unprejudiced reader may wonder that ABE so swiftly identifies the self-emptying Christ with a self-emptying God, as there is no immediate support for such a conceptual transfer in Phil 2. At least a wider selection of biblical references would be required to support this identification. The decisive thing is that Abe in the "self-emptying of God" sees a rapprochement between what has traditionally been spoken of as "Christian theism" and "Buddhist atheism" respectively. He observes a kind of "kenotic" convergence between the two religions. How is this judged in terms of dialogue after so ample a time to examine his proposal?

The seven respondents can all be observed as spokespersons of distinctive orientations, all with particular affinity to the issue. Three are well-known American "Process theologians", keenly interested in the ontological distinctions of being, non-being and becoming. One respondent speaks on behalf of "Feminist theology", another one is a Jew, and still another is an influential, if rather independent, spokesman of Continental mainline Protestantism. The last and most provocative member of the company may – with regard to our issue – in several regards be THOMAS J.J. ALTIZER, known as chief promoter of the "Death of God" break-through in American theology in 1966.[54] Even if the language of "the Death of God theologians" in the meantime has been swept away as too sensationalist, the basic concerns of Altizer have over the years been recognized as relevant by not unimportant segments of Western theology. One would immediately presume interesting links between the agenda of Altizer and Buddhist non-theism.

And so it turns out. In the vision of ALTIZER a declared concord between "radical Christianity" (BLAKE, KIERKEGAARD, DOSTOYEVSKY as his references) and dominant strains of Buddhism (referred to as "The Kyoto school" and "Mahayana Buddhism") steps to the fore:

> "... modern Christian visionaries have realized an opening to absolute emptiness itself ... the very center ... the Crucifixion of God ... the modern Christian will fully know that center only by becoming open to Buddhism ... a Buddhist ground ... in this perspective will inevitably be known as a Christian ground. The Kyoto school discovered a Christianity that it could know as a Buddhist ground, and discovered it by way of the Christian symbol of the death or kenosis of God, a symbol ... of an absolute and total self-emptying. Mahayana Buddhism has always known the self-emptying as total compassion, just as Christianity at bottom has always known the Crucifixion as the full embodiment and ultimate actualization of the love of God." [55]

---

[53] Ibid., 61.

[54] TIME MAGAZINE, Good Friday, April 8, 1966, cover story 'Is God Dead?' Cf. Thomas J.J. ALTIZER: The Gospel of Christian Atheism, 1966, and: The Self-Embodiment of God, 1977.

[55] Ibid., 77.

What ALTIZER expresses here, goes actually further than to a mere acceptance of ABE's vision. He refuses to observe a distinctive, limited identity for each of the two religions. But, at the same time, what he confirms as their common, fundamental insight, gives no indication of past contact or of palpable influence in one direction or the other. Altizer is an unblended mystic. His interpretation postulates a discovery common to two faiths: a spiritual reality valid independent of, and prior to, both of them, even if he is keen to observe the respective break-throughs in history.

How do the three "Process" respondents react to ABE's rapprochement? JOHN B. COBB JR. is one of the main promoters of dialogue in general and of Buddhist-Christian exchange in particular. We have already given him broad attention in our general survey of "inclusivism".[56] This time he chooses a kind of thematical detour in order to present a fundamental challenge, not specifically to Abe, but to Buddhism in general. Neither godhead nor christology is his immediate concern, but reality as such, more precisely: the unwillingness of Buddhist thinkers to examine "what differentiates one entity from another." Cobb does not reject a coherent concept of human relationship with reality, such as he sees it developed in Buddhism. It is the taking for granted, together with the massive application, of this relational perspective he wants to question.[57] But isn't this an issue so fundamental that it may hamper all serious exchange between Buddhists and Christians? We shall soon test Cobb a little more closely on precisely this topic.

SCHUBERT OGDEN, the second "Process" participant at the symposium, finds "striking similarities between the understanding of human existence" in the version of Buddhism represented by ABE, and his own Christian conviction. But he declines the idea of a "kenotic God", seeing kenosis as imaginable only in the case of some observable, limited individual – an assumption which would be a total misunderstanding in the case of God, "the universal individual".

> "Thus from the standpoint of Christian faith any individual who could conceivably be the kenotic God could not really be God at all but only an idol in whom faith could believe only by ceasing to be itself."[58]

This immediately corresponds with our observation that the kenosis passage in Phil 2 cannot be formally transferred, or applied, to God.

The third "Process" musketeer DAVID TRACY also takes reservation to ABE's use of the kenosis motif, but in a milder form: He does not "believe that Abe's formulation of the kenotic God and the kenotic Christ is the route for Christians to take." However, reflections on Abe's model of thought has helped him to change his "former Christian theological understanding of God in ways that needed changing."[59] Above all the Buddhist Abe has lead him to a new and deeper reading of Medieval Christian mystics – "apophatic theologians", as Tracy calls them: ECKHART and RUYSBROECK.

---

[56] Here, 4.2.3.
[57] COBB & IVES, 91–101.
[58] Ibid., 129 (125–134).
[59] Ibid., 136 (135–154).

He sees Abe's position quite close to that of Meister Eckhart: a total black-out of any conceptual representation of God. To Tracy this is no tenable conclusion at all, but completed by Ruysbroeck's trinitarian dialectic, it becomes a purifying observation en route to a mystical contemplation of the crucified Christ. In this way, Abe's proposal is not in itself a viable conclusion to Christians. It may, however, serve as a dynamic contribution to our contemporary search for, and progress toward, a clarified Christian identity.

In CATHERINE KELLER's: "On Feminist Theology and Dynamic Self-Emptying", a Feminist theologian "only with a sense of irony ... adds her voice to the Christian-Buddhist dialogue", since it is impossible to abstract from "the most obvious common denominator of these two world religions: their patriarchalism!"[60] With such a point of departure, an essential contribution to an exchange between two faith traditions can hardly be expected! But it is not difficult to see that in a wider setting of dialogue likely to come, the two religions will profit from comparing their experiences of social involvement – maybe even from sharing corresponding acknowledgements of failures and shortcomings. Maybe there will even be some opportunity for theological feminism to lend a voice to an important segment of such an exchange?

When inviting just one Continental participant to the literary ABE symposium, the editors COBB & IVES had good reasons for choosing JÜRGEN MOLTMANN, fervid advocate of what he sees as classical Christian trinitarianism, and correspondingly vehement antagonist to abstract monotheistic conceptuality. In his actual contribution "God is Unselfish Love" Moltmann exposes his relational understanding of godhead in opposition to abstract philosophical essentialism as well as to monolithic theism with Islam as its most eloquent representative. In this perspective he expresses genuine appreciation of Abe's kenotic approach. Few Christian comments on the focal passage in Phil 2 "are so profound and precise as this work of a Buddhist scholar."[61]

> "... Sunyata appears to come so close to creation that Christians can learn from Buddhists how to handle and how to live in this creation community ... In Sunyata the perichoretical structure of all things is realized." [62]

What, after all, MOLTMANN has to reproach Abe for, is for framing his kenotic concern in the conceptuality of traditional substance metaphysics, thus neglecting "the interpersonal categories of the social doctrine of the Trinity" and ending up with kenotic deity as "the great zero". ABE's 'kenosis' is understood as the self-annihilation of a transcendent Creator God – certainly a valid protest against a strong metaphysi-

---

[60] Ibid., 102 (102–115).

[61] Ibid., 116 (116–124).

[62] Ibid., 121. To Perichoresis (Greek: interpenetration), cf. 4.3.2.2. note 246. At this stage it may be additionally clarifying to add Moltmanns later observation: "... all relationships which are analogous to God reflect the primal, reciprocal indwelling and mutual interpenetration of the Trinitarian perichoresis: God in the world and the world in God ..." MOLTMANN 1985, 17.

cal strain in Christian theology through the centuries, but remote from the vision of a relational godhead in the biblical tradition.

What then has ABE's "Rejoinder" to say to this colorful bouquet of critical admirers?[63] First of all, he underscores naturally enough the importance of a joint Buddhist-Christian orientation in face of the strong and aggressive irreligious movements of the time. Further, he professes willingness to learn more from his critics about Christian trinitarian faith as expression of a relational God-language, and he shares their hope for a considerable enrichment of Buddhism through a more informative encounter with this essential dimension of the Christian legacy, as with that gospel of kenotic deity which he recognizes as his own spiritual horizon.

His main reservation is that his critics generally oversimplify the Buddhist understanding of transcendence. While totally void of substance, Sunyata as transcendent principle is neither good nor evil. This insight involves basic separation of ethic and religion: there is no such thing as divine commandments, and ethic has to be dialectically established in the religious dimension "through the realization of Sunyata …" This also reflects a dialectical understanding of reality. The distinctiveness of events and phenomena is not denied "in the socio-historical dimension". Such denial takes place only where meditative perception opens up a universe with no beginning and no end in time and with no cleavage in separate elements.

"Buddhist-Christian dialogue is also beginningless and endless. With a clear realization of the beginninglessness and endlessness of our dialogue we find ourselves at a new starting point for dialogue – not only at this moment, but also at each and every moment." [64]

5.2.2.2. A "Process" Approach to Buddhism: John B. Cobb Jr.

JOHN B.COBB JR., probably the most influential voice of contemporary Process Theology, has been mentioned and quoted several times, and his principal position on dialogue is among the ones already described and commented upon (4.2.3). We may now have occasion to observe more closely his preoccupation with Buddhism in particular.

Among his contributions, we have visited the epochal study *Beyond Dialogue – Toward a Mutual Transformation of Christianity and Buddhism*. This programmatical study was published in 1982. That is: prior to the literary explosion of the big dialogue boom, 1984. At that stage of events, the book offers more reflection on the principal foundations of interreligious dialogue than the title would make us presume today. "Mutual transformation" is established as the over-all aim of dialogue. At the same time there is no doubt that Cobb's choice of Buddhism as illustrative model is anything but arbitrary. Nor is the choice primarily due to his Californian site of residence, Claremont School of Theology, the main center of American and international Process thought, with a natural geographical orientation toward the Pacific …

---

[63] Ibid.,157–200.
[64] Ibid., 200.

In his vision Process thought has an immediate affinity to Buddhism: a common holistic approach to reality, an understanding of all phenomena and all events as integral parts of a universal dynamic – in a world which loses its meaning if atomized into fragments of matter or of separate events.

The two first chapters of Cobb's study outline the principles of a theology of dialogue in general. This was Cobb's first major appearance on the international scene of dialogue, and it is exciting to see how he establishes his stand as balanced, and at the same time explicitly "inclusivist", in a definite refusal of Hick / Knitter's "pluralist" theism as much as of "exclusivist" orthodoxy. This position of his has undergone little revision in the years that followed.

It is remarkable how his definition of Process principles fits in with his introductory presentation of Buddhism. But it is impossible to accuse him of manipulating the one or the other in order to make them fit. Could one imagine his horizon giving an equally flying start to a conversation with – say – Islam? Evidently not – which undoubtedly has to do with the role of underlying ontological suppositions.

Cobb's *no* to Hick / Knitter rests on a paradoxical-sounding accusation against the declared "pluralists" for a narrow concept of religious commonality. Their invocation of a universally adaptable idea of godhead as common denominator can impossibly apply to the great religions of the East, and to Buddhism less than to any. "We must be prepared to subject our views of divine transcendence to the test."[65]

Which then, according to Cobb, are the issues of particular importance for "a mutual transformation" of Buddhism and Christianity? And in which direction(s) does he see that process running? As could be expected, the central Buddhist concept of Nirvana – here translated as: Emptiness – becomes a main key to the exchange. The customary inadequacy of occidental interpretations of this category seems in recent years to be yielding place to increased listening and empathy.[66] Cobb offers a coherent interpretation of "emptiness", stressing the personal experience of a "passing over" as condition for grasping an ontological orientation profoundly different from that of the West.[67] But just as important is the "Coming Back": it is just in their difference that the two visions of reality enrich each other, and it is in their reciprocal awareness of own identities that the two religions undergo mutual transformation and "convert apparent contradictions into complementary contrasts."[68]

Christian belief in Christ as "the Truth", and readiness to share this conviction with others, does not tune down, but rather accentuates the obligation to explore "the deepest dimensions of reality". Precisely the conviction of Christ as truth universal, demands, in order to be credible, a confrontation with the truths of any people with whom we want to share that testimony.

[65] Cobb 1982, 45 (36–46).
[66] Ibid., 55–74.
[67] Ibid., 75–95.
[68] Ibid., 97 (97–118).

"In this way we can embody that Truth which leads to ever new truths rather than falsify it by presenting our limited truths as if they were the Truth."[69]

So far, one can say that the specificity of the Buddhist challenge has come little to the fore in COBB's reflection, except for the striking concentration on the difference not of conceptualized opinions, but of underlying ontologies in the two religions. From the very beginning, he has taken differences in way of thinking as an observation prior to, and determinant of, observable differences in thought. What Christians are supposed to receive from Buddhists, is defined not in terms of a doctrinal, but an epistemological widening of horizon. Encounter with an entirely different image of reality demands a break-up from the narrowness of traditional identification of Christ the Truth with a limited, conventionally Christian, collection of "truths". Precisely in that setting Nirvana, expression of the ultimate non-objectifiable character of truth, more than anything inspires veneration for the universal mystery of being = becoming. To Christians a sharing of this discovery will actualize ineffable dimensions in their own faith.

More explicit, however, is the corresponding proposition of a Christian contribution to the future development of Buddhism. COBB starts with "the universalist commitment, so central to Mahayana Buddhism", which has "its fullest expression so far in Pure Land Buddhism ... what is named Amida in Pure Land Buddhism is what Christianity calls Christ." This again leads to the brave assumption "that Buddhism can best advance through the recognition of the decisive incarnation of Amida in the historical Jesus."[70]

Here is how COBB sums up his vision of "mutual transformation" of the "two traditions", as he prefers to call them:

"A Buddhisized Christianity and a Christianized Buddhism may continue to enrich each other and human culture generally through their differences ... First, it is the mission of Christianity to become a universal faith in the sense of taking into itself the alien truths that others have realized. This is no mere matter of addition. It is instead a matter of creative transformation.... a Christianity limited to its own parochial traditions, cannot fulfill its mission of realizing the universal mission of Jesus Christ .... When it appeals for total commitment to so fragmentary a realization of Christ, it is idolatrous ... it is the mission of a self-transforming Christianity to invite other religious traditions to undergo self-transformation as well. There is nothing wrong with opening our doors to individual converts from other traditions. Indeed, if we begin seriously to undergo self-transformation we will need the help of those who have known the truths from within other traditions. But more important than the conversion of individual Buddhists, Hindus, or Muslims is the conversion of Buddhism, Hinduism, and Islam. I have tried to indicate what that might mean in the case of Mahayana Buddhism."[71]

---

[69] Ibid., 120, cf. 119–143.

[70] Ibid., 121, refers to a Japanese branch of Buddhism, emerging in the twelfth century. Amida means "infinite light", and signalizes, according to COBB, an appearance of Buddha as the great mediator of grace, to be met and embraced in faith.

[71] Ibid., 142, cf. 140–143.

It would take us too far to raise the issue of whether Cobb's observations on Mahayana ("the great vehicle") version of Buddhism might pertain to Buddhism in general, including those of the stricter Minayana – "the small vehicle" – observance. In any case it seems apparent that his reflections on Nirvana and ontological awareness contain a reference to Buddhism in general, irrespective of historical differentiations, far beyond the Amida experience of salvation.

Interesting in a special way is Cobb's 'Postscript: Buddhism, Christianity and the Philosophy of Whitehead'.[72] Not only does he express indebtedness to the father of 20th century process thought, who has equipped him with the philosophical instrumentality needed for a congenial approach to Buddhism. He goes beyond that, and voices regret that neither Whitehead nor his followers so far have explored Buddhism and its resources for human self-understanding. As much as Whitehead has – unintentionally – opened the gates of Buddhism to Cobb, Buddhism has widened his understanding of his own philosophical identity.

> "We Whiteheadians have consistently interpreted Whitehead in a way that reduces his radical break with substantialist and dualist modes of thought ... Whitehead himself was not able fully to carry through his own intentions."[73]

Evidently, there is no theological (and philosophical) school in the Western, "Christian" world which can claim an epistemological relationship with Buddhism like Process thought.

5.2.2.3. Katsumi Takizawa – A "Christian Buddhist"

Recalling the name of Katzumi Takizawa, we step outside the main arena of international dialogue. As a student of Karl Barth in Germany/Switzerland in the pre-dialogue era, this most conscious heir of Japanese Buddhist tradition(s!) relates to traditional trends of continental European Protestantism more than to ecumenical trends of post-war Christianity. His presentation is deeply marked by the fact that his medium of communication is German, not English.[74] His identity as citizen of two worlds is fascinating – and not a little enigmatic. In interwar Europe we meet a Buddhist student at the feet of Karl Barth, the die-hard advocate of Biblical revelation, with his rejection of modernity and of all attempts to compromise 'das Wort Gottes' with extra-biblical religion. What is a Japanese Buddhist doing there?

Takizawa's chef d'oeuvre must be his Reflexionen über die universelle Grundlage vom Buddhismus und Christentum.[75] Our first observation is his consistent attempt not to

---

[72] Ibid., 145–150.

[73] Ibid., 145f.

[74] Takizawa's life, his way to Christianity through Karl Barth, and his relationship with the various Buddhist traditions, are instructively reported by Schoen 1984, 137–150. Of interest is also Theo Sundermeier (ed.) 'Katsumi Takizawa: Das Heil im Heute – Texte einer japanischen Theologie', 1987, particularly Sundermeier's lecture in Fukuoka at the post mortem promotion of Takizawa to honorary doctor of theology (University of Heidelberg), with an analysis of his contribution to the "intercultural theological conversation", 11–24.

[75] Frankfurt a.M. / Bern / Cirencester 1980.

limit a Buddhist-Christian dialogue – as we have seen Cobb doing it – to a rendez-vous with Amida and the tradition of the "Pure Country" (Jôdo-shin-shu-Buddhism), the branch of Buddhism with which also Takizawa feels most closely related. He intentionally attempts also to remain in contact with a radically different Japanese branch of Buddhism, the profoundly philosophically oriented Zen.[76]

For Takizawa the clue, when comparing Buddhism and Christianity, is not the customary nirvana/kenosis, but "The Power of the Other and the Power of the Self."[77] Strangely, his reconciliation of Buddhism and Christianity proceeds by a reconcilia-tion of his two contrasting Buddhist traditions. He contends that the Amida of the "Pure Country" by no means implies a passive surrender of thoughts and ethical self-control, but a confidence in "das ganz Andere" (complete otherness), which opens up for "a responsibility including oneself and the whole world". Zen, on the other hand, must not be falsely interpreted as another brand of secularized individualism, which is frequently done in the West. Its fundamental allegiance to individual personhood rests fully in a vision of Buddha as mystically present in every human person.[78]

Confronting this dialectical specter of Buddhism with a corresponding intrinsic dynamic in Christianity, Takizawa draws a preliminary conclusion:

> "Auf diese Weise sehe ich das Christentum und den Buddhismus ... als jeweils besonderen Wiederschein oder besonderes Echo des wahren einen Logos oder Dharmas in dieser Welt ... im gemeinsamen Lebensgrund des ganzen Menschengeschlechtes ... Doch in der Religi-on kommt es sachlich weder darauf an, dass sie auf die Kraft des anderen wie im Shin-Buddhismus oder auf die Kraft des Selbst wie im Zen-Buddhismus Gewicht legt, noch, darauf, dass es in ihr eine geschichtlich erschienene Gestalt wie im Christentum in den Vordergrund tritt oder umgekehrt, wie im Buddhismus die ewig gegenwärtige Wahrheit, sondern vor allem darauf, was für eine 'Kraft des Anderen' oder 'Kraft des Selbst' dabei gemeint ist und in welcher Weise die geschichtliche Form für wichtig gehalten wird." [79]

On this background, it is with excitement that we follow Takizawa to dialogue with his teacher Barth. That discussion focuses on a remarkable footnote on 'Amida' in Barth's *Die Kirchliche Dogmatik*.[80] Here Barth expresses a certain, but dialectically balanced, appreciation of Amida as a remarkable expression of divine grace. He sees it as an ally in combating the general concentration of religions on merits and ratio-

---

[76] A sharper confrontation of the two traditions is found in van Straelen: Le zen demystifié, and: Ouverture à l'autre (both: 1982), further: L'église et les religions non chrétiens – Au seuil du XXIe siècle (1994). – van Straelen, himself a Catholic missionary in Japan for 40 years, and advocate of a rather conservative Thomist theology, expresses a remarkably sympathetic judgement on "Pure Country" Ami-dism (1994: 153–167) – a striking contrast to his restrictive attitude to non-Christian religions in gene-ral and to Zen Buddhism in peculiar. He accuses Zen of intellectual arrogance (169–192), but joins the respected progressive cardinal Henri S. de Lubac S.J. in describing Amida as "la fleur du bouddhisme", 167.

[77] Cf. headline, Takizawa 1980, 46.

[78] Ibid., 28–31.

[79] Ibid., 33f.

[80] Die Kirchliche Dogmatik (1932ff) I,2, 372–377, reproduced by Takizawa, 1980, 67–72.

nal bargaining. To Japanese readers that rather famous footnote may, after all, be rather disappointing. In certain of Barth's expressions they may easily identify "the self-sufficiency of Christians, the absolutification of Christianity so widespread in the West". This Takizawa refutes as a valid interpretation of Barth's theology in general, and he responds to the supposable criticism in two chapters carrying the headlines "The Double Meaning of the Name Jesus Christ in Karl Barth" and "New and Old Thinking in the Theology of Karl Barth".[81]

He maintains that BARTH speaks of Jesus Christ as "the original reference point between God and Man ... the God-Man, in whom God himself is at work as a real, existing human being." This is the Christ who "suddenly delivered the young Karl Barth from the old fettering of the Christian religion to the pitfall of modern liberalism and humanism." At the same time this means that in Barth's thinking "that side of the 'Man Jesus' falls completely away, with which a historically concrete, carnal person expresses God himself."[82] In spite of this, TAKIZAWA has certain difficulties in reconciling his image of Barth with his reading of the said footnote:

> "Wenn KARL BARTH sich noch einen Schritt weiter begeben und sich vom letzten Rest der 'Theologia naturalis' befreit hätte, indem er durch und durch bei dem Urfaktum, der ursprünglichen Beziehung zwischen Gott und Mensch, geblieben wäre, hätte er sicher nicht den Namen Jesus Christus verabsolutiert wie er es in seiner Fußnote tat."[83]

With this, TAKIZAWA leaves us in a double puzzlement. First: concerning interpretation of BARTH. Among Barth interpreters there is general agreement that a surprising opening-up to extra-biblical revelation takes place, but of a late date.[84] But in that regard, can we look away from the witness of Takizawa, who after all seems to have been one of Barth's closest informants and conversation partners in the matter of extra-biblical religion? Schoen sees Takizawa's proposal to distinguish two meanings of "Jesus Christ" in the work of Barth – the preexistent and the historical – as "helpful, to see more clearly in our task ... to sort out simple absoluteness."[85] Whether Barth for his part would have subscribed to such a statement of task, may, however, be a different issue.

More fascinating than a discussion about BARTH's stand, however, is a comparison of TAKIZAWA's Buddhist-Christian approach to that of MASAO ABE. Abe's focus on sunyata/kenosis may, as indicated already by our survey of the Honolulu Symposium

---

[81] TAKIZAWA 1980, 76–81 & 85–87.

[82] Ibid., 85: "Daher fällt bei ihm die Seite des 'Menschen Jesus' völlig weg, mit der ein historisch bestimmter, fleischlicher Mensch Gott selbst ausdrückt ..."

[83] Ibid., p. 87.

[84] Cf. our earlier observations on Barth (4.3.2), particularly 4.3.2. note 229! Also Ulrich SCHOEN, strong admirer av Takizawa and supporting his image of "the real Barth", voices divergence on chronology: "Dieser wahre Barth is derjenige, in dessen Denken von Anfang an ein fruchtbarer Keim enthalten war, der sich zwanzig Jahre später ... zu Aussagen entwickelte, die von einer 'von westlichen Christen unmöglichen, unerhörten ernsten Offenheit' gegenüber den nicht-christlichen Religionen zeugen. Leider kam diese Entwicklung zu spät ..." (SCHOEN 1984, 92)

[85] SCHOEN, op.cit., 148.

1984/ 1990, be seen as highly representative of contemporary attempts to bring Buddhism and Christianity together. But do not Abe's and Takizawa's projects conceptually move in diametrically opposite directions?[86]

To ABE, heir of traditional Buddhist "atheism", the appealing aspect of Christianity is that of divine kenosis, i.e. "emptying" = radical historicity. God, as proclaimed in and by Christ, is identifiable only in the shape of unmitigated servanthood. In terms of contemporary theological language this reflects a radical "christology from below". The transcendent mystery anticipated behind, may remind us of what fifth century Church Fathers spoke of as an 'apophatic' concept of godhead – unpronounceable while radically non-objectifiable.

TAKIZAWA's approach may be described in contrasting terms: a "christology from above". The preexistent, universal "Jesus Christ" is only for a limited, illustrative purpose to be spoken of as one specific character in history. Couldn't this vision be seen as reminiscent of what early Christianity called Docetism: the Divine Logos presented only in the seeming appearance of a human body? This, in case, would be in clear contradiction to Karl Barth's Nicene 'neo-orthodoxy'.

In spite of this, it is not difficult to see how the contrary approaches of ABE and TAKIZAWA unite in protesting the Nicene idea of Divine incarnation as one, unique, historically integrated unification of godhead and humanity. They just attack the synthesis from opposite sides, one of them retaining deity but exempt from the particularity of a historical appearance, the other retaining the appearance in history but emptying it of any resemblance for divine appearance.

Abe questions the very idea of divine presence as metaphysically impossible. But what with his attempt to identify biblical κενωσις with the nirvana of metaphysical emptiness? Wouldn't that change a unique historic event – the way κενωσις is explained in Phil 2 – into sunyata, presumably an ontologically permanent state of being? Is it logically meaningful to speak of kenosis and sunayata as complementary expressions of one unified concern?

---

[86] It may be illuminating to observe how Takizawa profiles his own attitude toward the main streams of (Japanese) Buddhism. His affiliation with Jodo-shin ("Pure Country") doesn't prevent him from a constructive dialogue with the Zen concept of ontological "otherness". Still more recommendable than in Zen he finds this concern expressed by the philosopher Kitaro Nishida, whom he compares with his Christian hero Karl Barth – with a slight preference declared to the latter. (TAKIZAWA 1980, 127ff.)

Jean-Claude BASSET in his extensive survey 'Le dialogue interreligieux, Histoire et avenir', 1996, introduces the dialogue initiatives of Keiji Nishitani and the "Kyoto School" as the key event not only in Buddhist-Christian conversation, but in contemporary interreligious dialogue as a whole. This Zen-based initiative on the Japanese stage in many ways resembles Abe's intervention in the international debate. – Nishitani's and his "school" are characterized by frequent references to radical Christian mystics like Meister Eckhart, and of a respectful reinterpretation of the biblical kenosis: "L'au-delà du dialogue' de la tradition zen apparait dès lors comme un nécessaire correctif au monopole occidental de la parole intelligible et à son anthropologie implicite ... à élargir et approfondir un rencontre ... pas seulement ... de deux systèmes de pensée ... mais de deux manières d'être, enracinées dans deux perceptions de la même réalité ultime. De tous les dialogues interréligieux contemporains, celui ... entre chrétiens et bouddhistes zen est assurément le plus exigeant et le plus prometteur ..." (BASSET, 384f, cf. the whole section 374–387)

TAKIZAWA, on the other hand, relativizes the historical event in its supposed uniqueness, seeing the incarnation, unification of godhead and humanity, as fulfilled in a timeless preexistence. But neither his teacher BARTH nor any New Testament author ever pondered the possibility of identifying eternal godhead and incarnation, thus reading the coming of Christ in "flesh" as pure reference to a mystery eternal (cf. John 1)!

In spite of these not undisturbing questions it may definitely be meaningful to ponder the question of ULRICH SCHOEN: What about "the task to sort out simple absoluteness"? Can not only christological meditation, but biblically oriented reflection on the relatedness of God and the world in its entirety, profit from the challenge of Buddhist ontology? Could reflection on this basic issue contribute to the purification of a theological language which, in the age of post-modernity, seems to have lost a good deal of its communicative power – possibly due to generations' preponderance of repetition over reflection? In few constellations of interreligious approach are the given frameworks of conceptuality more discrepant, and need more initial clarification, than in the case of the Abrahamic religions and the faiths of the Far East.

What then about the ethical implications of such an exchange, burning as everyday challenges may be in the context of today's world? That a Buddhist-Christian dialogue on ethics so far has been lagging behind – a good deal behind – the exploration of ontological foundations, must be due to the structuring of logical procedure more than to some joint estimate of priorities. Or maybe precisely such an estimate would have revealed a difference – Eastern contemplation versus Western activism – that in itself might explain why?

Ontological diversity causes reciprocal alienation also when facing a common responsibility for our contemporary world. There seems to be a joint fear of entering issues – be it with practical proposals as well as with political comments – as long as the danger of violating the identity of a dialogue partner feels more acute than does the urgency of shared responsibility. It is also easy to see why the distance so deeply felt between biblical faith in creation and a Buddhist concept of nirvana, induces immediate uncertainty in face of joint approaches to what have become more and more challenges in and on one common world. On that background, the temptation of lingering too long in ontology may become an obstacle to dialogical progress more than a clearing of the lane before us. But does that need to happen?[87]

---

[87] A promising sign of an extended Buddhist-Christian dialogue – thematically and geographically – could be observed in: DdR 1–95 92–95: 'Buddhisten und Christen für Gerechtigkeit, Frieden, Bewahrung der Erde – Internationales Symposion vom 17.–22. Juli 1994 ... Bad Schönbrunn' with the aim: "den christlich-buddhistischen Dialog voranzubringen und auch in Europa so zu etablieren wie dies in Nordamerika oder Japan schon seit geraumer Zeit der Fall ist." In any case, the practical orientation of that event did not seem to reflect a main thrust of Buddhist-Christian conversations in the other parts of the world mentioned up to then! – Cf. KVÆRNE: 'Økokrisen i buddhistisk lys' (in: ØSTNOR 1995, 206–212).

5.2.3. Hinduism

Hinduism is the matrix of Buddhism, and the latter can hardly be understood unless considerable attention is paid to that fact. The geographical expansion of Buddhism has, however, gone in directions away from the Indian continent, to Sri Lanka, to Indochina, Tibet, China and Japan. Thus Hinduism has remained *the* religion of the Indian mainland (ca. 80% of the population of India), an observation powerfully confirmed through the revival of Indian nationalism in the 20th century.

In terms of worldwide attention, the name of 'Hinduism' may be less celebrated than that of 'Buddhism'. But Hinduism as a complex source of spiritual currents seems by no means less present than Buddhism, its most mature daughter. In the last hundred years the spreading of Hindu impulses is identifiable under different labels, such as Theosophy, Krishna, Transcendental Meditation, a variety of Yoga schools and Guru communities. Hindu spirituality has shown an immense aptitude to enter into relationships with traditions of highly different origins.

In the 20th century break-through of dialogue, Hindu inspiration has plaid a visible role. We have already outlined the particular contribution of the professed Hindu-and-Christian RAIMUNDO PANNIKAR (4.1.3.). We have also seen how in the case of STANLEY SAMARTHA (4.1.3.), for years the trend-setting director of the World Council of Churches' Dialogue program, Hindu environments as formative horizon are easily recognizable in his presentation.

In the following we shall focus (1) on Hindu India as a cradle of dialogue, (2) on a specific Hindu emphasis in the theology of religions in contemporary Germany (MICHAEL VON BRÜCK), (3) as well as in the contemporary USA (DIANA ECK).

5.2.3.1. A Hindu Cradle of Interreligious Dialogue?

In his contribution to *The Myth of Christian Uniqueness* STANLEY J. SAMARTHA calls particular attention to the interaction between his Hindu reference background and his own entrance on the international scene of dialogue.[88] He traces the history of a coexistence in reciprocal tolerance between Hindus and Christians, ever since the 16th century arrival of Roman-Catholic missionaries in India. He sees such tolerance as deeply rooted in the Hindu way of thinking as well as in what he regards an authentic understanding of Christianity.

> "In no other country, therefore, does the claim for the 'uniqueness' of one particular religious tradition or the assertion of the 'normativeness' of one particular faith over others sound so rude, out of place, and theologically arrogant as in India." [89]

In his historical sketch SAMARTHA draws the scenery up to the present time with a climax in the remarkable openness to the person of Jesus in post-Gandhi India. The only requirement for Christianity in order to obtain a meaningful exchange with

---

[88] HICK & KNITTER 1987/88, 69–88.
[89] Ibid., 75.

Hinduism is, according to Samartha, to develop a "theocentric christology" void of what he sees as an "idolatrous" claim of uniqueness. The christology asked for, then, must

"... take into account at least two factors that have emerged out of India's long history of multireligious life. One is the acceptance of a sense of Mystery and the other the rejection of an exclusive attitude where ultimate matters are concerned."[90]

A slightly more differentiated image of the Indian stage is given by ISRAEL SELVANAYA-GAM some years later.[91] This author gives great importance to a series of initiatives aiming at dialogue between Christians and Hindus, started 1956 by the Christian Institute for the Study of Religion and Society and its founder/director P.D. DEVA-NANDAM, and continued by his successor, the well-known ecumenist M.M. THOMAS, for a period moderator of the WCC Central Committee.[92] Selvanayagam complains not only about a general unwillingness to dialogue within the Protestant churches in India. He also finds a certain ambiguity in Hindu readiness, confirmed not only by history, but by rather spectacular events in the present.

"The much celebrated Hindu tolerance stands exposed in the Ayoadhya issue ... While many view this as a deviation from the Hindu principle of tolerance, others argue quite justifiably, that there never has been tolerance in Hinduism beyond a limit ... Tolerance was a principle incorporated into bramanic Hinduism, but never fundamental to it".[93]

An issue of *Current Dialogue*, a regular World Council of Churches' information paper, a few years back reviewed five Hindu-Christian consultations in India, taking place in October 1995.[94] Two of these events were explicitly dedicated to the relationship between Hindus and Christians. The three others dealt with aspects of religious activities in the contemporary world in general, but under a horizon undeniably Indian. For our purpose it may suffice to throw a look at the first two.

An impressive task is set by the conference 'Working for Harmony in the Contemporary World: A Hindu-Christian Dialogue'.[95] But regrettably its focus is nearly exclusively on 'Harmony', as perceived by each of the two traditions respectively. In the conference report the question is hardly touched, of whether in our contemporary world 'Harmony' can be meaningfully explored by, and in, two traditions of faith without some orientative consultation with and about the surrounding world. It is

[90] Ibid., 75.

[91] 'A Dialogue on Dialogue' 1995, preface by SAMARTHA.

[92] Ibid., X ff. – The report from the Working Group on Hinduism at the consultation on "other faiths" held by the Lutheran World Federation in Bangkok July 1996, in its historical survey calls attention to the fact that Hindus in the mid-nineteenth century initiated a series of dialogues with Christians in order to seek impulses for what to them at the time seemed a necessary, purifying renewal of their own religion. In: MWAKABANA 1997 (LWFD 41), 129 (117–159).

[93] Ibid., 33. – In Ayodhya, India, in December 1992 the Babri Majid mosque was violently destroyed by a fanatic Hindu mob, cf. MWAKABANA 1997, 117.

[94] CD 29, January 1996.

[95] Madurai Kamaraj University, Oct. 9–11, 1995, with 40 participants, half of them Hindus, half of them Christians.

not brought clearly to the fore that social 'Harmony' is no simple function of philo-sophy and/or meditation. Today, no less than in the past, an integral study of 'Har-mony' will have to take important elements of culture, tradition, economy, politics etc. into consideration. In spite of its methodological limitation, however, the report concludes with a series of recommendations for everyday coexistence, several of them worth attention. But instructions for practical adaptation are rather vague.

Truly, it may be advisable, as is recommended by the Harmony conference, to start a Hindu-Christian exchange on 'Harmony' (= peaceful coexistence) precisely by in-specting differences of ontology and language. In this regard the premises seem little different from the exchange between Buddhists and Christians. Differences in the style of cognition and communication must be observed, before decisive progress can be made on "the issue". But it is essential to realize from the start that this task is not fulfilled with a bare clarification of principles.

The workshop on "Issues in the Hindu-Christian Relations", presented in the same issue of CD, speaks right to the heart of the dialogue issue. The aim of this event was an agreement on guidelines for future bilateral conversation between Hindus and Christians. This is completed in terms of "Some Guiding Principles" (§§ 10–21) and "Practical Guidelines ... At the level of school, college, university (§§ 22–30) ... At the level of village, town and city (§§ 31–41) ... National level" (§§ 42–50). It might be instructive to reflect on these rules: which are applicable to interreligious dialogue in general, which are relevant predominantly, or exclusively, in a Hindu-Christian (and / or, possibly, in a Buddhist-Christian) setting?

Most fascinating is, however, what HANS UCKO, leader of the WCC Office on Inter-Religious Issues in Geneva, reports about the working procedure of the work-shop, especially the daring idea to have the participants start by stating frankly their advance impression of the dialogue partner.[96] According to his description it was above all the frankness of the Hindu representatives which secured the success of the method, the Christians needing a little more time to overcome immediate shyness. As quoted in the report, the list of provocative reciprocal challenges is considerably shortened, and it is reproduced in a somewhat diplomaticized form:

"Challenges.

7. Our experience of dialogue makes us aware of some of the issues that make Hindu-Christian relationship difficult and at times even impossible. The Hindus find the absolute claims for the Church, for Jesus, the traditional methods of missionary activity and the labelling on non-Christians as sinners etc., very offensive. There are also such accusations as extra-territorial loyalties, de-culturalization, etc. already levelled against Indian Christians.

8. The Christians are uncomfortable with the tendency of their Hindu friends to mini-mize the differences that exist between religious traditions and make Hinduism as an all-inclusive umbrella of truth. Likewise, they find it difficult to understand the Hindu's pro-clivity to downplay the reality of suffering, oppression, and discrimination by reducing

[96] CD 29, 3–6. "This procedure was a bold move by the organisers, which very well could have put an end to dialogue," 3.

them all to Karma and fate. The age-old problem of Untouchability, socio-economic exploitation, and gender injustice still persists in the name of religious sanctions.

9. The Workshop identified the need to study these and other issues so that our dialogue helps us to grow in genuine religiosity, promoting human dignity and solidarity. We hope that our future meetings will enable us to clarify these areas, and also to identify concerns such as social justice which call for sustained cooperation and collaboration."[97]

It is not our task to enter into the discussion invited here. But it may be appropriate to observe the main issue as regarded from opposite sides by the two colloquial partners, namely: What about the character and handling of religious truth claims? Friendly embracement by Hindus of (non-exclusive) truth claims as voiced by other faiths – this, at least, is what it looks like – too, may be felt by Christians (as also by followers of other faiths, not least Muslims) as expressing a distinctive claim of moral superiority (being in itself a superior truth "umbrella", wide enough to shelter the rest of the world). But there may be reasons to observe this, rather annoying, trend as reflecting primarily dynamics of tolerance operative within the complex spiritual fellowship of Hinduism itself.

"Hindus have hindutva, six schools of Hinduism and no centralized system ... the Hindu society has not evolved around one single person like Christ. There is a plurality."[98] To the name of Christ could here have been added those of Buddha, Moses, Muhammed, Confucius ... In no other world religion with a historical collection of holy writings as foundation, is the face of a gründer missing in the way it is in Hinduism. This may to some extent account for the multiplicity of imagery, concepts and religious practices characterizing the Hindu constituency, loosely aligned as it is in terms of structure.

The model of one universal truth dressed in an infinity of garbs – so decisive to the Hindu interpretation of own identity – seems easily transportable from an intra- to an inter-religious stage. Even if this implies a wider, more distant and less obliging radius of orientation, it does not seem difficult for a Hindu eye to observe the wide realm of religions as an external orbit of a domestic spiritual precinct.

The only factor apt to destabilize this vision will be a truth claim refusing integration into such a preestablished model of universality. The challenge of an explicitly alternative claim will be a provocation, especially while experienced as a threat to the historical unity of Indian culture. In that case it is precisely the reputed Hindu tolerance which can, as ironically suggested in Selvanayagam's remark on the Ayoadhya episode, light the fires of protesting violence. Also the long-term armed conflict between Cinghalese Buddhists and Tamil Hindus on Sri Lanka may indicate the limitation of such an ideologically founded tolerance (proper to both the traditions concerned) in face of hard-core societal realities. Maybe a new and more radically motivated dialogue may help, a dialogue ready to let divergent truth claims really face each other in the ways each of them is prepared to present itself?

---

[97] Ibid., 11.
[98] Hans Ucko, ibid., 5.

5.2.3.2. A Continental Approach to Hinduism: M. v. Brück

We have already, in the general context of a pluralist theology of religions, dealt extensively with the Hindu-inspired reflections of MICHAEL VON BRÜCK, professor in Munich with several years of studies in India behind him.[99] At the same time it is of importance to see his magisterial study *Einheit der Wirklichkeit – Gott, Gotteserfahrung und Meditation im hinduisch-christlichen Dialog* (1986) in light of the same dialogue, where von Brück presents himself as a participant no less than an observer.

Hindu-Christian dialogue is not only the topic of his study, but just as much the structuring principle of it. VON BRÜCK is not primarily occupied with describing and analyzing the dialogue between two religions as an actually evolving process. Most important for him is to present an ideally constructed Hindu-Christian dialogue, such as it might proceed if faithfully respecting fundamental convictions of both.

> "Diese Arbeit möchte vor allem einen Beitrag zur Klärung und Deutlichkeit im theologischen Gespräch leisten. Der Dialogpartner ist ein Spiegel, in dem eigene Schwächen und Stärken erscheinen. Die gegenseitige Spiegelung ist ein Weg, zur vertieften Selbstverständnis zu finden. Der Höhepunkt des Dialogs liegt dort, wo der andere zur Quelle des Selbstverständnisses wird. Dieses Geschehen ist gleichzeitig der Inbegriff personaler Gemeinschaft, um die Menschen verschiedenen Glaubens ringen. Auf unsere Studie angewandt heißt dies, dass *Advaita* zur Quelle des Selbstverständnisses der Trinität werden kann." [100]

This lays a clear, if by no means uncontroversial, methodological foundation. The 'mirror principle' as we see it phrased here, must obviously be applicable to bilateral dialogues, whoever the partners may be in a concrete case. Notwithstanding that, it may invite reflection to ask: would a similar orientation have recommended itself so readily if Christians were facing not one of the great "mystery religions" of the East, but Judaism, Islam or declared followers of old Nordic religions? After all, the image of a mirror immediately suggests a difference in perceptive attitudes rather than disagreement on some substantial truth.

v. BRÜCK's programmatic remark about Advaita as a key to understanding the Christian doctrine of Holy Trinity is more extensively explained in the course of his study. What he attempts, is to explain Hinduism (supposedly unknown to the reader) through a face-to-face with Christianity (supposedly familiar). The aim of this procedure is evidently (1) to make an unknown religion known by relating it to corresponding elements in the reader's already existing universe of understanding, 2) to make the unknown productive, shedding new light on corresponding elements in the religion already known. In this way, new understanding and wider acceptance of the world of faiths will finally help the reader to relate more consciously to the orientation which is already his/hers.

This may not be the place to discuss the particular thesis on Advaita and Trinity, but maybe for observing a little more closely its role within a wider argumentative horizon. We observe that Advaita, the central Hindu principle of metaphysical one-

---

[99] Cf. our sequence 4.1.5.
[100] v. BRÜCK, 1986, 3.

ness, and Trinity are synchronized through the triple division of von Brück's study: "1. Non-Duality in Hinduism. 2. Non-Duality of the Doctrine of Trinity. 3. Unity of Reality." At first glance "non-duality" may sound rather trivial as common denominator of "unity" and "trinity". Neither 1 nor 3 is divisible by 2. An immediate impression of superficiality will, however, crumble as soon as the underlying concern is recognized: that of distinguishing a universal principle of integration. Two short quotations may illustrate this:

> "Wenn der Partner Quelle meines Selbstverständnisses wird, ist er auch Quelle meines Gottesverständnisses. Indem man die eigene kulturelle, sprachliche und theologische Relativität entdeckt, wird man frei, zu neuen Ufern aufzubrechen. Auf dieser Grundlage kann z.B. der Advaita Vedânta zur Quelle für das spezifisch christliche trinitarische Gottesverständnis werden, wie wir hier zu demonstrieren versuchen."[101]
>
> "... nicht nur ... die advaitische Erfahrung des einzelnen Menschen, wie sie in Jesus Christus anschaubar ist, sondern auf die Verwirklichung des Advaita von Gott und Menschheit bis hin zur universellen Integration, die wir mit dem Begriff der Einheit der Wirklichkeit bezeichnet haben. Wo immer diese advaitische Kraft des Geistes wirklich wird, ist das von Jesus verkündigte Gottesreich nahe."[102]

It is not easy to discover the intrinsic movement of dialogue – a two-way exchange – in statements like these. In his study, dedicated to the "hinduisch-christlichen Dialog", von Brück seems unilaterally occupied with (1) exploring Hindu conceptuality, and (2) reinterpreting Christian categories in light of that. What else can be the meaning of making "the Advaita Vedânta the source of the particularly Christian Trinitarian understanding of God" and – on this background – of subsuming the essence of both religions under the definition "realization of the Advaita of God and humankind all the way up to universal integration ... indicated by the notion 'the Unity of Reality' "?

Without either confirming or rejecting VON BRÜCK's thesis about Advaita and Trinity, we observe an apparent insufficiency in his method. One could speak of a reversed preferentialism: taking one's point of departure in the partner's religion, and testing its ability to (re-)interpret one's own faith in the direction of a maximal consonance – without wasting time on possible objections en route.

To start a dialogue with Hinduism on the issue of Advaita – the unexplorable mystery everywhere present and providing all things there are with a unifying sense, rejecting any ontological confrontation of spirit and matter, God and world – may seem not only well- advised, but simply inevitable. The only question is how Advaita, understood as the unifying principle of Hinduism (cosmologically and also epistemologically), can be introduced as hermeneutical principle for what seems to occupy an equally integrating role in Christianity: the Trinitarian understanding of Godhead. Does this give reasonable support to infer: in both cases the role of a globally

---

[101] Ibid., 243.
[102] Ibid., 252.

unifying principle is essential, so observing the solution in one case, will immediately instruct us how to accommodate it also in the other?

I would suggest a somewhat hesitant answer: such procedure may provide us with important and undoubtedly relevant insights. The condition for drawing a conclusion is, however, that our observations take place within an overall comparison of two faith traditions, allowing each of them to speak for itself – as far as such a synchronization proves practicable. As we have seen it developed, VON BRÜCK's constellation of Advaita and Trinity scarcely implements that demand for fundamental equality of the partners.

I would hesitate to see this as primarily due to some particular spell of Hinduism on Westerners impressed by the idea of some universal conceptual integration. But attention should be given to the highly complex appeal of such a promise to observers tired of contemporary cultural fragmentation. With that reservation, the Oriental plea for cognitive integration may be worth both study and contemplation. But, as it indirectly appears from VON BRÜCK's advance, much epistemological clearance is needed before such exchange becomes real dialogue and not, in plain speech, a reversed monologue.

5.2.3.3: A North-American Approach to Hinduism: Diana L. Eck

When we choose to proceed with a quick review of DIANA L. ECK: *Encountering God – A Spiritual Journey from Bozeman to Benares*[103], it has to do with the extraordinary and, at the same time, unmistakably representative character of that document. In spite of its personal form, it is a scholarly account of a "typical Westerner" meeting and discovering the religious East. Years after her epochal discovery Eck, as professor at Harvard, looks back on that experience and its remaining imprint, now with the eyes of an expert, existentially motivated and academically equipped for an analytical reflection on a 'pilgrim's progress' which she is likely to share with a good number.

In its principal orientation her book relates to faith and to faiths, globally. The author presents herself as "a Christian ... a seeker ... who has traveled the path with Hindus and Buddhists, Muslims and Jews, Jains, Sikhs, and Native Americans". She is writing a book about how "my encounters with people of other faiths have challenged, changed and deepened my own faith." But for good reasons Hinduism comes first, as it becomes particularly clear already in the section on "The Names of God".[104]

The author reports her spiritual journey from growing up as a mid-stream Protestant (Methodist) of North-European descent in a small town in Montana, and how her interest in the great religions one day made her member, later moderator, of the WCC Working Group on Dialogue with People of Living Faiths.

A dramatic situation is reported from the (all-Christan) Dialogue conference in Chiang Mai 1977, where DR.ECK was assigned to conduct a morning worship, and was shocked to observe that 2/3 of the (all-Christian) audience did not join in the

---

[103] 1993.
[104] ECK, IX, cf. ibid., 45–80.

common reading of a series of Bhagavad Gita texts. – As one of the participants present in Chiang-Mai, and as one of that somewhat demonstrative majority, I certainly remember the event. In order to understand that reaction, it could be helpful to see it not only – maybe even, not primarily – as a stand on the particular, still much debated, issue of devotional fellowship across faith borders, or of the possible role of devotional exchange within the process of dialogue at large. The reaction may have responded just as much to the surprise effect of an unprepared challenge, and to some unpleasant feeling of being caught in a trap. A conference summoned to discuss premises and possible limits of interreligious dialogue felt itself invited to accept some important conclusion before having had the opportunity to face the basic issues implied. As I read her careful wording now, Eck in posterity may not be far from accepting my interpretation.

The most fascinating thing in her book is, however, how she explains Hinduism and uses it as a hermeneutical entrance to the understanding of the world of faiths at large. Facing the visionary complexity of the Veda world, her universal theory of religious reality takes its final shape.

> "The Hindu tradition is both monotheistic and polytheistic. Oneness and manyness are not seen as true opposites ... If something is important, it is important enough to be repeated, duplicated, and seen from many angles. There are many gods (devas), many divine descents of the gods (avataras), many ways of salvation (margas), and many philosophical systems (darshanas) ... Manyness is valuated; indeed, it is seen as essential. Hindu polytheism is simultaneously one of the most significant and one of the most difficult matters for Westerners to grasp in attempting to understand Hindu religious life ... One might, in fact, question whether Hindus "believe in Gods" at all. Rather, Hindus perceive the manyness of the Divine in a way that is both complex and helpful in our inquiry into the meaning of God. India's thinkers have explored the complexities of manyness more thoroughly and persistently than any on earth. Whether one is charmed, perplexed, or repulsed by India's unabashed polytheism, Hindu theological strategies for thinking about the manyness of God might enable us to get out of our conceptual routines and think about God in new ways."[105]

This is so far certainly an appropriate as well as challenging observation, inviting reflection rather than response! The only remark immediately to be made, is that speaking of manyness in such a language, automatically invokes oneness as the "reverse side of the coin". Not the oneness of God, the supreme Being, as presupposed in the "Abrahamic" religions, but of Being, prefigured as an overarching unity of existence visible and invisible. Here also lies, in spite of overwhelming differences in outward appearance, the basic commonality between Hinduism and its emancipated daughter Buddhism. In any case: a basic theme for East-West dialogue be hereby announced!

Let us follow ECK, as she turns and returns to conclusions with a more principal, universal – but even this, an unmistakably Hindu inspired – orientation:

---

[105] Ibid., 60f.

"Recognizing God is not an easy task. It is not the simple affirmation that all the visions of God are the same – they are not. And there are places and communities where I as a Christian do not have the experience of recognition. For me to recognize God as I know God in Vishnu and Shiva and for Mr. Gangadaram to recognize Shiva in Christian worship and language ... can only be the fruit of real encounter ... There are no easy, uncritical theological equations here. Yet as we are open to real encounter in the give-and-take of learning and un-learning our recognition of the one we call "God" can only become larger and clearer."[106]

The bearing of this statement may be a little diffuse. Does it relate exclusively to the subjective aspect: it is always difficult to see with the eyes of people from a culture other than one's own, particularly where fundamental issues of human existence are concerned? In that case the opinion voiced will probably not be contested by any reflective observer in any faith tradition. If, on the other hand, it is taken to prescribe distinctive borders to conflicting truth claims, how viable is a strategy of mutual rapprochement by limitative prescriptions?

5.2.4. Judaism

Judaism is in several regards a case of its own – not only when observed from the standpoint of Christianity. Historically, the Church must be seen as an offshoot of the Synagogue, and the New Testament is through and through based on the Old. In addition, the geographical presence of numerous Jewish communities within the precincts of a nominally "Christian" civilization has through the centuries fostered lamentable tensions and outbursts distinctive from everything else in world history. To some extent Judaism is also special, seen from the viewpoint of Islam, which recognizes divine origin of the Hebrew Bible and a far-reaching validity of a common prophetic legacy. But apart from these inner dynamics of "the Abrahamic family" – what is particular about Judaism when seen in the full perspective of worldwide dialogue?

Between the dialogue partners facing each other in the actual world of faiths, Judaism holds a position very much its own, due to its matchless combination of religion and nationhood, as well as to the historical role – in more than one regard dramatic – of the Jewish people. Beyond all discussion, the community of Jewish faith must be seen as the historical matrix of Christianity.

5.2.4.1. Peculiarity of Jewish-Christian Exchange

The Hebrew Bible – known in the Jewish tradition as three separate collections of scriptures: the Torah (Law), the Nebijim (Prophets), and the Ketubim (Writings) – has from the dawn of Christianity made up The Old Testament, an irreplaceable first half of its Holy Writ. More annoying to the relationship of the two faiths than the unnegotiated loan of scriptures, however, is the constitutive claim of Christianity.

---

[106] Ibid., 198.

From its very beginning it has presented Jesus as fulfilment of the Messianic promise – a "promise" already for centuries fundamental to the Jewish vision of salvation history.

Precisely this common ground of the two faiths, historical, conceptual and geographical – has caused more painful conflict, and for a longer time, than between any other two religions. Early Jewish measures of repression are reported through Christian sources, particularly the book of Acts. Certain examples of Jewish tolerance also recorded (e.g. Act 5:34ff, 17:10ff), were – alas – not equally remembered by Christian posterity. Remembrance of such primeval persecution, together with accusations against the Jewish people as collectively responsible for the murder of Jesus the Messiah, have been amply accentuated by nominal (often including official) champions of Christianity, from early Medieval times up to the twentieth century Holocaust.

In our day the Jewish-Christian dialogue distinguishes itself from other branches of interreligious dialogue. First, because it, to such an overwhelming extent, has taken place under the standard of repentance: Christians seeking expiation and reconciliation after the gloomy history of the Holocaust. Second, because the world has been obliged to respond to the establishment of the state of Israel, a response which seems to imply a theological stand no less than a political one.

Fundamentalist branches of Christianity, generally reserved to dialogue with other faiths, in most cases take an emphatically different attitude to Judaeo-Christian relations. Above all, their reading of the Bible encourages a vigorous support to the state of Israel, which they acclaim as a literal fulfilment of prophetic promise. "The International Christian Embassy" in Jerusalem, based on multinational cooperation between Christian groups sharing such a conviction, is a rather eloquent expression of what we are talking about. But it would inevitably cause more confusion than clarity if we subsumed this type of politico-religious support under the label of "Interreligious Dialogue".

5.2.4.2. What is "Israel"?

Closely attached to the issue of "biblical promise" and the contemporary state of Israel with its entanglement in the international power game, is a problem less striking to the general public, but which may well call for dialogical clarification in the years ahead. *"Israel: Race, People – or What?"* So the renowned Old Testament scholar SIGMUND MOWINCKEL phrased his question shortly after the proclamation of the state of Israel.[107] Judaism is fundamentally different not only from Christianity, but from all the big religions in its unmatched integration of ethnic and religious identity, of Jewish nationhood (by no means to be equated with Israeli citizenship, which is available also to non-Jews!) and allegiance to the community of Mosaic faith. Even those identifying themselves as "secular Jews", usually explain their ethnic identity

---

[107] Book title: 'Israel – rase, folk – eller hva?' Oslo 1949. – Cf. the article "Nationalism", in 'The New Standard Jewish Encyclopedia', Jerusalem 1975, col. 1414–17.

historically by referring to the Hebrew Bible, and take it for granted to have their domestic life framed by the Bible-based Jewish calendar.

Conversion to another faith – even to Christianity, which is founded on the same scriptures – is seen not only as religious apostasy, but as a desertion of Jewish nationhood. For that reason also, Israeli legal practice remains in a certain tension with the idea of religious freedom as understood in the Western world.

"A Christian Jew" is immediately taken for a contradiction in terms, and is also incompatible with the classificatory system of Israeli law. The same observation would apply to "a Muslim Jew" or a "Buddhist Jew". Jewish identity is manifestly based on a more than 3000 years old idea of divine covenant, chosen people, promised land. And it is powerfully reaffirmed by a unique solidarity developed by the history of the Jewish people. Above all, the complex Judaeo-Christian relations may have contributed to that incomparable synthesis of ethnic and religious self-understanding. How can that particular fact and its complicating influence on dialogue be approached – through dialogue? As far as can be seen, this methodological prerequisite has not yet, at the turn of millennium, been systematically explored by architects of Judaeo-Christian dialogue.

5.2.4.3. Developments in Jewish-Christian Dialogue

Peculiar to Jewish-Christian dialogue is the active cooperation of a permanent joint agency: The *International Council of Christians and Jews (ICCJ)*, founded in 1974.[108] It is worth observing that America had its *National Conference of Christians and Jews* already from 1928, and England had its *Council of Christians and Jews* from 1940. These pre-Dialogue occurrences may, when seen in a global perspective, be due not least to a substantial joint presence in a shared geographical room. In addition to these particular agencies, Jewish-Christian dialogue is today incorporated in the dialogical structures of The Roman-Catholic Church and The World Council of Churches, parallel to dialogue with other world religions. During the last decades a considerable number of churches in the Western world have made official declarations on Jewish-Christian relations, generally with explicit regrets of own deficiency in face of the Holocaust catastrophe (and the centuries long history that prepared for it.)

Representatives of mainline Christian dialogue engagements may in many cases be just as occupied with the wider "Abrahamic Dialogue" as with Judaism as a particular case of its own. Such dialogue will comprehend and compare the three "biblical faiths": Judaism, Christianity and Islam, making their common Abrahamic and

---

[108] It sounds promising for further exchange when the Theology Committee of the ICCJ in a general presentation of Judaeo-Christian dialogue (CD 28, 1995, 10) underscores the importance of noting "an obvious asymmetry" between the partners. But it is too narrow, when this "asymmetry" is identified only in terms of the one having its historical roots in the other, a circumstance – of course – beyond all reciprocality. Undeniably true, but ... ! Asymmetry seems just as much founded in the fact that the triangle: congregation-people-land so fundamental in the one case, has no parallel, and thus, traditonally, evokes little understanding in the other.

Mosaic legacy a distinctive and in itself stimulating precinct of dialogue.[109] HANS KÜNG, even in his close to 800-page volume on "Das Judentum" (1991), gives primary importance to that perspective:

> "Man hat nicht ohne Grund die drei Religionen, die sich auf ihn, Abraham, berufen und in denen der Mensch 'vor' Gott (coram Deo) steht, sich ganz auf Gott verlässt und so 'an' Gott (in Deum) glaubt – im Gegensatz zu den mystischen Einheitsreligionen Indiens oder auch den Weisheitsreligionen Chinas – als *Glaubensreligionen* bezeichnet. Abraham erscheint so als der gemeinsame Stammvater aller drei großen Religionen semitischen Ursprungs, die man deshalb auch die drei abrahamischen Religionen nennt. Sie können ... als ein großes religiöses Stromsystem nahöstlichen Ursprungs verstanden werden, das sich von den Systemen indischen oder fernöstlichen Ursprungs wesentlich unterscheidet"[110]

KÜNG's project is to approach Judaism, like he approaches Islam,[111] by a Christian vision which gives prominence to the appearance of Jesus from Nazareth as the main prophet within a more comprehensive biblical tradition, granting only secondary, critical attention to the dogmatic christology of what he judges as hellenized Christianity.

Even if KÜNG by this christological approach may have opened a lane to the hearts of his 'abrahamic' dialogue partners, he seems less successful in his apologetic treatment of another main issue of offence in Judaeo-Christian history: that of the Law (Torah) and the traditional Christian accusation against what has been seen as Judaic "legalism".

In the 'festschrift' for KÜNG's 65th birthday an impressive section is dedicated to "Dialog mit dem Judentum."[112] A selection of Jewish reactions to his big book on Judaism from 1991, already mentioned, is collected and presented from various sources, and Küng responds to his critics. Here are a few samples:

> "Das traditionelle christliche Gesetzverständnis wird nun leider auch in HANS KÜNGS neuem Buch *Das Judentum* fortgeführt ... eine Nichtachtung des Gesetzes durch Jesus postuliert ... Die Tradition ist im jüdischen Verständnis ... eine eingebaute Progressivität ... Das rabbinische Judentum ist die Krönung der biblischen Botschaft und das Mittel für ihre Verwirklichung." [113]
>
> "Schwierigkeiten hat KÜNG auch mit den Lehrern der jüdischen Tradition, die er offenbar mit ihm unliebsamen Erscheinungen in seiner Kirche zu identifizieren sucht. Dazu muss er dem "Gesetz" eine Rolle zuschreiben, die dem Judentum fremd ist ... Wenn er damit die Torah und ihre Auslegung meint, so kämen hier Begriffe wie Weisung, Deutung, Gebote, Pflichten, Legenden, Gleichnisse eher in Frage als der den Quellen unadäquaten Begriff von 'Gesetz'." [114]

---

[109] For presentation, see particularly KUSCHEL 1994, observed here 5.2.1.4.

[110] Ibid., 33f.

[111] Ibid., 388f, as to Islam cf. KÜNG a.o. 1984, 31–204. – For the wider setting in Küng's observation of church history, see his: Das Christentum, 1994, 89–335.

[112] HÄRING & KUSCHEL 1993, 519–586.

[113] Nathan Peter LEVINSON, P–F 14–2–1992.

[114] Ernst Ludwig EHRLICH, WW 13–2–1992.

"KÜNG gelingt es nicht, den wahren Zweck dieses Unternehmens ('des Gesetzes') zu bestimmen, nämlich die göttlichen Werte in den prosaischen Akten des täglichen Lebens zu erhalten. Er ... weist ihre intellektuelle Kraft als Kasuistik zurück."[115]

KÜNG defends his criticism of Jewish "legalism" with fervor:

"Wer als Theologe unvoreingenommen Parallelen zwischen der Orthodoxie allüberall wahrnimmt, ob im Judentum oder im Christentum, wer vergesetzlichte Strukturen überall der Kritik unterzieht, seien sie vom Jerusalemer Oberrabbinat oder vom Vatikan garantiert, gerät leicht von beiden Seiten unter Beschuss. Denn es ist nun einmal für Orthodoxen, wo immer sie leben (ob in Rom, Jerusalem oder Teheran), unbequem, sich anhören zu müssen, wie sehr sie das Prophetische in ihren eigenen Traditionen domestiziert haben, wie sehr Lehrgesetz."[116]

Whatever one may judge of KÜNG's conclusions, his type of argument is interesting in more than one regard. Whether it may be valid or not, his image of rabbinic legalism may be typical of Christian criticism of Judaism through the centuries. At the same time his ready admittance of horizon: he is criticizing various versions of Orthodoxy, Christian and Jewish, as samples of a common legalistic attitude – implies in itself a certain mitigation of his judgement on the Jewish Halaka (rabbinic ethical code). At the same time it contains a provocative confirmation of joint dialogue as a general means of detecting and critically exploring tendencies common to more than one religion.

It would evidently be a gross simplification to characterize Küng's study on Judaism as just another echo of his conflict with the Vatican. However, his readiness to confirm and restate traditional Christian criticism of Judaism in at least one ostentative regard – a strategy rather divergent from contemporary Christian approaches to Mosaic religion, and remarkably different also from his own mood of addressing extra-Christian faith communities – is hard to understand apart from his existential involvement with "legalism" as problem universal.

On the background of this vivid exchange in 1992/93, so unconventionally exposed in a "festschrift", an issue is indirectly put on the agenda, but is definitely left unresolved: Should the floor be reopened for the classical argument between Jews and Christians on the "Law" and on the importance of divine commandments for human salvation? If so: on which terms? Could this eventually be done in a less confrontative way than of old? At the root of the controversy on "the Law" lies, as one may have noticed, a focal dilemma already bordered in the first generation of Christians. Jews are reported by Christians to have accused them of "speaking words against ... the Law"[117], a topic fervidly discussed by the rabbinic ex-student Paul, particularly in his letters to the Galatians and the Romans.

As to the other capital dogmatical issue of Jewish-Christian argument throughout the centuries – the Messianic claim on behalf of Jesus – it is obvious that the two

---

[115] Anthony M. BAYFIELD, CT 27–3–1992.
[116] KÜNG (in: HÄRING & KUSCHEL 1993), 563.
[117] Act 6:13.

topics of dispute are interrelated. But it is also clear that the two discussions may evolve differently so that distinctive lanes of exchange may develop. In the last two generations, the developing conversation between Jews and Christians has either – in the shadow of the Holocaust – been on recent Jewish-Christian relations, or it has been on the Jew Jesus and his importance for (the non-Jewish segment of) human-kind.

5.2.4.5. "Common Religious Basis" – A Stage or a Stalemate?
Jews and Christians in Search of a Common Religious Basis for Contributing towards a Better World is the title of a document issued by the ICCJ in 1995.[118] It starts by an over-all allocation of Judaeo-Christian dialogue. First it outlines "A Traumatic Past": Christianity as traditionally depriving itself of identity by neglecting its Jewish roots, and – worse still – preparing unconsciously the climate in Europe for the Holocaust. Then it turns its attention forward and proceeds to describing a joint orientation "Towards a Better World", hopefully to be pursued in togetherness.

From here the reflection starts by presenting two corresponding sections on "Je-wish (/resp. Christian) Perspectives Concerning Communication and Cooperation with Christians (/resp. Jews)." Actually, the two presentations are rather incongruous. The first starts by reviewing "Attitudes in Judaism towards Non-Jews and Chris-tians", generally underlining an open and inclusive demeanor, with exception for some deviations in rabbinical evaluations of Christianity through the times. Listed next are "Bases for Jews to Enter into Relationship with Christians". These are gene-rally uncontroversial, calling attention to manifest social-ethical concerns, and to the importance of honoring God's name in open-minded communication with people of other faiths ready to do the same.

The section on Christianity is rather differently constructed. It starts with "Over-coming Obstacles Stemming from Shared Roots" and identifies a series of barriers to Jewish-Christian understanding residing in traditional Christian theology:

> "1. the teaching that the Torah has been replaced by Jesus Christ as God's ultimate revela-tion; 2. the proclamation of Jesus of Nazareth as the Messiah promised to Israel; 3. the denigration of the national character of God's Covenant with Israel by considering the latter replaced by a divine covenant with all who 'are in Christ'; 4. the rejection of the Land promised to Israel as a meaningful theological category for the Jewish people."[119]

Following next is an exposition of "Current Christian theological thinking that seeks to deal with these obstacles ..." The proposal is to replace the four offensive state-ments with interpretations unmistakably acceptable to Jewish thinking. This means that convictions essential to historical Christian thinking in all its major traditions are frankly abrogated: all indications of Christianity as a fullfilment of, or a successor to, Old Testament Judaism, are replaced by some model of a mutually acceptable

---

[118] CD 28, 1995, 9–15.
[119] Ibid., 12.

juxtaposition. Jesus is no more a pretender to the throne of the Jewish Messiah, and it is agreed that "proselytizing of Jews, often referred to as missionary activity ... is theologically untenable."

That many Christians may be inclined to question this as a "theologically tenable" exposition of New Testament writings like Acts and the letters of Paul, is not commented upon in the document before us. This immediately recalls the question about the epistemological prerequisites of dialogue so emphatically thrown into the discussion by Paul J. Griffiths: the necessary observation of confronting truth claims essential to the historical identities of each of the religions in conversation, if movement is to be made towards authentic understanding at all. In that perspective, abandoning *a priori* a controversial standpoint, in order to avoid a confrontation of conflicting claims, is judged as contrary to the basic idea of dialogue.[120] One may doubt whether the quick escape from history undertaken in the quoted ICCJ declaration will survive confrontation with that criterion.

The ICCJ case must also raise questions about the bearing of guilt and expiation as dominant motivations for dialogue. They signalize an emotional imbalance which may be adequate enough in an acute situation of human reconciliation, but may – if allowed to dominate the orientation of long-term dialogue, heavily damage the criteria of historical observation and assessment. It is easy to see that if materialized as a kind of peace bargain, moral repair in itself cannot serve as foundation of lasting dialogue without creating a new and confusing kind of imbalance.

In Jewish-Christian exchange we have never observed explicit demands for Christians to tune down traditional theological standpoints as a compensation for antisemitic assaults through the centuries, or as atonement for theological militancy of the past. But the searchlight is frequently set, as in the actual ICCJ statement, on a supposed interaction between the ancient theological model of the Church as the final messianic event – a new "Israel" spiritually replacing "the old" – and the sad history of antisemitism in Europe. For clarification of such an accusation as this, methodological distinction must be made between indisputable logical consequence and actual, historically conditioned connectedness. In a dialogical context, one must take account of the possibility that doctrinal formulations, by virtue of historical circumstances, may have acquired meanings and supported developments different from, and even contrary to, their original purpose. If such developments are seen by the dialogue partners as lamentable and calling for reversal, it is not immediately granted that it is the initial formulation which needs revision. Intermediary circumstances may have exploited and distorted the original meaning of the words, and it would be an inefficient remedy to do away with initial statements as such. In some cases it could just as well serve to turn attention away from the root conflict!

In a concrete case it demands both research and reflection to explore how principle and practice affect each other. To judge concepts of faith by their societal fruits – fruits previewed, observed, discerned, supposed, suggested – may, if dialectically un-

---

[120] GRIFFITHS 1991.

questioned, prepare for a purely pragmatic concept of truth. On the other side: to argue "truth" without reviewing possible, or even probable, consequences to fellow humans, to society and to the world at large, may, if no worse, isolate truth in a sphere of idle theory.

5.2.4.5. Jewish-Christian Dialogue – A Paradigmatic Perspective

The instance of Jewish-Christian confrontation may, more than other bilateral relations, expose the complex interaction of competing faith convictions and historically biased patterns of coexistence. Would it serve the further development of dialogue if the Church gave up what, according to all sources available, must have been its prime definition of own identity, namely as "the Messianic people" of God?

A preparatory answer may be to let another question go between: Could Christianity – without compromising its primeval claim of representing biblical fulfilment – dress its self-interpretation in a language more apt to encourage dialogue between Jews and Christians? Can Christianity, without deserting its primeval idea of historical legacy, adopt a language less assaultive to Jewish self-understanding – rabbinical and Mosaic – than has been the case for twenty centuries?

Certainly, the ugly habit once so wide-spread in Christendom, of loading the Jews with collective guilt as "murderers of Christ" has long been banned from official and responsible Christian discourse, not primarily for the sake of reciprocal politeness, but for the very authenticity of the Gospel: "There is no difference, all have sinned and fall short of the glory of God"(Rom 3:23). Observations of antisemitic disturbances around the world, not at least in ex-Communist Europe, show that misguided "Christian" revengefulness may still be operative and may have hibernated even in regions where it has seemed extinguished for decades.

For that reason it may be extremely appropriate to keep Christian language under critical observation, including that of the New Testament – particularly of the Johannine writings. It should be remembered that New Testament references to "the Jews", even in polemical contexts, reflect a historical phase with a confrontative situation different from that of the following centuries – and of today. Christians were political and social outsiders, and the possibility of Christians doing violence to Jews in the name of Christ was utterly remote. It did not take many centuries for things to shift.

More than any other interreligious exchange, Jewish-Christian dialogue, due to its complex and gloomy antecedents, needs to be instructed that authentic dialogue does not start with a fixed agreement about final accomplishments, but with some viable agreement on a direction in which to go in order for an approach to start. In this regard, Jewish-Christian dialogue is by no means unique. It is exemplary, in unveiling with so unmatchable clarity methodological aspects essential to all dialogue: dynamics highlighting the interaction of principle and practice, particularly the demand for apologetical authenticity as a prerequisite of real reconciliation. This observation of possibilities contains in itself no generalizing judgement on what is today in process of committed Judaeo-Christian exchange.

5.2.5. Indigenous Religion(s)

"Indigenous religion" or "Tribal religion" has become the prevalent designation of what a hundred years ago was generally referred to as "Primitive religion". "Natural religion", "Non-literary religion", "Traditional religion" signalize different approaches to the same phenomenon. Geographical designations have been in supplementary use. "African religion" is easily heard as a rather unambiguous reference. "American religion" echoes more ambiguity. Should it refer to worship life in a Native American reservation, or to religious marketing in the shadow of Manhattan skyscrapers — or what?

5.2.5.1. The Burden of Terminology
An interesting remark is made by HANS-JÜRGEN GRESCHAT in an encyclopedial article on the German term "Stammesreligion" – which literally corresponds with "Tribal religion" and which, in terms of connotations, comes close to "Indigenous Religion". He finds that designation acceptable as a scientific term only as long as a better one is not found. Previous terms have all been exchanged or supplemented, while gradually recognized as incomplete or misleading.[121]

The most eloquent example of a biased terminology may be "Primitive religion". It contains a scarcely disguised value judgement, reflecting a 19th century evolutionist approach to the history of religions, blended as it was with occidental trust in own cultural superiority. In later time, "primal religion" has also been in use. That notion contains an observation of religion as pertaining to the primeval identity of a particular culture. It implies no value judgement and contains no implicit suggestion of progressive evolution.

"Natural religion" may point in a slightly different direction. Originally it speaks of religion as determined not by specific revelation or by some identifiable initial event, but by insight pertaining to persistent laws of creation. This is a term in correspondence with the old Enlightenment (and before that even: Scholastic) focus on "natural truths/natural rights etc.". But to a modern ear it may just as well refer to religion as observant of divine presence in expressive manifestations of 'Nature', be they located on the ground or in the sky. A deficiency of "nature"/ "natural" as directive attribute of "religion" may be a screening of the fact that any religion will be marked by some history which grants cultural presuppositions and repercussions of its own. On that background "natural" may be heard as stressing commonality at the cost of diversity – of imagery, recitals and customs – between as well as within families and branches of tribal religions.

"Non-literary religion" may adequately underscore one important point, in signalizing the absence of normative holy writings as well as of written documentations about the origin and development of the religious community considered. This may in an overwhelming number of cases be seen as reflecting the absence of a written

---

[121] Article "Stammesreligion" in: 'Wörterbuch des Christentums', Gütersloh 1988, 1186.

language on the whole. Written records of myths and cultic usages will frequently be owed to observers from outside: casual reports by foreign visitors over the centuries or – more recently – fruits of some ethnographically related research. Evaluative communications by authors grown up in, and more or less identifying themselves with, such religion, are of more recent date, but will prospectively be increasing in number, and maybe rapidly so. Such authors may contribute to making the spirit of a non-literary community more accessible also to outsiders, but can scarcely give new access to its primeval history as such. In any case the negative designation "Non-literary religion" offers an unacceptably narrow characteristic of the phenomenon under observation.

"Traditional religion" may to some extent overcome that narrowness, especially in the ears of those who know that "tradition" (Latin: tra-ditio) does not signalize static 'custom', but dynamic 'passing on', an uninterrupted process of furtherance. Precisely while not being stored and preserved in written texts, the contents of "traditional religion" must be continuously carried on as oral event. The possible weakness of this designation may be that, to the broad public, it is easily confused with the opposite, namely the image of something established, a social phenomenon being there simply by virtue of custom. This again means something stiffened, something irrelevant to the contemporary process of dialogue.

"Indigenous religion" gives full meaning only when used "on location", as referring to a concrete appearance: a religion autochthonic to an identifiable area. We are all "indigenous": natives of some particular region, and as persons we could rightfully be labeled so within our geographical territory – there, just there. Correspondingly, everything that someone has received and adopted from, and within, his own domestic territory, makes up his/her indigenous inventory. When applied to religion, the word "indigenous" suggests a contrast to religion imported from a different region, especially to what is generally known as "world religions". It follows from this, that the word "indigenous" may be most meaningfully employed when combined with some geographical referent. Or when, as in our present case, it is used as classificatory term in a setting of principal reflection.

An interesting feature in contemporary dialogue is that indigenous religion is on the move, and cannot be immediately written off as reminiscent of a remote past. "Indigenous religions" spelled in the plural are many and not easily counted, simply because it is impossible to decide where the territory of one ends and that of another begins. In some cases it would give meaning to count a few hundred adherents, in others it would be more informative to speak of millions. We don't face corporations likely to nominate official delegates for conferences and consultations around the world. A tribe will usually negotiate on issues of immediate interest through the chief, or of someone he appoints. And as long as ethno-political and religious community in these cases tend to be identical, a certain practice of interreligious dialogue with neighbors is likely to take place. Interesting for our review of the status quo and the future possibilities of dialogue, is not the distinctiveness of one tribal territory versus another, but common characteristics distinguishing the world of indigenous from that of other religions. Amazing common features can be observed among indigenous religions around the world, in spite of a splendid lack of exchange possibilities from times immemorial.

5.2.5.2. A Contemporary Challenge?

As we are observing, the appearance on the contemporary scene by indigenous religion(s) as an alarming question to the family of Abrahamic religions, has a good deal to do with the coming to awareness of an environmental crisis, from around 1970. For a world suddenly confronted with Nature as a long forgotten divine challenge, it was highly appropriate to summon, and to listen to, testimonies about "Nature" by incontestably nature-oriented religion(s).

In July 1996 the Lutheran World Federation concluded a major study project on "Theological Perspectives on Other Faiths" with an international consultation in Bangkok. The official Documentation, published the following year, shows that one of five Working Groups had been discussing "African Religion".[122] One may ask why African religion as the only segment of indigenous religion should be examined at a consultation in East Asia. The answer may first of all be that the consultation, and the wider study project to which it was related, had a global orientation. In order to assess indigenous religion as an invitation to dialogue, it may be meaningful to focus on one representative, geographically relatively surveyable area. Beyond doubt, Africa is the continent where indigenous religion still has its main residence and is most vividly alive, whereas Asia, where Bangkok is situated, generally is observed as a continent of literature-based religions with a traceable history. One observes with special interest the Kenyan dr. JOHN MBITI, author of several highly respected introductions to African religion, as member of the said Bangkok Working Group.

The start of the corresponding group report may be enlightening:

"African religion (AR) is an indigenous system of beliefs and practices integrated into the cultures and the world views of the African peoples. Although diverse in its local manifestations, it has common basic elements which testify to its unity regionally and on a continental level. Among the main beliefs of AR is the affirmation and acknowledgement of one God who is the creator and sustainer of life and of all things ... The basis of AR lies in the strong belief in the unity of the cosmos, where religion embraces the natural and the supernatural, the sacred and the secular. Religion permeates all aspects of life making the whole person a religious being in a religious world ...

Judaism, Christianity, Islam and later Hinduism and others, have now also found a home in Africa. Statistically, it would seem that the adherents to AR have decreased due to conversions to these new religions of Africa, but in reality this is only at face value. People continue to be influenced by and to treasure AR in their total life, whether they recognize it or not. It is pluralistic in nature and quite hospitable to other forms of belief systems. This calls for a deeper understanding of AR and its encounter with other religions, a process which has already started."[123]

[122] MWAKABANA 1997: Report of Working Group on African Religion – with bibliography, 21–47.
[123] Ibid., 21f. – For a more differentiated image of African religion as viewed by an African, cf. Kwesi A. DICKSON: Theology in Africa, 1984.

This must be taken for an empirical description, but only with certain reservations. First of all, it is evident that a picture of so vast a number of unassociated, or only vaguely associated, religious communities on a big continent must be selective and generalizing at the same time. Besides, the Bangkok participants, eager to encourage new dialogue, are not projecting some critically balanced assessment of a potential new partner in view, but an ideal presentation with suggestion of expected challenges they feel immediately ready to face. For that purpose the group constructs patterns of meaning, coherence and universality in the complex world of indigenous African worship – a method which is definitely acceptable as long as one keeps the limitation of such a simplificatory perspective realistically in mind. Within that setting a few critical questions are also suggested in the report, sufficient to indicate (hardly more) that the foreseeable profit of the new dialogue intended, ought to be reciprocal.

Recording "The Study of African Religion So Far", the same report is extremely critical to the negative image of African religion traditionally given by Western observers, including missionaries and theological scholars. Under fire are stereotypes still very much alive among ordinary people, not only in the West, but also among Africans raised in, or personally converted to, Christianity. In recent years this study has, however, to a large extent changed in character, the group says, not least through becoming a normal part of the curriculum in African universities. Recent development indicates that in days to come the same study will hopefully provide essential material also for a prospective dialogue.[124]

A review of basic theological and anthropological ideas as perceived in African religion, results in a list of suggested items for dialogue. The report ends with certain practical suggestions, of which it may be of interest to note:

> "It is recommended ... That efforts be made to educate people in our churches so that they come to appreciate and accept the positive contribution African religion can make in enriching our lives holistically. There are taboos and mores and practices that tend towards subjecting the individual to what is less than respectful and dignifying, if not downright inhuman. These religio-cultural demands call for further investigation and critical appropriation ... That churches (at their theological institutions and at other study centers) make an effort to engage in the kind of research work that will help to unearth the hidden treasures in our cultural and religious heritage that can make the Christian faith even more meaningful in the African continent."[125]

5.2.5.3. Limits to Dialogue

It goes without saying that organized dialogue with indigenous religions so far has been practically awkward. Generally these religions are lacking in corporate structure, in written documentations and even in common literacy. They have been made objects of literary description and scholarly observation mainly by observers from other cultures, and, following them, by alienated progenies: children and grandchild-

---

[124] Ibid., 22–27.
[125] Ibid., 45f.

ren of practitioners. These latter are generally observers already shaped by a Western education, frequently provided in mission schools.

Signs of a critical reaction to this are seen when a third generation of "ex-pagans" throws a critical eye on the massive condemnation of their spiritual ancestry so willingly accepted by the first two generations of new Christians. An opposite reaction, as seen in the late 20th century, to a large extent reflects the turn of tides in international (Occident-based) studies of religion: a massive rejection of Occidental cultural superiority. Even if the number of academically educated reconverts to traditional religion seems so far extremely modest, and of a political more than a religious motivation, the number of critics – Christians of indigenous, or of "foreign", background, pleading for attentive listening to the "old" religions in their ecological awareness and harmonious symbiosis with nature – is becoming impressive. In many eyes this seems to imply a hope of exploring neglected sources for a timely readjustment of "Abrahamic", theistic "domination of the earth" (Gen 1:28, Ps 8:7).

It is, however, easy to see that such dialogue will be of a somewhat unconventional kind. It will rarely be carried out as a balanced exchange in an organized encounter between representatives of two belief systems. To a wide extent it may have to be carried on as a self-critical exchange between reflected Christian observers, some with, others without, ancestral roots in the said belief systems. Christianity, like the other world religions, will to a major extent have to converse with indigenous religions through interpreters, in many cases: descendants of "pagans" converted to Christianity (some presenting themselves as, partly or totally, re-converted to the ethnic legacy of their great-grand-parents). A growing number of them may have made the "old" faiths object of special study, and will possibly want to restore their image and reputation. A particular exchange may in some geographical regions expand between Christians unconditionally rejecting their "pagan" heritage – at least verbally – and Christians ready to revalue aspects of it.

If roads in the future are to be paved for regular conversation between structured "historical" and hitherto unstructured "natural" religions, the latter will presumably be represented in the dialogue not by pre-literate practitioners who have themselves grown up in an indigenous culture,but by academically trained reconverts from Christianity (or from Islam). These may consciously have chosen the faith of their great-grandparents in opposition to their immediate forebears, whom they will reproach for a too quick prostration to a – once – dominant, North-Atlantic (or Arabian) civilization.

5.2.5.4. Observations for Reflection

Two impressive experiences, dating back already to the mid-eighties, made these prospects for the first time come alive to the author's reflection. The first commemorates the programmatic presence of North American natives ("Indians") at the Assembly of the World Council of Churches (WCC) in Vancouver BC in 1983. The other relates to a smaller and thematically more specialized conference a little further south on the same Pacific coast, namely in Burlingame CA, two years later. In the first case

I was an ordinary delegate together with several hundred others, in the second I was one of the persons sharing organizing responsibility.

In Vancouver a semi-official presence of regional indigenous culture was accommodated in an impressive way. This is how it is described in the assembly report:

> "A native arbour, 'a sacred meditative area among the trees', was set aside on the campus of the University of British Columbia. A sacred flame burned nearby for the duration of the Assembly. Appropriately, it was lighted by an elder of the Musqueam tribe, on whose lands the university now stands. A 15-metre high totem pole, carved by Native inmates of Agassiz Mountain Prison to symbolize humanity's spiritual quest through the ages was raised on the campus during the Assembly. It will find a permanent home in Geneva. Through plenary presentations and public forums, participants became aware of the thinking of Native Canadians particularly concerning land claims."[126]

Even if the official voice of Vancouver is directed more to the political than to the spiritual importance of Church solidarity with native Canadians, the participants were, as I can personally confirm, not less impressed with the implicit stimulus of dialogue communicated in the process of events.

At that time, a particular and much celebrated text was in the mind of many Christians familiar with the ecumenical information network: the chief Seattle's famous speech to the President of the United States (1855), which had been brought to the highlight in the official liturgy of the 1981 World Prayer Day for Women.[127] This speech, in a lofty poetical language, praises the mystery of the created universe, and impressively opposes awed adoration of the Creator against the greediness of upcoming modern civilization. Unmistakably present in the words of the chief is a spirit of awe which at the same time makes it easy to perceive how the religious universe of indigenous North Americans once made it easy for them to embrace the Bible as a source of spirituality and to accept integration into a Christian faith community.

It is a remarkable thing how the North American continent, with its numerous tragic collisions between aboriginal and immigrant land interests, in the 19th century became a close to unmatched example of easy missionary conquest.[128] In this perspective, nothing came more natural than the fact that chief Seattle, with his crushing and yet compassionate exposal of the covetousness of the white man, became a kind of patron saint to the environmental theology of the 1980's. – From where in the world can observations, constructive and destructive, be gathered for a reflection on the prospectives of exchange between Christianity and native religion like it can from the indigenous scene of America?

---

[126] David GILL (ed.): Gathered for Life ... 1983, 15. The picturesque totem pole today occupies an impressive site in front of the WCC headquarters in Geneva. – This symbolic gesture should be seen in close connection with the 'Resolution on the Rights of the Aboriginal Peoples of Canada' adopted by the same Assembly, ibid., 164.

[127] About this speech and its remarkable contribution to the expansion of ecological awareness in Western theology in the 1980's, see LØNNING 1989, 46f.

[128] Cf. H.W. BOWDEN: American Indians and Christian Mission 1981.

An experience more painful to me was one connected with the conference on *'Creation and Culture – The Challenge of Indigenous Spirituality and Culture to Western Creation Thought'* in Burlingame CA, USA, in 1985.[129] In that symposium, North American minority cultures: Native American, Hispanic American, Black American and Asiatic American – were invited to challenge representatives of Western theology and church life. Attention was paid to a double aspect: "Creation speaks on culture, and culture speaks on creation." Which light does creation faith throw on the variety of cultures in the world, and how does this variety confirm or question existing ideas of the unity of creation? In either regard, the minority participants were encouraged to express observations and reflections challenging dominant Western theology, as seen from the actual socio-cultural situation of their own respective communities.

The minority cultures invited to Burlingame described their relationship with Christianity and with Western religious establishment very differently. The majority of Asiatic Americans define their religious identity as related to some religion rooted in their continent of origin.

Hispanic Americans generally present themselves as Christians, most of them with traditional ties to Roman Catholicism, although several with a remarkable charismatic leaning. Some local Hispano-American communities may also be visibly imbued with impulses from old ethnic religions, sometimes an amazing blend of Latin American and African impulses.

Black Americans have for generations shown strong Christian convictions, and reminiscences of African ways are more easily observed in moods of expression (worship style, music) than in religious language or theology. In the last generation, however, the much observed phenomenon of 'Black Muslims' – a movement which can only to a limited extent be seen as cultural import or as a fruit of planned Islamic mission – is an eloquent expression of a nascent opposition to what is characterized as 'White' religious oppression: Islam is propagated as the religion of the colored races against white economic and cultural dominance.

Seen in our present context, the most interesting partners at the Burlingame consultation were the spokesmen of Indigenous American culture. Of the two "Indians" present, the one was a conscious champion of indigenous religion (a proclaimed reconvert), the other a theologian, church employee, with outspoken, critical observations on the relationship between established Christianity and the old religious culture of his people.

The first of them, VINE DELORIA JR., professor of political science at the University of Arizona, is known as author of a most provocative book *'God is Red'*. He is

---

[129] Held under the auspices of the Lutheran World Ministries, USA, and the Institute for Ecumenical Research, Strasbourg, and reported in David G. BURKE (ed.): Creation and Culture – The Challenge of Indigenous Spirituality and Culture to Western Creation Thought, LWM, New York 1987. – Cf. the introductory presentation of the conference as part of the more comprehensive Strasbourg study project 'Creation – an Ecumenical Challenge?', by Per LØNNING, ibid., 7–12. Likewise the condensed report of the consultation: LØNNING, ER, October 1985, and his more comprehensive evaluation in: Creation – an Ecumenical Challenge? MACON 1989, 43–72.

himself the son of a Lutheran clergyman, and at one point he interrupted his own training for a clerical ministry and declared his return to the faith of his ethnic ancestors. In his reflections on the topic *'Christianity and Indigenous Religion: Friends or Enemies? – A Native American Perspective'* [130] he produced a sharp confrontation between the two. Even if his reference background is unmistakably American, he gives to the term "tribal religion" a noteworthy universal orientation. Here are his conclusions:

> "The tribal idea of nature is a tapestry or symphony – creation cannot be completed unless every entity plays its part. The Christian idea of nature is loneliness and alienation. Humankind can never enjoy companionship with other life forms and has been pitted against nature since the expulsion from the Garden of Eden ... Christianity produces an adverse social milieu. Tribal religions produce an advocacy milieu. Tribal religion must change before tribal religion gives way; Christian culture must change if Christian religion is to have an impact on people ... Tribal religions are living religions in the sense that new revelations and ceremonies are still possible. Christianity is dead insofar God has said anything he wants to say. Tribal communal activities are consonant with the nature of creation – communal. Christian individual salvation is a fraud in that it suggests the possibility of a completely isolated individual ... Tribal religions show by example, Christianity uses many tactics to demonstrate its validity – but primarily it is a religion of force and oppression. Tribal religions are at home in the world and are designed to solve its problems; Christianity cannot live in the world with any competitor next to it, for fear it would be revealed as a fraud." [131]

This is not precisely a language of dialogue. DELORIA's sharp distinctions with their emphatic value judgements were not apologetically encountered in Burlingame. A confrontative response would hardly have served the purpose of the conference. His challenge was taken seriously by the audience not as a statement of avowed facts to be rejected or received by the public, but as a reflective description of an impression obviously spreading among indigenous Americans in our time. As such it must be accepted without reservation by Western, Christian dialogue partners – accepted and self-critically explored: How have "we" contributed to such an alarming cultural collision, up to now hardly observed by official Christendom? In this perspective the "green" criticism against traditional "Abrahamic" theology for lack of environmental awareness, a criticism so omnipresent in the 1970's, in the 1980's found its radicalized succession in an indignant indigenous voice like that of Deloria.

Still more typical of the time than Deloria's uncompromising polemic was, however, that of his brother-in-blood the Lutheran clergyman GEORGE TINKER. Besides acting as "Red" respondent in Burlingame, Tinker has contributed an overall confe-

---

[130] 'Creation and Culture', 31–43.

[131] Quotations are from a written survey presented by the speaker to the consultation participants together with the oral performance in Burlingame (quoted more extensively in: LØNNING 1989, 48f). The original wording – but certainly not the substance – is lacking in the final, published version. Cf. our notes 130, 131.

rence assessment in the official report.[132] Here he speaks in the name of his people more than in that of his church. Even if the tone is much milder than DELORIA's, and his criticism is formally directed not against teachings of the Bible, but against the so-called Christian praxis of white Americans, his critical statements go very much in the same direction as that of the former.

"The Black church functions with a primary attachment to the same Scriptures as the dominant European-American culture of this continent, however differently they interpret those Scriptures. American Indian peoples, I would argue, do not. The primary attachment of Indian peoples, even those who have been converted to some type of Christianity for several generations back, is still to their tribal traditions. There is something about being Indian that Christianity has not been able to change, just as there is something about the Black church that has irrevocably changed Christianity – even if it is the case that some people have not yet noticed."

Opposing the unifying vision of American Indian ontological cosmology to that of Euro-American fragmentation, TINKER concludes by expressing hope

"...that their stories and their ways of reverencing Creation will some day win over the immigrants and transform them."[133]

As already indicated, indigenous religions have entered the stage of international dialogue, not originally and not primarily through confrontative confessors fighting for survival in competition with the established world religions. That challenge is possibly coming next, paradoxical as it may sound. TINKER's way of reacting must be seen as historically prior to DELORIA's, and both of them may be more easily imaginable in the Americas than in Africa. If Deloria's approach seems to leave little space for real exchange except for the very fact that he is ready to offer plain speech, Tinker presents several of the same thoughts in terms of a generous invitation to joint reflection.

The most intriguing question to this constellation may be whether the further flow of events will change the Tinkers of today to Delorias of tomorrow. With regard to the future of Christianity among the descendants of aboriginal civilizations in America and elsewhere, the answer may not least depend on the readiness of the church to invest in unprestigious listening and unrestricted readiness to dialogue.

There may be little reason to add reflection on attempts in recent years by marginal groups in the Western world (Germany, the Nordic countries – most spectacularly, maybe, Iceland) to reintroduce pre-Christian religion, the old Asa faith, occasionally under the provocative standard of "Paganism" ('hedenskap'), mainly as a stern challenge to established Christianity in the ideological tensions of the day. Apparently, the agents of such, hitherto marginal, attempts, view the mythic pantheon of old Nordic religion as distant as does the rest of the population today. What they acclaim, is the vision of human potentialities behind.

[132] Ibid., 1–6.
[133] Ibid., 4, 6.

Beyond doubt, old Nordic/Germanic/Roman/Greek religion held basic orientations in common not only with each other, but to an amazing extent also with indigenous religions as we know them from their reminiscences around the globe today. And there may still be sparsely observed residues of ancient cultic usages, in quotes and in customs, scattered around even in Euro-American culture. But this hardly makes up for the alienating effects of any attempt to revivify a religious culture after a thousand years of uninterrupted defunctionalization. As purely poetical garments of a philosophy extolling what is supposed to be the all-determinant powers of nature, such an enterprise of revivification would eventually produce a counterpart – not a dialogue partner – most different from what we have so far been observing as indigenous/primeva/natural/tribal religion.

6. Dialogue and Biblical Orientation

In Christianity, the intrareligious exchange is, like all theological deliberation, intimately linked with biblical study. This exchange reflects a spectrum not only of competing textual expositions, it echoes differing understandings of biblical authority, ranging from absolutizing fundamentalism to relativizing modernity. Corresponding tensions may be found in substance as though the decisive issues were settled by some unprejudiced reading of the texts alone.

In intrareligious dialogue, arguments are not infrequently heard which pretend to distill some unquestionable theory of dialogue right out of the Book. Such procedure would, however, presuppose that no conflicting opinions could be found within the collection of writings known as "the Bible" – with its more than a millennium long history of origin – and that centuries of intermediate occupation with the texts, including the interpreter's own involvement up to date, would have no disturbing influence on the immediacy of communication between the biblical writers and their readership.

The task of the following chapter, then, is not to prove this or that theory as "*the* biblical doctrine of interreligious dialogue*" – which could be meaningful only on theological premises comprehensively explained and sustained in general. The aim is to show how biblical resources for a contemporary Christian reflection on dialogue can be sought and found, and how appropriate, promotive questions may be asked to and through the old texts, questions which safeguard the authenticity of the historical texts – as of our contemporary reception.

It goes without saying that our exposition of biblical texts, like our observations of the dialogical profiles of non-Christian religions, will be highly summary, both in selection of texts and in handling of interpretational diversity. The description will be based on widely accepted text interpretations, with few references to specialized studies, and with the intrinsic coherence of the emerging display as a carefully considered criterion of verification.

6.1. Types of Texts Relevant

Obvious point of departure: the Bible does not speak to or speak about dialogue in our contemporary sense of the word. Dialogue between different faiths does not occur as an event particularly observed, even if conversations pertaining to faith between people of different religious commitments are reported as natural events from the days of Abraham on. The closest we come to "dialogue" in our meaning of that word, may be the reports in Acts on Paul's exchanges with Jewish communities.

In these cases the verb διαλεγεσθαι– to converse – is used.[1] But the same terminology may also be used about his teaching in a Christian congregation.[2] It may be worth observing that the noun διαλογος occurs nowhere in the New Testament. Yet biblical scriptures relate to our topic, and this in several regards. They are full of observations and comments on non-biblical faiths, and full of reports on exchange between people domiciled in the sphere of biblical revelation and partners of extra-biblical commitments.

1. The first question, then, must be this: Biblical *texts which speak explicitly on non-biblical religion*, precisely what do they say? Are they intrinsically geared to "religion" in singular as a universal topic, or do they limit their scope to particular religions, eventually observed in settings where principal implications must be rather limited? – From such observations questions arise concerning the extent of consequences to be drawn from a specific text. Does a meeting of people of different faiths illuminate primarily (a) some other, non-dialogical circumstance in the recital, (b) specifics of the particular religion or family of religions in focus, (c) extra-biblical truth claims in general? (d) Or could it have some other function relevant to dialogue? (e) Do other biblical records contain directions which contradict, or at least seem to question, the one(s) thus observed?

2. Are there *reports, narratives, descriptions of persons and events* which – without focusing foreign religion as their central topic of interest – expose characteristic attitudes vis-a-vis people of other faiths? Accepting or repugnant – how do such sections eventually combine together with other expressions of corresponding or contrasting attitudes, and how do they relate to the more concise statements which we have already recorded?

3. Further, *the issue of "syncretism"*: to which extent does a religion declare, and/or practice, openness to impulses from other faiths? And to which extent does actual development in past and present indicate an openness, or an exclusiveness, not immediately compatible with its pronounced ambitions? Making Christianity the test case: How may the Bible reveal influence from extra-biblical sources? Which elements in biblical religion – language, concepts, usages – unveil observable impulses from other faith traditions? How do shifting trends in the history of biblical religion reflect changing impressions received from the outside world? Which dynamics may – consciously or unconsciously – have steered the adaptation of developing biblical tradition to its non-biblical environments? These are also the core issues in the, for several years rather heated, discussion on dialogue and "syncretism".

4. Finally, *the self-image of a religion* will always encompass, if not a strict theory, then at least some implicit understanding of the realm of human faiths in general, including some unspoken judgement on the value of other religions. Does my faith observe the existential dilemma of humankind in a way that allows for more than one answer – or possibly: for more than one expression of one common answer? If so be the case: how does this admission delimit the range of varieties acceptable?

[1] Acts 17:2 &17. 18:4 & 19. 19:8f.
[2] Acts 20:7.

This may suggest that some *elements of a theology of religion(s)* – certainly not the same – *may be seen as inherent* in any viable religion, even if a considerable variety of understandings may encompass such elements within the domestic camp. Two representatives of the same faith community disagreeing on dialogue – be it dialogue in general or be it one particular dialogue project – may hold less disparate images of their prospective dialogue partners than of their own faith. Can tensions of a similar variety be observed within the Bible?

6.1.1. Straight Biblical Statements

The adversaries of faith as viewed in the Bible are not foreign religions: more or less established structures of belief, worship, ethical regulations. Adversaries are the "false gods", idols claiming an allegiance rightfully due to the Creator alone, the One who has revealed himself to his chosen people Israel under the name of Yahweh: He-Is-Who-He-Is (Ex 3:14).

A non-negligible difference may be there between a more ancient and some subsequent orientation. According to the first, Israel, Yahweh's people, delivered from slavery in Egypt and pledged to him by holy covenant, owes loyalty to him alone, whereas neighboring peoples may be rightfully committed to their (presumably: less valiant?) deities. In the later orientation, Yahweh as Creator of the universe claims allegiance of the whole world, a claim which presupposes the nullity of any godhead that could be mentioned.

"Will you not possess what Chemosh your god gives you to possess? And all that Yahweh our God has dispossessed before us, we will possess," speaks JEPHTHAH the Judge to the king of the Amorites.[3] This is probably the oldest type of argument we can verify. Such language could, of course, be understood as one of dialogical diplomacy, saying in a gentle way: "As acting on your premises, you will certainly accept that I act on mine, so let us get along!" At the same time, the Old Testament flows over with indications that Israel's argument with Canaanite neighbors was not about the existence of one god versus the other, but rather about the authority and power of godheads recognized to exist by both sides in the discussion. Jephthah does not attack the idea of a foreign godhead protecting a foreign people, he just refuses the authority of such a godhead over the people of Israel.

Correspondingly, the voice of "the fool" in the Psalm: "There is no God",[4] must in the framework of Hebrew semantics be understood not as a metaphysical denial of divine existence. In the mocker's mouth it is rather a refusal to accept God as an actual presence powerful enough to fashion the existence of humans in this world. Even if this suggests a universal perspective, and thus marks a significant distance to

---

[3] Jud 11:24.
[4] "Æin Elohim", Ps 14:1. – To the meaning of 'non-being' in the Old Testament, consult the word "AIN", in Hebrew dictionairies!

the ethno-theology of Jephthah some hundred years earlier, it supports it in giving actual presence priority over pure, metaphysical existence.

"The gods of the people are idols" – this heavy psalmistic statement goes in the same direction.[5] It may be unclear whether the word "Elil", traditionally translated as "idol" (German: Abgott), is originally a tendentious derivative of "El", the basic semitic word for "God". In Hebrew "Elil" is ultimately used as a universal term for "nothingness" without explicit religious connotations.

Claus Westermann in his compendium of Old Testament theology[6] sees the concept of divine oneness / exclusiveness developing in three stages: (1) "I am the Lord, your God, who led you out of Egypt ...You shall have no other gods beside of me" = Monolatry demanded of Israel through unique divine intervention in the history of the people. (2) "Yahweh, our God, Yahweh is one" = Monolatry confirming the oneness of God, the One facing Israel in actual worship. (3) "Before me no God was there, and after me there will be none ... beside me there is no savior" = Monotheism universally commanded by the One and only God who deserves unlimited sovereignty over humankind.[7]

Verbal testimony of religious identity appears not only as finite statements. Prior to syntactic constructs vocabulary speaks for itself. Words, single elements of language, occurring generally in correspondence with surrounding religions – not least as names and titles attributed to godhead – are in this setting important, but let this correspondence of religious terms be a theme for reflection in the following section of our study!

The world of the Old Testament is anything but narrow in terms of religious variety and reported encounters of faiths. Expanding roughly from the emigration of Abraham from Ur in Chaldea to the rule of the Maccabeans in Jerusalem it covers the ground of a good 1600 years. With all their changes in political, economical and cultural framework one important feature remains: during all that time some conversation with people of neighboring faiths has taken place: Chaldean, Egyptian, Canaanite, Persian, Greek ... as a gross review.

For the majority of OT writers, times of confrontation and spiritual struggle for life seem more interesting and occupy more attention than periods of comparatively peaceful cohabitation. And if any unalterable feature of the past – and present – is remembered, it is how the identity of the chosen people calls for conscious and constant guard. If its religious identity is blotted out, Israel's historical vocation – the focal theme – is gone. Without this presupposition in mind, it is impossible to look into the historical fate of the Jewish people as conceived by itself through the millennia, and even to interpret the classical self-understanding of the Christian church as "the New Israel", the pilgrim people persistently on march through the desert of Sinai to the promised Canaan.

[5] Ps 96:5, cf. the article "ÆLIL" in W. Gesenius: 'Hebräisches und Aramäisches Wörterbuch', 17. Aufl. (1962) 42.
[6] 'Theologie des Alten Testaments in Grundzügen' 1985, 2.ed., 25–27.
[7] Ex 20:2f. Deut 6: 4. Jes 43:10.

Proceeding to the New Testament, we observe a double change of reference frame as, in the course of a generation, the new Messianic community becomes sturdily dissociated from the Synagogue and finds its shape as Εκκλησια (a public gathering of people) understood as: a people of God, gathered by divine vocation. In less than two generations the stage expands from limited Palestine to the cosmopolitan arena of Greco-Roman civilization.

JESUS, as portrayed by the four evangelists, had been open to contact with the most different kinds of people in need of his help, especially those lacking integration in the Jewish society at large. In several cases these were ethnic and religious strangers: Samaritans (Luk 17:16, Joh 4:4ff), Canaanites (Mt 8:28ff, 15:22ff), Romans (Mt 8:5ff, Mk 15:39). The Master may even recommend the spiritual attitudes of religious outsiders, seeing them as models for his own people, notwithstanding their alien religious belonging. His praise of "the men of Nineveh" and "the queen from the South" points in a similar direction (Mt 12:38–42).

Are there statements by JESUS referring explicitly to extra-biblical religions? That could perhaps be the cryptic allusions in the gospel of John to "the sheep which are not of this flock" with the promise that some day "there will be one flock and one shepherd" (John 10:16). But as a matter of fact, the meaning of this statement is far from unambiguous. Can it refer to people of other nations who will soon enter the Church and share fellowship with the Jewish followers of Jesus? To individuals of other faiths who will change religious orientation and join in with his disciples at some coming stage of events? Or to people who may already unwittingly be receiving his blessings in their own communal setting, and who will eventually recognize his presence only on the The Last Day?

Closely linked with this question and equally impenetrable is the Johannine suggestion of a mysterious predestination: Certain people "given" to JESUS by the Father, and who will certainly not fail to realize him as their final destiny (6:37ff, 10:29, 17:2). This may in some way correspond with the fundamental idea in the same gospel, of Christ as the Logos, universal meaning of creation (John 1:1ff).

At the same time the Gospel of John emphatically, over and over again, links salvation with faith in Christ, mostly through explicit quotations of JESUS himself. And it is in the same book we find the "exclusivist" statement *par excellence* by Jesus: "I am the Way, the Truth and the Life, no one comes to the Father except by me" (14:6). Immediately, those words sound as a categorical refusal of anybody with a religious belonging outside Christendom. Interpreters who, through the ages, have shrunk from that radical consequence, assume that Christ may be invisibly at work also where knowledge of him is absent, and that a face-to-face encounter with him – for which a variety of religions, if ever so unconsciously, might hopefully prepare – will take place at the end of time. In the same perspective it might be asked: could Jesus in Joh 14 be speaking with the voice of the universal Logos, and could this Logos in the course of time have spoken similar claims through mouths other than his, without signalizing an essential conflict with John 14?

Evidently no such modifying theory can be proven as an authentic interpretation

of the provocative statement by Jesus in John 14. Decisive for our theological exposition is finally the integration into a global understanding of that gospel, and of "the
Gospel", primeval Christianity, in general.

Confrontations between early Christian mission and surrounding religious establishment, Jewish as well as Greco-Roman, stage the show in the book of Acts as well
as in the letters of Paul and in the remaining New Testament. Our object of research
is not the policy of religious tolerance and intolerance in the living Roman Empire, nor the
dynamics of encounter between Apostolic mission and local communities, Jewish or
"pagan". Our attention is directed to the view of other religions voiced by early Christianity, and what this may signalize of readiness to enter interreligious conversation.

The most illustrious attempt known at a dialogical approach to the extra-biblical
world in Apostolic times is Paul's famous Areopagus speech (Acts 17:16ff), where he
observes an altar in Athens with the inscription ΑΓΝΩΣΤΩ ΘΕΩ: To a God
Unknown. From there his point is developed:

> "What therefore you worship as unknown, this I proclaim to you. The God who made the
> world and everything in it, being Lord of heaven and earth, does not live in shrines made by
> men ... since he himself gives to all men life and breath and everything. And he made from
> one every nation of men to live on all the face of the earth ... that they should seek God if
> they might feel after him and find him. Yet he is not far from each one of us, for *'In him we
> live and move and have our being'*; as even some of your poets have said, *'For we are indeed his
> offspring.'* Being God's offspring we ought not to think that the Deity is like gold, or silver,
> or stone, a representation by the art and imagination of man. The times of ignorance God
> overlooked, but now he commands all men everywhere to repent, because he has fixed a
> day on which he will judge the world with righteousness by a man whom he has appointed,
> and of this he has given assurance to all men by raising him from the dead."

Up to this point the majority, so the record, has listened with sympathetic curiosity.
But making the last point, the apostle is interrupted by unrest and by split reactions.
Some deride him, manifestly provoked by the idea of a resurrection. Even if the
reporter does not state it explicitly, it seems likely that the negative outbursts relate to
Paul's determinant vision of uniqueness: one particular person at one particular point
in history as unparalleled unification of humanity and God.

Apart from Paul's strategic plea to his public, what does he really say by his recognition of Athenian religiosity? His fascination about the sanctuary for a God
Unknown can hardly be taken for an authorization of religious ignorance or as an
expression of some purely apophatic idea of deity. The whole speech is geared to a
fundamental human quest for meaning, which he proclaims as fulfilled in an all-
embracing historical event. Indirectly, however, Paul accuses his public of idolatry, a
reification of godhead which – confronted with their own manifest insights – is unveiled as a betrayal of their own human dignity.

A similar confrontation takes place in Lystra, where Paul and Barnabas, after a
miracle of healing, are celebrated by the public as Zeus and Hermes (Acts 14:8ff).
Distressed by that idolatrous conduct, the missionaries cry out their denunciation of
"these vain things" and encourage "conversion to the living God who has created

heaven and earth". This call is supported by the observation that the Creator, who "in the past generations allowed all the nations to walk in their own ways", has by no means "left himself without witness", shedding, as he is, the manifold blessings of "rain and fruitful seasons from heaven".

This confrontation makes an impression similar to that of the Areopagus account. The apostolic proclamation fully endorses the listeners' concern for a global commitment, combined with a fundamental rejection of "vain things": idols = objects of religious veneration falsely occupying the position of God, the One. The sovereignty of the Creator over against intruding idols is the issue, not the position of one religious community over against some other.

Doctrinally more reflected is the following statement in the introductory passage of the Letter to the Romans, where the same PAUL starts by summing up the premises for his understanding of salvation:

> "What can be known about God is plain to them ... Ever since the creation of the world his invisible nature, namely, his eternal power and deity, has been clearly perceived in the things that have been made". (Rom 1:19f)

The remarkable thing about this statement is its contextual function. It does not serve to explain or to support some religious insight universally accepted in the world. On the contrary, it sustains a general accusation against humankind for self-contracted religious ignorance. People ought to have known, but actually they don't! Observations available to everybody would suffice to prove the presence of the Creator and to instruct obedience to his will, but "they" chose not to honor him as God. Thus, "claiming to be wise they became fools ... and worshipped and served the creature rather than the Creator" (vv. 22. 25).

The strongest statement in a Pauline letter concerning the futility of extra-biblical religion must be the one in a letter to formerly non-Christian readers in Asia Minor:

> "Remember that you were at that time separated from Christ, alienated from the commonwealth of Israel, and strangers to the covenants of promise, having no hope, and without God in the world!" (Eph 2:12)

Whether PAUL is himself the author of Ephesians or the letter has been edited in the circle of his disciples, has been a matter under dispute. But that is of minor interest to our research. The important thing is to observe the specter of New Testament statements ranging from the praise of a universal "God Unknown" on Areopagus to the total dismissal of "God and hope" from pre-christianized Ephesians – enough of a contradiction to call for particularly careful consideration.

Finally, the complex fabric of the Apocalypse (Revelation of John), echoing a situation of extreme confrontation with the Roman Empire towards the end of the first century A.D., gives profile to a church with extreme awareness of its distance from the surrounding religious – and irreligious – world.

The dialectical complexity of explicit biblical statements on the theme of "religions" is manifest.

6.1.2. Figures, Events, Situations – a Selection

Let us show, by a quick circumspection, how interreligious relations are elucidated by a number of biblical details in texts which are not particularly geared to other faiths as a theme of instant reflection. This may exemplify, and also indicate the importance of, some further research hopefully to be extended a good deal beyond what has been done in connection with the dialogue debate so far. An optimal utilization of such a heuristic method would undoubtedly require a wider, more systematical selection of texts and a more thorough analysis of each sample than can be offered within the framework of our present study.

The Old Testament 'Heilsgeschichte', its continuous history of divine salvation, starts with the story of Abraham (Gen 11:27 – 25:11). We observe the patriarch's origin in Ur in Chaldea, an important religious center of the day. We also note the later Hebrew recollection of ancestors "on the other side of the Euphrates" as worshippers of "other gods" (Jos 24:2).

Conspicuous are ABRAHAM's numerous, highly official contacts with chiefs and princes of various peoples (Gen 12:10ff, 12:17ff, 20:1ff, 21:22ff). In this connection one event distinguishes itself with its ostentative elements of a *communio in sacris*. Abraham, victorious in battle, is received with a ceremony of blessing by MELCHI-ZEDEK, the mysterious "king of Salem" and "priest of God Most High". To this priestly king Abraham offers "one tenth of everything" (Gen 14:18ff). The same Melchizedek appears as a typological figure in a cultic Psalm with apparently strong ties to the temple of Jerusalem (Ps 110:4), and subsequently, in the New Testament, in a sequence which most impressively interprets Jesus as sacrificial high priest (Heb 5 & 7).

Salem has traditionally been identified as Jerusalem, which, nearly a thousand years after ABRAHAM, became the site of David's royal rule and of Solomon's temple (Ps 76:2). 'God Most High' (EL 'ELYON) contains in itself a predicative statement (cf. Ps 78). But evidently there is more to it than that: it is a designatory construct. Like a great number of similar constructs in the semitic world of that day, it links Godhead (EL) with a particular cultic tradition, and in that way it exercises a name-giving function.[8] The many composites which combine EL with a determinant seem to reflect an underlying interaction of monolatric and polytheistic presuppositions more complex than observers readily fancy today. In the OT a number of such composites are in use to signify One God, the Creator. But it should not be taken for granted that they reflected such a monotheistic orientation from the beginning.

As presented in Genesis, MELCHIZEDEK is the priestly king of an Amorite (/Jebusite) community, the extension and ethnic affiliations of which we do not precisely know. Abraham honors him as a legitimate representative of God and – in that capacity – as superior to Abraham himself. As designation of God the composite EL-'ELYON is sparsely used in the OT (In addition to Gen 7, only Ps 78:35). But

---

[8] Cf. articles on EL, on 'ELYON and on ELOHIM in W.Gesenius (cf. our note 5).

'ELYON can be similarly connected with the Hebrew ELOHIM – obviously a derivative of EL – or with the divine name specifically related to the Mosaic covenant:
YAHWEH. 'ELYON may also occur alone ('The HIGHEST').[9] In all these cases the
predicative function of 'ELYON seems to prevail over the nominative. This also corresponds with the observation that 'ELYON and other metaphors of "height" are
frequently predicates of God in the Psalms, as – for understandable reasons – it can
be in liturgical language in general.

The salient point is that the Genesis narrative, recorded around 1000 years after
the presumable event, seems to accept unrestricted fellowship of faith with such a
"foreign" tradition of worship. Such a presentation may, at the time of David and his
progenies, have served a particular purpose, namely to give legitimacy to Jerusalem,
new capital in Israel and fresh center of Israelite worship. Which again means: it
authorized the Davidic kingdom as legitimate channel of the Abrahamic blessing.

But – the other way around – it may equally well have served to preserve some
cultic tradition of ancient Salem, including the priestly succession of ZADOK, king
DAVID's and SALOMON's high-priest, whose person seems to have been an important
link between Jebusite Salem and Israelite Jerusalem.[10] Cultic remembrance of the
communion between MELCHIZEDEK and ABRAHAM seals the new state of affairs, in
the words of Psalm 110. This Psalm is more frequently quoted by the New Testament
than any other, and then as herald of Christ the sacerdotal King above all.[11] Finally,
this Jerusalemic communion of Abraham and Melchizedek, of David and Zadok, is
christianized by the unforgettable typological interpretation offered in the Letter to
the Hebrews (Heb 5–7). Through the intermixture of Psalm 110, the NT transforms
"Melchizedek King of Salem" to a model of Jesus the Christ, "Son of David". This
kind of an inclusivist procedure may be not irrelevant for a principal assessment of
interreligious exchange. It may also be read as a striking apropos to our following
section on "syncretism" (6.1.4).

A character who plays as pivotal a role in the history of biblical revelation as Abraham, is MOSES. The Israelite tribes, addressed and organized by Moses in the land of
Egypt some 500 years after ABRAHAM, must – when seen with the eyes of posterity –
have been badly in need of spiritual renewal and political organization. Moses is
encountered by Yahweh – 'The one who is who he is' (Ex 3:14) – in a burning bush in
the desert, and the covenant with Israel is sealed at the mountain of Sinai (Ex 19ff).
But can impulses from other religions have played a traceable role at so revolutionary
events?

They can. MOSES, a refugee from Egypt, has found his shelter in the house of "the
priest in Midian", whose daughter Zippora he is some day going to marry (Ex 2:16ff).

---

[9] With ELOHIM: Ps 57:3. 78:56. With YAHWEH: Ps 47:3. Alone: Num 24:16. 32:8. 2 Sam 2:14.

[10] The root ZDK is obviously the same in Zadok and Melchi-Zedek, so already etymology invites to
opt for some Jerusalemic priestly succession taken over and continued after the conquest by David. Cf.
Sigmund MOWINCKEL: Offersang og sangoffer, Oslo 1951, 36, 134ff.

[11] Quoted 25 times, according to index in (ed. ALAND a.o.) Novum Testamentum Graece, Stuttgart
1968, 897ff. Next comes Ps. 47, namely 10 times.

Later, when Israel under the leadership of Moses is tarrying at the foot of Sinai, JETHRO, his priestly father in law, arrives, bringing with him Moses' wife and his two sons (Ex 18). At this occasion Jethro, after praising Yahweh as "greater than all gods", performs a liturgical act of sacrifice, and is afterwards reported to have assisted Moses in organizing a legal system.

There have been various hypotheses concerning the role of the people of Midian in the emergence of Israelite religion.[12] Even the name Yahweh has been suggested to have Midianite roots. The remarkable thing is that the texts unveiling MOSES' relationship with Midian have been fashioned at a time when Midian and Israel for centuries had been dissociated from each other, even through bloody warfare. Midian was powerfully defeated by GIDEON (Jud 6–8). "The Day of Midian" became an eloquent figure of speech (Jes 9:4). Common political considerations would have recommended ancient contacts with that people for oblivion, particularly memories connected with Moses and the exodus from Egypt, events so decisive for the foundation of Israelite identity.

Irrespective of the many questions which remain unsolved with regard to Midianite influence on early Israel, another powerful testimony of openness to extra-Israelite influence at an important stage of the biblical formation process has been observed.

In the OT, a prevalent attitude toward neighboring peoples is one of distance and of a certain fear. As worshippers of gods other than Yahweh, they might seduce Israel to apostasy: to exchange Yahweh with foreign godheads, or to accept others "beside" him (Ex 20:3–5). This invited a policy of uncompromised non-fraternization (frequently bordering on "ethnic cleansing") in the generations of invasion and land conquest. After that followed centuries of constant endeavors of segregation vis-s-vis surrounding Canaanite cultures and communities. The conquest of Jerusalem by King DAVID established a hitherto unmatched cultural melting pot, of religious importance not only through adaptation of cultic customs and corresponding ideas – usually strongly resisted by the prophets – but also by developing more intimate patterns of neighborly cohabitation and exchange.

The preaching of the prophets, at the same time as it denounces infiltration by 'pagans', emphatically warns Israel against relying on own prerogatives. "The peoples" (goyim) must not be regarded as less valuable in the eyes of the Creator than the Israelites, or less embraced by his providing care. "'Are you not like the Ethiopians to me, O people of Israel,' says the Lord, 'Did I not bring up Israel from the land of Egypt, and the Philistines from Caphtor and the Syrians from Kir?'" These are the words of AMOS, the most provocative of the judgement prophets (Am 9:7). No less important: "the peoples" and their rulers are, if ever so unconscious of the matter themselves, instruments in the hands of the Lord, even when he sends them to chastise "his own" people Israel. For that purpose he "whistles for the fly which is at the sources of the stream of Egypt, and for the bee which is in the land of Assyria" (Jes 7:18).

---

[12] Cf. Gaalyah CORNFELD (ed.): 'Archeology of the Bible: Book by Book', 1976, 40ff, 55ff.

No foreign ruler is, however, seen in so immediate a relationship with Yahweh and his universal rulership as the Persian king CYRUS, eagerly awaited as liberator by the deported Jews in Babylon. This situation is directly reflected by the author usually referred to as DEUTERO-ISAIAH. The passage where he deals explicitly with Cyrus, Is 44:28–45:9, is remarkable in several regards.[13] Not only that, beyond all reservation, it authorizes a "pagan" ruler as Yahweh's envoy, but that, at the same time, it contains a proclamation of Yahweh's universal sovereignty unmatched in the whole Hebrew canon.

At this point in history the question also emerges whether, and eventually to which extent, Old Testament statements may reflect lasting impressions of Persian Mazdaic (Zoroastrian) dualism. It is difficult not to hear the words in DEUTERO-ISAIAH as a polemical demarcation against the absolute polarization of light and darkness in Mazdaism:

> "I am Yahweh, and there is no other. I form light and create darkness, I make weal and create woe, I am Yahweh who do all these things." (Is 45:6f.)

At the same time it is evident that in the room of dialectical oscillation between monism and dualism, a remarkable shift is noticeable in the Hebrew writings of the immediately following centuries. The appearance of Satan, "the Enemy", in some of the later books – a character absent in the Hebrew literature before 500 BC – above all his picturesque role in the story of Job, may be the most eloquent expression of this (Job 1 & 2). In early Christianity striking similarities with mazdaic dualistic language may be found, particularly in the Johannine writings (use of the polarities: light/darkness, truth/lie, life/death).

6.3. The Issue of "Syncretism"

Observations of biblical material have led us back to the controversial issue of "syncretism", a word with a multiplex and highly challenging history from Plutarch via Nairobi 1975 up to our day. An instructive summary is presented in THEO SUNDERMEIER's article "Synkretismus" in *Evangelisches Kirchenlexicon*.[14] His observation is incontradictable enough: "Wertneutral ist der Begriff nie gewesen."

Even if the word "syncretism", up to our own time, has generally indicated some synthetic mixture of elements of different origins – a perspective which has produced predominantly negative reactions – new approaches of system analysis have in the last fourth of the 20th century tended to bestow new dignity on the concept. More and more has it been accepted as a confirmation of important historical dynamics: a

---

[13] The fact should not be overlooked that Persians and Jews had good reasons for political friendship, sharing the now disintegrating Babylonian empire as main enemy. Regarding Cyrus as liberator and protector of the Jewish people, cf. 2 Chron 36:22f, and the books of EZRA and DANIEL.

[14] 1996, Vol.4, col. 602–607.

culture can only survive and preserve vitality by adopting and integrating impulses from other, to a certain extent differing, traditions.

Christianity conquered the Roman Empire, as later it conquered the Germanic territories, by its boldness to reinterpret and incorporate pre-Christian terms, images and cultic practices. Particularly important was a transformation of the ancient calendars, which refashioned the annual cycle of nature into commemorative celebrations of biblical salvation history.

A sympathizing understanding of "syncretism" had been launched already in the beginning of the century by the "religionsgeschichtliche Schule" in Germany. At that time such an embracement was easily combined with the idea of religious evolution and Christian cultural superiority. Single elements adopted from "lower" religions will not signalize a spiritual setback, but rather a step of progress, if transformed and contextually integrated on a "higher" level. Syncretistic openness may secure longtime survival as well as growing influence to a receptive partner in a reflective dialogue, and no less to the proficient winner of a passionate altercation.

In the meantime, "syncretism" became a more suspicious word than ever in the epoch of Barthian theological reaction, most eloquently profiled in HENDRIK KRAEMER's theology of mission.[15] The issue was again pushed into the center of theological debate a generation later. In fact, it functioned as fuse of the exploding dialogue confrontation at the WCC Assembly in Nairobi 1975. The focal role of the word in the Nairobi discussion was not at least determined by the moderator M.M. THOMAS's introductory report with its provocative plea for "a Christ-centered syncretism".[16] When reading Thomas's report over again more than twenty years later, and when comparing it with his own rather conciliatory role in international debate in the following years,[17] it may be a little difficult to understand the commotion it aroused in Nairobi, and which can only be explained by a tense communicative situation then and there.[18]

THEO SUNDERMEIER, whose analysis of the concept has already been quoted,[19] makes a basic distinction. On the one side he sees "symbiotic syncretism" as an expression of vital "enculturation": a religious system gains influence within a culture only by integrative openness to what is already there (language, customs, patterns of thought). On the other side he lodges "synthetical syncretism": a more or less selective linking together of elements from various traditions, directed by a conscious strategy of some kind.

---

[15] Cf. 'The Christian Message in a non-Christian World', 1938. Kraemer's concern is powerfully followed up by W. VISSER't HOOFT, at that time general secretary of the WCC, in: ' No Other Name' 1963. Cf. the section 'Syncretism – Ancient and Modern', 9–49, which counts four "waves" of syncretism in history from the days of ancient Babylon up to modern times. With regard to the subsequent fate of the word in the WCC, it is striking to observe the harsh criticism from the council's own chief official only twelve years prior to the Nairobi assembly.

[16] David M. PATON: 'Breaking Barriers – Nairobi 1975', 236.

[17] Cf. his contribution to the famous "Uniqueness" debate in: D'COSTA 1990, 49–62.

[18] Cf. our summary record of the WCC dialogue debate, here 3.2.

[19] Cf. here, note 14.

It is obvious that the strong opposition to "syncretism" voiced in the Nairobi debate, mainly challenged connotations in the latter direction. If we understand Sundermeier rightly, he sees a certain, basically unintended "syncretism" as constitutive in a context of expanding socio-cultural – including religious – communication. He is not ready to draw a similar conclusion about strategic "syncretism". In addition to examples known from ancient history, he points to "New Age" and cases of recently emerging religious blends, where not least an inorganic mixture of East and West serves the cause of innovative fascination. This must, in his view, be as remote from genuine enculturation as it is possible to imagine.

SUNDERMEIER also underlines how divergent, emotionally embedded attitudes to "syncretism" in public debate depend not only on differing connotations and various width attributed to the concept itself, but also on a fundamental difference in understanding of "divine revelation". In the more recent phase of the syncretism debate, it is remarkable how even a leading "mainline" theologian like WOLFHART PANNENBERG[20] makes reflective use of the word for a constructive purpose.

In this connection we may suggest that the acceptance of "syncretism" as a respected term in Occidental theology in recent years – closely related as Sundermeier sees it with the spreading of "system-theoretische Überlegungen" (theories of system analysis) – may have part of its background in the renaissance of Hegelian thinking in Continental social philosophy (JOACHIM RITTER, HELMUTH SCHELSKY, NIKLAS LUHMANN a.o.), where a certain "syncretistic" interpretation of history interacts with the structuring presence of a thesis-antithesis-synthesis scheme. This dynamic of history, then, is understood as only partly promoted by the controlling power of intensive reflection.

Without entering further into this discussion, it may suffice to conclude by warning against a one-sided sloganish use of the term "syncretism", and to underscore the necessity of a certain distinction. Observable imprints of lasting exchange between systems of faith in communicative contact with each other, may be inseparable from the process of communication itself, and must be distinguished from syntheticized ideologies as well as from unreflected capitulation to the consequences of some incalculable "laisser-faire". This again confirms our general observation, that the results of interreligious communication – including dialogue – are unpredictable, but by no means independent of conscious strategies.

If we stick to the customary assortment of exclusive, inclusive and pluralist theologies of religions, it may be clarifying to proceed by etymology and make the following inference. – "Exclusivism" will stand for the principal repudiation of syncretism, understanding it as a particularly provocative kind of spiritual pollution. – "Pluralism" will basically keep a relaxed attitude, while, in principle, seeing all religions as equally true. Truth is neither increased nor diminished through an interchange of opinions and practices, provided that none of the parts exercises undue pressure on the other. "Inclusivism" is more dialectical in its approach to "syncretism" than this simple "Yes

---

[20] About PANNENBERG: here, particularly 4.3.2.2.

or No". It makes a fundamental distinction between what may be the fruits of an open-minded, open-ended exchange, and those which reflect disregard, conscious or unconscious, for differing historical identities.

In any case, the challenge suggested by the word will have to be finally tackled in concrete situations of encounter, and with a solid element of critical self-awareness implied.

6.4. An Implicit "Theology of Religion(s)"?

Attention should be given to the usually unspoken evaluation of other faiths, which is indirectly, but efficiently operative through the definition by a religious community of its own identity.

We have already seen that in addition to the opinions on other faiths more or less explicitly expressed by a religion in its normative sources – be they geared to one particular or to "foreign" faiths in general – several other and less officially observed factors have contributed to stabilizing the attitudes of one religion to another, or to others, through the years. Memories kept of confrontative historical events and circumstances may in this setting have exercised an influence still more transparent to observers than to those directly exposed to it. Also, patterns of behavior once established in a religion for historical reasons forgotten today, and transported through the centuries by more or less unchallenged custom, accompanied by none or by highly vicarious reflections, may reactivate feelings of confrontative identities with considerable motivating power.

All these dynamics are observable factors, blended, and varying in relative strength from one case to another, at the same time as the attitudes under observation more or less interact with that vision of own identity which any religion is inclined to claim as its own main constitutive. Such variations can be observed not only from one religion to another, but between various social and theological segments, and between different geographical regions or historical epochs, of one and the same religion.

A complex variety of factors, then, determines actual attitudes toward interreligious dialogue within a given religious constituency. However, as long as a community is upheld by the vision of some corporate identity grounded in divine guidance, such identity will exercise a permanent influence on its appreciation of, and its relation with, any "foreign" community geared to the issue of "ultimate concern" like itself. Any religion will contain a "latent theology of religions". This theology does not need to make its presence felt as long as there is no event to stir it up, but it is kept on the alert as long as some consciousness of own identity stays alive.

The bearing of conscious identity on the appreciation of foreign faiths may generally be oriented by two questions: What is the ultimate destiny of humanity? – and: how does my own religion contribute to fulfilling that aim? Of these topics, the latter may be the easier one to visualize. Implicitly, it arranges the faiths of the world in a specter extending from the modesty of a tribal religion which restricts ambitions to its own local territory, to the self-absolutization of a sect – maybe even only the size of a tribe – which claims that divine presence in the world is offered through its own attendance alone. Between these extremes there may be innumerable shades of inter-action between the notion of a truth absolute and some recognition of own limita-tion. Common to the whole specter seems an obvious correspondence between defi-nition of own identity and valuation of other faith communities – even if a solid margin for "accidental" factors is taken into consideration.

The most complex of the two questions may finally be the underlying supposition: How does some comprehension of a universal meaning direct a particular religion in its concepts of human life and, eventually, of "eternal salvation"? In order to disagree with each other, discussion partners must first agree = delineate together the issues on which they don't agree. For dialogue to take off, there must be an underlying certain-ty of a common concern: to which extent do our differing answers respond to the same questions? Can one fundamental theme be identified which links our discrepant issues together to a wholeness and makes of our divergent concerns a unity in disuni-ty – so as to make dialogical conversation fit?

Starting with PAUL TILLICH's famous definition of religion as "ultimate concern",[21] we may take this formula not only to signify unconditional priority, but to integrate aspects like aim, totality and meaning. According to Tillich this does not automati-cally mean that one religion is *the* ultimate and that all the others are at the best penultimate. Even if he maintains some uniqueness of biblical revelation, he differs from his contemporary KARL BARTH in maintaining a "correlation" between revelati-on as an event in history and religiosity as a timeless universal. A capital question put to Tillich by posterity is, consequently, how his construction of 'religion' really relates to the existing world of religions in its concreteness.[22] A universalized concept of religion, however inclusive, hardly signalizes the most promising start to a clarifying interreligious dialogue, geared as such dialogue should be to exchange between live faiths in their complexity.

An introductory constructional approach may, however, also have certain advan-tages, namely as a unifying reminder of a shared platform. Evidently it could be useful to raise the question in togetherness: "What is religion?" – What do our faiths hold in common, that makes them fit together as partners for dialogue? Before that question materializes in conversation between religions couplewise, it could provide illumination if it were raised multilaterally, inviting (as fellow agents) and at the same time embracing (as fellow objects) any potential partaker of interreligious dialogue.

TILLICH's concept of "ultimate concern" may be a constructive starting point for a reflection on the role of religion / religions, also with particular reference to dynamics

---

[21] Paul TILLICH: Systematic Theology I 1968 (1953), 14ff.

[22] Cf. SCHOEN 1984, 103–11. – "Tillichs Anliegen ist, aufzuweisen, wie das, was mich unbedingt angeht – das Absolute – sich in nur relativen Formen manifestiert. Die Beziehungen zwischen den Religionen, bei denen sich relative Formen konfrontieren, sind für Tillich bloß ein Beispiel für dieses allgemeine Anliegen. Er lebt nicht wirklich mit den anderen Religionen und wird nicht von ihrem Anders-Sein bedroht und zerdrückt ..." op.cit., 110.

in the contemporary world. Such a reflection would naturally expand to include the role of one religion in relationship to the others. In this perspective any religion will understand itself as one among many responses to a common quest – a quest more fundamental than all others, the quest for a meaningful integration of all human quests into a clarifying totality. The mutual relation of these religions, then, will be partly confirmative (as to general purpose), partly alternative (as to particular realization). The pursuit of an ultimate quest can only take place in the perspective of a capital gain-or-loss.

A key word for integrative implementation could then be "salvation". There may be several corresponding expressions pointing to existential loss/lostness as overcome. However differently religions view the essential content of "lost" and "saved", the idea of an ultimate good to be pursued incorporates that of an ultimate failure to be avoided. A concern – ultimate or intermediary – indicates some possibility of fulfilment yet to be realized. Things do not work out all by themselves. When related to ultimacy, failure will be the fundamental disaster of human existence. The possibility of gain is hardly imaginable without the alternative of loss.[23]

More need not be said to support a preliminary conclusion. An obliging agreement on the importance of ultimacy opens up for a wide range of differing answers: Which of the "ultimate realities" proposed by various faiths is the authentic one which can rightly claim the role of ultimate concern? Common acceptance of ultimacy as the structuring referent of human orientation, then, could have as its first effect to "ultimatize" (= absolutize) any structurally integrated conflict between faith communities.

The reflection of TILLICH intended to prevent such a consequence, distinguishing, in a rather Platonic way, ultimacy as the ideal orientation of "religion", and actually existing religions as highly approximative realizations of that idea. One consequence of this distinction may be that the authenticity of any actual religion could be tested by its recognition of its own distance to the purity of absolute "religion".

> "In TILLICHS philosophisch inspiriertem Denken ... wird die Religion als eine Funktion des menschlichen Geistes begriffen – mit der unvermeidlichen Folge, dass sie nun als der Versuch erscheint, sich des Unbedingten zu bemächtigen und es dadurch zu verfälschen ... Ihr Gegenspieler ist die 'absolute' Religion, die aus der 'lebendigen' Beziehung auf eine letzte göttliche Wirklichkeit lebt ... Hier gibt es keinerlei Brücken: Vor der Offenbarung der Unbedingtheit Gottes ist alle Religion – nichts. ... den Religionen, das Christentum eingeschlossen, steht das, was den Menschen 'letztlich angeht', als ... Maßstab gegenüber. Die Religion müsste imstande sein, sich selbst als geschichtlihe Religion zu überwinden. Das ist aber unmöglich."

---

[23] It goes without saying that "ultimacy" in an existential analysis like Tillich's should not be conceived of as an objective, metaphysical category such as "the end of the world", "eternal salvation / damnation" etc. Its focus is on finality as existential orientation, not on a final destiny as a foreseeable or non-foreseeable state of "affairs".

This critical observation is made in a report on interreligious dialogue by an official committee of the Protestant churches in Germany, chaired by the professors CARL HEINZ RATSCHOW and THEO SUNDERMEIER.[24] The observers may be right in questioning Tillich's use of an ideal construction as critical standard for religious truth, but hardly in resenting – as it seems – a dialectical confrontation of faith in ultimate truth (faith transcending management by the faithful) and faith as penultimate realization (empirical religion).

In defining itself and its legacy on the background of a basic ("ultimate") human quest, a religion implicitly decides also on the role of other religions and stages its own relationship with them. And it would be good to find a way to combine the vision of ultimacy ("absoluteness" of commitment) with a critical estimate of one's own religious practice, thus admitting, indirectly, an equal dignity – and disgrace – of human truth ambitions, channeled as they may be by different religious traditions and communities.

For a community of faith it must be vital to relate to ultimate truth without monopolizing it, making itself some neatly circumscribed center of human society. But where all is true, nothing is true – and truth claims become essentially irrelevant. A balancing principle, prescribing some standard of mutual recognition based on give-and-take, can hardly be expected to find universal acceptance – at least in a foreseeable future. Momentous obstacles to an agreement based on stated standards are obviously (1) that the constitutive self-understandings of different religions leave different space for acceptance of alternative doctrines, and (2) that in different cultures historically given standards of tolerance exercise different degrees of influence, positive and negative, standards which reflect themselves also in the attitudes of religious communities – whether they themselves would (and/or could) claim paternity to these standards or not.

Applying these observations to the situation of Christianity may contribute to clarification in two directions. By raising general questions of heuristic importance it helps us to understanding intrareligious dialogue as going on in the Christian community in light of universal dynamics, active in the whole world of religions. At the same time it exemplifies these dynamics and so contributes to clarifying the presuppositions of interreligious dialogue in general.

Which are, in such a setting, the main doctrinal components in historical Christianity that most immediately affect the evaluation of other religions? In the history of Christian reflection as well as in the Biblical writings there is a basic tension between a universalistic and a particularistic drive. The first is grounded in the vision of the world – its totality – as God's creation, and of human beings, irrespective of ethnic and religious differences, as shaped in 'God's image' (Gen 1). But, paradoxically enough, there may also be a strong strain of universality in the proclamation of a "no

---

[24] 'Religionen, Religiösität und Christlicher Glaube' (ed. Arnoldshainer Konferenz & VELKD) 1991, 22f.

difference" participation in a common human fall with subsequent dependence on divine forgiveness (Rom 3). The particularizing trend resides in the understanding of sin as separation from God, to be overcome only by the self-sacrificial intervention of Christ, received in faith.

Salvation = full realization of human identity in openness to ultimate reality, may, structurally, be defined as the common aim of all religions. But this, purely formal, delimitation, leaves us with at least three questions unanswered: (1) How can that "identity in correspondence" be described in more than simply formal terms? (2) What barriers would eventually suspend it? (3) By what power are human beings "saved" (= restored) into this unconditional identity of theirs?

The most persistent tension in Christian history must be that between an optimistic anthropology/ cosmology, arguing the once-for-all given integrity of God's creation, and a pessimistic view stressing the gravity of human fall and the universal dependence on divine grace. Apparently, it will be easier to reconcile an accepting attitude to various religions with the former than with the latter of the two orientations. Elements of a similar tension are present in other religions too, particularly in the two of an Abrahamic background. But we should not overlook the fact that the critical concept of universal human deceitfulness also may have reconciliatory effects, even if more indirectly. In terms of equality and companionship, the message may come out identically if we say: "Their practice is as good as ours" or: "Ours may be no better than theirs."

The author of this study will never forget the impression it made when, as a youth consultant at the Assembly of the World Council of Churches (WCC) in Evanston IL in 1954, he listened to the UN General Secretary DAG HAMMARSKJÖLD concluding his greeting by expressing that no corporation in the world might have a resource for human peace and cooperation to offer, equal to the faith which speaks, in the words of Paul in Rom 3:22f: *"For there is no distinction, since all have sinned and fall short of the glory of God."*

The unifying effect of creation belief is not primarily the assumption that most religions (and most of the people on the earth?) share some idea of a common human origin. Even religions worshipping a divine mystery as source of the universe, may see this belief in an ontological, cosmological and/or anthropological framework which makes the notions of creator and creation come out rather differently. Not to forget that a similar diversity may, even if on a minor scale, be observed among believers of one and the same religion. –

Our unifying factor is above all the assurance: all people created in the image of God possess equal dignity and are driven by a common quest for an ultimate meaning of life – irrespective of how each individual or each community may think of that matter themselves. Not only is there a consciousness-building effect of such an insight to all who share it. Beyond that, essential expressions of createdness are universally operative prior to all awareness – so must a reflective creation faith confirm. Whether a person is created by God or not can impossibly depend on his/her own opinion about it.

After the doctrine of "creation", the concept "sin" may be the one to have the most immediate consequences for the attitude taken by a particular religion to dialogue. Concerning "sin" as a theme especially challenging to dialogue, three distinctions should be observed.

First, dialogue may start by actualizing the concept of "sin", the betrayal of human fellowship. What about observing honestly, every partner for him/herself, whatever might be discernible of deficit in confidence and in genuine readiness to cooperation here and now, i.e. in the concrete situation of dialogue? Or, would it be better not to invite the role of human egocentricity in religious disunity as a theme of exchange at too early a stage of interreligious dialogue ? Rather might it profit from some previous confidence-building through exchange on less soul-searching and prestige-promoting items. In intrareligious exchange it may be different, as there must be reason to welcome critical examination of common motives in the domestic camp at any stage of procedure.

Second, the variety of interpretations is supposedly a good deal more ostentative in the more closed domain of "sin" and "salvation" than in the open field of "creation" and "preservation". So, the difficulties of mutual understanding and the urgency of dialogue become even more acute and more complex when the problem of evil is brought on the table.

Third, continuing with "salvation", the most essential idea common to religions must be that of effecting a vital change in the lives of its adherents. This again implies some concept of a situation to be overcome and a new state of affairs to be introduced. Between the destructive *terminus a quo* and the salutary *terminus ad quem,* there must be fundamental correspondence, the dominance of the one being understood as oppression by the other and vice versa. Probably no question may divide faith communities like this: How do we understand radical evil – how, and by whom, can it be cured? Even if far-reaching agreement is there about practical repercussions in every-day life, the discrepancy of diagnostic explanations as well as of therapeutic prescriptions may be tremendous. So, beyond the issue of agreement and disagreement: which saving power does my faith accord to religious approaches other than its own?

Immediately, the tolerance embedded in religions of a fundamentally ethnic orientation is apparent. This does not relate exclusively to tribal religions. Primarily geared to a veneration of nature as such religions are, they will experience kinship to neighbors oriented toward whichever element of nature as expression of the one life-giving power, even if bloody collisions of tribal interests may acquire religious overtones. Our general observation applies in an even more striking way to deeply historical religions like Hinduism and Judaism. In spite of highly different concepts of truth – regarding the mood of divine communication as much as the content of it – these two religions have something remarkable in common. Each of them is affiliated with the life of one people with its own very distinctive culture, but in a way which, at least in the first round of reflection, invites a comprehensive recognition of other religions as supposedly corresponding exponents of historical authenticity for other peoples.

But this is a tolerance strictly delimited by ethnic borders. The vision of the suggested ethno-religious unity tends to demand political restrictions against religions trying to extend their mission in a way infringing upon ethnic borders. India and Israel are both states with a certain reputation of curtailing "mission" by law. A similar tendency in Muslim countries (not necessarily limited to those of them under Islamic law) may show less of the – to Western eyes paradoxical – combination: religious tolerance, ethnic self-preservation.

For a religion with a universal truth ambition, the plea for tolerance will naturally be of a different kind. Politically it will appear more tolerant, in terms of missionary ambitions it will at least look less tolerant. For the sake of logical consistency, it has to accept equal rights of mission in both directions. It can demand no restrictions against foreign mission in its domestic territory which it is not ready to respect in its own "mission fields". On the other hand, as herald of a message insisting on universal validity, it will definitely have a limited margin for equalizing claims of universality from other salvation messages. In that regard universality – paradoxically enough – may represent a narrowing when compared to ethnocentricity.

How far can universal validity of a message be resolved from its historic (institutional, doctrinal, ritual) expressions, and – condensed to some substantial core – be recognized as present also in other, in many, or perhaps in all, faith communities? Such a core, then, would have to be fancied as a kind of universal insight, essentially independent of historic appearances. In other words: some illuminating inner experience, addressable through various vocabularies (and methods of communication) – the geographically unlimited presence of some divine power. Viewed by Christianity, no such alternative would seem meaningful as a presentation of ultimate reality. In their a-historicity they are hardly synchronizable with the messianic role attributed to Jesus from Nazareth in the New Testament, and they seem incompatible with any personal face-to-face with godhead. To other faiths, especially of an Eastern extraction (Bahai, Taoism, various shades of Buddhism) this may look different. But in any case, such an assumption of truth universal, cannot be declared as the foundation of dialogue universal. For those believing in it, it will rather have to be set as an aim, hopefully to be conveyed to partners through dialogue.

Attempts have been made, ever since the first centuries of Christian history, to highlight "the Logos" (John 1:1ff) in the Fourth Gospel as a metaphor of omnipresent divine wisdom, and – a consequence of this – to raise question about possible footprints of the "Logos become flesh" (John 1:14) also in other religions. Such speculations sometimes expanded to suggesting a salutary presence of Christ also beyond the borders of biblical history. That discussion, which borders on that of "anonymous Christians", shall not be continued here. Our present aim is to show an intimate connection between the soteriology (doctrine of salvation) of a particular faith and its own theology of religions. This involves again: presenting the situation of Christianity as reflecting a dilemma suggestibly essential to all religion in dialogue. Even if concrete issues may be different from one to another of them, the question in the questions may be essentially the same.

At the same time, the intrinsic link between the self-understanding of Christianity and its implicit understanding of other faith communities is – as now indirectly observed – confirmed not only by some general concept of salvation, but by the overarching function of christology. Who Christ is, and what presence of his can eventually be imagined outside the reach of Christianity, is the question which will, more than any other, shape a Christian theology of religions.

This is manifest also in contemporary projects of a revisionist foundation of intra-religious dialogue. Already the coordinate titles of JOHN HICK's two anthologies *The Myth of God Incarnate* and *The Myth of Christian Uniqueness*[25] testify to this. So does the book title of another champion of "pluralism" STANLEY J.SAMARTHA: *One Christ – Many Religions. Toward a Revised Christology.*[26] As clearly suggested, this is an attempt to show how a "pluralist" theology of religions recommends and supports a doctrine of Christ – one must say – emphatically different from that of Nicene orthodoxy, up to now the foundation of Christian ecumenics.

Also HANS KÜNG, with his more moderate, "inclusivism"-oriented theology of religions, is determined to link dialogical concern with a reexamination of the christological decisions of the Ancient Church. He sees Nicea as expression of a Hellenization of Christianity, a process which, in his view, dramatically confirmed the division between Jewish and Christian identity, and subsequently served to radicalize nascent Islam as a movement of protest against institutionalized Christianity.

His plea for a reexamination of traditional christology was a major issue when in 1979 KÜNG was deprived of his authorization as teacher of Roman Catholic theology. It may be worthwhile, however, to note that this took place some years before his fervid involvement with dialogue. At the same time, his concern about christology and interreligious understanding differs from that of HICK/KNITTER/SAMARTHA. Their worry is of a principal kind: a "unique" Christ will inevitably disqualify any extra-Christian approach to God. Küng's worry is more historically founded: the Hellenistic-speculative drive of the Nicene development having, as he maintains, served to tear the three semitic religions apart, notwithstanding an originally common footing in Old Testament monotheism. A de-hellenized christology is thus, according to KÜNG, recommendable especially for "ecumenical" reasons.[27] An elo-

---

[25] HICK1977, and HICK & KNITTER 1987/88.

[26] 1991. In CD 38, Dec. 2001, (official WWC publication!) – an issue entirely consecrated to the memory of Stanley J. SAMARTHA, his christological challenge is particularly described (and seemingly uncritically endorsed?) by his WCC successor Wesley ARIARAJAH, 15–29. Still more remarkable it is that Lukas VISCHER, former secretary of Faith and Order, gives a "Faith and Order Perspective", 30f, with no observation at all on Samartha' frontal collision with the rather trend-setting Faith and Order Paper No. 153 'Confessing the One Faith' (1991).

[27] This point is advocated with strength already in Küng's analysis of the relationship between Christianity and Islam in 'Christentum und Weltreligionen', 1984:
"Aber im ökumenischen Zusammenhang ... bedrängt mich die Frage: Wie kann ich einen Muslim (oder Juden) verständlich machen, warum Christen an diesen Jesus als den Christus, die Offenbarung Gottes, glaubt? Und mit dieser Intention habe ich durchaus das Recht, auf die ... ursprüngliche christologische Option aufmerksam zu machen, die noch jahrhundertelang von den zerstreuten judenchristli-

quent example of how dialogue between religions has demanded – and in the future still more may demand – retrograde influence on doctrinal decisions within a participating religious community!

This brings us once more back to our thesis about an implicit theology of religions – and thus of dialogue – as a given function of any religious self-understanding. To which extent, then, can an elaborate theology of dialogue – developed more or less in conscious emancipation from that pattern – exercise a retrospective influence on the doctrinal profile and, thus, presumably, on the identity, of a given religion? Accepting dialogue in itself as a motive for reorientation of identities would be to equip a procedure of consensus-building with cognitive authority in itself, which would lend rather massive priority to pragmatism: dialogue has to succeed for the sake of dialogue, so…! One thing is to assign to dialogue the role of questioning, and suggesting amendments to, fossilized elements of thinking and handling. A different thing would be to authorize it to refashion our interpretative framework and to decide the location and role of essential truths. The integrity of dialogue demands that the conviction of a constitutive identity be kept intact. Truth cannot be changed for reasons other than truth. Substance can only be questioned through substantial reflection.

That dialogue may bring about changes in the self-understanding of individual participants is to be expected. What else is dialogue there for? But the accomplishments of dialogue will be rather meager if a change affecting the partakers is not shared by their respective communities in a way which affects relationship on a communitarian level. The real dilemma starts, however, at an earlier stage of reflection: can dialogue be founded on a self-presentation by the partners which already deviates from the common self-understanding of their respective communities, possibly because they have been reinterpreted for the sake of dialogical rapprochement? Should dialogue prepared, prior to dialogue done, be invited to depart from the historically grounded positions of the respective faith communities, in case that could be presumed to hurry up agreement around the table? As far as Christianity is concerned, this question seems illustrated in a thought-provoking way by the attention given to christology by the authors we have quoted.

In any case, any idea of own identity includes some view of one's surrounding partners, and any alteration in relationship with these partners may effect or reflect a fluctuation in the image of own identity. Such reciprocity will apply to relationship between collectives as well as to those between individuals. Already for reasons of logic, a theology of interreligious dialogue cannot terminate itself in an intrareligious

---

chen Gemeinden ... überliefert wurde. Und ich frage mich, ob hier möglicherweise nicht doch Kategorien, die diesen Jesus als die Offenbarung Gottes Juden und Muslimen verständlicher machen als die hellenistische Zwei-Naturen-Lehre." 197.

The same viewpoint is defended and more broadly developed by the same KÜNG 10 years later in 'Das Christentum – Wesen und Geschichte', particularly in the sections on 'Das jüdisch-apokalyptische Paradigma des Urchristentums', 89–144, and 'Das ökumenisch-hellenistische Paradigma des christlichen Altertums', 145–335.

dialogue narrowly understood: dialogue among fellow believers reviewing their dialogue with alien believers. The necessary dialogue on dialogue to be held in a domestic community can be accomplished only in the setting of an open exploration of own identity. Only when included in a context of global theological reflection does dialogue on dialogue receive meaning and give meaning.

The understanding of own identity and that of dialogical commitment define each other reciprocally. Such a correspondence is evidently there already at an ingressive stage, prior to being observed, reflected upon, and responded to. Which of the two understandings may, in concreto, be the one to set the game, may ensue differently from case to case – the old story of the hen and the egg. It is in full awareness of this hermeneutical interaction that we must test our criteria in the ongoing intrareligious dialogue discussions – including also the argumentative use of biblical references.

7. Dialectic of Dialogue

The first conclusion to be drawn from our comprehensive consultation, is that dialogue is vital – for principal as well as for practical reasons.

Practical: concern for peace and a maximum of "common" human cooperation gets more and more urgent as the constructive, as well as the destructive, possibilities of expanding technology and communication present themselves.

Principal: such reasons will remain the same at all times, whether observed or not. The quest for an ultimate truth raises concerns well beyond the self-protection of separate religious traditions, and beyond any particular theory of dialogue. How silly it would be to canonize my own community – its actual constitution, its declarations and decrees – as domicile of truth in its fulness! And how could I presume that maxims and practices of other communities, such as they are understood and venerated by their faithful, be void of any truth at all? Modest as these self-examinatory avowals may sound, they at least leave the stage open for conversation and joint reflection, inviting in this way a worldwide movement of mutual rapprochement. A process of authentic dialogue may have started. A platform of developing confidence may be bordered, resting precisely on the assurance that no limitative condition is stated and that no profile of a final agreement is declared – prior to the confidence-building exchange.

7.1. Dynamics of Exchange

In this perspective the interaction of inter- and intra-religious exchange shows its trend-setting importance. The process of mutual clarification between dialogue and dialogue-on-dialogue reflects a double orientation of vital significance to any partner in dialogue, as a responsorium between alterable and unalterable givens. An exchange takes place, each participant representing a self-image in face of another self-image. The neighbor's identity should be respected no less than my own – and mine no less than the neighbor's, for that matter. So far, the challenge of dialogue will reflect an all-encompassing demand of tolerance in all truly human relationships. But in addition to that comes the particular religious aspect: an orientation in the direction of ultimacy = unconditional finality, which makes the confrontation of contradictive-looking concerns more painful than on a finite level of non-ultimacy.

In terms of psycho-social dynamics it is easy to see why the confrontation of competitive truth claims is so frequently understood as intolerant and intolerable, and why several agents of dialogue try to eliminate the dilemma by fencing out what may seem to be unconditional claims in advance. The presupposition is obviously that participants in dialogue, when thinking consistently, are left with a simple alternative. *Either* to absolutize truth as accommodated in their own community: doctrines, cult, ethical practices – exclusivism in a rather literal meaning of that word. *Or* to identify equal rights for each of the partners to have one's own truth claims accepted: which would be close to unmodified pluralism. Positions commonly labeled as 'inclusivist', may try to place themselves in-between, advising opposite-looking claims to reconcile on some looser theory of mutual acceptance. But in-between positions are easily rejected as logically or existentially intolerable by the champions of a clear-cut either-or. A characteristic example may be PAUL KNITTER's condescending treatment of HANS KÜNG in his reported Rubicon argument.[1]

The non-dialectical approach of unmitigated 'exclusivists' is particularly visible in what is today generally referred to as "fundamentalism". If we define "fundamentalism" as an attitude which unrestrictedly identifies truth with formulations on display in one's own community,[2] it is clear that such a position excludes everything we can profitably call dialogue. Fundamentalist attitudes seem in our day to be just as present within a majority of world cultures and religious communities as ever – even where they are by no means proclaimed as written rules of religious corporations or political society. Experience so far forbids us to reduce fundamentalism to a phenomenon bound, by some irresistible power of progress, to disappear from the surface of the earth in a foreseeable future.

As seen in so many contexts, the main prerequisite for dialogue may be identified as equality: equal right and duty for each of the partners to present their own identity as they themselves sense it, with corresponding acceptance of the same right/duty for the partner(s). Such mutual recognition will inevitably produce a double consequence.

First, I cannot – in the name of tolerance, and for the sake of apparent "peace" – restrict truth ambitions essential to the community I represent, as that would do injustice also to the conversation partner, directly and indirectly. Directly, it would leave him in a fatal mistake, presenting him with a false image of the community which I represent. Indirectly, it would invite false strategies for reciprocal rapprochement and most likely demand him to present his own community in an equally adaptable "light version".

Second, I cannot, in the name of honesty, and for the sake of uncompromised encounter, make the understanding of truth cherished by my community, into a methodological prerequisite of interreligious dialogue. Faith commitment must be present, and at the same time absent, in the conversation. Present, as an indispensable thematic ingredient of the exchange; absent, as a presupposition in one way or the other craving control of the conversation procedure.

[1] Again: 'Hans Küng's Theological Rubicon', in: SWIDLER 1987, 224–230. Cf., here 4.2.2., especially our notes 161–164.
[2] LØNNING 1997, 177–184.

It is easier to detect a deficit in the neighbor's account than in my own. So, as an example helping to raise reflection, may we once more be reminded of that undialectical blend of faith and empirical knowledge, which we had opportunity to note in contemporary Muslim polemic.[3] Here, the truth of the Qur'an and of the New Testament are compared, the first as infallible by virtue of dogmatically sustained claims, the other as full of errors, witnessed by modern historic criticism.

The prime requisite of dialogue must be equal standards of argument. Inability to arrive at equal standards may be due to different cultural assumptions and is in itself an essential topic of discussion. It may have to be sought through dialogue before it can be practiced in dialogue. Our prime demand is equality of standards to be employed by the same judge in face of truth claims by various discussion partners – own claims not excluded. Equal chances for different faiths to be heard, to be understood, and to be fairly evaluated! Two sets of holy scriptures under comparison must be subject to the same historical and moral scrutiny

Certainly, it is a deep-going difference between two religions if the one declines any historical-critical approach to its holy book, and the other is ready to adopt such procedure. But this difference can least of all justify the use of double standards by one and the same authority. At the same time it is clear that different attitudes to Holy Scripture and critical research as part of different religious legacies, will be a dialogical issue of top importance. But these two regards are priorities on different levels. Matter and method should certainly be distinguished!

7.2. Between Fundamentalism and Pluralism

So far we have addressed a fundamentalist attitude which denies to others a protective shield which it claims for itself. Additionally, it denies for itself the acid test of scientific criticism which it conjures for its competitors. These two procedures of attack, logically irreconcilable as they are, are not usually apparent in Occidental branches of fundamentalism. These branches would commonly limit themselves to promoting own absolutist claims, thereby excluding other, competitive claims as impossible to reconcile with them – in itself a more logical operation, faltering just on a scientifically superficial evaluation of supporting "facts".

"Les extrèmes se touchent" – however. Opposite to fundamentalism, in every regard – except, usually, in final conclusion – is that theology of religions which refers to itself as "pluralist". As its most representative expression so far, we have had several occasions to inspect *"The Myth of Christian Uniqueness"* (1987),[4] and its counterpart *"Christian Uniqueness Reconsidered ... "* (1990).[5]

A criticism frequently voiced against "pluralism" is that, in not unimportant regards, it turns out to be the opposite of what if pretends. It claims to be open, tole-

---

[3] Cf., here 5.2.1.3.
[4] Particularly, here 4.1.1 & 4.1.3.
[5] Here 4.1.1 & 4.2.4.

rant, impartial, and liberating. But the fact is that, categorically relativizing all truth claims, it excludes from dialogue potential partners unready to comply with the pluralist idea of truth equally divided and possessed by all. Whoever insists on bringing particular truth claims along to dialogue, will certainly be excluded from the good society!

We have seen REINHOLD BERNHARDT making himself the defender of leading pluralists against such accusations. He sums up and claims to defeat the most common objections against "pluralism", and we commented on his observations, in which we found reasons to remark several weaknesses.[6]

We have noted as an elementary failure of the "pluralist" school – with JOHN HICK as its most outspoken herald – the proclaiming as common foundation of religious authenticity a (18th century type of) theocentricity, neglecting among other things how powerfully this excludes the great religions of the East. More fatal still is, however, the consequence of obstinately modifying all truth ambitions allowed in dialogue, to a preestablished standard of Occidental modernity. For good reasons this has been judged, especially by voices in the "Third World", as expression of the traditional cultural arrogance of the white man, yea, as an attempt by old colonial powers to dictate mutual relationships on the world scale.

May the core of the issue be a manifest confusion of two, mutually exclusive, concepts of equality? (1) Equal possession of truth by all – a methodological condition to be endorsed, as well as a final conclusion to be embraced, by all – and: (2) equal opportunity for all to explain and defend their own relationship with truth.

In the first case the task of dialogue itself will be reduced to exposing and explaining a common platform, in principle already proclaimed. Aim as well as end of the process are clarified (by a purely intrareligious approach?) and seen as ideally present from the very beginning of interreligious exchange – namely as a fairly unified acceptance of some fundamental consensus now to be further developed and embraced by all. The show starts and ends with a joint agreement about the non-significance of all disagreements. Dialogue, then, just serves to make a consensus, already recognized in principle, obvious in its practical consequences, with the aim of hopefully promoting mutual respect and cooperation. No religion, then, is allowed a concept of salvation which puts a question mark at the concepts of finality held by the others.

The great issue is whether this ideal image of equality also grants equality in a more elementary and palpable sense: freedom for each to express his / her own claims, unrestricted by, and at the same time not restricting, a corresponding freedom of opposition from the others? Where all are equally right, do all enjoy equal rights? Where truth, by authority of indisputable rules, belongs to all, freedom fundamentally belongs to none. Restrictive, regulative opinions authorized in advance decide the design of the building.

If, as we propose, equality of methodological rules is established as the one condition fundamental to dialogue, it does not follow that the one or the other can impose

6 Here 4.1.5.

his rules on the partner(s). The point is that none of them can practice contrasting standards for judging an apparent controversy with the partner. To the extent that one part feels pledged to criteria unlike those of the other, this is in itself an issue to be noted on the agenda of dialogue.

Each of the partners may have preferences as to format and character of the consensus hopefully to result, but no concrete expectation can be imposed as normative. Nor can a partner enter dialogue determined to push the process to such or such an end, without submitting first his enterprise to dialogical response and corrective. Dialogue as authentic exchange demands freedom to find its own course. It cannot be staged by one or the other, even in the name of nominally freedom-loving pluralism.

How, then, do we accommodate the fact that some commonality of purpose obviously must be there, in order to initiate dialogue as a joint, unifying enterprise? A mutual will to rapprochement is required: an idea of main direction combined with a readiness to consultation and adjustment along the way. But the "pluralist" theory goes far beyond that, in a direction – paradoxically enough – of uniformity, not by way of stated purpose, but by way of inescapable consequence. Pluralism claiming general allegiance, as it virtually does, rather deserves the name of "uniformism".

In addition, the following should not be overlooked. The partners invited to dialogue are not the various religions such as each of them would describe itself. They are the respective religions as seen through the glasses of Occidental modernity. When standing face-to-face, observer and object are both carrying their respective loads of history, entangled as they have been, and still may be, in their respective social, cultural and political networks. For each of them it is rather essential to keep this duplicity clear as a contribution to dialogue itself.

So, dialogue demands of each partner a readiness to relativize and, to a certain extent, even to denounce, own confrontative manners in past and in present. In order to defend convincingly the truth of its inheritance, it must reflect critically on its history. It cannot raise universal truth claims in its own name – as an institution eager to confirm own formulations, own regulations, own customs and traditions – only on behalf of some superior, non-manipulable vocation. This again means to accept that vocation as judicial of own actual appearance. When presenting itself in its manifest complexity, it places itself under judgement by its own claim to an identity founded in ultimate truth.

7.3. Christianity – A Universal Paradigm?

Undeniably, Christian churches did play a leading role in the emergence and development of interreligious dialogue in the 20th century. This may mainly be due to two factors: their great advantage as to resources (organization, economy, international network of contacts) – and a crisis of conscience with a corresponding readiness to

penitence, caused by the role of the "Christian World" in the era of colonial imperialism now coming so unmistakably to its end.

A question about own committedness had, and has, to be asked first by Christians
to Christians, Muslim to Muslims, Buddhists to Buddhists etc. Each should be called
to self-examination: To which extent may the predicaments we, for our part, face as
to interreligious exchange, reflect complexities of universal impact? To put the question a little paradoxically: Can understanding of own barriers to understanding wake
understanding of corresponding (or contrasting) barriers with the other(s), encouraging thus a spreading spirit of communication? Or, expressed in positive terms: Can
intrareligious dialogue in faith community A as domestic wrestling with the challenge of interreligious dialogue, when earnestly passed on to community B for information, throw light on B's own perplexities in the same area, thus leading it (through
own intrareligious dialogue) to clearer self-awareness in a way likely to be promotive
of interreligious understanding? If that be so, what could be a more eloquent demonstration of the constructive interaction of intra- and interreligious dialogue?

The initial, trendsetting understanding called for may be an agreement – in whatever words or signs – of the urgency to walk toward increased mutual understanding
together. The pledge should be to proceed in cooperation as far as, at any time, a
common lane may open up through honest exchange of reciprocal convictions. What
such a progress requires is obviously communication based on common rules and
equal rights, with full bi-/multi-lateral openness about disagreements. The latter
would include a declared willingness both to ask and to answer critical questions, and
this in ways proper to challenge one's own prestige. In detail, the grammar of dialogue will have to take shape en route, in light of confirmative (and negative) observations stepwise confirmed by joint experience. In this way, theory and praxis must
be allowed to shape each other mutually. Dialectic, expressed as constant reflection
on what the conversation is doing to ourselves and to our partner(s), may be needed
in plain interreligious dialogue no less than in previous (and successive) intrareligious
dialogue.

It is evident that intrareligious dialogue, responding to the prime responsibility of
each communion to clarify its own readiness for dialogue, will be of limited value
unless the accomplishments are passed on to the wider arena of interreligious exchange. This not only in terms of ready-made resolutions from back home, but as an
open account for domestic premises and for confrontations as well. Secrecy about
one's own uncertainty is not a great promoter of confidence. The frankness thus
recommended, may invite others to admit and to combat, a corresponding uncertainty of their own. Such sharing of information prepares interreligious dialogue
as a joint exploration of similarities/differences in expectations and approaches.

Further, it invites to share discoveries of presuppositions genuinely common, even
if frequently diversified in historically conditioned guise. Critical self-examination by
each religion in intrareligious research may produce a reference material of vital importance for interreligious understanding, accounting for similarities in differences
no less than for differences in similarities. In this way a variety of single processes

(intrareligious dialogue, proper to each religion separately) indirectly inform and instruct the one great process (of interreligious dialogue, common). Similarity may be
there with the many minor rivers adding up to the big flood on its way to the sea. A
universal dialogue, on subject as well as on method, can only take shape gradually,
through a dialectical interplay of single dialogues (intrareligious dialogue feeding
interreligious dialogue and vise versa).

Does this sound too specific and biblically related to illustrate cross-denominatio-
nal universality? The recipe may sound comparatively easy for Christianity with its
language of sin and forgiveness, dying and resurrecting, or – as we have seen in the
contemporary dialogue with Buddhism: of self-emptying, κενωσις. Even in religions
where such language gives little emotional echo, a rational understanding may be
there of a fundamental distinction to be made between a pledge to ultimate truth and
defense of structurally integrated positions.

In contemporary dialogue it would sound ridiculous to claim infallibility for an
established community or for any identifiable element of its appearance. Each dialogue participant has – for reasons of its own integrity as well as of viable dialogue –
to admit the difference between given complexity and intended simplicity in its self-
presentation. Struggle for truth and struggle for self-preservation must be fundamentally distinguished, at the same time as practical connections must be explored: After
all, for a message to survive and for the community transmitting it to survive, some
interaction between the two is needed.

This general demand distances itself from that of "equal truth to all" set forth by
the "pluralists", in that it accepts the right and plight of each colloquial partner to
sustain the truth claims of its own conviction – provided only that this be done in a
frame-work of searching and self-criticism without any insistence on own irreproach-
ability.

There may be reasons to claim universal validity for the suggested non-relativizing
dialectic of self-trial. As a meaningful foundation of interreligious dialogue, it may be
difficult to point out an alternative which to the same extent combines the conviction
of uncompromisable truth with a conscious openness to critical assessment. A coun-
tering question may, however, be hard to escape, for after all: isn't this an Occidental
model of reflection ever so much as that of relativizing pluralism? And by introducing
it, isn't this precisely what we have accused the "pluralists" of doing: we prescribe a
model of dialogue of Western provenance to be adopted by the peoples of the earth?

Not precisely. Terminology and exemplification will always reflect the environments in which a theory was formulated, but that in itself does not preclude the
possibility of a universally valid reflection. The point of our "dialectical" theory is to
unite a demand – presumably of all faiths – to formulate their own truth claims (a
right denied them by the pluralist ban on all pretensions of "uniqueness"!) with maximal readiness to invite and listen to criticism from outside. And it may function
without restricting the freedom of the partner to choose his own strategy. He is encouraged to formulate his truth claims himself. He may also contest the category of
"ultimacy", even if I will do my best to prove the impossibility of rejecting a transcen-

dental category : in this case, the formative horizon of integrative thinking (terminology as such may be debated). He may gratify my plea for criticism precisely to the extent he likes. And he decides how much or how little he will follow along and invite criticism.

Additionally, our dialectical recipe of dialogue should primarily be seen as an outline for intrareligious dialogue : intended to be received and accommodated for practical use by one particular religion. Its subsequent role as prospective guideline for interreligious dialogue should probably be delayed until the questions it responds to, emerge unsought through the very dynamics of dialogical exchange.

As already shown, this dialectic has no particular affinity to Christianity which contradicts its claims of impartiality, neither with regard to methodological equality as irreplaceable presupposition, nor to an open-ended future as the orientative direction. As far as a certain bias of language and exemplification may seem inevitable, this has been observed in a way which hopefully encourages the translations needed for necessary dialogical transmissions. The dialectic called for can be described and concretisised in different vocabularies and cognitive frameworks.

The dialogue suggested does not call for an advance agreement on end, method or procedure. A ready-made theory of dialogue is not the prime requisite for an adequate orientation of dialogue. The initial, basic agreement called for, must be an implicit understanding – in whatever words or signs – of the urgency of a walk toward increased mutual understanding, an understanding which immediately includes readiness to accept a communication based on common rules and equal rights, with full openness about fundamental convictions, and determined willingness to ask and to answer critical questions based on the principle of reciprocity. A more detailed grammar of dialogue can be expected to materialize only as it is tested out. Theory and practice should be allowed to shape each other reciprocally. Dialectic seems needed *in* plain interreligious dialogue no less than in dialogue *on* dialogue (intrareligious dialogue as a reflective topic of interreligious dialogue).

Does this mean that dialogue on dialogue, which we have basically presented as the legacy of intrareligious exchange will to a certain degree be extended and transferred to the level of interreligious dialogue ? It might be a more clarifying description to confirm that intrareligious reflection as a primary responsibility of each religion per se, will be of limited value unless its accomplishments are channeled on to the interreligious setting and thus meaningfully related to the dialogue of religions all the way through. Religious communities in dialogue with each other should be kept constantly informed of the dialogue on dialogue going on in each of the communities respectively. Not only does such information serve interreligious dialogue as a joint exploration of difference in expectations and approaches. It just as much invites a shared discovery of presuppositions genuinely common, but hidden in different guise in the various traditions.

The self-search by each religion produces a non-dispensible reference material for interreligious dialogue, as illustration of similarities in differences no less than differences in similarities, such as they project themselves in live actuality. In this way a multitude of processes (intrareligious dialogues, as proper to each community separately) indirectly inform and advise the one great process (of interreligious dialogue, common), adding to a universal dialogue, on subject as well as on methodology, within the framework of a constantly developing exchange.

This is also what, in this context, we have referred to as dialogue. And it indicates the reason why a study on dialogue like ours, largely limited to intrareligious reflection in its Christian version, can hope to contribute – and contribute essentially – to molding the role of intrareligious dialogue in its multiple diversity, which actually means: preparing the event of an interreligious dialogue universal.

7.4. "Is Christ a Christian?"

Tracing now our "dialectical" concern in the opposite direction, straining in this way the legacy of intrareligious exchange to the utmost: is there in Christian faith anything indispensible, which a Christian in dialogue cannot surrender, not even conceal, without, by so doing, ceasing to speak as a Christian? This may be read as the final issue also in the dispute of different theologies of religions: exclusivism – inclusivism – pluralism – in whatever version.

Contrary to what a superficial look may suggest, this question is of paramount interest also to non-Christian partners ready to engage in a truly existential dialogue with Christians. It puts their observation of Christianity as a reliable conversation partner to a basic test, and so the seriousness of a mutual dialogue program. This implies: setting an example, a standard of dialogical honesty, in calling to mind that soul-searching (ultimate expression of intrareligious dialogue!) which each of the partners may have to go through as a purging preparation for dialogue universal.

In authentic dialogue, the possibility must exist that some participant at the end may arrive at the conclusion: "I have changed my opinion, I may have to transfer my allegiance from one faith to another." Dialogue ceases to be dialogue if the conversion of conversation partners is seen as the very aim of it. But so it does if the possibility of accepting the partners' testimony of truth is formally prohibited.[7] For this, as for several other, reasons, clear distinction must be made between the participants as individuals and as representatives of their respective communities. Collective conversion by one religion to another is certainly not a possibility to be foreseen. Hardly to be wanted, either. But a wide variety of possible rapprochements could be hoped (and prayed for), even if, in advance, a logical analysis of various scenarios would offer a survey no less complex than would a review of psycho-/socio-logical dynamics at work.

In recalling what in Christianity has been described as "a stumbling block to Jews and folly to Gentiles ... Christ crucified ... the power of God and the wisdom of God"

---

[7] Once more we remind of John Cobb's reflections on interreligious conversions as a possible resource of impulse sharing, COBB 1982, 142.

(1 Cor 1:23) we highlight a radically controversial claim of uniqueness, not on behalf of the Church as establishment or as authoritative interpreter of truth, but to its founder, who is in person the focus of attention in its faith confessions. Indeed, a truth claim presented in a language demanding defense, be it by an institution or by a single person!

As we have seen along the road, there have been – and there are – several ways to reconcile salvation in Christ with some concept of salvation available even in spiritual environments where the name of Jesus of Nazareth is unknown. KARL RAHNER's much debated concept of "anonymous Christians" does not explicitly recognize a presence of Christ communicated through non-Christian religions, but observes individual persons in a way that makes the presumptive support of their respective religions an issue of little import. To Cobb and KÜNG there is no salvation apart from Christ – for Christians. That they, scared by apparently imperialistic consequences of RAHNER's theory, concede salvation importance also to other religions without postulating any extra-Christian presence of Christ, makes them vulnerable to accusations, both from the left and from the right, of lacking coherence in their respective approaches.

More consistency may be claimed by recently expanding theories a bit "further to the right" (PANNENBERG, several contributors to "Christian Uniqueness", American "evangelicals"), where distinction is made between the objective uniqueness of Christian faith (proclaiming Christ as the only savior of humankind) and subjective faith as individual assurance of one's own salvation. Salvation, then, in ways beyond human exploration, is taken for available also to people who are not actually informed about the Christ event, and it is not definitely excluded that other religions, in ways hidden to themselves and equally undetectable to others, may prepare individuals for receiving that salvation. Confer PINNOCK (4.3.1.) with his elaborated distinction between Christ as the unique "ontological" foundation of salvation independent of actual "epistemological" grounds!

The most explicit theory in that direction may be that of GEORGE LINDBECK about a person's final decision visualized at the border of life, where Christ in his "second coming" is recognized or not recognized by individuals according to criteria entirely separate from their previous knowledge of him. No less venturous, compared with his own theological standards, is CLARK H. PINNOCK, in working out his distinction between the unconditioned "ontological" and the conditioned "epistemological" significance of Christ for human salvation. Christ the author of human salvation is not to be restricted to Christ an object of human faith. Salvation by faith is emphatically distinguished from faith in own salvation.[8]

There is no reason why the approaches of LINDBECK and of PINNOCK could not be unified – on the contrary! And certain suggestions by continental theologians like

---

[8] Here 4.2.4. and 4.3.1, cf. George LINDBECK: The Nature of Doctrine, 1984, and Clark H. PINNOCK: A Wideness in God's Mercy, 1992.

MOLTMANN and PANNENBERG could be added into a joint assumption that openness to the great mystery of divine generosity – in the Bible declared as "grace", and seen as definitely realized on earth in Christ – can develop within different settings of religious community, without this assumption abolishing to Christians the obliging character of the Great Commission: to make Christ, the unknown source of salvation for humankind, known (Mt 28:16). In that context even a couple of suggestions by authors we have observed in less conservative theological camps deserve to be brought to attention. In spite of earlier critical remarks, we refer, although with some hesitation, to v.BRÜCK's understanding of Hindu Advaita as corresponding with a trinitarian experience of divine presence, and, with a little less hesitation, to the role of Amida as fountain of grace in "Pure Land" Buddhism (COBB, VAN STRAELEN). In any case, do such observations justify the suggestion that a basic experience of divine generosity as the bearing dynamic of our cosmos, could give substance to a hope that seekers of truth finally will recognize their leading ambitions as fulfilled in Christ?

The spectrum we have indicated of – call it – "split solutions", fulfills in some way our request for a dialectical approach: full respect for what is observed as the distinctive character of one's own faith (in this case Christianity), combined with full equality not only in facing common rules for dialogue, but in searching for a final hope for every person made in the Creator's image!

How would such a captivating vision fit with a biblical panorama of ultimate judgement? Differing answers will be given by regular Bible readers, including representatives of academical scholarship. But the best-supported observation may be that of the Bible containing an impressive variety of eschatological models, models reflecting, not least, various stages in the historical process of formation. An important number of observations will have to be confronted and reciprocally adapted if taken to sustain some unifying model of thought.

It is not easy to see *that, why,* and *how* some eschatology with direct prospects for eternity should be a prerequisite for dialogue. Our programmatic combination of methodological equality and doctrinal confrontability demands a horizon of openness. In that case a desirable balancing of truth claims is bound to take place a posteriori – that is: as a consequence, not as a condition of dialogical commitment. Premature conclusions on issues of content would unduly restrict the field of vision, and thus the essential challenge, of dialogue. When we refrain from discussing the doctrinal aspects of the proposals just recited, it is not because they are seen as unimportant, it is precisely because a conclusion would be irrelevant in the present context – and that for the reasons just stated.

Returning to our provocative question: "Is Christ a Christian?" – it may now be paraphrased a little less enigmatically: How can the presumptive core of Christian orientation: an unconditional loyalty to Christ, the ultimate reference of human commitment, combine with a critical (including self-critical) distance to Christianity in its historical (including its contemporary) appearance? How can the suggested interaction of commitment and critical awareness foster openness vis-a-vis people of other faiths? How can involvement in dialogue differentiate between Christ as undisputable focus of spiritual allegiance and Christianity[9] as social and psychological frame-work? These questions may be supposed – but, for reasons of principle, not declared in advance – to have structural parallels in other faiths. And they may, like in Christianity, be urgent not primarily for the sake of dialogue, but for the intrinsic identity of each religion. Each of them may be challenged to approach itself critically, as a highly duplex phenomenon, a divine legacy presented in garbs unmistakably human.

Our answer is that the correspondence and possible interaction of split identities can unveil itself and become instrumental to dialogue only in the developing process – a challenge which has been largely overlooked in the discussion so far. "The process", then, does not refer unilaterally to intrareligious or to interreligious dialogue, but to the dialectical back-and-forth which both separates and unites the two. In this way self-examination in each of the camps is encouraged through correspondence with the wider interfaith exchange. But each partner keeps the right of a final, as well as initial, self-definition. Interfaith exchange can progress only when constantly enriched in two-way communication with its intrafaith pendant.

This means that a choice: exclusivism – inclusivism – pluralism, or whatever alternative theories may appear – is principally postponed. Not *ad calendas graecas*, but rather *ad* some unknown *calendas Domini*. In the meantime, the discussion can be carried on, but definitely not brought to an end, within each of the respective constituencies separately, if so they wish. But it can hopefully be carried on with less of confrontative elan than in the somewhat sloganish confrontation at the borders of "the river of Rubicon".[10]

Christ is no Christian in the meaning of one authorizing, and one incorporated into, Christianity – i.e. into the highly complex socio-cultural entity which that word has come to circumscribe in "ordinary" language. Nor is he available as general guarantor of human achievements, in however good faith they may be presenting themselves to the world as "Christian". The image of the Church as "corpus Christi" is a vision of faith which lends no special claim of superiority, moral or political, to claims made by individual Christians or by ecclesiastical establishments in their own names.[11]

---

[9] It must be clear that "Christianity" here primarily serves as a psychological more than a sociological referent. The possibility of substituting it by "the Church" or by "Christendom" for a clarification of purpose, has been considered – and rejected. "The Church" would suspect the institution in itself for being the actual referent. This might easily camouflage the real culprit under persecution: fundamental confidence in own religious identity as distinguishing oneself from others, a reliance which may just as well express itself in privatized adaptations of Christian imagery and conceptuality as in institutionalized churchmanship. – "Christendom" would better take care of a religio-geographical sphere transcending concrete establishment, but could also offer an easy escape to those cherishing more individualistic shapes of Occidental self-confidence.

[10] Cf. "the Rubicon discussion", 4.2.2. our notes 161–164, and 7. note 1.

[11] In this context there is ample reason to record that the word Χριστιανός – Christian – occurs only tree times in the New Testament, and is of no major importance as tool of doctrinal reflection: Act 11:26, and 26:28, further 1 Pet 4:16. – To the image "body of Christ", see especially Rom 12:4f and 1 Cor 12:12ff.

Thus, it will be erroneous to glorify empirical Christianity as possessor of some religious value distinctive from, and superior to, comparable socio-cultural entities on the earth. In this world of relations and of relativity, truth cannot be seized, exposed and proven as some item safely parked in a proprietor's hand. A possessive fist must give way to a humble but confident finger, pointing in a direction, steady and apt to take all attention away from the pretended advantages of "me and my own camp". That means: pointing without excluding the possibility that someone differently positioned and for that reason pointing in a different direction – whether realizing it or not – may finally be pointing towards the same aim. It is not, for that reason, necessary to arouse new misunderstanding by referring to him or her as an "anonymous Christian".

Certain things still remain to be seen, and may do so for a good while yet. That is what makes dialogue possible. That is what makes dialogue promising. And that is what makes dialogue urgent.

Literature

ABE, MASAO: Kenotic God and Dynamic Sunyata (in: COBB & IVES 1990, 3–65, 157–200).

–: "Leuchtende Finsternis". Zum Verständnis von "Letzter Wirklichkeit" in Buddhismus und Christentum (in: HÄRING & KUSCHEL 1993, 623–650).

ALTIZER, THOMAS J.J.: Buddhist Emptiness and the Crucifixion of God (in: COBB & IVES 1990, 69–78).

ARIARAJAH, S. WESLEY: Can We Pray Together? Interreligious Prayer: A Protestant Perspective, PD 1998: 258–265.

–: Some Glimpses into the Theology of Dr. Stanley Samartha, CD 38, Dec. 2001: 15–29.

AUGUSTIN, GEORG: Gott eint – trennt Christus? Die Einmaligkeit und Universalität Jesu Christi als Grundlage einer Theologie der Religionen ausgehend vom Ansatz Wolfhart Pannenbergs, Paderborn 1993.

BARTH, KARL: Die kirchliche Dogmatik, München 1932ff.

BASSET, JEAN-CLAUDE: Le dialogue interreligieux, Histoire et avenir, Paris 1996.

BAYBROOKE, MARCUS: Inter-Faith Organizations 1893–1979: A Historical Directory, New York and Toronto 1980.

–: Pilgrimage of Hope. One Hundred Years of Global Interfaith Dialogue, London 1992.

–: A Wider Vision: A History of the World Congress of Faiths, London 1996.

BERGER, PETER L.: From Secularity to World Religions (in: WALL 1981, 21–28).

BERNHARDT, REINHOLD: Deabsolutierung der Christologie? (in: v.BRÜCK & WERBICK 1993, 144–200).

–: Der Absolutheitsanspruch des Christentums. Von der Aufklärung bis zur pluralistischen Religionstheologie, Gütersloh 1990.

–: Ein neuer Lessing? Paul Knitters Theologie der Religionen, ET 1989, 516–528.

–: Zur Diskussion um die Pluralistische Theologie der Religionen, ÖR 43/2, 1994, 172–189.

BETHUNE, PIERRE F. DE: The Bond of Peace – A few Theological Reflections on Interreligious Prayer, PD 98, 159–165.

BONHOEFFER, DIETRICH: Widerstand und Ergebung, München 1951.

BOOKMAN, TERRY A.: The Holy Conversation: Toward a Jewish Theology of Dialogue, JES 32:2, Spring 1995.

BOROWITZ, EUGENE B.: Dynamic Sunyata and the God Whose Glory Fills the Universe (in: COBB & IVES 1990, 79–90)

BRAATEN, CARL E.: No Other Gospel! Christianity among the World's Religions, Minneapolis 1992.

BROWN, STUART E.: Meeting in Faith – Twenty Years of Christian-Muslim Conversations Sponsored by the WCC, Geneva 1989.

BRÜCK, MICHAEL VON: Einheit der Wirklichkeit – Gott, Gotteserfahrung und Meditation im hinduisch-christlichen Dialog, München 1986.

–: Heil und Heilswege im Hinduismus und Buddhismus – eine Herausforderung für christliches Erlösungsverständnis (in: v.BRÜCK & WERBICK 1993, 62–106).

– & WERBICK, JÜRGEN (ed.): Der einzige Weg zum Heil? Die Herausforderung des christlichenWahrheitsanspruchs durch die pluralistischen Religionstheologien, Freiburg 1993.
BSTEH, ANDREAS (ed.): Beiträge zur Religionstheologie, Mödling.
  Band II: Der Gott des Christentums und des Islams, 1978, Nachdruck 1992.
  Band III: Erlösung im Christentum und Buddhismus, 1982.
  Band IV: Sein als Offenbarung im Christentum und Hinduismus, 1984.
  Band V: Dialoge aus der Mitte christlicher Theologie, 1987.
BUREN, PAUL M. VAN: Probing the Jewish-Christian Reality (in: ed. WALL 1981, 67–73).
CHANDRAN, J.RUSSEL: Theological Assessment of Interreligious Prayer, PD 1998, 197–207.
CLARK, DAVID K. (a.o., ed.): Procedings of the Wheaton Theology Conference, vol. 1, 1992.
CLARK, FRANCIS (ed.): Interfaith Directory, New York 1987.
CLARKE ANDREW D. & WINTER, BRUCE W. (ed.): One God, One Lord, Grand Rapids 1992.
CLOONEY, FRANCIS X., S.J.: Reading the World in Christ. From Comparison to Inclusivism (in: D'COSTA 1990, 63–77).
COBB, JOHN B. JR.: A Critical View of Inherited Theology (in: WALL 1981, 74–81).
–: Beyond Dialogue – Toward a Mutual Transformation of Christianity and Buddhism, Philadelphia 1982.
–: Beyond 'Pluralism' (in: D'COSTA 1990, 81–95).
–: Interreligiöser Dialog, Welt-ethos und die Problematik des Humanum (in: HÄRING & KUSCHEL 1993, 589–606).
–: On the Deepening of Buddhism (in: COBB & IVES 1990, 91–101).
–: Order out of Chaos: A Philosophical Model of Inter-Religious Dialogue (in: KELLENBERGER 1993, 71–86).
–: Toward a Christocentric Catholic Theology (in: SWIDLER 1987, 86–100).
– & IVES, CHRISTOPHER (ed.): The Emptying God. A Buddhist-Jewish-Christian Conversation, New York 1990.
– & BIRCH, CHARLES: The Liberation of Life: From the Cell to the Community, Cambridge 1981.
CONCILIUM (C) 1/1986: Christianity among World Religions.
D'COSTA, GAVIN (ed.): Christian Uniqueness Reconsidered – The Myth of a Pluralistic Theology of Religions, New York 1990.
–: Christ, the Trinity and Religious Plurality (in: D'COSTA 1990, 16–29).
–: Theological evaluation of Interreligious Prayer: The Catholic Tradition, PD 1998, 254–257.
CRAGG, KENNETH: Muhammad and the Christian – A Question of Response, London/New York 1984.
CURRENT DIALOGUE (CD) 30 (Dec. 1996): Jewish-Christian-Muslim Meeting on Jerusalem.
– (CD) 38 (Dec. 2001): Tributes, Messages and Reflectons in Remembrance of Dr. Stanley Samartha.
DEAN, THOMAS: Universal Theology and Dialogical Dialogue (in: SWIDLER 1987, 162–174).
DIALOG DER RELIGIONEN (DdR) 1/95: Sprache im Dialog.
DICKSON, KWESI A.: Theology in Africa, London 1984.
DINOIA, J.A. O.P.: Varieties of Religious Aims: Beyond Exclusivism, Inclusivism, and Pluralism (in: MARSHALL 1990, 249–274).
–: Pluralist Theology of Religions: Pluralistic or Non-Pluralistic? (in: D'COSTA 1990, 119–134).
DRIVER, TOM: The Case for Pluralism (in: HICK & KNITTER 1987, 203–218).

DURAN, KHALID: Interreligious Dialogue and the Islamic "Original Sin" (in: SWIDLER 1987, 210–217).

ECK, DIANA: Encountering God – A Spiritual Journey from Bozeman to Benares, Boston 1993.

ELSHAHED, ELSAYED: Die Problematik des interreligiösen Dialogs aus islamischer Sicht (in: HÄRING & KUSCHEL 1993, 663–672).

EVANGELISCHE THEOLOGIE (ET) 49/6 1989: Dialog der Religionen?

EVERS, GEORG: Die "anonymen Christen" und der Dialog mit den Juden (in: VORGRIMLER 1979, 524–536).

–: Mission – Nicht-christliche Religionen – Weltliche Welt, Münster 1974.

FALATURI, A.: Islam und säkulares Denken, DdR 2–95, 122–128.

FEIL, ERNST: Religio, Göttingen 1986.

FERNANDO, ANTONY: A Tale of Two Theologies (in: SWIDLER 1987, 112–117).

FITZGERALD, MICHAEL L.: Où en est le Dialogue Interreligieux? PD 91, 1996/1, 36–38.

–: "Overview": Plenary Assembly 1995, Pontificium Consilium pro Dialogo inter Religiones, PD 92, 1996/2, 149–151.

FRIEDLI, RICHARD: Synkretismus als Befreiungspraxis: Asiatische und afrikanische Modelle im Dialog, DdR 1/95, 42–66.

FRIES, HEINRICH / KÖSTER, FRITZ / WOLFINGER, FRANZ (ed.): Jesus in den Weltreligionen, St.Otilien 1981.

GEFFRÉ, CLAUDE: Toward a Hermeneutic of Interreligious Dialogue, (in: JEANROUND & RIKE 1991, 250–269).

GILKEY, LANGDON: Plurality and Its Theological Implications (in: HICK & KNITTER 1987, 37–50).

GRIFFITHS, PAUL J.: An Apology for Apologetics. A Study in the Logic of Interreligious Dialogue, New York 1991.

– (ed.): Christianity Through Non-Christian Eyes, New York 1990.

–: The Uniqueness of Christian Doctrine Defended (in: D'COSTA 1990, 157–173).

HALLENCREUTZ, CARL F.: Dialogue in Ecumenical History 1910–1971 (in: SAMARTHA 1971, 7–71)

–: Kraemer towards Tambaram – A Study in Hendrik Kraemer's Missionary Approach, Lund 1966.

HÄRING, HERMANN & KUSCHEL, KARL JOSEF (ed.): Hans Küng – Neue Horizonte des Glaubens und Denkens. Ein Arbeitsbuch, München 1993.

HEIM, MARK S.: Eine Weite in Gottes Barmherzigkeit – Evangelikale Theologie überdenkt religiösen Pluralismus, DdR 1/95, 67–76.

HELLWIG, MONIKA K.: Christology in the Wider Ecumenism (in: D'COSTA 1990, 107–116).

HICK, JOHN: A Religious Understanding of Religion: a Model of the Relationship between Traditions (in: KELLENBERGER 1993, 21–36).

–: God has Many Names. Britain's New Religious Pluralism, London 1980.

–: Pluralism and the Reality of the Transcendent (in: WALL 1981, 60–66).

–: Problems of Religious Pluralism, London 1985.

–: The Non-Absoluteness of Christianity (in: HICK & KNITTER 1987/88, 16–36).

– & KNITTER, PAUL F. (ed.): The Myth of Christian Uniqueness, New York 1987/88, London 1988.

HILLMAN, EUGENE: Many Paths. A Catholic Approach to Religious Pluralism, New York 1989.

HUANG, YONG: Religious Pluralism and Interfaith Dialogue: Beyond Universalism and Particularism, IJPhR, vol. 37 no. 3, June 1995.

HUBER, WOLFGANG / RITSCHL, DIETER / SUNDERMEIER, THEO (ed.): Ökumenische Existenz heute, 1, München 1986.

HUNTER, ALASTAIR G.: Christianity and Other Faiths in Britain, London 1985.

INADA, KENNETH K.: Christocentrism – Buddhacentrism (in: SWIDLER 1987, 104–111).

JEANROUND, WERNER D. & RIKE, JENNIFER L. (ed.): Radical Pluralism and Truth – David Tracy and the Hermeneutics of Religion, New York 1991.

KASPER, WALTER: Das Christentum im Gespräch mit den Religionen (in: BSTEH 1987, 105–130).

KAUFMAN, GORDON D.: Religious Diversity, Historic Consciousness and Christian Theology (in: HICK & KNITTER 1987, 3–15). New York 1993.

KELLENBERGER, J. (ed.): Inter-Religious Models and Criteria. Papers from Claremont Philosophy of Religion Conference 1992, New York 1993.

KELLER, CATHERINE: Scoop up the Water and the Moon Is in Your Hands: On Feminist Theology and Dynamic Self-Emptying (in: COBB & IVES 1990, 102–115).

KIRCHNER, HUBERT: Die römisch-katholische Kirche vom II Vatikantkonzil bis zur Gegenwart, Leipzig 1996.

KNITTER, PAUL F.: Hans Küng's Theological Rubicon (in: SWIDLER 1987: 224–230).

–: No Other Name? A Critical Survey of Christian Attitudes Toward the World Religions, London 1985.

–: Nochmals die Absolutheitsfrage. Gründe für eine pluralistische Theologie der Religionen, ET 1989, 505–516.

–: Toward a Liberation Theology of Religions (in: HICK & KNITTER 1987, 178–200).

– & HICK, JOHN: see Hick.

KRAEMER, HENDRIK: The Christian Message in a Non-Christian World, New York 1938.

–: Religion and the Christian Faith, London 1956.

KRIEGER, DAVID J.: The New Universalism – Foundations for a Global Theology, New York 1991.

KROEGER, JAMES H.: Encountering the World of Dialogue, SID 3/3 1993, 71–92.

KÜNG, HANS: Christianity and World Religions: Dialogue with Islam (in: SWIDLER 1987: 192–209)

–: Das Christentum – Wesen und Geschichte, München 1994.

–: Dialogfähigkeit und Standfestigkeit – Über zwei komplementären Tugenden, ET 1989, 492–504.

–: Das Judentum, München 1991.

–: Projekt Weltethos, München/Zürich 1990.

–: What is True Religion? Toward an Ecumenical Criteriology (in: SWIDLER 1987, 231–250).

– & JULIA CHING: Christentum und chinesische Religion, München 1988.

– & JOSEF VAN ESS, HEINRICH VON STIETENCRON, HEINZ BECHERT: Christentum und Weltreligionen – Islam, Hinduismus, Buddhismus, München/Zürich 1984.

– & KARL JOSEF KUSCHEL (ed.): Erklärung zum Weltethos – Die Deklaration des Parlamentes der Weltreligionen, München 1993.

– & KARL JOSEF KUSCHEL (ed.): Weltfrieden durch Religionsfrieden – Antworten aus den Weltreligionen, München/Zürich 1993.

KUSCHEL, KARL-JOSEF: Streit um Abraham. Was Juden, Christen und Muslime trennt – und was sie eint, München/Zürich 1994.

– & HÄRING, H.: see HÄRING.

KVÆRNE, PER: Religionene og etisk pluralisme (in: ØSTNOR 1995, 11–20).

–: Økokrisen i buddhistisk lys (in: ØSTNOR 1995, 206–212).

LEEUWEN, AREND TH. VAN: Christianity in World History – The Meeting of the Faiths of East and West, London 1964.

LEIRVIK, ODDBJØRN: Images of Jesus Christ in Islam, Uppsala 1999.

–: Religionsdialog på norsk, Oslo 1996.

LEUZE, REINHARD: Möglichkeiten und Grenzen einer Theologie der Religionen, KuD 24, 1978, 230–243.

LINDBECK, GEORGE: The Nature of Doctrine – Religion and Theology in a Postliberal Age, London 1984.

LINDHOLM, TORE: Menneskerettigheter i islam og kristendom (in: ØSTNOR 1995, 153–167).

LOHTE, EGIL: Å formidle østlig etikk i et vestlig samfunn (in: ØSTNOR 1995, 132–150).

LØNNING, PER: Creation – An Ecumenical Challenge. Issuing from a study by the Institute for Ecumenical Research, Strasbourg, France, Macon GA 1989.

–: Der begreiflich Unergreifbare – "Sein Gottes" und modern-theologische Denkstrukturen, Göttingen 1986.

–: Dialogue: a Question about "Religiology", ER 1985, 420–429.

–: Die Schöpfungstheologie Jürgen Moltmanns, KuD 1987, 207–223.

–: Fundamentalisme – Ord til fordømmelse – ord til fordummelse? Bergen 1997.

– (ed.): Religionenes verden – en utfordring til dagens kristendom? Oslo 1981.

LUBBE, GERRIE: Could the Practice of Interreligious Prayer Continue? How? PD 1998: 216–222.

MACHADO, FELIX: Interreligious Dialogue in the Various Regions of the World, PD 93 1996/3, 267–270.

MARTINSON, PAUL: Explorations in Lutheran Perspectives on People of Other Faiths (in: MWAKABANA 1997, 207–237).

MBITI, JOHN: The Encounter of Christian Faith and Africal Religion (in: WALL 1981, 53–59).

MILBANK, JOHN: The End of Dialogue (in: D'COSTA 1990, 174–191).

MILDENBERGER, MICHAEL: Denkpause im Dialog, Frankfurt a.M. 1978.

MITRA, KANA: Theologizing through History? (in: SWIDLER 1987: 79–85, 251–253)

MOLTMANN, JÜRGEN: The Challenge of Religion in the '80s (in: WALL 1981, 107–112).

–: God is Unselfish Love (in: COBB & IVES 1990, 116–124)

–: Gott in der Schöpfung – ökologische Schöpfungslehre, München 1985.

–: Is 'Pluralist Theology' Useful for the Dialogue of the World Religions? (in: D'COSTA 1990, 149–156)

–: Trinität und Reich Gottes, München 1980.

MULDER, DIRK C.: A History of the Sub-Unit on Dialog of the WCC, SID 2/1 1992, 136–151.

–: Interreligious Dialogue and Social Ethics, SID 1/1991, 70–79.

MUSLIM-CHRISTIAN RESEARCH GROUP (1987): The Challenge of the Scriptures: The Bible and the Qur'an, New York 1989.

MWAKABANA, HANCE A. (ed.): Theological Perspectives on Other Faiths – Toward a Christian Theology of Religions (LWFD 41/1997).

NAGUIB, SAPHINAZ-AMAL: Religion og etikk i islamsk lys (in: ØSTNOR 1995, 78–96).

NEUNER, JOSEPH, S.J. (ed.): Christian Revelation and World Religions, London 1967.

NEWBIGIN, LESLIE: The Gospel in a Pluralist Society, Grand Rapids/Geneva 1989.

–: Religion for the Marketplace (in: D'COSTA 1990, 135–148).

OGDEN, SCHUBERT: Faith in God and Realisation of Emptiness (in: COBB & IVES 1990, 125–134)

–: Problems in the Case for a Pluralistic Theology of Religions (in: JEANROUND & RIKE 1991, 270–295).

O'NEILL, MAURA: A Model of the Relationship between Religions Based on Feminist Theology (in: KELLENBERGER 1993, 37–57).

ØSTNOR, LARS (ed.): Mange religioner – én etikk?, Oslo 1995.

OPSAL, JAN: Lydighetens vei. Islams veier til vår tid, Oslo 1994.

PANIKKAR, RAIMUNDO: Begegnung der Religionen: Das unvermeidliche Gespräch, DdR 1/94: 9–39.

–: Der unbekannte Christus im Hinduismus, Mainz 1986.

–: The Invisible Harmony. A Universal Theory of Religion or a Cosmic Confidence in Reality? (in: SWIDLER 1987, 118–153).

–: The Jordan, the Tiber and the Ganges (in: HICK & KNITTER 1987, 89–116.)

PANNENBERG, WOLFHART: Die Religionen als Thema der Theologie. Die Relevanz der Religionen für das Selbstverständnis der Theologie, TQ 1989/2, 99–110.

–: Religion und Religionen. Theologische Erwägungen zu den Prinzipien eines Dialogs mit den Weltreligionen (in: BSTEH 1987, 179–196).

–: Religious Pluralism and Conflicting Truth Claims (in: D'COSTA 1990, 96–106).

PETERS, TED: Confessional Universalism and Interreligious Dialogue, DIAL, Vol. 25, 1986, 145–149.

PINNOCK, CLARK H.: A Wideness in God's Mercy – The Finality of Jesus Christ in a World of Religions, Grand Rapids 1992.

PRABHU, RONNIE: My Experience of Interreligious Prayer, PD 1998, 223–225.

PRO DIALOGO (PD) 94, 1997/1: L'évangile de Jésus-Christ et la rencontre des religions traditionnelles.

– (PD) 98, 1998/2 [in cooperation with CURRENT DIALOGUE (CD)]: Interreligious Prayer.

PULIKKOTTIL, GEORG P.: An Orthodox Perspective of Interreligous Prayer and Relations, PD 1998, 247–253.

RACE, ALAN: Christians on Religious Pluralism, New York 1983.

RAHNER, KARL: Das Christentum und die nicht-christlichen Religionen, in: Schriften zur Theologie, Band V, Einsiedeln/Zürich/Köln 1964[2], 136–158.

RATSCHOW, CARL HEINZ (ed.): Der christliche Glaube und die Religionen, Berlin 1967

–: Die Religionen, Gütersloh 1979.

– & SUNDERMEIER, THEO (ed.): Religionen, Religiösität und christlicher Glaube. Eine Studie im Auftrag der VELKD und der ARNOLDSHEIMER KONFERENZ, Gütersloh 1991.

RUETHER, ROSEMARY R.: Feminism and Jewish-Christian Dialogue (in: HICK & KNITTER 1987, 137–148).

RUOKANEN, MIIKKA: The Catholic Doctrine of Non-Christian Religions According to the Second Vatican Council, Leiden 1992.

SAMARTHA, STANLEY J.: Between Two Cultures – Ecumenical Ministry in a Pluralist World, Geneva 1996.

–: Christen im Verhältnis zu Gläubigen anderer Religionen – Entwicklungen und Perspektiven, DdR 1/94: 39–50

–: The Cross and the Rainbow. Christ in a Multureligious Culture (in: HICK & KNITTER 1987, 69–88).

–: One Christ – Many Religions. Toward a Revised Christology. New York 1991.

– (ed.): Living Faiths and the Ecumenical Movement, Genève 1971.
– (ed.): Faith in the midst of faiths. Reflections on Dialogue in Community, Geneva 1977.
SANDERS, JOHN: No Other Name – An Investigation into the Destiny of the Unevangelized, Grand Rapids 1992.
SCHAEFFLER, RICHARD: Wahrheit, Dialog und Entscheidung (in: BSTEH 1987, 13–41).
SCHOEN, ULRICH: Das Ereignis und die Antworten – Auf die Suche nach einer Theologie der Religionen heute, Göttingen 1984.
SCHWÖBEL, CHRISTOPH: Particularity, Universality and the Religions (in: D'COSTA 1990, 30–46).
SECRETARIATUS PRO NON CHRISTIANIS: Religions – Fundamental Themes for a Dialogistic Understanding, Roma 1970.
SELVANAYAGAM, ISRAEL: A Dialogue on Dialogue. Reflections on Inter-faith Encounters, Madras 1995.
–: Christian Theology and Mission in the Midst of Many Theologies and Missions (in: MWAKABANA 1997, 181–201).
SHEARD, ROBERT B.: Interreligious Dialogue in the Catholic Church Since Vatican II. An Historical and Theological Study, Lewinston/Queenston 1987.
SIDDIQUI, ATAULLAH: Christian-Muslim Dialogue in the Twentieth Century, New York 1997.
DA SILVA, ANTONIO BARBOSA: Den traditionella afrikanska synen på familjen, äktenskapet och kvinnan. Et inlegg i debatten om en global etik (in: ØSTNOR 1995, 168–205).
SMITH, WILFRED CANTWELL: Idolatry – In Comparative Perspective (in: HICK & KNITTER 1987, 153–168).
–: The Meaning and End of Religion (1962), New York 1978.
–: Theology and the World's Religious History (in: SWIDLER 1987, 51–72).
SOTTOCORNOLA, FRANCO: Biblical Perspectives on Interreligious Prayer, PD 1998, 166–185.
STEWART, CHARLES & SHAW, ROSALIND: Syncretism/Anti-Syncretism. The Politics of Religious Synthesis, London & N.Y. 1994.
STRAELEN, HENRY VAN, S.V.D.: L'église et les religions non-chrétiennes – Au seuil du XXIe siècle, Paris 1994.
–: Le zen démystifié, Paris s.d.
–: Ouverture à l'autre, Paris 1982.
STROLZ, WALTER: Heilswege der Religionen – Christliche Begegnung mit Hinduismus, Buddhismus und Taoismus, Freiburg 1986.
SUCHOCKI, MARJORIE HEWITT: In Search of Justice. Religious Pluralism from a Feminist Perspective (in: HICK & KNITTER 1987, 149–161).
SULLIVAN, FRANCIS A., S.J.: Salvation outside the Church? Tracing the History of the Catholic Response, London 1992.
SUNDERMEIER, THEO: Konvivenz als Grundstruktur ökumenischer Existenz heute (in: HUBER / RITSCHL / SUNDERMEIER 1986, 49–100).
SURIN, KENNETH: A 'Politics of Speech'. Religious Pluralism in the Age of the McDonald's Hamburger (in: D'COSTA 1990, 192–210).
SWIDLER, LEONARD : After the Absolute. The Dialogical Future of Religious Reflexion, Minneapolis 1990.
–: Interreligious and Interideological Dialog: The Matrix for All Systematical Reflexion Today (in: SWIDLER 1987, 5–50).
– (ed.): Toward a Universal Theology of Religion, New York 1987.

TAKIZAWA, KATSUMI: Reflexionen über die universelle Grundlage von Buddhismus und Christentum, Frankfurt 1980.

–: Das Heil im Heute – Texte einer japanischen Theologie (ed. Theo Sundermeier), Göttingen 1987.

THANGARAJ, THOMAS: A Theological Reflection on the Experience of Interreligious Prayer, PD 1998, 186–196.

THOMAS, M.M.: A Christ-Centered Humanist Approach to Other Religions in the Indian Pluralistic Context (in: D'COSTA 1990, 49–62).

TRACY, DAVID: Dialogue with the Other. The Interreligious Dialogue, Louvain 1990.

–: Kenosis, Sunyata and Trinity (in: COBB & IVES 1990, 135–154.)

TÜBINGER DIALOGGESPRÄCH: Pluralismus und Identität im Dialog der Religionen, DDR 2/91.

VALLÉE, GÉRARD: Mouvement Oecuménique et Religions non Chrétiennes, Paris 1975.

II. VATICAN COUNCIL: Nostra aetate – Declaration on the Relationship of the Christian to Non-Christian Religions (Oct. 28, 1965).

VISCHER, LUKAS: Stanley Samartha (1920–2001) – Faith and Order Pespective, CD 38, Dec. 2001, 30f.

VISSER'T HOOFT, W.A.: No Other Name. The Choice Between Syncretism and Christian Universalism, London 1963.

VORGRIMLER, HERBERT (ed.): Wagnis Theologie – Erfahrungen mit der Theologie Karl Rahners, Freiburg 1979.

WAARDENBURG, J.: Religion und Religionen, Berlin/New York 1986.

WAGNER, FALK: Was ist Religion? Studien zu ihrem Begriff und Thema in Geschichte und Gegenwart, Gütersloh 1986.

WALL, JAMES M. (ed.): Theologians in Transition, New York 1981.

WEGER, KARL-HEINZ: Überlegungen zum "anonymen Christentum" (in: VORGRIMLER 1979, 499–510).

WERBICK, JÜRGEN: Heil durch Jesus Christus allein? Die 'Pluralistische Theologie' und ihr Plädoyer für ein Pluralismus der Heilswege (in: v.BRÜCK & WERBICK 1993, 11–61).

WILLIAMS, ROWAN: Trinity and Pluralism (in: D'COSTA 1990, 3–15).

WORLD COUNCIL OF CHURCHES: Dialogue in Community, Statements and Reports of a Theological Consultation, Chiang Mai, Thailand 1977, Geneva 1977.

–: My Neighbour's Faith and Mine – Theological Discoveries Through Interfaith Dialogue. A Study Guide, Geneva 1984.

YADAV, BIBHUTI S.: Anthromorphism and Cosmic Confidence (in: SWIDLER 1987, 175–191).

–: Vaishnavism on Hans Küng: A Hindu Theology of Religious Pluralism (in: GRIFFITHS 1990, 24–246).

YAGI, SEIICHI: "'I'" in the Words of Jesus' (in: HICK & KNITTER 1987, 117–134).

ZEBIRI, KATE: Muslims and Christians Face to Face, Oxford 1997.

ZEHNER, JOACHIM: Der notwendige Dialog – Die Weltreligionen in katholischer und evangelischer Sicht, Gütersloh 1992.

ZIRKER, HANS: Wegleitung Gottes oder Erlösung durch Christus? Zum Heilsverständnis und Geltungsanspruch von Christentum und Islam (in: v. BRÜCK & ZIRKER 1993, 107–143).

Abbreviations

C	Concilium
CD	Current Dialogue
CT	Church Times
DdR	Dialog der Religionen
Dial	Dialog (USA)
EK	Evangelische Kommentare
ER	Ecumenical Review
ET	Evangelische Theologie
IJPhR	International Journal for Philosophy of Religion
JES	Journal of Ecumenical Studies
KuD	Kerygma und Dogma
LWFD	Lutheran World Federation, Documentation
LWM	Lutheran World Ministries
ÖR	Ökumenische Rundschau
PD	Pro Dialogo
P-F	Publik-Forum
SID	Studies in Interreligious Dialogue
ThQ	Theologische Quartalschrift
VELKD	Vereinigt Evangelisch Lutherische Kirche in Deutschland
WW	Die Weltwoche

Index of Names

V&R
Vandenhoeck
& Ruprecht

DIALOG DER KIRCHEN

Veröffentlichungen des Ökumenischen Arbeitskreises evangelischer und katholischer Theologen. (Koproduktion mit Herder Freiburg)

Am 31. Oktober 1999 wurde in Augsburg von hochrangigen Vertretern des Lutherischen Weltbundes und der römisch-katholischen Kirche der Prozess der Verständigung über die „Rechtfertigungslehre" durch feierliche Unterschrift besiegelt. In den voraufgegangenen Auseinandersetzungen um den von einer gemeinsamen Kommission erstellten Textentwurf wurden in der ersten Reaktion des Vatikans vor allem auch Anfragen an die Fassung des (lutherischen) Grundsatzes „gerecht und Sünder zugleich" gerichtet, dessen Klärung nach den Worten Kardinal Lehmanns „eine Nagelprobe auf die gemeinsame Beschreibung der Wirklichkeit der Rechtfertigung des Menschen" ist.

Der „Ökumenische Arbeitskreis evangelischer und katholischer Theologen" hat diese Aufgabe in Angriff genommen und eine Klärung herbeigeführt, die in einem gemeinsam verantworteten Text verabschiedet wurde.

V&R
Vandenhoeck & Ruprecht